STEEDS
OF
STEEL

STEEDS OF STEEL

A History of
American Mechanized Cavalry
in World War II

HARRY YEIDE

ZENITH
PRESS

First published in 2008 by Zenith Press, an imprint of MBI Publishing
Company, 400 First Avenue North, Suite 300, Minneapolis, MN 55401 USA

Zenith Press titles are also available at discounts in bulk quantity for industrial
or sales-promotional use. For details write to Special Sales Manager at
MBI Publishing Company, 400 First Avenue North, Suite 300, Minneapolis,
MN 55401 USA.

To find out more about our books, join us online at www.zenithpress.com.

Yeide, Harry.
  Steeds of steel : a history of American mechanized cavalry in World War II /
by Harry Yeide.
    p. cm.
  ISBN-13: 978-0-7603-3360-0 (hbk.)
  1. World War, 1939-1945—Cavalry operations. 2. World War, 1939-1945—
Tank warfare. 3. United States. Army—Armored troops—History—20th
century. 4. United States. Army. Cavalry—History—20th century. I. Title.
D769.32.Y45 2008
940.54'1273—dc22

                                                            2007039576

Maps: Harry Yeide
Designer: Kou Lor

On the cover: Troopers exercise at the Cavalry Replacement Training Center
in April 1942. *Signal Corps photo*

On the back cover: Pre-war maneuvers still relying on the horse. *Signal
Corps photo*

Printed in the United States of America

"The mission of the cavalry is to fight."

Lt. Col. Charles Hodge,
117th Cavalry Reconnaissance Squadron, Mechanized

To those who fought.

CONTENTS

PREFACE

Steeds of Steel is intended to be a portrait of the mechanized cavalry troopers and their units rather than an all-encompassing treatise covering every twist and turn of organizational, equipment, or doctrinal change. This book is the soul mate of my earlier works *Steel Victory* (2003), on the separate tank battalions in the European theater of operations (ETO), and *The Tank Killers* (2005), covering tank destroyer battalions in North Africa, Italy, and the ETO. This time, I have included the Pacific theater, which was possible because so few mechanized cavalry formations fought mounted there that the task was manageable.

The separate tank battalions were a conceptual sideshow for men far more interested in creating the big, flashy armored divisions. After the war was over, the tank battalions found permanent homes within the infantry divisions. The tank destroyer battalions arose from the minds of clever men looking for a novel way to deal with the German armored blitzkrieg. Crafted from theory rather than experience, they served extremely well in ways unforeseen by doctrine but were deemed a flawed concept and disbanded after the war. The mechanized cavalry squadrons, groups, and troops emerged because the closed minds of horse soldiers cost the Cavalry branch the ownership of the armored force, and their creation was a belated move to get the cavalry into the coming modern war. Despite the best efforts by doctrinal theorists to ignore experience, the mechanized cavalry served well enough to validate the idea of machine-mounted cavaliers, and it lives on today in the form of the armored cavalry.

As always, I have had to make choices about what and what not to include. Several imbalances may be apparent to the reader. First, because so few mechanized cavalry formations participated in the North Africa, Sicily, Italy, and southern France campaigns, the squadron-size formations that did so get much more extensive treatment than squadrons that fought entirely in the ETO. Even within the ETO, I have highlighted several squadrons to lend a sense of continuity to the work. Second, those outfits that left behind good, detailed records get more coverage than those that did not. Third, the mechanized cavalry troopers who served with the infantry divisions did so in company-size reconnaissance units. Formations that small tend to become abstractions in the official battle narrative, receiving brief summary mentions. This work highlights the experiences of the few such troops that left behind more extensive accounts and assumes that they well represent the experiences of outfits that remain unacknowledged.

One of the cavalry's wartime roles, night patrolling, was a highly individualized experience that I have not attempted to cover in any depth. I heartily recommend Fred Salter's superb memoir of his time with the 91st Cavalry Reconnaissance Squadron, *Recon Scout*, to any reader interested in a deep look at that dangerous profession.

It may not be apparent to the casual reader, but it is darn hard to tell exactly what happened so many years ago. Contemporary reports written by separate participants in any given incident are likely to differ, sometimes substantially. On top of this, later accounts introduce additional flaws of memory or self-justification. The reader should view this work as the closest the author was able to get to what really happened.

I have not attempted to rewrite the history of World War II. Nevertheless, I have provided the big picture as a framework to help the reader understand the context and impact of the stories of the individual mechanized cavalry units and troopers; the actor needs the backdrop to help set the scene. The backdrops here are widely varied, from African desert to Pacific jungle to European mountains, plains, and villages.

I have crafted this work out of strict chronological order. The first half of the book covers the periphery, so to speak—North Africa, Sicily, Italy, and the Pacific, where the cavalry fought in relatively small numbers. The second half of the book tackles western Europe, where the bulk of the mechanized cavalry fought, even though events there overlap chronologically with earlier material on Italy and the Pacific.

Some readers may note that the chapter on southern France covers much of the same ground as in one chapter of *First to the Rhine*, which I wrote with Mark Stout. Rest assured that I have refocused the discussion on the mechanized cavalry and have included significant new material, while removing matter unrelated to the cavalry.

One note on photographs: images of the mechanized cavalrymen doing their job are scarce. This is not surprising given that they were often closer to the enemy than anybody else.

I have taken small liberties with texts drawn from the military records and personal accounts to correct grammatical errors and spelling mistakes and to introduce consistency in references to unit designators, equipment, dates, and so on. I have used the word *jeep* throughout for the quarter-ton truck because of its universal familiarity. Mechanized cavalrymen called the vehicle a "bantam" or, if assigned to an armored division, a "peep."

—Harry Yeide
October 2006

ACKNOWLEDGMENTS

I thank my wonderful wife, Nancy, for putting up with her husband writing another book, plus, more generally, for being wonderful. David Keogh, at the U.S. Army's Military History Institute, was of great assistance in uncovering material from veterans of the mechanized cavalry. Joseph Balkoski, 29th Infantry Division historian, enthusiastically aided in researching the 29th Reconnaissance Troop. I would also like to thank the cheerful and efficient public servants at the National Archives and Records Administration's (NARA) document and still-photo reading rooms in College Park, Maryland. My particular thanks to Greg Bradsher, NARA, who shared his research into the intelligence records covering the battle at Hill 700 on Bougainville.

Robert Lutz, a veteran of the 117th Cavalry Reconnaissance Squadron, was extremely generous with his time and his work on the 117th's history, as was Leonard Daloia in sharing his writings about the 37th Reconnaissance Troop and the outfit's Bougainville deployment. Lieutenant Colonel Joseph Haines generously allowed me to use his recollections of the 106th Reconnaissance Troop at the Battle of the Bulge. Vernon Brown contributed his wonderful memoirs of serving with the 94th Cavalry Reconnaissance Squadron and gave generous permission to use his wartime photos.

Other members of the veterans' community provided helpful assistance, rec- ollections, and materials, including Robert Beutlich, Thomas Price, and Milton Galke (6th Infantry Division); Wesley Johnston (7th Armored Division); Royal Call (18th Cavalry Reconnaissance Squadron); Don McKee and Bob Moscati (29th Infantry Division); John D'Agostino, Harold Smith, and Salvatore Tamburello (29th Reconnaissance Troop); George "Trent" Trentacosti (37th Reconnaissance Troop); Cyril Sedlacko (37th Infantry Division); Mrs. Edward Hunt, Robert Buschur, and L'Cainian Evans (40th Reconnaissance Troop); Robert Flynn and Ben Rosenthal (45th Reconnaissance Troop); and General William Knowlton, retired (87th Cavalry Reconnaissance Squadron).

I am indebted to Lt. Col. Scott Cunningham, a serving armored cavalry-man, for reviewing the manuscript. I am equally grateful to Steven Zaloga and Mark Reardon, who both reviewed the manuscript, each with the combined wisdom of a military historian and a mechanized warfare expert. All remaining errors are mine alone. Finally, cheers to Michael Ard for titular inspiration.

CHAPTER 1

FROM HORSE TO HORSEPOWER

The bayonet charge and the saber charge are the highest physical demonstrations of moral victory. The fierce frenzy of hate and determination flashing from the bloodshot eyes squinting behind the glittering steel is what wins.

—Maj. George S. Patton Jr., 1922

The U.S. Army's mechanized cavalry force served in an astounding variety of ways in World War II—certainly a greater variety in one three-year period than any other cavalry force in human history. Mechanized cavalrymen fought from tanks and armored cars, battled on and from the sea in tracked amphibians, stormed beaches from landing craft, slipped ashore in rubber rafts from submarines, climbed mountains, battled hand-to-hand on foot like any GI, and even occasionally rode horses. The troopers learned to outwit the enemy in African desert, on Italian peaks, in European hedgerows, and in Pacific jungles. Wherever an armored or infantry division waged war, the mechanized cavalry was there. Often, the cavalrymen worked alone, miles ahead of the nearest friendly units. This is their story.

When World War II broke out in September 1939, the U.S. Cavalry was still mainly a proud, horse-mounted force, as it had been since the nation's founding. Within a year, the Cavalry branch had lost its horses and very nearly its mission. The cavalrymen took to new steeds of steel, carved out a place on the modern battlefield, and restored their role and pride.

★★★

The U.S. Cavalry had seen virtually no action in the Great War, which one might have expected to provoke a deep reappraisal among cavalrymen in the United States of the mounted arm's role. Perhaps the problem was that the horsemen, relegated mostly to securing the Mexican frontier, had suffered no combat disasters that would have stripped away emotions that clouded analysis. The poetry and romance of the cavalier were deeply embedded in history and military tradition, and no amount of theoretical reappraisal was going to root out old beliefs absent such a shock, no matter how lethal industrial-age war had proved on the battlefields of western Europe. The utility that mounted units had shown on the Russian front—where vast distances created conditions that the U.S. Army was unlikely to face in a major war—and in small colonial actions also gave horse devotees straws at which to grasp.

The believers in the continued battlefield utility of the horse did not fit any caricature of doddering old schoolers. Major George S. Patton Jr. had fought with the Tank Corps in World War I and was to become one of America's greatest practitioners of armored warfare. Nonetheless, in 1922 even he enthused:

> Little of interest in purely cavalry tactics is at present available as a result of the World War in the west. . . . A general survey of the tactical tendencies at the close of the World War seems to me to point to greater, and not lessened, usefulness and importance for cavalry. The necessity, due to air observation, for most marches of concentration being made at night adds vastly to the destructive power of the mounted man, because charges with the saber or pistol or surprise fire by machine rifles will be terribly effective and most difficult to prevent. . . . The machine gun and automatic rifle, which at one time we considered so prejudicial to our usefulness, have in fact made us more effective. They give us the fire power dismounted which we lacked before.

Patton anticipated that the cavalry would use automatic weapons to pin down the enemy while mounted elements attacked from the flank or rear. Mounted men would seek out wooded and broken country to conceal themselves from highly lethal weapons, which would amount to a complete revolution in the concept of "good cavalry country," heretofore conceived to mean open, unfenced pastureland. Patton anticipated that some such attacks would be conducted on foot; those actions would have to be fast and sharp because the cavalry could not cart around the heavy equipment that the infantry would be able to employ.[1]

Patton anticipated that cavalry tactics would simplify into several categories: delaying or harassing action against infantry; attacks against flanks or thinly held sectors; offensive action against enemy cavalry; action against enemy lines of communication; actions by patrols; and actions against strong positions, where either cover or obstacles prevent maneuver.

Patton at least was a realist at the same time: "Still another development of the war, and one from which we shall surely hear in the future, was the enthusiast of the special arms—the man who would either bomb, gas, or squash the enemy into oblivion, according [to whether] he belonged to the Air, Gas, or Tank Service. All these men, and I was one of them, were right within limits; only they were overconfident of the effectiveness of their favorite weapon. In the future there will be many more such, and we must accept all they say and give them a trial, for some may be right. . . ."[2]

About the same time that Patton wrote these words, The *Cavalry Journal* took note of the decision by the French Army to establish within the Cavalry arm fourteen battalions of armored cars carrying 37mm guns. Each cavalry division had a total of forty-two armored cars.[3] American officers also were exposed to European thinking about the possibilities for using motorized vehicles to enable horse cavalry to move quickly from place to place.[4]

★★★

The U.S. Cavalry was never opposed to mechanization, per se. Its great mistake lay in missing the opportunity to embrace the transformation wholeheartedly. Had it done so, it probably would not have been marginalized when the army created the Armored Force in July 1940.

Major General Herbert Crosby, Chief of Cavalry, in 1927 held maneuvers in Texas, in part to try out limited motorization of transport and artillery. Crosby believed that some degree of mechanization would increase the Cavalry's role. After the exercises were completed, he created a new, trimmed-down cavalry division of some five thousand men that incorporated an armored car troop. He even considered adding a light tank troop.[5]

Impressed by the lessons of British maneuvers in 1927, during which a mechanized force defeated a traditional one, the U.S. Army in 1928 issued its first clear statement endorsing large-scale mechanization. The secretary of war, Dwight Davis, instructed the army to begin testing mechanized formations at Fort Leonard Wood—now Fort Meade—in Maryland.[6] General Charles Summerall, the army chief of staff, made it so, scribbling on a piece of pink paper "Organize a Mechanized Force. C. P. S." and passing it to the organization branch in the G-3 (operations). Nothing but a preliminary study of role, organization, or mission had been made.[7]

The Experimental Mechanized Force tested recent War Department thinking in a series of maneuvers between July and September 1928. Armored cars from the Cavalry joined World War I–era Mark VIII heavy tanks, Cunningham light tanks, truck-borne infantry, field artillery, engineers, antiaircraft artillery, and other elements. Most participants were surprised to learn how far automotive technology had progressed; even heavily loaded trucks were capable of reaching forty miles per hour on a road. Unit commanders were granted the freedom to experiment with new approaches rather than being held to and graded on existing doctrine.

Major C. C. Benson, one of the cavalry officers who participated in the exercises, offered his view to his colleagues in the branch: "In the absence of authoritative opinion, I submit the following: The purpose of a mechanized force is to provide army and higher commanders with an additional powerful weapon, which will combine firepower, shock, and speed to a much higher degree than now exists in any one combatant arm. Specifically, units of a mechanized force could be used to great advantage for advance, flank, and rear guards; to seize and hold, temporarily, distant key positions or critical areas; to cover tactical or strategical concentrations; for raids, wide envelopments, turning movements, exploitation, and pursuit."

Although Benson supposed that such a force would not completely supplant the horse cavalry because it could not operate in swamps, mountains, and forests, his insightful analysis must have shocked many of his comrades in arms, who could foresee most of the traditional glorious roles of the horse soldier slipping away if this vision came to pass. Indeed, the future was bleaker for the horse soldier than even Benson could imagine, for the mechanized cavalry in fact eventually operated in swamps, mountains, and forests, too.

Benson also raised an issue that would roil the army for more than a decade to come: Who should control the tanks? He suggested that they would mesh well with the cavalry and its missions, but he also noted that the infantry was developing a capable system for training armored troops. Perhaps, he suggested, the army should resurrect the Great War's Tank Corps.[8]

After the experimental mechanized unit was disbanded, the G-3 conducted its first detailed assessment of the prospects for mechanization in light of the latest technical developments. That study reached one bedrock conclusion: Tanks could not be used alone. They were noisy and blind and had difficulty defending themselves. Other types of vehicles would have to be employed with them to offset their vulnerabilities.[9]

★★★

A doctrinal inclination for the employment of machine-mounted cavalrymen emerged like an original sin, and it was to plague the force throughout the coming war. Troop A, 1st Armored Car Squadron, was the first armored car unit to be organized in the U.S. Army. Under the command of Capt. H. G. Holt, it joined the 1st Cavalry Division in November 1928. The armored car's role was to be primarily one of reconnaissance. Although commanders recognized its combat value under certain circumstances, they judged that reconnaissance should always have a higher priority.[10]

Troop A fielded six medium and two light armored cars divided evenly into two platoons, and only a single vehicle was outfitted with an SCR-127 radio. The troop headquarters was equipped with a light scout car and two trucks. The armored cars, most built by Ordnance, carried a mix of .30- and .50-caliber machine guns. Troop personnel built two of the vehicles themselves to try out some of their own ideas, such as using a ring mount rather than a pedestal mount for a machine gun.[11]

Maneuvers quickly revealed several facts. In delaying actions, the cavalry's armored cars were extremely effective at hindering the opposing force, which had to bring forward antitank guns to make any headway. And each platoon had to have its own radio.[12]

★★★

The horse-loving cavalrymen did not take the threat of modernization lying down; rather they sought to encourage the faith of their soul mates. The *Cavalry Journal*, in the same January 1929 issue that carried Benson's startling vision of the future, ran a lead commentary by Field Marshal Viscount Allenby, which read in part:

> The functions of the cavalry have, admittedly, been affected by the advance of modern invention.
>
> Distant reconnaissance has become mainly the business of the air force. Tactical reconnaissance, too, is increasingly being carried out by mechanized means. Tanks, armored cars, and the like have proved their value; their assets—as regards firepower, mobility, invulnerability, endurance—are real and great; nevertheless, their claim to have superceded cavalry cannot be accepted.
>
> The work of contact and linking up of units on wide battle fronts will still fall to the cavalry; the eyes of that arm are not

hooded, it has clearer vision than the purblind armored car, its mentality is more alert. The more invulnerable the machine, the blinder its crew. . . .

Modern invention has not rendered obsolete the mounted arm. The cavalier retains all his old power, his quick intelligence, his aggressive spirit; his good friend, the cold steel, is ready to hand. . . .[13]

Patton and Benson together countered that whatever cavalry's virtues and the limitations of mechanized forces, cavalry forces were bound to run into armored forces in the field, as well as be vulnerable to air attack. Mounted men would not survive such encounters unless the cavalry took full advantage of mechanized war machines to protect them from such dangers.[14]

The Missed Opportunity

It is no surprise that when the tipping point toward mechanization came, the Cavalry arm missed its chance to become the lead actor in the new form of mobile warfare that lay just over the horizon. Old thinking in key minds combined with resource constraints of the moment to hide the future from all but a few visionaries. Many officers had become obsessed with the platform—the horse—and lost sight of the mission.[15]

General Summerall, as his last act as the army chief of staff, in October 1930 ordered the establishment of the army's first permanent mechanized force, to be stationed at Fort Eustis, Virginia. He still viewed the cavalry as a primarily horse-mounted arm—to be supported in its reconnaissance mission by mechanized elements.[16] Indeed, by then the cavalry division had been authorized one company of light tanks (infantry) and one squadron of armored cars (cavalry). No fast tanks were yet available, however, and even armored cars were in short supply.[17]

Some officers had understood the opportunity that the looming change would create and had tried to sway their fellow cavalrymen to seize it. Lieutenant Colonel K. B. Edmunds, writing several months before Summerall acted, urged the horsemen, "Our Cavalry is instinctively hostile to any machine which may supplant the horse and inclined to disparage its effect. We are retreating to mountain trails and thick woods, hoping that no fast tank can follow. Our policy, on the contrary, should be to encourage the new arm, experiment with it. . . . The cavalryman is best able to understand its potentialities."[18]

Then came the moment that was missed: Gen. Douglas MacArthur, who replaced Summerall in 1931, judged that firearms had eliminated the horse as a weapon. MacArthur instructed that mechanized cavalry was to be organized to "fulfill the normal cavalry role, substituting the vehicle for the horse." These missions included mobile offensive combat, mobile strategic reconnaissance, fighting for the "theater" of reconnaissance, seizing points of strategic importance, tactical reconnaissance, pursuit, delay of hostile advance, exploitation of breaks in the enemy line, reserve for a larger formation, and operations on the flank and against the enemy's rear.[19]

At the same time, MacArthur probably unwittingly created conditions that enabled the army to field a globally competitive armored force nearly a decade later. MacArthur decentralized authority to make decisions regarding mechanization to the autarchic Infantry, Cavalry, and Artillery branches. Mechanization advocates such as Col. Daniel Van Voorhis considered this a major mistake; they believed that any mechanized force should consist of the combined arms.[20] Nevertheless, the infantry was free to continue to develop the line of medium tanks—which were of no interest to the cavalry—that resulted in the M4 Sherman models, which formed the backbone of the armored formations not just of the United States but also its western allies. Moreover, the army was able to adopt the basics of combined-arms warfare in time to fight the war, despite decentralization.

The new Mechanized Force, the command and support staff of which arrived at Camp Knox (soon renamed Fort Knox), Kentucky, in November 1931, absorbed the 1st Cavalry Regiment, which became the 1st Cavalry Regiment (Mechanized) in 1932. The battalion-size regiment controlled a combat car (tank) squadron and a "covering squadron" made up of armored car and scout car troops. The War Department also in 1932 established the headquarters for the 7th Cavalry Brigade (Mechanized), which was to incorporate the 1st Cavalry Regiment (Mechanized) and a battalion (two batteries of 75mm howitzers) of the 68th Field Artillery. The 13th Cavalry was mechanized in 1936 and subordinated to the brigade, and two more batteries of artillery were added as well.[21]

Had the Cavalry seized on this as the model for its future, the odds are good that when the armored divisions came along, they all would have belonged to the men who wore crossed sabers. This did not happen, although by 1933 some consensus had emerged in thinking about the role of mechanized cavalry formations. Their mobility and firepower offered the greatest payoff in offensive roles; they were unsuitable for holding ground except for brief periods; and offensive action was likely to produce the best results even when they were on the defensive. Nevertheless, officers continued to argue over whether mechanized cavalry was suited to some traditional roles such as deep exploitation into the enemy's rear. Some thought an affirmative answer self-evident; others argued that mechanized elements would be quickly incapacitated if cut off from supply.[22] The latter argument implicitly played to one of the rationales offered by horse cavalry advocates: Horses and men could live off the land.

For cavalrymen uncertain as to the relative merits of the horse and the machine, the latter might not have looked like a good career bet. When planners at this time thought about the future battlefield environment, they concluded that given the high cost of mechanized formations—especially in the mental context of Depression-era America—no army would be able to field more than a few such brigades.[23]

By late 1936, the Germans were defying that expectation by creating mechanized divisions and corps, which appears to have changed some American officers' thinking about where resources would flow if war were to come. Signs emerged that turf considerations were coming into play. Cavalry officers were well aware that there was no significant difference between the combat cars fielded by their formations and the light tanks in use by the infantry. Against this backdrop, Maj. Gen. Leon Kromer, then Chief of Cavalry, wrote a letter to Brig. Gen. Daniel Van Voorhis, commanding the 7th Cavalry Brigade (Mechanized), in which Kromer fulminated that the infantry appeared to be holding its light tanks in reserve during exercises. "This indicates their intention to take over the Cavalry mission of exploitation."[24]

★★★

In the decades before World War II began, doctrine foresaw two overarching roles for cavalry regiments, the direct forebears of most mechanized cavalry outfits. Independent cavalry was to operate several days' march ahead of—or on the wing of—the army. Its missions were both strategic reconnaissance—in cooperation with air assets and mechanized units—and combat. Combat was expected to be of low intensity and short duration. Cavalry attached to infantry divisions was to perform tactical reconnaissance in the area of operations of the controlling division.[25]

During 1937, horse-cavalry advocates mounted a campaign to reduce the number of tanks in the mechanized brigade and replace those lost with scout cars. The advocates' apparent aim was to push the new-style formation into a purely reconnaissance role, thereby preserving other traditional cavalry combat missions for horse-mounted units.[26] This effort may have led to doctrinal formulations issued six years later when the standardized wartime mechanized cavalry reconnaissance troops, squadrons, and groups were organized. If so, these Luddites achieved their aims eventually in words, but not in practice.

By 1939, maneuvers had provided lessons that foreshadowed experience in battle. Brigadier General Adna Chaffee told an audience in September that his mechanized cavalry brigade was too weakly manned with riflemen to have adequate "holding power." He judged that it would be necessary to add a gun capable of defeating medium and heavy tanks (at that time thought to be a 37mm weapon). Chaffee added that the formation also badly needed a reconnaissance element beyond that of the subordinate regiments—a sure sign that the brigade was rapidly becoming mainly a fighting force. Indeed, the general noted, "Mechanized cavalry, due to its great fire power, surprise effect, and crushing ability, has a decided adverse morale effect on [opposing] ground troops." Reconnaissance from unarmored vehicles was of "doubtful value" and likely to lead to high losses of men and machines.[27]

The Cavalry's Little Bighorn

As of mid-1939, with war clouds gathering on the horizon in Europe, Maj. Gen. John Herr, Chief of Cavalry, still thought that the proper proportion of horse to mechanized cavalry was three divisions to one.[28] He could point to the example of the German Wehrmacht, which, although increasingly mechanized, fielded eight horse-mounted cavalry divisions.[29] That same year, however, the Germans broke up thirteen cavalry regiments to provide each infantry division with a reconnaissance battalion organized into three "squadrons" mounted, respectively, on horses, on bicycles, and in armored cars.[30] These battalions employed cavalry tactics in reconnaissance, counter-reconnaissance, screening, flank protection, and covering withdrawals.[31]

Germany's swift destruction of the Polish Army using its mechanized formations as a slashing saber provided the shock to horse advocates that they had not received in the Great War. Poland fielded the world's second-largest horse-mounted cavalry force when Germany invaded on 1 September 1939.

The Poles employed some of the tactics that the U.S. Cavalry intended to use to deal with mechanized enemy forces and had even equipped horse units with some light armored vehicles, much as was the case in American formations. Even Major General Herr finally acknowledged the role that the machine was going to play in the next war, and he ordered the conversion of two regiments to fifty-fifty "horse-mechanized" formations—a last-gasp bid to preserve some role for the steeds of flesh. (The horse-mounted elements were to be "porteed" from place to place in large, slat-sided truck trailers.)[32] The problem seemed to remain of what to do with the other ten Regular Army, eighteen National Guard, and twenty-four Organized Reserve horse-mounted regiments.[33]

In reality, the horse-mechanized formation was still a problem, not a solution. The 101st Cavalry, for example, was inducted into federal service on 27 January 1941 as a horse-mechanized outfit. Charles Graydon, a company-grade officer at the time, commented on the lessons learned during the Carolina maneuvers that autumn:

> As the maneuvers progressed, it became clear to many that the inclusion of horse and mechanized units in one regiment was a mistake. Their capabilities were completely different, nor did they complement each other in the completion of missions as the field manuals said they were meant to do. Furthermore, the use of tractor-trailers to move men and horses from one battle area to another was difficult. They were unwieldy and impossible to camouflage. In one instance the column commander was embarrassed in finding himself on a narrow dead-end road. It took half a day to get the column turned around. In another situation the tractor-trailers became bogged down in a field after an all night rainstorm, thereby preventing them being moved for almost an entire day.[34]

Moreover, despite Herr's reluctant shift, a crisis was brewing for the Cavalry branch. Chaffee and other mechanization advocates had been calling for the establishment of "cavalry divisions, mechanized" built roughly along the lines of the German panzer divisions that had swept through Poland, to be manned by personnel stripped from the Regular Army's horse cavalry.[35] During army-level maneuvers in May 1940, the 7th Cavalry Brigade (Mechanized) formed part of a provisional armored division, along with the infantry's Provisional

Tank Brigade from Fort Benning, Georgia, and the 6th Infantry Regiment (Motorized). The provisional division dominated the exercise.[36]

This was the future of mobile warfare, and it was not going to belong to the Cavalry. On 25 May, Brig. Gen. Frank Andrews, the War Department assistant chief of staff, G-3 (operations), met in a high school basement in humble Alexandria, Louisiana, with Maj. Gen. Adna Chaffee and other officers from cavalry and mechanized units fresh from Third Army maneuvers nearby. Colonel George S. Patton Jr. was one of those present.[37] The men at the meeting advocated a unified approach to mechanized development free of the Chiefs of Cavalry and Infantry.[38] Within a month, Lt. Col. Willis Crittenberger (operations officer, or S-3, 7th Cavalry Brigade [Mechanized]) informed mechanized cavalry advocate Maj. Gen. Daniel Van Voorhis that the G-3 had recommended organizing a separate armored corps that would incorporate all of the army's mechanized formations, and Chief of Staff Gen. George C. Marshall had approved the proposal. A formal plan reached the War Department General Staff on 10 June. Detailed consideration followed. Despite opposition to the proposal from the Chiefs of Cavalry and Infantry, the War Plans Division began altering mobilization plans to include armored divisions.[39]

The G-3 proposed to establish two mechanized divisions, one based at Fort Knox and the second at Fort Benning. Mechanized units would be redistributed among them to ensure that the divisions started from roughly the same basis. The infantry's light tank formations were to be reorganized along the lines of mechanized cavalry regiments, and cavalry officers would be spread among the two divisions, where they were expected to wield strong influence. On the other hand, the new divisions inherited the organization of distinct light and medium tank battalions, a concept approved by the War Department in 1938 to meet the declared needs of the Infantry branch.[40]

The adjutant general on 10 July 1940 authorized the creation of the Armored Force as a "service test," which sidestepped the need for congressional approval and allowed the War Department great flexibility in modifying the organization. Chaffee, appointed Chief of the Armored Force and commanding general, I Armored Corps, had full authority over tactical and training doctrine for all subordinate units as well as a research and advisory role in equipment procurement. The Armored Force consisted of the 1st and 2d Armored divisions and the separate 70th Tank Battalion (Medium), a General Headquarters (GHQ) "reserve" battalion.

Stripped of much of its mechanized strength, the Cavalry retained only two horse-mechanized regiments, the 1st Cavalry Division's armored car squadron, and the armored car troops belonging to eight active horse regiments. Only the cavalry division's squadron retained any light tanks.[41]

President Franklin Roosevelt in September ordered the entire National Guard into federal service for one year, which created much of the manpower pool that was to serve in the mechanized cavalry. The New Jersey National Guard's 102d Cavalry Regiment (Essex Troop), for example, was part of the 21st Cavalry Division when it was called up in November 1940 and separated from the division. The regiment mobilized on 6 January 1941, with orders to move by train to Fort Jackson, South Carolina. Prior to departure, the regiment reorganized as a horse-mechanized outfit; one squadron, including Troops A–C, remained on horseback, whereas the second squadron, with Troops D–F, was converted to two armored car troops and one motorcycle troop. On 6 April 1942, the 102d Cavalry reorganized as a fully mechanized regiment.[42]

The New Mechanized Cavalry

With the eclipse of the Cavalry branch by the Armored Force, the mechanized cavalry took on three basic forms, determined by attachment to an armored or infantry division or organization as a separate squadron. The army decided in May 1942 to leave the two active cavalry divisions horse mounted and to mechanize non-divisional regiments and squadrons and the cavalry components of infantry and armored divisions.[43]

The Armored Division's Reconnaissance Element

Initially, each armored division had an organic reconnaissance battalion, which was for all intents a mechanized cavalry squadron, and each regiment had a reconnaissance company. The 1st Reconnaissance Battalion, for example, was activated on 15 July 1940 as part of the 1st Armored Division, with its personnel drawn from the 7th Cavalry Brigade. It was redesignated in May 1941 as the 81st Reconnaissance Battalion and again in January 1942, when the armored divisions reorganized with two instead of three tank regiments, as the 81st Armored Reconnaissance Battalion. The reconnaissance battalion consisted of a headquarters element, two armored reconnaissance companies equipped with scout cars and motorcycles, a light tank company, and a half-track-mounted rifle company.[44]

The reconnaissance battalion provided the division commander with the capability to conduct distant, close, and battle reconnaissance. The last category included assignments when the division was engaged in combat, such as locating the enemy's flanks and rear, observing the flanks for indications of hostile reserves or reinforcements, harassing hostile command and supply installations, and seeking gaps or soft spots in the enemy's line. Secondary missions included security (for example, guarding key fords across rivers), delaying actions, seizing and holding key terrain, pursuit, and forming a division reserve.[45] In 1942, Field Manual (FM) 17-22 explicitly included combat in the list of additional missions.[46] These were the classic cavalry tasks.

A reorganization in 1942 eliminated the rifle company and made the armored reconnaissance battalion closely resemble a cavalry reconnaissance squadron, the main difference being that reconnaissance battalion reconnaissance platoons were issued an assault gun. The doctrine, too, changed to emphasize reconnaissance and avoid combat.[47]

Men in the armored division reconnaissance elements initially suffered even greater spiritual dislocation than that felt by those merely making the jump from the horse to the machine. "There was some loss of identity," recorded the history

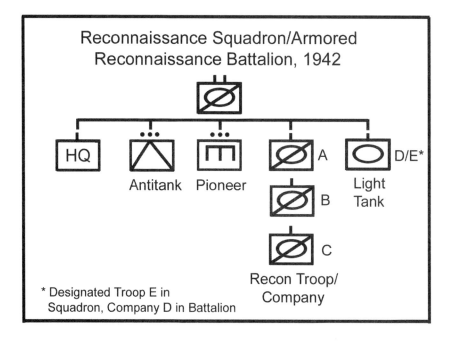

Reconnaissance Squadron/Armored Reconnaissance Battalion, 1942

HQ Antitank Pioneer A D/E* Light Tank
B
C
Recon Troop/ Company

* Designated Troop E in Squadron, Company D in Battalion

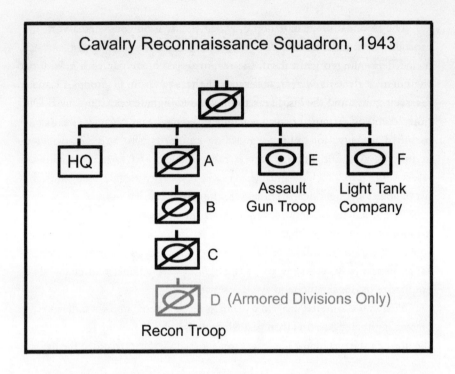

Cavalry Reconnaissance Squadron, 1943

HQ — A — B — C — D (Armored Divisions Only) — Recon Troop

E — Assault Gun Troop

F — Light Tank Company

of the 89th Armored Reconnaissance Battalion. In 1943 it had left the 2d Cavalry Division, in which it had been the 92d Reconnaissance Squadron. "[T]he squadron became a battalion; the troops, companies; the hat braid turned from yellow to Armored Force green and white; but in merging with the larger unit, the 89th still proudly retained its basic cavalry heritage."[48]

Another Armored Force reorganization in September 1943 created light armored divisions without a regimental structure, at which time the reconnaissance battalions were formally labeled cavalry reconnaissance squadrons, mechanized. This was good news to old cavalrymen: "[T]he squadron again emerged," recorded the 89th Cavalry Reconnaissance Squadron, "as a Cavalry organization, complete with red-and-white guidons and a standard of Cavalry yellow."[49] (The guidon dated back to 1834, when it was established by regulation for companies of dragoons.) William Knowlton, a lieutenant with the 87th Cavalry Reconnaissance Squadron, agreed, saying, "We were very conscious of being Cavalry."[50]

Being Cavalry meant something to the troopers that is difficult to quantify— a body of self-perceptions and standards of excellence derived from the experience and lore of centuries. The cavalryman was audacious, clever, and instinctively aware of the best moment to strike. Troopers shared an esprit de corps that was unique within the army's ranks.[51]

Under the reorganization, the reconnaissance companies from the two armored regiments were transferred to the squadron as Troops D and E (assault guns), and the light tank troop was redesignated as Company F. Only the 2d and 3d Armored divisions retained the old heavy organization, and the 1st Armored Division did not reorganize as a light formation until July 1944.

The Squadrons and Groups

In January 1941, the army created the prototype for the cavalry reconnaissance squadron that would serve through the coming war. The original provisional armored car troop was redesignated as Troop A of the newly formed 1st Reconnaissance Squadron, which was organic to the 1st Cavalry Division. The squadron consisted of a headquarters element and four troops. Troops A and B fielded scout cars and conducted reconnaissance missions, Troop C was made up of riflemen mounted in jeeps (or "bantams"), and Troop D was the "reserve troop" and employed thirteen light tanks organized into four three-tank platoons and a headquarters. The field manual specified that Troop C was to have motorcycles, but then-Capt. Hamilton Howze, a horse soldier who had taken charge of the troop and was later to become the father of the air cavalry, recalled that his was the only entirely jeep-mounted troop in the army. Total strength amounted to 657 men and 33 officers. In May, the unit was redesignated the 91st Reconnaissance Squadron. Altogether, this battalion-size unit had a remarkable 450 automatic weapons (light and heavy) and 140 rifles at its disposal.

The 2d Cavalry Division received a matching reconnaissance element in July 1941 with the establishment of Troop A, 2d Reconnaissance Squadron (Provisional). The troop was formally designated Troop A, 92d Reconnaissance Squadron, on 1 November 1941, and Troops B–D were created with personnel inducted after Pearl Harbor.

The chief mission of the new squadrons was scouting and patrolling. Nevertheless, given their great firepower, they were available to form part of a combined-arms team in the attack, in delay, and in harassment of the enemy.[52] Doctrine anticipated that "the squadron must fight at some time in the execution of any mission it may be assigned," and noted that the squadron had a tank troop to enable the reconnaissance troops to act aggressively. Fighting dismounted was discouraged, and an envelopment of one or both enemy flanks was commended as the usual tactic to employ.[53]

In early 1942, Chief of Staff Gen. George Marshall ordered the conversion of all non-divisional cavalry regiments into mechanized formations (in the end, two were dismounted instead).[54] In December, the War Department established a system of groups that were to control multiple battalion-size elements that were administratively and logistically self-sufficient, including mechanized cavalry, combat engineers, field artillery, and antiaircraft artillery. Separate tank and tank destroyer battalions were already organized along these lines.[55] As a half-step, some reactivated regiments, such as the 2d Cavalry (15 January 1943), were converted to mechanized regiments with two provisional squadrons.[56]

The vast majority of mechanized cavalry squadrons were created in 1943 with the reorganization of the non-divisional cavalry regiments into groups consisting of two squadrons each, plus one additional separate outfit, the 117th Cavalry Reconnaissance Squadron. (The 11th Cavalry Group briefly controlled three squadrons during the summer of 1943.) The squadrons were attached to, not organic to, the groups and were administratively self-sufficient. The 91st Reconnaissance Squadron reorganized in 1943 into the standard cavalry mechanized reconnaissance squadron configuration.

Like tank (later "armored") and tank destroyer groups, the cavalry group consisted of little but a headquarters element, which was capable of directing squadrons and other elements attached to it. Unlike the other two group types, the cavalry groups routinely functioned as a command element in combat. Normally, a group was assigned to each corps in the European theater, but not in the Mediterranean or Pacific theaters.

The standardized 1943 cavalry reconnaissance squadron had a headquarters and a service troop, with 12 officers and 123 enlisted men, four armored cars, five half-tracks, ten jeeps, and thirteen 2 1/2-ton trucks; three reconnaissance troops (four in light armored divisions), each with 5 officers and 140 enlisted men, twelve armored cars, four half-tracks, twenty-three jeeps, and one 2 1/2-ton truck; an assault gun troop with 4 officers and 89 men (5 and 111 respectively, in armored divisions), three two-gun platoons (four platoons in armored divisions), eight half-tracks, two jeeps, and one 2 1/2-ton truck; and a light tank company, with 5 officers and 92 men, seventeen tanks, two jeeps, and one 2 1/2-ton truck. The troops and the tank company had a tank retriever each, and the headquarters troop had a heavy wrecker. The 2d and 3d Armored divi-

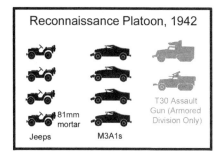

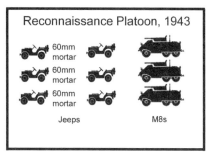

sions retained their armored reconnaissance battalions, as did the 1st Armored Division until it reorganized as a light division.[57]

Throughout the war, the cavalry squadrons were deemed by their commanders to have too few riflemen to hold ground. Moreover, cavalry troops were not issued items that the infantry took for granted, such as entrenching tools and wire communications equipment.[58]

In both the squadron and the troop, the reconnaissance platoon was the key action element. From 1943 on, the platoon consisted of an armored car section with three M8s, three jeeps with .30-caliber machine guns, and three jeeps carrying 60mm mortars (which replaced the 81mm mortars used up to that point).

The Infantry Division's Reconnaissance Troop

The army in 1940 instructed the Cavalry branch to create an entirely new strategy for its employment—specifically to design a reconnaissance element for each of the new "triangular" (three-regiment) infantry divisions.[59] The concept was mechanized from the start, and each infantry division was given a cavalry reconnaissance troop—one-third the size of the reconnaissance battalion available to a German division commander, and one-fifth the size of a British infantry division's reconnaissance regiment after the creation of the Reconnaissance Corps in 1941. Some personnel were drawn from the horse cavalry, but they mixed with other soldiers from the division, such as infantrymen and military police to whom cavalry traditions were new. "You got KP if you called it a company," recalled one veteran.[60]

From the outset, the Cavalry branch doctrinally limited the troops in infantry divisions to conducting reconnaissance by stealth and avoiding combat. Initially, the troop consisted of a headquarters section and three platoons, each equipped with four scout cars, up to twelve jeeps, and two motorcycles.[61] After 1943, the organization was the same as that in the cavalry reconnaissance squadrons.

The infantry division's reconnaissance troop in combat often was spared difficulties caused by low rifle strength because it could draw on the parent formation. According to one troop commander in Europe:

> In a rapidly moving situation, when the infantry cannot maintain contact with the enemy, the reconnaissance troop [can]. By riding eight or 10 infantrymen "pig-a-back," a reconnaissance platoon gives to the following infantry first-hand information whenever it is stopped temporarily by enemy action. By the same token, no time is lost by the infantry main body in becoming disposed for action, because the mounted point has the situation "diagnosed. . . ." Usually, the fire power of the reconnaissance platoon is sufficient to reduce local resistance, and handling of prisoners by two of the infantrymen allows the platoon to proceed without delay.[62]

Nonetheless, the troop, when committed to man a line, defend a road-block, or advance as infantry, sometimes was left on its own; in such cases, low rifle strength and the lack of infantry training came to bear. In December 1944, for example, the 9th Cavalry Reconnaissance Troop was expected to fill a six-thousand-yard gap with eighty-five men in outposts, a decision that resulted in five hundred German troops infiltrating through the sector.[63]

Training

Many of the first cavalrymen to enter training were housed in pyramidal tents, fending off the winter cold with three blankets and a sheet, while the rapidly expanding army built barracks to house them. Training was arduous and intensive.[64] Basic training featured the usual: long marches and basic familiarization with small arms and vehicles. Medical personnel earned real-world experience taking care of blisters and accident victims. In the 2d Cavalry, the men sang, "They say this is a mechanized war. Then what the hell are we marching for?"[65]

Cavalrymen were provided a unique set of soldier skills. They received some instruction in dismounted combat and reduction of roadblocks. Recognizing that troopers would often fight under conditions that precluded rapid supply of replacements for casualties, the army trained each man to drive the vehicle to which he was assigned, to use every weapon on board, and to operate the radio. Mounted drill taught men to work together as a unit, though nobody expected that drill formations would be used in combat. Personnel were trained to observe and report any information that might be of value to the current operation, and officers received intelligence training to enable them to discern important information to pass up the chain so that higher echelons would not be deluged by trivia.[66]

For veteran cavalrymen, the transition was huge. One member of the 102d Cavalry Regiment recalled, "Few cavalrymen found the transition from the horse to the scout car or the motorcycle easy to accept. It was, as many a good horseman found out, one thing to care for a mount, as ornery as some of them could be. It was something else to care for a mechanized monster, whether you were thinking in terms of affection or of maintenance."[67]

The 43d Reconnaissance Troop, by contrast, was organized to be the 43d Infantry Division's mechanized reconnaissance element from its creation in February 1942 without ever seeing a horse. The unit history records:

> In June 1942, the troop received 10 scout cars and other of its basic equipment. It began an intensive mounted reconnaissance and combat training program, which included two successful night attacks on the Hattiesburg Airport, which was defended by a battalion of infantry. Included in this training was air-ground coordination work, at which time a Piper Cub was attached to the troop. It was during this period that the troop became proficient in the use of its vehicles in mounted reconnaissance and combat; use of radios, machine guns, 37mm anti-tank guns, and 81mm mortars; scouting and patrolling, and all other functions required of a reconnaissance troop.[68]

Charles Raney joined the army on 5 October 1942 and went to Fort Leavenworth, Kansas, for cavalry basic training. He was assigned to the newly formed 89th Cavalry Reconnaissance Squadron, part of the 9th Armored Division, at Camp Funston, Kansas, joining a cadre of old 2d Cavalry horse soldiers from Fort Riley, Kansas.

Raney recalled, "I was placed in Troop D, 1st Platoon. We trained during the winter in Kansas in tanks, M8 [armored cars]; then to the Mojave Desert near Needles, California, for summer desert maneuvers in half-tracks; then on to Camp Polk, Louisiana, for more maneuvers in the pines and swamps all winter in jeeps. I qualified as a radio operator, voice, swimming, and combat village instructor, rank of corporal. Trained to use efficiently, the .30- and .50-caliber machine guns, .45-caliber Tommy gun and automatic pistol, 37mm, German small arms, and grenades. Learned map reading and orientation, fire direction, and demolition."[69]

Sergeant Ivan Marion, who served with the 91st Cavalry Reconnaissance Squadron throughout the war, concluded that the cavalry, indeed all combat troops, should have received infantry training.[70] Somebody must have had some inkling as to what could happen on the real battlefield, because the final test given to the 101st Cavalry (Mechanized) in the autumn of 1942 was a dismounted attack on a fixed position, "one thing that cavalry was not trained, organized, or equipped to do," commented Col. Charles Graydon later.[71] Nevertheless, such training was not added to the program.

Lieutenant Colonel Phillip Davidson, 3d Cavalry Group, told an interviewer in late 1944, "The training received in preparation for [corps and army] tests was very good. . . . It was, however, close-range stuff and not a progressive, integrated training necessary for combat. . . . In my opinion, the biggest mistake made in training was not to tactically train reconnaissance teams and platoons as units. . . . Some of this was done, but not nearly enough. . . . In practically all combat situations encountered by the 3d Cavalry Group, such combat situations have been met by platoon and team action."[72]

The situation appears to have been generally similar for the squadrons and battalions in armored divisions. Training included a great deal of work with equipment and participation in large-scale exercises, but platoon-level work was the rare exception in the States. In the armored division, the reorganization from the heavy to light configuration consumed time that could have been spent otherwise.[73] Once divisions shipped to the UK, most instruction had to be done in garrison because of limited training area facilities, which prevented much fieldwork at the troop or platoon levels.[74]

Iron Horses: Equipping the Force

The Cavalry branch oversaw the design of vehicles during the mid-1930s that would fit its operational needs, including the half-track, armored car, and scout car. It rejected light tanks with two turrets—which the infantry wanted so crews could aim machine guns at more targets—in favor of a single-turret design. The branch demanded speed, power, and mechanical reliability from its armored vehicles and therefore avoided thick steel plate. It needed the ability to maneuver cross-country, so wheeled vehicles had to have four-wheel drive. Other goals were to have tanks that could travel a full day without resupply and be able to fire on the move, have as many vision ports as possible, and have turrets that could traverse quickly.[75]

In 1938, Maj. R. W. Grow, who worked in the office of the Chief of Cavalry, described mechanized cavalry's vision of its equipment needs on the battlefield:

> From its earliest conception, it was recognized that "tanks" or combat cars must initially form a part, and an important part, of mechanized cavalry. In fact, combat cars today are the backbone of the mechanized cavalry, but their independent employment is *never* contemplated. They invariably form but the nucleus of a balanced, tactically homogeneous whole. Cavalry must above all things be capable of fighting unsupported by infantry. . . . Therefore, mechanized cavalry must fight mounted, dismounted, or by combined action.
>
> Our attempts to meet this requirement to date have resulted in a variety of machines which, in a measure, have worked. Breeding and cross-breeding are being carried out in arsenals and shops to develop an IRON HORSE as a Cavalry mount. Such an iron horse must be fast and surefooted, enable his riders to fight mounted or to readily dismount and fight on foot, must have good "eyes" and a "tough skin" and be constitutionally a good "keeper" and a light "feeder." This is not a "tank" in the sense of a mechanical weapon to be propelled against a hostile position in support of other troops. It is a mechanical HORSE for cavalrymen to employ on all cavalry missions. So far, we have failed to attain the ideal "iron horse" and have been forced to be content with a variety of vehicles for special purposes. These have included combat cars, armored cars, scout cars, half-track cars, motor mounts, etc. . . .
>
> More and more we find mechanized cavalry employing dismounted action, utilizing its iron horses for rapid maneuver on the battlefield and presenting constant threat of mounted action. . . . Scouting and patrolling, outposts, and security detachments demand soldiers with their feet on the ground. Mechanized cavalry has always recognized this.[76]

★★★

As Grow had conceded, the vehicles with which the mechanized cavalry went to war generally fell far short of the ideal. Still, the hardware did allow the troopers to move relatively quickly, to fight mounted, and to dismount with alacrity.

The reconnaissance men would go to war riding the M3A1 scout car, which was designed for "high-speed scouting duty" and was standardized in June 1939. A lightly armored open-topped body—one-quarter inch of steel all around except for a flip-down, half-inch armored cover for the shatterproof windshield—was mated to a commercial four-wheel-drive chassis. The vehicle's in-line six-cylinder 110-horsepower engine could move the car at fifty-five miles per hour on a road. Armored shutters controlled by the driver protected the radiator. Normal armament consisted of one .30-caliber and one .50-caliber machine gun mounted on a skate rail around the interior of the body. Space was provided for a radio.[77]

After training with the M3A1 in North Africa and fighting with it in Sicily, the 45th Cavalry Reconnaissance Troop offered this observation: "The M3A1 scout car has very little if any cross-country capabilities or maneuverability, its armor is of no value, and it is out-gunned by any of the enemy's armored cars. It is hard to replace, maintain, and obtain parts for. It is 'duck soup' for ambush, particularly with hand grenades."[78]

The M8 armored car (dubbed the "Greyhound" by the British) was standardized in June 1942, but contract talks delayed serial production until March 1943, and cavalry units did not begin to receive them until late that year. The vehicle was initially designed as a fast, light tank destroyer but was adopted to replace the M3A1 scout car in cavalry units. The six-wheel-drive vehicle used the same engine as the M3A1 and could reach fifty-five miles per hour despite its 17,400-pound bulk. The M8 had five-eighths-inch-thick upper front armor and three-eighths-inch-thick armor on the sides and rear. The bottom was unarmored.

The 37mm main gun was installed in an open-topped turret in a combination mount with a .30-caliber coaxial machine gun. The main gun could elevate twenty degrees and depress ten degrees. The weapon fired its shell at a muzzle velocity of 2,900 feet per second and could (in theory) penetrate 1.8 inches of face-hardened armor plate at a thousand yards with the armor-piercing capped (APC, often simply rendered AP) round. The requirement for cavalry M8s to carry two radios, both AM and FM, reduced ammunition stowage for the main gun to sixteen rounds, but many outfits found ways to carry more. No antiaircraft machine gun was fitted on the turret until mid-1944, but many units installed .30- or .50-caliber weapons on their own.

The cavalry did not think much of the M8 when it received a test model. The vehicle had the same power plant as the M3A1 scout car but was much heavier, so its cross-country capabilities were suspect. Nonetheless, many who used the M8 in battle liked it well.[79] This held true even under some fairly awful conditions, such as unending mud. The 96th Cavalry Reconnaissance Troop, after its experience on Leyte, in the Philippines, would report, "[The M8] performed more satisfactorily than anticipated. With chains, which are extremely necessary, its mobility is comparable to a 2 1/2-ton truck, 6x6." The troop removed the mud shields so the wheels would not jam.[80]

A turretless utility version, the M20 armored car, was used by some cavalry units; it appears to have been universally disliked. It was difficult to enter and exit and had little room for cargo.[81]

The M2 half-track car, standardized in 1940, weighed 19,800 pounds and had a six-cylinder gasoline engine that could move it along at forty miles per hour. The half-track carried sixty gallons of fuel and had a cruising range of 175 miles. Various radios could be mounted in the vehicle as needed.

Armor plating one-quarter-inch thick protected the entire vehicle except for a hinged half-inch plate that could be swung down over the windshield. The armor was calculated to be stout enough to stop small-arms fire, but the half-track earned a bad name among the troops regarding protection as early as the fighting in North Africa. One soldier, when asked by an officer if German aircraft bullets would go through the half-track, replied, "No, sir. They only come through one wall and then they rattle around."[82]

The M2 had a short bed and could transport ten men when equipped with seats in the cargo space. A gun rail ran around the upper wall of the cargo area and typically supported three machine guns; the layout precluded a back door, so men had to mount and dismount over the walls.

The M3 half-track personnel carrier, also standardized in 1940, was essentially an M2 fitted out with a longer bed, a rear door, and a pedestal-mounted machine gun; the new layout boosted hauling capacity to thirteen men. The M2A1 and M3A1 models added a ring mount for a .50-caliber machine gun over the passenger seat in the cab.[83]

The half-track was equipped with either a roller or a winch on the front, the former intended to lift the nose to prevent embedding when crossing ditches.

With the winch, the half-track was deemed the most reliable "get through" vehicle available by at least some troopers who fought in the deep Pacific mud.[84]

The famous jeep, or quarter-ton truck, served with the cavalry throughout the war. Ironically, horse cavalry advocates were influential in spurring development of the jeep, which they wanted to haul around .50-caliber machine guns and 37mm antitank guns to protect the cavalry division against enemy armor. The first vehicles from Bantam were delivered for testing in January 1941, and the suspiciously similar version contracted for by the army with Willys went on to play a key role in mechanized outfits as well as in the rest of the military.[85]

The four-wheel-drive jeep could reach sixty-five miles per hour on a level road and climb a 60 percent grade on the strength of its four-cylinder, fifty-four-horsepower engine. The vehicle was equipped with a baseplate in the back for mounting a machine gun. Space was provided for a radio.[86] An amphibious version, allegedly similar in capability and reliability, was authorized for the pre-standardized reconnaissance squadrons, though it was disliked when used because it could not maneuver well on sand or rough ground.[87]

The jeep "iron pony" warmed the hearts of reconnaissance men. It was quiet, excellent at cross-country maneuver, and light enough to be ferried across streams on makeshift rafts. The vehicle's low silhouette made it perfect for the point of a column.[88]

Some officers hoped the jeep would displace the Harley-Davidson motorcycle, used by dispatch riders and troopers who were supposed to segue into dismounted action. The army went to war with motorcycle-mounted cavalry despite the lessons of maneuvers, which showed how extremely vulnerable they were on the battlefield and how poor they were at cross-country maneuver.[89] When the 101st Cavalry began receiving jeeps to replace motorcycles in April 1942, commented Charles Graydon, "this was a relief to many of those who had risked their lives riding them in the snow of New England and mud of the Carolinas."[90]

The Harley-Davidson motorcycle was a standard police bike outfitted with a holster for a submachine gun, a bracket for extra ammunition, and combat-zone safety lighting. The twenty-three-horsepower engine could drive the motorcycle to sixty-five miles per hour.[91]

The M3 light tank, nicknamed the Stuart by the British, entered series production in March 1941 and provided the firepower for the light tank companies in the squadron-size reconnaissance units that would fight in North

Africa. The M3 weighed a bit over thirteen tons and had front armor one and a half inches thick and plate on sides and rear one inch thick. Turret walls also were one inch thick.

The turret had a manual traverse system, which was not a terrible deficiency given its small size. The M3A1 standardized in August 1941 incorporated several improvements, including powered traverse. The 37mm main gun's characteristics were the same as for the M8 armored car. The M3 had stowage for 103 rounds (37mm), which would typically be a mix of APC, high-explosive (HE), and canister shells. Canister rounds were highly effective against infantry to a range of two hundred yards and could be fired on the move.[92] Four additional .30-caliber machine guns were provided: one in the hull for the bow gunner (who was called the "bog"), two in the side sponsons, and one on the roof for antiaircraft defense.

The 27,400-pound M3, powered by a seven-cylinder 250-horsepower Continental radial aircraft engine, could reach thirty-six miles per hour on level ground but had a cruising range of only seventy miles. Disposable fuel tanks could be attached, which boosted reserves from 56 to 106 gallons.

Crews thought highly of the M3-series tanks, which were mechanically reliable. Fighting in North Africa was to show that the tank was too light and under-gunned to serve as a battle tank, but users thought it had proved effective for reconnaissance in force, exploitation, wide harassing attacks, and hit-and-run attacks. That view was to change as German tanks got steadily bigger and tougher, but the M3 and its generally similar M5-series successor never fell behind Japanese armor in the Pacific.

The M5 and M5A1 light tanks differed from the M3 series mainly in having sloped front armor in place of the M3's vertical slabs (which eliminated the sponson machine guns) and twin Cadillac engines in place of the radial motor. The various changes boosted the vehicle's weight to 33,000 pounds, but there was no loss in speed.[93]

Fighting in North Africa was still under way when the army concluded that it needed a light tank with the punch of a 75mm gun and improved mobility. Ordnance authorized development of the new tank in March 1943. The M24, called the Chaffee by its American creators, was standardized in July 1944 and was the most powerful light tank in the world. But it did not begin to reach mechanized cavalry outfits in Europe until early 1945 and was never issued to the cavalry reconnaissance troops in the Pacific.

The M24 represented a design break from the M3/M5 light tank series and was closer kin to the M18 tank destroyer and M26 heavy tank. The low-silhouette hull was supported by a torsion-bar suspension. The sleek new turret housed the commander, loader, and gunner; the driver and bow gunner remained seated in the hull. The turret had power traverse.

The lightweight, gyrostabilized, short-recoil gun was based on a 75mm design built for use by ground-attack bombers, but it fired the same ammunition at the same muzzle velocity as the weapon mounted in the M4 medium tank. A .30-caliber coaxial machine gun was supplied, as was a .30-caliber bow gun and a .50-caliber antiaircraft (AA) machine gun mounted on a prominent pintle on the turret roof. A 2-inch mortar was incorporated into the turret top. Organized stowage was provided for 75mm rounds (48), .30-caliber rounds (3,750), and .50-caliber rounds (440), plus 14 smoke and fragmentation mortar shells.

One inch of sloped frontal armor provided the ballistic protection of two and a half inches; armor on the sides was one inch thick and the rear amor was three-quarters of an inch thick.

To simplify production, the twin Cadillac engines were retained from the M5, but with an improved manual shift transfer unit to manage the two Hydra-Matic transmissions. The vehicle weighed in at nearly twenty tons but could reach a top speed of thirty-five miles per hour on level ground.[94]

Crews were overjoyed when they received the M24. The tank had all the advantages in speed that cavalrymen needed, and they had a gun for the first time that could knock out even a heavy panzer if the gunner could get a fairly close shot at the flank or rear.

The half-track-based T30 assault gun, a stopgap similar to the ad hoc first-generation M3 tank destroyer, initially equipped reconnaissance outfits. The T30 consisted of an M3 half-track with an M1A1 75mm pack howitzer mounted in the bed pointing forward over the cab. The gun could be elevated 50 degrees, depressed 9 degrees, and traversed 22.5 degrees to either side. Firing a 14.6-pound projectile at a muzzle velocity of 1,250 feet per second, the piece had a maximum range of 9,610 yards. The vehicle had stowage for sixty rounds of 75mm ammunition, and although the howitzer was not designed for antitank use, there was a high-explosive antitank (HEAT) round available. According to Ordnance, it could penetrate three inches of armor plate "at howitzer range." The T30 had a gun shield that was three-eighths-inch thick and was designed to stop a .30-caliber round at 250 yards.

The half-track was outfitted with a .50-caliber machine gun on a pedestal mount for antiaircraft defense. The crew numbered five. The T30 was equipped with an SCR-510 radio.[95]

The M8 howitzer motor carriage (HMC) entered production in 1942 and began to replace the T30 in the assault-gun role in cavalry units in the field in late 1943. An open-topped turret housing an M2 or M3 howitzer (75mm) was mounted on a slightly modified M5 light tank hull, which retained the M5's engine and drivetrain. Except on the upper front hull, the armor was slightly thinner all around than on the M5 because the design goal was to provide protection for the four-man crew against small-arms fire only.

The gun could elevate forty degrees and depress twenty degrees. The weapon could lob a high-explosive shell 9,610 yards and fire an armor-piercing round at a muzzle velocity of 1,250 feet per second. There was stowage for forty-six 75mm shells in the small vehicle, which was not much in light of the weapon's maximum rate of fire of twenty-five rounds per minute. A .50-caliber machine gun in a ring mount was provided for antiaircraft defense.[96]

The troop headquarters detachment's antitank platoon in 1942 and 1943 received the M6 gun motor carriage, which featured a 37mm gun mounted on a four-wheel-drive Dodge three-quarter-ton weapons carrier. The gun could traverse 360 degrees but would shatter the windshield if fired forward. A one-quarter-inch shield offered the gunner and loader minimal protection. The gun's capabilities were identical to those of the gun mounted in the M8 armored car. The in-line six-cylinder engine was capable of pushing the vehicle to fifty-five miles per hour on a road surface. Four men crewed the truck and gun.[97] The arrival of the M8 armored car in cavalry units rendered the M6 superfluous.

An investigating board in the European theater of operations in March 1944 considered the desirability of including the newly available and speedy M18 tank destroyer in the organization of the cavalry squadron. Although there was support for adding four M18s to the assault gun troop or substituting them for a platoon of light tanks, this step was not taken.[98]

★★★

The radio was arguably the main weapon of the mechanized cavalry, because with it the cavalrymen could set in motion events leading to the destruction of enemy forces they observed. The mechanized cavalry used the radio equipment designed for the armored force. The SCR-245 FM set was the chief tank radio in 1940, but development work began immediately on the SCR-508 FM family of radios, which became the workhorse in armored units. The line-of-sight SCR-508 system reached out to a maximum of fifteen miles; in broken terrain reconnaissance units at times had to use armored cars or half-tracks as relay stations. The SCR-508 had a transmitter and two receivers, whereas the variant SCR-528 had a transmitter and one receiver, and the SCR-538 had a receiver only. The SCR-510 was a manpack version with receiver and transmitter. Under the standardized 1943 Table of Organization and Equipment (TO&E), each armored car carried an SCR-508, and three jeeps in each reconnaissance platoon were equipped with the SCR-510.

By 1943, every armored car was also outfitted with the SCR-506 AM radio, which could reach up to a hundred miles and tie into other radio nets, such as artillery. The maintenance section also had one SCR-506, so it could hear about problems in distant elements of the troop. All told, the 1943 reconnaissance troop in a squadron fielded twelve AM radios and twenty-three FM radios, whereas an infantry division's troop possessed one more of each.[99]

★★★

The carbine was the cavalry's traditional firearm because of its lighter weight and shorter barrel as compared with the rifle, but the mechanized cavalry went to war with a mix of small arms. The 91st Reconnaissance Squadron used World War I–vintage .30-caliber Springfield rifles throughout its service in North Africa, supplemented by the .45-caliber Tommy gun and some carbines. When it re-equipped at the end of the campaign, it received the new .30-caliber M1 Garand rifle.[100] The 81st Armored Reconnaissance Battalion in North Africa appears to have used at least some of the new .30-caliber M1 carbines. Anecdotal accounts suggest that troopers outside the Pacific much preferred the Garand because the carbine lacked stopping power.

Under the standardized 1943 TO&E, the mechanized cavalry reconnaissance troop was allocated ninety-one carbines, twnety-eight .45-caliber submachine guns, and twenty-six M1 rifles. Adding weapons assigned to other elements such as the light tank company and assault gun troop, the totals for a mechanized cavalry squadron (non-armored division) were 465 carbines, 205 submachine guns, and 90 M1 rifles—plus 3 pistols. The reconnaissance troop also fielded thirteen .30-caliber machine guns (54 per squadron) and three .50-caliber machine guns (25 per squadron), plus the weapons mounted on armored cars, tanks, and assault guns.

The Cavalry's First Combat

The cavalry first went to war in the Philippines after the Japanese invasion on 10 December 1941. The troopers involved were horse cavalry fighting under the very conditions that the old school thought still guaranteed the horse a place on the modern battlefield. The 26th Cavalry Regiment, Philippine Scouts, had the mission of fighting a classic delaying action to cover the withdrawal of American forces to the Bataan Peninsula. Notions of staying on rugged terrain to avoid tanks proved ridiculous because the cavalry had to fight where the Japanese were, and they were using the roads to advance from town to town.

Colonel Clinton Pierce, commanding, told a correspondent:

> We fought 'em in the streets and nipa shacks of Damortis all day [22 December 1941]. Then late in the afternoon, the Japs got some tanks ashore farther north and came after us with planes and tanks. We pulled back to Rosario during the night, and the next day they were on us again. . . .
>
> The next day we fought them at Pozzorubio, which we reached during the night, and it was the same story. They couldn't hurt us until their planes and tanks came. Had we any tanks and planes, it would have been different.[101]

Once trapped on the Bataan Peninsula, the surviving troopers had to eat their mounts when rations ran out. One must concede that mechanized cavalry could not have done that.

★★★

Mechanized cavalry was about to find out how much better it could do. In late June 1942, the 91st Reconnaissance Squadron received orders that detached it from the 1st Cavalry Division to prepare for shipment to North Africa.[102] By this time, the squadron had reorganized so as to have three reconnaissance troops and a light tank troop with thirteen M3s. Each reconnaissance platoon now had its own artillery in the form of an 81mm mortar, and the troop anti-tank section had two M6 gun motor carriages. Fred Salter, who had joined the horse cavalry earlier in the year and had just transferred to the 91st Squadron, recalled, "When we left the States in 1942, the end of the war seemed an eternity away."[103]

CHAPTER 2

NORTH AFRICA: A CONCEPT TESTED

As you go into combat, always remember to have boldness of action and rapidity of movement.

—Lt. Col. Harry Candler to his
cavalrymen in North Africa, 1943

The first mechanized cavalrymen to engage the enemy appear to have belonged to the 1st Reconnaissance Troop, 1st Infantry Division, which landed near Oran, Algeria, at about 0830 hours on 8 November 1942 as part of Task Force Center in Operation Torch. The task force had sailed from England, as had the Eastern Task Force, which was landing British and American troops at Algiers. The Western Task Force deposited troops brought from the United States near Casablanca, Morocco. Mounted in scout cars and jeeps and feeling out the infantry's route of advance, the 1st Reconnaissance Troop encountered French resistance at Ste. Jean Baptiste crossroads at about 2130 hours on 9 November. The men withdrew and reported the encounter to the commander of the 2d Battalion, 16th Infantry, who immediately ordered his force to engage the foe while the cavalrymen pulled back to screen the rear. This first encounter resulted in no losses of men or material.[1]

The 3d Infantry Division's Reconnaissance Troop, which landed at Fedala as part of the Western Task Force, had been scheduled to be the first cavalry outfit into action. The men wore special black uniforms for their pre-dawn assault on Yellow Beach. But a series of mishaps in lowering and loading boats prevented their landing until daylight. The troop returned to the transports rather than conduct a frontal attack across a well-defended beach in broad daylight. Elements of the 2d Armored Division's 82d Reconnaissance Battalion

did reach shore as part of the armored landing team of the same task force, but they do not appear to have engaged in battle that day.[2]

Both the 3d Reconnaissance Troop and 82d Reconnaissance Battalion performed roles close to the one advocated by those who believed that mechanized cavalry should not fight during the 3d Infantry Division advance toward Casablanca beginning 10 November, which was supported by Combat Command B, 2d Armored Division. The 2d Platoon, Company C, 82d Reconnaissance Battalion, was probably with the point, identified only as five light tanks, when it ran into French resistance west of Bou Guedra at about 1700 hours. The column slipped around the French to continue to Casablanca, and the reconnaissance elements led the way during the lights-out night march. They reached Mazagan about daylight, and the French garrison surrendered. During the day an armistice was signed, which ended hostilities in Morocco. The 2d Armored Division, with its reconnaissance battalion, spent the remainder of the North Africa campaign guarding the frontier with Spanish Morocco to deter any Axis attempt to cut Allied lines of communication from there.[3]

Tunisia: Meeting the Real Enemy

At dawn on 31 January 1943, the second squadron-size mechanized cavalry formation to reach North Africa, the 1st Armored Division's 81st Reconnaissance

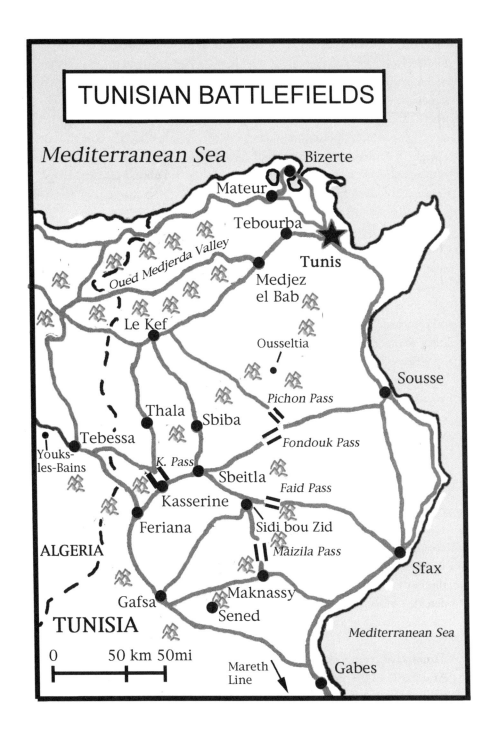

Battalion, went into action for the first time at Station de Sened, in Tunisia. During November and December, the Germans had managed to land enough troops in Tunisia to stall the Allied advance and had even reclaimed the tactical initiative in some zones, particularly that held by the under-equipped French, who had joined the Allied cause after the armistice. By January, the winter rains had produced impassable mud across the front and convinced Lt. Gen. Dwight Eisenhower that he would have to call off offensive operations. Although ordered by Eisenhower to go over to the defensive, Maj. Gen. Lloyd Fredendall, commanding II Corps, wanted to capture Maknassy, east of Sened, with the 1st Armored Division before he did so.

The 81st Reconnaissance Battalion was to support an attack by Combat Command D by scouting routes of advance through the olive groves in the valley and surrounding foothills, by protecting the flanks, and if possible by cutting off the enemy's escape route from Sened. Company C and a platoon of light tanks from Company D, the first battalion elements to reach the front, had participated in a raid with Combat Command C the night of 24–25 January across this very same ground. Elements of the Italian 50th Special Brigade supported by some tanks from the 21st Panzer Division held Sened.[4]

The first job of the mechanized cavalryman was to find people to shoot at him. Lieutenant Colonel Charles Hoy, who commanded the 81st Reconnaissance Battalion, characterized its business this way: "The reconnaissance platoon, moving by bounds, comes under accurate enemy fire; it has gained contact. Long-range antitank and artillery fire cannot be considered contact with the enemy. The platoon must get in under this fire. Usually it can be done mounted, but once under accurate short-range fire, the men will generally have to dismount."[5]

In North Africa, the "meeting engagement" rarely involved two maneuvering forces encountering each other; instead, the most common situation was an attempt by reconnaissance elements to reestablish contact after the enemy had withdrawn to a new defensive position. The forward platoons generally had some idea where the enemy was, either from the G-2 (intelligence) or a map study that identified logical places that would favor a defender.[6] At Sened, the Axis positions were known in the most general terms.

The savvy recon man, Hoy would later explain, knew that if he passed through artillery fire, contact with the enemy was imminent. In principle, scout cars would lead each section in a platoon, followed by one of the assault guns.

The commander of the first car would head for cover—not reverse course—when he discerned accurate incoming small-arms or antitank fire. The second scout car would lay down return fire, and the assault gun would come into action as quickly as possible. Under this covering fire, the crew of the first scout car would dismount and seek to identify the nature of the opposition. The other two sections, meanwhile, would attempt to bypass the opposition, or at least establish observation posts on one or both flanks, typically supported by .30-caliber machine guns taken from the jeeps. In a meeting engagement, the enemy could often see the positioning of the new observation post (OP), and the men had to be prepared to defend it. The recon men would then set about establishing a new OP using stealth, possibly waiting until after dark.[7]

But this was a first fight, and some of these were lessons yet to be learned. On that January day, the 81st Reconnaissance Battalion, with Company C leading, made some progress until coming under heavy artillery fire and grinding to a halt. Lieutenant Colonel Hoy committed the light tanks of his Dog Company to the attack, but to no avail. L. E. Anderson recalled that the company's commanding officer inexplicably sent his maintenance and supply vehicles just behind the M3 light tanks. The tanks fanned out to bypass Sened and take it from the rear. Instead, German positions bypassed by the tanks opened up with mortars and machine guns, and explosions erupted around the support vehicles.

Confusion set in as several vehicles caught fire, and gasoline and ammunition blew up. "Unexpectedly, the lead tanks returned," Anderson remembered, "coming over the hill at full speed, heading for the rear." German tanks were said to be in pursuit, and the entire company fell back in disorder. Company B followed.

Indeed, sharp-eyed scouts had reported German Mark IV tanks—far more than a match for the M3s—and Italian armored cars in Sened and a suspected artillery position hidden in an olive grove. After six hours of shelling and air attacks, the green reconnaissance troopers pulled back, abandoning five scout cars, three jeeps, and two assault guns in the process.

The battalion, under frequent attacks by Stukas and Messerschmidts, made no more progress the next day. Companies A and C were dispersed along a rocky slope. Each scout car mounted a .50-caliber machine gun, and although most of the men took shelter in slit trenches, one man per car blazed away at any aircraft that came within range.

Finally, on 2 February, the recon men pushed onto high ground and overran some Italian troops and equipment. The outfit's first battle had cost two men killed, nine men wounded, and another fifteen gone missing.[8]

The Cavalry at Kasserine

The 81st Reconnaissance Battalion was attached to Combat Command A on 11 February and rolled to the area southeast of Sidi bou Zid, a small town just west of Faid Pass in the Eastern Dorsal range. Unfortunately, the new area of responsibility lay in the path of the German counterattack, which came to be known as the Battle of Kasserine.

German lieutenant general Erwin Rommel, having been pushed back across Libya to the Tunisian frontier by British general Bernard "Monty" Montgomery's Eighth Army, conceived of a plan to use the Germans' interior lines to combine with the Axis forces facing the Allies to the west and strike a crushing blow against the Americans. Forces under Gen. Curt von Arnim were to attack out of the Eastern Dorsal Mountains, where they had retaken key passes from the French, while Rommel attacked toward Gafsa.[9]

The 81st Battalion recon men had set up OPs and begun patrolling the area on 12 and 13 February, clashing occasionally with German patrols and enduring a terrific sandstorm. The battalion learned that the Germans appeared to be gearing up for a stiff defense or an attack. Just past midnight on 14 February, Company A's listening posts reported the sounds of enemy tanks on the move.

The Germans on 14 February drove out of several mountain passes and generally westward through the American line. While two battle groups of the 10th Panzer Division engaged the 168th Infantry Regiment, 34th Infantry Division, just to the north of the 81st Reconnaissance Battalion's zone, mobile elements from the 21st Panzer Division hit Company C north of Maizila Pass. At 1020 hours, the company reported that thirty tanks were approaching its positions in a V formation, and soon a hundred trucks bearing infantry were spotted behind the panzers.

A platoon of light tanks supported Company C. Sergeant Herbie Bush had backed his M3 into a draw to provide protection for his flanks and rear. Bush and his gunner, George Kajawa, watched the approaching panzers with feelings of awe and impending doom. Kajawa opened fire with his 37mm when the tanks came into range, only to watch his shells bounce harmlessly off two of them. Then a tremendous force struck the little M3 and lifted it briefly off the ground. The German round had penetrated the turret and wounded Bush mortally, although the crew got him out of the tank just before it burst into flames. Bush ordered them to leave him and escape, which they accomplished over the next four grueling days with little food or water. Bush was never accounted for again.

The recon men mounted a brief delaying action but were unequipped to fight off an armored attack. Company D lost more than half its light tanks. Company A, meanwhile, was attached to the 168th Infantry and by afternoon was isolated well east of much of the German armor.

The 1st Armored Division operations report recorded on 14 February, "Enemy tank attack started on wide front. Djebel [Hill] Lessouda surrounded by more than 40 tanks. Our positions held even though Djebel Ksaira surrounded by more tanks and infantry. The whole operation was supported by continuous and heavy air bombardment." Combat Command A (CCA) estimated that it had been hit by a tank force twice its own size. Division intelligence correctly deduced that it faced a substantial portion of all German armor in North Africa.[10]

Over the next two days, German operations mostly surged by Company C as well as Company B, which had taken up positions north of the Sbeitla-Faid road. Company A was cut off and in only sporadic radio contact, but its brief messages indicated that it was taking a pounding from air and artillery attacks. Late on 15 February, the recon men watched tank hulks burn in the distance, left behind by Combat Command C's failed counterstroke toward Sidi bou Zid. The foray resulted in the loss of most of a tank battalion and spelled the end of serious efforts to hold any ground east of Kasserine Pass.

At dusk on 16 February, the 81st Battalion withdrew with the rest of CCA to the area of Sbeitla. The battalion had been assigned about thirty native French troops (*Goumiers*) to serve as guides and translators, and each platoon had three or four of them attached. Company B found itself cut off at one point and turned to its *Goumiers* for salvation. The native troops found an unguarded pass that the Germans had considered incapable of being traversed by vehicles, and the company made its escape. (The 91st Reconnaissance Squadron also later used native troops in North Africa and found them to be excellent night fighters and a boon on patrols.)

That night, Company A—along with troops from the 168th Infantry Regiment, which was surrounded on Djebel Ksaira—destroyed its equipment and tried to walk to American lines. Only fourteen recon men made it. The next day, the depleted reconnaissance battalion withdrew behind the defenses at Kasserine Pass, and its role in the debacle came to an end.[11]

Rommel, worried about Montgomery's Eighth Army at his back, decided to end his offensive on 23 February. By 25 February, German forces had withdrawn to the line Faid Pass–Gafsa, and the following day the battered 1st Armored Division went into corps reserve.[12]

That day, the 81st Reconnaissance Battalion's Company C was one of the first formations to probe into the vacuum left by the retreating German troops. The recon men found the roads mined and the bridges blown, and the towns of Kasserine, Thelepte, and Feriana heavily booby-trapped.

Indeed, from this point on in North Africa, the men learned that mines were the greatest hindrance in any advance to reestablish contact with the foe. The Germans laid them not so much to cause casualties but to delay. Each platoon had a mine detector, but because speed was essential, Lieutenant Colonel Hoy ordered his troops to lead with their heaviest vehicles. Hence, most minefields were discovered by detonation, which resulted in some serious injuries, although no fatalities. After spotting a minefield, the men cleared a narrow path by hand, and the advance continued. There was some underlying consistency to where the Germans planted mines, and some of the men developed an almost psychic ability to divine the location of a minefield. Nevertheless, one lieutenant in Company C named his third scout car replacement "Mine Detector No. 3."[13]

Eisenhower deemed the Kasserine line stabilized as of 26 February.[14]

Back on the Offensive

While rebuilding after the battle, the 81st Reconnaissance Battalion reorganized as an "armored reconnaissance battalion." But because of its losses, it had to eliminate Company D and parcel out its light tanks among the other three line companies. Company A was reconstituted.

On 12 March, orders arrived from Division: It was time to go back on the attack at the very place where the battalion had first seen action, Station de Sened. The battalion was to provide flank protection for the main 1st Armored Division thrust aimed at Maknassy. Operations kicked off on 15 March, and the battalion advanced eastward, struggling through rain-soaked wadis and encountering the occasional minefield and brief stand by German troops in company strength.[15] The Axis defenses under the command of Italian general

Imperiali were just short of collapsing when a battle group from the 10th Panzer Division arrived on 23 March to stabilize the line.

On 24 March, near Maknassy, elements of *Kampfstaffel* Rommel's reconnaissance battalion stopped the 81st Armored Reconnaissance Battalion's advance at Leben Wadi.[16] The route to the high ground that dominated the terrain was devoid of cover, so, after dark, Lieutenant Lydle, Company B, infiltrated the German lines and set up an OP. After two days of undetected observation, the patrol left the OP to obtain food and a replacement radio battery. While creeping back to the OP in the dim pre-dawn light, Lydle's men noticed that there was a German OP just a few yards away. The Americans shot first and killed a German artillery observer and a noncommissioned officer (NCO) and wounded another soldier. After stripping papers from the bodies—including a map marking all German positions—and absconding with a German radio range finder, the recon men returned to their own spot to continue their work. The Germans were onto them, however, and soon hostile infantrymen started up the slope. Lydle reported the situation, and the battalion's three assault guns hidden in the wadi opened fire. The patrol returned to American lines under the cover of this fire with all of its prizes.

Farther down the same ridgeline, another lieutenant led a patrol through the German positions and established a replacement OP on commanding ground. For two days he directed artillery fire on the defenders; he pulled back on the third night only because the team's food and water were exhausted.[17]

It is worth noting that the German commander in this instance was using his reconnaissance battalion in accordance with his own tactical doctrine. Like American mechanized cavalry doctrine, German doctrine specified that reconnaissance units were to avoid fighting unless absolutely required by the situation to accomplish their missions. Nonetheless, it was expected that reconnaissance elements would often have to fight for information, and battalion commanders were admonished not to dissipate their strength because "superiority of means" would often be essential to success. If a reconnaissance unit were to be given a security mission, as at Leben Wadi, the unit was to be reinforced by other units: for example, by machine gun, light artillery (an observer was present in this case), antitank, and engineer troops.[18] Indeed, German practice frequently employed armored reconnaissance battalions and infantry division reconnaissance battalions as highly mobile combat troops, normally reinforced by some armor or tank destroyers.

***

As this case illustrated, the American reconnaissance men learned that in Tunisia they were going to have to gather most of their information dismounted. Because there was generally no coherent front line, they could use stealth to get close to or even bypass enemy positions to set up their observation posts.[19]

A visual OP normally filed "first light" and "last light" reports that summarized everything of interest—negative or positive—in its field of vision. It was crucial to maintain contact with the enemy at night, when he was most likely to pull back to new positions. Listening posts were critical after dark and were typically sited near a main road, a pass, or a road junction. Normally, three men would move to the previously reconnoitered position once darkness fell; if their vehicle could not be parked in the immediate vicinity, they would dismount the radio and carry it forward. Reports were expected at least once an hour.[20]

Lieutenant Colonel Hoy judged that a good reconnaissance leader had to possess "insatiable curiosity . . . , a 'yonder-pastures-are-greener' attitude." He always had to be looking for a better OP.[21]

During operations, each company in the 81st Armored Reconnaissance Battalion tried to keep one platoon in reserve for each five-day stretch. This was the time to service vehicles, eat hot meals, wash clothes and bodies, get haircuts, and write letters home. The battalion had three doctors and a dentist assigned. One doctor remained with the headquarters element, and the other three physicians deployed with the line companies to handle the sick and wounded.[22]

The First Cavalry Squadron Enters Battle

While the 1st Armored Division slogged away at Maknassy, Montgomery on 20 March tried to rout the Afrika Korps along the Mareth Line. His operation fared poorly, but he shifted at the right moment to flank the Axis line and by 7 April had driven the foe into retreat. At 1600 hours on 7 April, elements of the 899th Tank Destroyer Battalion, operating with the 1st Armored Division, established contact with the Eighth Army.[23] There was now only one front in North Africa.

Lieutenant General Omar Bradley replaced Patton, who had taken charge after the Kasserine debacle, at the head of II Corps on 15 April so that the latter could return to overseeing the planning for the invasion of Sicily. Pinched out of the line by the steady shrinkage of the Axis perimeter, II Corps shifted behind the British lines and took on responsibility for the left flank along the coast. The new objective was Bizerte.[24]

The 91st Reconnaissance Squadron entered the line on 19 April attached to II Corps' 9th Infantry Division after completing a 1,083-mile march from French Morocco. The men had gotten their first inkling of their destination only while aboard ship from the States, when they had been handed booklets on Arab culture. The baptism of fire had been at the docks in Casablanca, which the Germans had bombed while the squadron was disembarking. Arriving at the front, the wide-eyed soldiers noted that the land between the 9th Division headquarters at shell-ravaged Djebel Abiod and the squadron's new home was littered with American, British, and German graves, and the road was lined with the shells of Allied and Axis vehicles.

The squadron's first assignment was to conduct a "vigorous reconnaissance" to the east to draw attention from 9th Division operations farther north and to establish an OP on the high ground at the Djebel Tebouna mine (roughly twenty-nine miles west of Mateur), which was held by elements of the Division von Manteufel. II Corps was to push off in four more days to capture Mateur as part of an Allied offensive intended to finally wrest Tunis from German hands. The recon men discovered that their 1:50,000 maps would be next to useless. What looked like small hills and ridges on a map turned out to be steep slopes, small cliffs, and sharp ridges. Most of the unimproved roads and trails on the map were nonexistent in the real world. The cavalry was going to need engineers to move its vehicles forward—all except perhaps the nimble jeeps.

Troop A relieved the British 4th Recce on a high ridge, where the 9th Division tied into the neighboring 1st Infantry Division, to the south. Each British infantry division by this time fielded a seven-hundred-man reconnaissance regiment, such as the 4th Recce, which was—much like the mechanized cavalry—equipped with a mix of light armored cars and tracked Bren carriers, motorcycles, and unarmored vehicles. The regiments combined the cavalry ethos—they were organized into squadrons and troops—with twice the firepower of an infantry regiment. The British press characterized these as elite formations on par with commandos and paratroops.[25]

The tank platoon attached to Troop A, commanded by Lt. Dan Coffee, advanced in the direction of the Mine du Djebel Semene, the first of several French metal mines in the area that the Germans had converted into fortresses. Blocked by a wadi with vertical banks a full 1,400 yards from the objective,

Coffee fired his 37mm gun at the mine's buildings. German troops came boiling out of the mine entrance to take up positions in fieldworks. Machine-gun bullets pinged off the tank armor, and bursts of white phosphorus from mortar rounds sprang up around the M3s. Coffee pulled back his tanks. The 91st Reconnaissance Squadron had made its first contact with the enemy.

The next day, a jeep-mounted patrol tried to work its way across the wadi, but the terrain was so rough that the team had to press ahead on foot. The Germans had their own patrols out and sprang a trap. Half the Americans and two jeeps were captured; the crews in two other jeeps made a narrow escape.

The squadron spent the next two weeks patrolling and probing the German lines, mostly on foot. The light tanks of Troop E were detached on 23 April and sent north to support the French. That night, five tanks were sent forward on reconnaissance—a terrible misuse of vehicles that had limited vision even in daylight. Captain James Green Jr.'s tank turned over under enemy fire, and three other tanks were knocked out. Three sergeants burned to death in their tanks, two other men were seriously burned, and another sergeant died in a hail of machine-gun fire while escaping on foot.[26]

★★★

If the troopers in the 91st Reconnaissance Squadron thought they were going to avoid much real fighting, that delusion evaporated fairly quickly. On 28 April, Troop C received orders to recapture high ground that the squadron had briefly occupied the preceding day but then lost to a counterattack. One platoon had been reduced to eight men after it was cut off during the retreat.

Troopers dismounted the machine guns from their jeeps, picked up their Springfield rifles and Tommy guns, and moved forward. A map overlay marked the place simply as objective "A," but someone had dubbed it Plymouth Hill. The troop advanced on the German flank and attacked the height from the south. Four M3 tank destroyers from the 601st Tank Destroyer Battalion had been attached to the troop, although it is unclear whether they provided supporting fire. After climbing a slope, the men reached a flat area containing only two stone huts. German fire cut loose from the ridge beyond that, and the troopers hit the dirt as bullets whipped by like a swarm of hornets.

Corporal Fred Salter led his squad farther to the flank with an eye toward taking out one troublesome machine-gun nest. Working through brush that provided good concealment for the creeping men, Salter crawled around a boulder and was shocked to see a German kneeling with his machine pistol at the ready but faced away. Some small noise must have alerted the man, for he looked over his shoulder, then turned with all the speed he could manage, firing even before he could get his muzzle in line. Showered by rock fragments, Salter squeezed his trigger and, facing death for the first time, burned through his entire thirty-round clip. The stream of .45-caliber slugs tore the German in half. Salter examined himself and found two bullet holes in his left sleeve.

The rest of Troop C had already pulled back when Salter withdrew his squad. The troop had failed to take its first real objective. The next day went no better. The place was to go down in squadron lore as About-Face Hill.[27]

The following morning at 0400 hours, after nearly half the exhausted and demoralized surviving troopers had refused a direct order to attack again, squadron commanding officer Lt. Col. Harry Candler personally led a skirmish line of the remaining reluctantly obedient cavalrymen up the hill one last time. The men moved as silently as they could, yet one trooper stumbled. Everyone froze, but there was no reaction from the Germans. The colonel, using a "cricket" to signal his commands with clicks, ordered the line to move forward, then stop again. A moment passed.

"Charge!" Candler yelled into the darkness. Warned beforehand to expect this moment, the troopers—most of them southerners—loosed a rebel yell as they surged forward firing their Tommy guns and rifles. Grenades arced over the muzzle blasts of MG34 machine guns and silenced the nests. German mortar rounds exploded around the cavalrymen, but they quickly subsided when the enemy crews realized that the Americans were into their lines.

Troop C was on its objective. "Plymouth Hill has been taken," Candler reported to the 9th Infantry Division command post (CP).[28]

★★★

Some fifteen miles to the south of the 91st Squadron's positions, the 81st Armored Reconnaissance Battalion had made contact with the Germans at Djebel Badgar and set up an OP within four hundred yards of the enemy line. The 1st Armored Division had moved into the area to be ready to exploit any breakthrough that the infantry divisions managed to achieve that would open the door to Mateur. The Germans decided to remove the nuisance posed by the OP and sent forward a platoon of riflemen to do so. A Company C lieutenant in the OP spotted the movement and called forward two supporting light tanks from hidden positions two hundred yards to the rear. The tanks swung around the knoll hosting the OP and opened fire into the German ranks with canister rounds from the 37mm main guns. Only seven of the attackers survived to be taken prisoner.[29]

★★★

On 3 May the Germans pulled back, and the 91st Reconnaissance Squadron moved forward on foot to reestablish contact. Three Troop B men died in shell fire that greeted them, and two more men were lost to machine-gun fire—one when a bullet set off a hand grenade hanging from his suspenders—as contact was obviously reestablished. That same day, the 1st Armored Division was unleashed to exploit the German withdrawal.

The German retreat continued the next day, and the 91st Squadron passed through Mateur, moving quickly now on its mounts for the first time and slowed only by occasional minefields and air attacks. Elements of the 81st Armored Reconnaissance Battalion had reached Mateur just ahead of the 91st Squadron. That evening, the squadron was detached from the 9th Infantry Division and attached to the 1st Armored Division.

The Germans had taken up positions east of Mateur, and the 91st Squadron received orders to clear Djebel Achkel, a mountain northeast of Mateur that initial patrols determined contained another French metal mine. The prominence was surrounded by a swamp that prevented vehicles from approaching any closer than a mile. None of the squadron's weapons-carrier-mounted 37mm antitank guns would be able to get in close. Instead, the 81mm mortar teams moved to the swamp's edge during the night and dug hasty positions from which they would be able to fire their mortars directly, almost like rifles, after discarding the bipods.

Before dawn on 6 May, the squadron attacked from west to east, with Troop C on the left and Troop B on the right. Troop C worked through the swamp and surprised the defenders, who belonged to the elite Hermann Göring Division, thirty of whom surrendered. The alerted Germans spotted Troop B just as it reached the lower slope and unleashed a storm of rifle and machine-gun fire.

A battery of division artillery, the antitank platoon's 37mm guns, and the troops' mortars commenced pounding the German positions. But as darkness fell, the enemy again slipped away, leaving only a few snipers to harass the Americans.

Having detached Troop A to clear the snipers, the 91st Reconnaissance Squadron pursued the retreating Germans eastward on 7 May at a speed that no horse cavalry could have imagined. The squadron's light tanks and jeep-mounted recon men led the way for two tank battalions of Combat Command A in the squadron's first real mounted cavalry action in the campaign. The Troop E tankers spotted two German batteries northwest of Ferryville, some eight miles northeast of Mateur on the road to Bizerte, firing "full blast." Shells from one 88mm gun in a cactus grove brought the tanks to a stop. The tank platoon commander moved into a hull-defilade position while Troop C's three 81mm mortars set up in a draw just to the rear. The tankers directed mortar fire onto the gun, and it fell silent.

Two men in a jeep who had rolled out to assess the situation spotted the gun crew hightailing it into an olive grove about 175 yards away. The jeep stopped with its hood under the muzzle of the disabled gun, and one man jumped out with his carbine to fire on the gun crew. At that moment, a camouflaged 88mm in the olive grove opened up and destroyed the jeep. The recon troops replied with everything they had. A direct hit from an 81mm mortar round knocked out the second gun.

Under covering fire from some Sherman tanks, Troop B rolled into Ferryville with the loss of two soldiers killed. The overjoyed French citizenry mobbed the troops, shoving flowers and wine into the men's hands.

The squadron pressed on while the 81st Armored Reconnaissance Battalion moved in behind to mop up in Ferryville. From atop the next ridge, the men saw a vast stream of German vehicles heading east and a German infantry formation reorganizing below them. Using a tank radio, an observer brought artillery fire down on these tempting targets.

On 8 May the understrength 3d Platoon, Troop C, rolled out at 0600 hours to reestablish contact with the enemy. Its orders were to report its position every quarter mile; when the combat command heard German guns open fire on the patrol, it would know where the new German defensive line was. A scout car took the lead, followed by machine-gun jeeps. Corporal Fred Salter commanded the last jeep in line.

After traveling several miles, the patrol dipped into a wadi. When Salter's jeep began its descent, German troops hidden on the high ground ahead unleashed a deadly fusillade, starting at the back of the column so that none of the American vehicles could turn and bolt to safety.

Salter's driver took a fatal round almost immediately, and Salter and his machine gunner dove into a ditch, although it would provide the barest safety from the lethal fire. Salter fired at Germans who exposed themselves in a desperate effort to deter them from advancing and wiping out the platoon's survivors at point-blank range. Salter shook his companion out of anguished prayer, and soon two rifles covered the beleaguered platoon. Fortunately, friendly artillery soon opened up, and now it was the troopers' turn to watch the Germans take a beating.

The squadron was held up by Germans defending a ridgeline with infantry, machine guns, and antitank guns, including eight 88mm guns. The fight dragged on until 1530 hours, when Combat Command A decided to bypass the problem with a tank assault on the north end of the German line. The attackers had to cross five miles of open ground covered by German fire.

A platoon of light tanks commanded by Lt. Dave Termin plus Troop C accompanied one tank battalion into the assault. "It was the nearest thing to a mechanized charge I have ever seen," commented squadron commander Lt. Col. Harry Candler later. German fire claimed two medium tanks, but the attack was a success. The advance pushed on.

Salter could hear 1st Armored Division tanks arriving and shortly spotted one working its way into the wadi. The tank opened up on the Germans and was soon joined by several more Shermans. Salter recalled, "To be caught between two opposing armies on a battlefield, with shells coming from both directions, is beyond description."

Suddenly, as if on a signal, the German guns fell silent. A white flag appeared on the high ground. The Shermans gradually ceased their cannonade, and an eerie silence settled over the battlefield. Soon, the surrendering Germans marched toward the Americans, four men abreast. Salter found his bandoliers to be empty, and only three rounds remained in his rifle. Every vehicle in the 3d Platoon had been destroyed.

In a daze, Salter walked to meet the German officer at the head of the column. He accepted the officer's proffered pistol, and added the man's excellent binoculars. Turning back toward friendly lines, Salter raised his right arm and lowered it slowly in front of himself, the old horse cavalry command for "Forward, ho!"

★★★

Lieutenant Coffee's tank platoon with a reconnaissance platoon attached was ordered forward to feel out the situation. Coffee soon "came in" on the radio. "Have captured a battalion, about seven hundred officers and men." The command had overrun a six-gun Italian naval shore battery located on the road to Bizerte. A column led by a reconnaissance jeep appeared back at the squadron positions before dark. Behind it marched a group of thirty German soldiers followed by the Italians. Coffee's tanks brought up the rear.[30]

Lessons Learned

With the collapse of German resistance in Tunisia by 12 May, the North Africa campaign was over. The mechanized cavalrymen had measured themselves against the enemy. They concluded that the Germans were well trained, well armed, and well led, whereas the Italians were none of those things. They also believed that German combat vehicles were better than their own, a view that would never dissipate entirely even after later improvements.[31] Numerous observers reported back to Army Ground Forces that the self-propelled 37mm gun in particular had been condemned by the troops as ineffective. One War Department observer who interviewed armored division, combat command, and armored reconnaissance battalion commanders at the end of the campaign reported that they believed that "it is seldom that the desired information can be obtained without fighting for it. It is therefore vital that the reconnaissance battalion (squadron) have the necessary armament to carry out its mission without undue losses. . . ."[32] (Interestingly, the Germans about this time responded to being forced onto the strategic defensive by replacing reconnaissance battalions in infantry divisions with "fusilier" battalions, which were essentially light rifle battalions that could conduct reconnaissance or fight as infantry. Some cavalry elements that had been disbanded to form reconnaissance battalions were reconstituted for use in the Balkans and on the eastern front.[33])

The 34th Infantry Division equipped its reconnaissance troop with seventeen M5 light tanks because, to quote the troop commander, "a jeep had a hard time beating a German heavy armored car mounting a 75."[34] In the course of sixty days of combat, the troop had lost nine jeeps, a command vehicle, and a scout car. The troop fought with this unusual configuration until March 1944 in Italy, when the outfit traded in its tanks for M8 armored cars before the division shifted to the Anzio beachhead.[35] Unfortunately, the division's and the troop's skimpy battle reports give no sense for how the division exploited this asset.

The 9th Infantry Division, commenting on its reconnaissance troop, which it had used mainly for patrolling, filling gaps, and clearing minefields, concluded that the mechanized cavalry was the most flexible arm attached to the division and that when it was used properly, it was indispensable. The division judged that it needed a cavalry squadron, not just a troop—a conclusion presumably based on the attachment of the 91st Cavalry Squadron in northern Tunisia. "The men *must* be given relief," the after-action report (AAR) added, "due to the extremely nerve-racking type of work they do."[36]

Major General C. P. Hall, an observer who toured North Africa in March and April 1943, reported that commanders would have liked to have had more mechanized cavalry available during the final stages of the campaign. Commanders said they would have used the cavalry to great advantage for reconnaissance and filling gaps between units.[37]

Another observer team that interviewed personnel from every cavalry and armored reconnaissance outfit to fight in North Africa encountered some sentiment that horse cavalry would have been useful. When the question was put to Eisenhower, he replied, "There were many uses for and requests by subordinate commanders for horse cavalry during the North Africa operations. . . . However, the advantages of horse cavalry did not outweigh the need for shipping space, which was and still is critical and vital. To have been of value during the North African campaign, it would have been necessary not only to transport the animals, but also the grain, for only green forage is available. . . . In Europe, the above factors are equally applicable. . . ."[38]

Lessons Unlearned

While the first mechanized cavalry units fought their way across North Africa, the army gradually did away with organized horse cavalry in 1942 and 1943. The Office of the Chief of Cavalry was abolished in March 1942, as were those of the other combat arms chiefs. The Army Ground Forces, which took control over the whole shebang, quickly pushed the mechanization process. The 2d, 3d, 11th, and 14th Cavalry regiments were dissolved, re-formed as armored regiments with the same numbers, and subordinated to the newly raised 9th and 10th Armored divisions. The 2d Cavalry Division was inactivated except for its 4th Cavalry Brigade; the division was briefly reactivated but closed down for good by May 1944. The 1st Cavalry Division in December 1942 received orders to move to the Pacific theater, where it was to fight as an infantry division.

In mid-1943, all non-divisional cavalry regiments were broken up to form groups and squadrons, as were federalized National Guard regiments. The War Department mandated that mechanized cavalry units were to be organized, equipped, and trained to perform reconnaissance missions employing "infiltration tactics, fire, and maneuver," a philosophy formalized in a new field manual issued the following year. Elements were to seek out unopposed routes of advance. The doctrine acknowledged that cavalry squadrons would sometimes have to fight for information, but they were to engage in combat only when necessary to accomplish that mission or to avoid destruction and capture.[39] As one veteran from the 91st Cavalry Reconnaissance Squadron put it, "Go ahead, contact the enemy, no return fire, turn around and get back."[40] The same philosophy was supposed to apply to the armored reconnaissance battalions, too.

Charles Raney, with the 9th Armored Division's 89th Cavalry Reconnaissance Squadron, recalled, "We were not a fighting troop, as such, but scouts for other outfits of the 9th Armored Division. We were not to engage, purposefully, in any fighting or action but to get back with information. This we did except for a few times when forced into fire fights to get out of a tight spot after being detected."[41]

The pendulum was swinging too far away from the old cavalry doctrine. Cavalrymen were not making the big decisions at Army Ground Forces, and much of the branch's talent pool was serving in the Armored Force. Those who were in charge did not seem to recognize the lessons that had been learned in North Africa. It had been the role originally assigned to the armored reconnaissance battalions that had best anticipated actual conditions in battle—including the inevitable involvement of mechanized cavalry in classic cavalry tasks. The British understood this, and its Reconnaissance Corps, in the words of historian Sir Arthur Bryant, was evolving into "swift, adaptable and superlatively mobile fighting units with fast vehicles capable of taking heavy punishment, highly concentrated fire power, and a complicated but efficient wireless network designed to convey, under the most trying conditions imaginable, accurate and balanced information to the general's battle map."[42]

But this doctrinal problem was not to matter all that much. From the day the new doctrine was imposed, most mechanized cavalry formations and the units they supported simply ignored it. As the same 91st Cavalry Reconnaissance Squadron veteran said, "I'm not going to stand there and let somebody shoot at me. I'm going to shoot, fire back, and that's what [happened]. The book we threw away, no such thing."[43]

CHAPTER 3

SICILY AND ITALY: MECHANIZATION MEETS THE MOUNTAINS

The tactical employment of the troop for reconnaissance purposes was limited in that the terrain was not suited for motor operations. . . .

—AAR, 36th Cavalry Reconnaissance Troop

The mechanized cavalry was about to enter a battleground where notions of stealthy mounted maneuver for reconnaissance would suddenly seem absurd much of the time. Even traditional cavalry missions had never foreseen troopers riding point for a column on the only road anywhere around, surrounded by impassable terrain, and facing an enemy who knew very well that an attacker was going to have to use that road.

Sicily: Taking the War to the Axis

Four enlisted men chosen as scouts for the 45th Infantry Division were the first mechanized cavalrymen to land in Sicily as part of Operation Husky on 10 July 1943. The troop had undergone scout and raider training in Florida back in February. "We were trained so well we were crazy," commented one veteran later.[1]

Under the command of a naval officer, the four scouts—dressed in black and with blackened faces and hands—braved waves as high as the deck of the *Susan B. Anthony* to jump through inky darkness into a landing craft, into which they had lowered their rubber raft. The troopers were armed only with pistols and one grenade each. They were ferried to a drop-off point and slipped ashore about midnight, then located the road exit off Blue Beach and marked the channel with buoys. The first shells of the preparatory bombardment dropped only several hundred yards away from the men at 0300 hours. They scooted back out to sea, climbing aboard the transport by 0500. That morning,

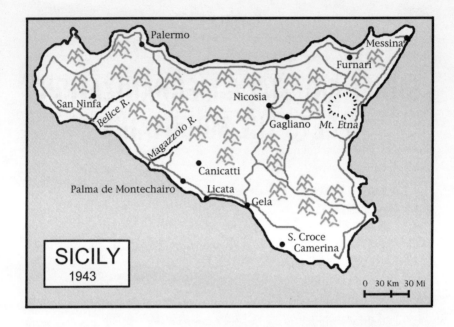

SICILY
1943

0 30 Km 30 Mi

a vast armada of nearly 2,600 ships put seven Allied divisions ashore on Axis home territory—the British Eighth Army on the right, and Lt. Gen. George S. Patton Jr.'s U.S. Seventh Army on the left.

The 1st Platoon, 45th Cavalry Reconnaissance Troop, landed at 0640 hours near the right end of Seventh Army's zone and at 1000 received orders to reconnoiter to the southwest of the division area. At 1300 it ran into fire from an Axis pillbox near S. Croce Camerina. The troop's 37mm gun chipped away at the bunker, as did .50-caliber machine guns. The pillbox fell silent, and 125 Italian soldiers surrendered. The troop's baptism of fire had gone well.[2]

Two officers and fourteen men from an advance detachment of the 91st Reconnaissance Squadron were the second cavalry team to reach shore, at 0730, with the 1st Infantry Division's 16th Infantry Regiment in the central landing zone. These troopers, however, did not have an immediate battle task.[3]

The 1st Platoon, 3d Cavalry Reconnaissance Troop, meanwhile, crossed the beach at Licata just eighty minutes behind the 3d Division's assault wave on the American left. The troop's mission was to screen the exposed left flank and make contact with the enemy. One mile east of Palma de Montechairo, the recon men came upon a large bridge wired for demolition by a half ton of TNT. The troopers cut the wires, posted a guard, and moved on.

Two hundred yards past the bridge, the platoon encountered light artillery and machine-gun fire from a ridge up ahead. Lieutenant McCloskey directed his vehicles to take cover, then set off with eight dismounted troopers. The men spotted a strongpoint consisting of two concrete pillboxes protected by triple bands of barbed wire and dug-in infantry. The scouts tried to work around the flank but were seen and peppered by rifle, machine-gun, and mortar fire, which left the scout sergeant wounded. Creeping and crawling as they had never done before, the remaining troopers advanced to a point from where they could survey the entire position as well as an enemy OP on another hill. A radio report to Division produced a crushing artillery barrage that destroyed the position entirely.[4]

★★★

The 2d Armored Division's Combat Command A, including Company B, 82d Reconnaissance Battalion, landed late on D-Day after spending hours on their ships under continuous air attack. The command was attached to the 3d Infantry Division to provide tank support. Combat Command B (CCB), including the remainder of the reconnaissance battalion, arrived several hours later and was attached to the 1st Infantry Division.[5]

By the end of the first day, the Allies were firmly established on the island. Resistance had been light except in the American center, where counterattacks by mobile and armored forces hit paratroopers from the 82d Airborne Division—which had dropped inland from the invasion beaches—and elements of the 1st and 45th Infantry divisions.[6]

Patton's Drive to Palermo

The most desperate fighting to confront American troops on Sicily erupted on 11 July as Axis forces strove to push the invasion force back into the sea. Under constant attack from the Germans, the Americans had little need for reconnaissance that day. Panzers nearly reached the beach at Gela, in the 1st Infantry Division's zone. Combat Command B tanks and howitzers firing over open sights eventually stopped the assault, but not before the 82d Reconnaissance Battalion's Companies B and C had been deployed with only their personal weapons to defend the division CP.[7]

Meanwhile, Maj. Gen. Lucian Truscott, commanding the 3d Infantry Division, ordered Combat Command A to seize Naro and Canicatti, in the hills, to forestall German armored counterattacks along that axis. Naro proved to be unoccupied, and Company B, 82d Reconnaissance Battalion, was dispatched toward Canicatti. Before reaching town, the point spotted some Italian soldiers in the narrow mountain pass. Lieutenant W. R. Neilson led two light tanks forward but halted when he realized that four large-caliber guns controlled the road. Two 37mm self-propelled guns arrived to help, but at this point Italian infantry on the high ground opened fire. The cavalry had found the enemy! Neilson and company backed out of the trap and summoned the armored infantry to deal with the problem. The Italians held firm until dark, then slipped away.[8]

Starting 12 July, Seventh Army took back the initiative and started to drive inland. Eighth Army, however, was running into determined resistance on the east coast, and its commander, Gen. Bernard Montgomery, on 13 July persuaded Gen. Harold Alexander, commanding the overall invasion force, to shift the inter-army boundary westward. This deprived Seventh Army of a main highway to the north, which infuriated Patton. The Americans were convinced that they were being shunted aside so that the British could claim the glory of reaching Messina, just across the straits from the toe of Italy.

Patton cast about for a way to get back into the game and settled on a drive to Palermo, Sicily's capital, on the northwest corner of the island. He first wangled authorization for a "reconnaissance" led by the 3d Infantry Division starting 15 July. He then added the 2d Armored and 82d Airborne divisions on the 3d Division's left to create a "provisional corps," which had orders to dash the hundred miles into Palermo.[9]

★★★

The provisional corps, with the 82d Reconnaissance Battalion directly attached, pushed off on 20 July. Company C spearheaded the advance by the 82d Airborne Division along the coast, contacted the enemy that day at the Magazzolo River, and took fifty prisoners. The next day, the Italian garrison in Alcamo surrendered to the company with great pomp. During this period, the 2d Armored Division waited, ready to charge when the moment was right.

The moment came on 22 July, when Combat Command A followed the reconnaissance battalion's Company C north across the Belice River toward Palermo. The recon men captured San Ninfa at 0930 hours, and one of the prisoners reported that the road ahead was mined and covered by antitank guns. The troopers moved out, driving up a steep road that switched back and forth in hairpin turns. They spotted the mines, which still sat beside the road.

Thirty more Italians appeared and surrendered. One of them indicated that there was something just ahead. Lieutenant Donald Chase eased his scout car forward a hundred yards, conducting reconnaissance by fire. Heavy weapons responded; the second shot destroyed the scout car. Everyone opened up, and the Americans called down artillery fire, which knocked out the gun.

The scene repeated itself at the next pass, minus the burning scout car; then that was it. The road to Palermo was open.

Combat Command B now joined the advance and plowed ahead against decreasing resistance. About noon, the first patrol from Company B, 82d Reconnaissance Battalion, rolled into the Sicilian capital.[10] Patton would get his newspaper headlines.

The 2d Armored Division drew a lesson from the first extensive use of its reconnaissance battalion in battle: "Heavier caliber antitank guns and .50-caliber machine guns are recommended for reconnaissance units. Practically all initial contact is against troops protected by some armor or fortification. Machine guns mounted on 1/4-tons should be mounted directly in front of the assistant driver to permit their immediate use."[11]

★★★

The 3d Cavalry Reconnaissance Troop, meanwhile, led the 3d Division's advance toward Palermo against generally light resistance. On 21 July, ten miles south of the objective, the point platoon spotted a number of Italians moving around what appeared to be a gun position protected by large boulders 300 yards to the left front. Captain A. T. Netterblad, the troop commander, led a dismounted patrol forward about 150 yards to a ridge. From there he could see four Italian guns, plus one German 88mm on another ridge some 800 yards away.

The patrol notified the infantry, which decided to send forward its cannon company. The noise of the guns advancing alerted the Italians, who opened fire. Cannon Company's howitzers fired back, directed by Netterblad. The captain also ordered forward two .50-caliber machine guns, which drove the enemy crews to cover. The infantry surged forward under this fire and took eighty-seven prisoners.

The troop entered Palermo on 22 July and was rewarded with four days of well-deserved rest.[12] The next day, General Alexander ordered Patton to strike eastward to Messina because Montgomery had again bogged down on the east coast.

Can the Cavalry Ride Mountain Goats?

While Patton's left was driving toward Palermo, Lt. Gen. Omar Bradley's II Corps, consisting of the 1st and 45th Infantry divisions, pushed northward to cut the island in two. Action for the advanced detachment of the 91st Cavalry Reconnaissance Squadron, still attached to the 1st Infantry Division, over the first few days reflected the pattern that was to characterize the entire Sicilian experience for the outfit: a road-bound journey from enemy strongpoint to enemy strongpoint. The remainder of the squadron arrived by 20 July and immediately moved out to conduct reconnaissance in the direction of Nicosia and to screen the division's right flank, maintaining contact there with the Canadian 1st Division.

Troop A contacted the enemy at Villadoro early on 22 July. The Axis force was far too powerful for the cavalry to handle, so the 16th Infantry Regiment moved in to clear the town. Troop B operated adjacent to the Canadians on the right. As the squadron's history recorded, "[T]he rugged terrain and lack of roads or trails forced [the troop] to fall back to Leonforte and push north on Highway 117 toward Nicosia."

Troop A was advancing up a parallel road toward Nicosia when it ran into heavy German fire from Hill 845 on 25 July. One patrol was pinned down, and only aggressive fire from an attached medium tank platoon enabled the men to pull back. The tanks tried to maneuver off the road to bypass the resistance, but three of them became stuck among the rocks, and the recon men had to return the earlier favor by protecting the tanks until they could be hauled loose after dark.

Troop A and a patrol from Troop B stormed the hill at dawn the next day and established an OP. The observers directed mortar fire against antitank guns covering the road, which allowed the medium tanks to advance and destroy several machine-gun nests and trucks loaded with men and ammunition. Again, however, several tanks became stuck.

The Germans at this point counterattacked in strength and drove the weak American outpost off the hill. They then set the immobilized Shermans ablaze. Troop A, undaunted, moved to a nearby hill and set up a new OP. From here the recon men directed artillery fire against the Germans on Hill 845, while the Germans did the same to them. Troop A attacked once more on 28 July but was driven back. Patrols that afternoon found the Germans gone, perhaps because Troop B had worked its way around the position and continued up Highway 117 toward Nicosia.

★★★

The 45th Cavalry Reconnaissance Troop left a record of this brief radio conversation during this period:

Assault battalion commander: What is your position?

Platoon leader: My position is [map coordinates].

Battalion commander: What's holding you up? Air reconnaissance shows nothing along that road for twenty miles.

Platoon leader: I don't give a damn. There's at least four machine guns up here, five Mark IV tanks, two self-propelled 90mm's, and some mortars.

Battalion commander: How do you know?

Platoon leader: Godammit, they're shooting at me![13]

★★★

Troop B, 91st Reconnaissance Squadron, entered Agira on 30 July and again made contact with the Canadians. The Germans had blown a large crater in the road south of Gagliano, and a reconnaissance security detachment was dispatched to protect engineers who were working to repair the road.[14]

Here the men ran into a small detachment of the 29th Motorized Division. Staff Sergeant Gerry Kisters was awarded the Congressional Medal of Honor for his role in the small firefight that ensued. His citation reads, "On 31 July 1943, near Gagliano, Sicily, a detachment of one officer and nine enlisted men, including Sergeant Kisters, advancing ahead of the leading elements of U.S. troops to fill a large crater in the only available vehicle route through Gagliano, was taken under fire by two enemy machine guns. Sergeant Kisters and the officer, unaided and in the face of intense small-arms fire, advanced on the nearest machine-gun emplacement and succeeded in capturing the gun and its crew of four. Although the greater part of the remaining small-arms fire was now directed on the captured machine-gun position, Sergeant Kisters voluntarily advanced alone toward the second gun emplacement. While creeping forward, he was struck five times by enemy bullets, receiving wounds in both legs and his right arm. Despite the wounds, he continued to advance on the enemy, and captured the second machine gun after killing three of its crew and forcing the fourth member to flee."

This was the story as the 91st Reconnaissance Squadron worked its way across Sicily: leading the advance, pushing Germans off hills to establish observation posts, directing artillery against the next group of dug-in infantry. At times the recon men were operating several miles ahead of the infantry. On 6 August the squadron was attached to its former partner in North Africa, the 9th Infantry Division, which had entered the line a day earlier.[15]

On 10 August the 2d Platoon, Troop C, followed a Sicilian guide over a mountain trail, often having to push the platoon's single scout car, and reached positions at Furnari that afforded a sweeping view of Sicily's northern coast. The village was full of Germans, and the troopers set up hidden machine-gun positions for defense because they knew they could never retreat under fire over that terrain with their vehicles. The patrol broke radio silence to report its position, which II Corps initially refused to believe was accurate because it was twenty miles behind German lines. Fortunately, the next day friendly Sicilians told the German commander that a huge American force was about to attack his position from the rear, a story he believed after one of his patrols spotted a couple of 2d Platoon troopers. The Germans pulled out, the town was spared a battle, and the troopers escaped with their lives.[16]

On 16 August the squadron went into reserve for the brief remainder of the campaign. Lieutenant Colonel Charles Ellis, who had replaced Candler as the squadron commander, took action that would serve his outfit well in the Italian mountains. He obtained special authorization to acquire engineering equipment, including an R4 angle dozer, a compressor, motor-driven saws, a Barco hammer, and hand tools. The cavalrymen would now be able to deal with German demolitions without having to wait for engineers to show up, which would allow them to press forward and maintain contact with the foe.[17]

The Cavalry Grabs the Golden Ring

Seventh Army worked its way eastward along the northern Sicilian coast as the Germans prepared to evacuate the island. Brilliant German delaying actions in the mountainous terrain, as well as heat and malaria outbreaks, slowed the advance to a crawl.[18]

Lieutenant McCloskey's platoon, 3d Cavalry Reconnaissance Troop, was the lead unit working down the coast road toward Messina on 31 August. The Germans had blown the bridges and were defending the obstacles, so McCloskey sent a dismounted patrol into the hills, where it discovered a trail looping from the main road toward Messina. Captain Netterblad ordered Lieutenant Gunter's platoon to advance over the trail. The cavalrymen were

pleasantly surprised to encounter no resistance as they entered the city at about 0700 hours. Lieutenant Phillips' platoon, meanwhile, had dismounted and bypassed the blown bridges on foot to join Gunter's men in Messina. The last Germans had just left for the mainland.

About an hour later, British tanks rolled into town. The brigadier commanding expressed surprise to find American recon units already there and rounding up officials. At 1045 the recon men escorted Lt. Gen. George S. Patton Jr. to the city hall so that he could revel in the glory of having beaten Montgomery to Messina.[19]

★★★

The 9th Infantry Division, which had operated with the 91st Reconnaissance Squadron attached throughout its part in the Sicilian campaign, concluded, "Reconnaissance troops when given the mission of maintaining contact with the enemy must be prepared to follow closely on his heels with foot patrols, and the organization of reconnaissance squadrons and reconnaissance troops should be modified to provide foot patrols capable of sustained operations and fighting on foot. The present reconnaissance units are designed to operate and fight from their vehicles. In the Sicilian campaign, the road net being extremely limited and demolitions and mining very heavy, reconnaissance units were delayed by being road-bound and could not maintain contact with the enemy. Portee horse cavalry would have been extremely valuable in this campaign."[20]

Major General John Lucas, in a report submitted on the Sicilian campaign, agreed with this last point. "Many German troops escaped us," he wrote. "I believe that a division, or even a brigade, *of horse cavalry* could have gotten to the enemy's rear, stopped the retreat, and allowed us to destroy him."[21] The old horse cavalrymen could always hope.

Whatever the shortcomings of mechanized cavalry in mountainous terrain, the recon men had nonetheless demonstrated that they could play a vital role in locating the enemy for the main force to engage. Indeed, the difficulty in maneuvering mounted in many cases gave greater weight to "sneak and peek" reconnaissance than to fighting for information. The 82d Armored Reconnaissance Battalion's run to Palermo demonstrated that even in rough terrain, the mechanized cavalry could exploit into the rear of a weak enemy.

Into Italy

At one minute after midnight on 9 September 1943, riflemen of the 141st and 142d Infantry regiments, 36th Infantry Division, began descending from troop transports into waiting landing craft off the Italian coast in Salerno Bay. There was no naval bombardment under way—which was an attempt to achieve surprise. The Germans recovered quickly if they were surprised at all, and laid down a murderous fire after the first soldiers had reached land. With the coming of light, four groups of tanks from the 16th Panzer Division counterattacked the tenuous beachhead.[22]

The 36th Infantry Division had split its reconnaissance troop into four "flying columns," which were to land in the fourth wave, then rush inland to reconnoiter the terrain. Each column had three jeeps, each with a machine gun and an "extra"—one with a bazooka, one with an 81mm mortar, and one with a mine detector and a demolition kit. Each column also had an amphibious jeep with a long-range AM radio and an M6 weapons carrier with a 37mm gun. The remainder of the troop, which was to land later, was outfitted with jeeps, 3/4-ton trucks, two half-tracks, and a 2 1/2-ton truck.

No tanks or tank destroyers had been committed to the assault wave. By the time the flying columns hit the beach, German armor was already pushing back, and the cavalrymen suddenly became a key piece in a very tenuous antitank defense of the infant beachhead. An unidentified member of Flying Column 1 related, "During the approach to the beach, the craft and beaches were under heavy artillery and small-arms fire. The two boats that carried [us] hit the beach at 0510 hours. . . . We deployed our vehicles and took cover, because the beach was being heavily shelled at the time. We were on Blue Beach about an hour. During this time, a German Mark IV tank moved into position about 800 yards to our right flank and laid a heavy concentration of [cannon] and machine-gun fire on us and the advancing infantry. Two of our men . . . jumped to their 37mm gun and took the tank under fire, knowing all the time that they could not penetrate the tank armor at that range. The two boys did, however, drive the tank away."

Flying Column 2 got as far as the ridge behind the beach before seven Mark IV tanks opened up on it with machine guns. The outfit's report stated, "Sergeant [James] Bunch, Pvt. [Elmer] White, Pvt. [Billy] Gibson, and Sgt. [Stanley] Patton manned the .50-cal and managed to knock the track off a Mark IV. Meanwhile, Corporal [Clyde] Kitchens and Pvt. [Robert] Reaney left with a rocket launcher and a rifle-grenade launcher. Corporal Kitchens' shot missed, but Private Reaney's grenade struck fairly only to break into three pieces instead of exploding. The six remaining tanks withdrew . . . while we finished off the crew from the seventh."

The other two flying columns got to shore under heavy fire but were still able to move inland and begin their missions. The fourth column spotted the dust of a coming attack by Mark IV tanks and drove to the division CP to report this fact. The men were ordered to protect the CP. The outfit's report said, "While the tank attack was in progress, our 37mm gun commanded by T/5 Bernard Jasin and fired by Pvt. Jesus Gonzales bagged two Mark IVs at a range of 170 yards. (We later paced it off.) One of the tank crews was captured by Sgt. [Daniel] Carvajal and an unidentified lieutenant. Our mortar crew did some excellent work in keeping the tanks out in the open, enabling the artillery and our 37mm to pound away at them."

The troop spent the coming days conducting patrols and establishing contact with units that had dropped out of communication in the heat of battle.[23]

★★★

The 45th Infantry Division, which had been VI Corps' floating reserve, landed beginning 10 September and plunged quickly into the heavy fighting. The first recon men belonging to the 45th Cavalry Reconnaissance Troop's 4th Platoon, a temporary non-standard organization, landed near Paestum and received oral orders to lead the advance for the 179th Infantry. The troopers scouted until they reached a blown bridge, then fired on an antitank gun crew guarding the crossing.[24]

Up the Boot

Field Marshal Albert Kesselring strove to drive Fifth Army into the sea and very nearly succeeded, but on 16 September he ordered a slow fighting withdrawal to the Volturno River line, which he intended to hold until 15 October. Beyond that, his engineers were busily preparing more fortified belts across the isthmus.[25] On 18 September VI Corps troops found nothing to their immediate front.

The remainder of the 45th Cavalry Reconnaissance Troop had arrived from Sicily on 16 September, and four days later the troop led the division's advance past Eboli. The following journal entries for that day reveal the kinds of things the recon men spotted during an advance against a fighting withdrawal:

> **1530:** Message from 2d Platoon—observes three enemy armored cars and one motorcycle at [map coordinates].
> **1600:** CO reports—five enemy armored cars sighted—enemy mortar, artillery, and small-arms fire coming from about [map coordinates]. Have two foot patrols out trying to determine the situation.
> **1700:** CO reports—self-propelled guns, one 20mm gun, one tank (Mark IV) firing at them at [map coordinates] approximately from [map coordinates]. Eight Germans sighted mining bridge at [map coordinates].[26]

The 3d Infantry Division's reconnaissance troop landed across the beach at Salerno on 20 September, and the next morning the troop moved out to scout the division's route of advance. The 3d Platoon established contact with the British from the Salerno landing force (10 Corps) on the left, while the other two reconnaissance platoons got their first look at Italy's realities. "Enemy demolitions and impassable mountain trails [make] vehicular reconnaissance nearly impossible," recorded the troop's after-action report.[27]

Captain A. T. Netterblad, the troop commanding officer, filed a report upon his return to the States in early 1944 that provides a picture of the troop's operations during this period. The troop, although theoretically subordinated to the G-2, received most of its orders verbally from the division commanding general or his chief of staff. Roughly half of its patrols were conducted on foot and half mounted. Netterblad spread his Italian-speaking soldiers across the recon platoons, and they proved invaluable for gathering information from the locals. For night patrols, troopers joined infantry patrols, where they proved better able than the GIs to gather useful information because of their specialized training. Netterblad often flew in a Cub plane above his men; from there he could see them and the enemy and drop messages to the troopers.[28] There was some talk in the theater of assigning a Cub to each division's reconnaissance troop, but nothing came of it.

By 6 October Fifth Army had liberated Naples and had generally reached the line of the Volturno River. The British Eighth Army, which had landed on the "toe" of Italy prior to the Salerno operation, had fought up the east side of the peninsula and pulled into line to the right of Fifth Army.

The 45th Infantry Division held the craggy ground at the far right of the VI Corps line. Second Lieutenant Robert Flynn served with the 2d Platoon, 45th Cavalry Reconnaissance Troop. A former National Guardsman and infantryman with the 26th Infantry Division, he had entered officer candidate school in 1942. Flynn had briefly been assigned to the 94th Infantry Division, then was sent overseas to join the 45th Division in Sicily. Now he and his comrades were patrolling on foot as the division readied to attack across the Volturno.

Under static conditions, nighttime patrolling duties often came the way of cavalry reconnaissance men, and it was a nail-biting test of courage that could put a man almost on top of his enemy with no warning. Flynn related how he was wounded for the second time since reaching Salerno: "I was on a night patrol near [Piedemonte D']Alife, and there is nothing as bad as night reconnaissance work. You can't see where you're going, and it's easy to lose track of your terrain even if you've studied it during the daytime for a long period. Suddenly, almost out of nowhere, a Jerry machine gun opened up on us. It couldn't have been more than 10 feet away. I knew I was hit because I could feel my knee give way, but I still let my grenade go. And so did the other men." The machine-gun nest was destroyed.[29]

The 3d and 34th Infantry divisions forced the Volturno River line the night of 12–13 October, while the 45th Infantry Division drove through the mountains into the Volturno valley on the corps' right wing. Most of the crossings by VI Corps' running mate, British 10 Corps, succeeded on the Fifth Army's left wing. But Field Marshal Kesselring had anticipated this development and was well prepared to wage a fighting withdrawal to, first, the Barbara Line, then to a daunting band of fortifications that became known as the winter position, while he prepared the Gustav Line behind the Rapido and Garigliano rivers.[30]

★★★

On 10 October 1943 the 91st Reconnaissance Squadron, in Sicily, received orders attaching it to Fifth Army, on the mainland, and the troopers moved into staging areas. There the squadron obtained six half-tracks equipped with 75mm guns (probably surplus M3 tank destroyers) and issued them to its antitank platoon to replace its 37mm guns.[31]

The squadron arrived in Italy in early November 1943 and was attached to II Corps, which was stymied in the winter position. It went into reserve because, as the squadron's history records, "at this time, II Corps was heavily engaged with the enemy in the mountainous terrain commanding the Mignano Pass, and neither the situation nor the terrain warranted the employment of mechanized reconnaissance."

The squadron saw brief periods of activity, generally patrolling at the troop level, over the next several months. It received forty of the new M8 armored cars on 24 January 1944 while attached to the 36th Infantry Division near the Rapido River. The squadron in March 1944 moved out of the line to San Agata, where it reorganized as a standard cavalry reconnaissance squadron. The reorganization established Troop E, initially comprising six T30s assault guns, and relabeled the light tank troop as Company F. The reconnaissance platoons retained their 81mm mortars despite the official TO&E, which called for 60mm mortars, and would keep them for the duration. (In a demonstration of the unpredictable nature of equipment deliveries, the 117th Cavalry Reconnaissance Squadron, which was still sitting in North Africa, a month earlier had been able to trade in its T30s for the new M8 howitzer motor carriage.)

The men underwent intensive training in dismounted combat in mountainous terrain and night operations. Troopers learned from Italian mountain troops and a few advance members of the 10th Mountain Division how to climb up cliffs and rappel down them.[32]

★★★

The 1st Armored Division arrived in Italy in mid-November and bivouacked near Capua. The division formed Fifth Army's reserve, ready to exploit a breakout into the Liri Valley, which did not materialize. Nonetheless, when hopes were still high, a five-man patrol from the 81st Armored Reconnaissance Battalion set out on 13 December to scout the Rapido River, the last barrier before the valley. Deep behind enemy lines, the men hid in a cave at dawn. An Italian farmer discovered the patrol, but rather than turn the men in, he provided civilian clothes so they could make a daylight reconnaissance of the area. Mission accomplished, the patrol returned to American lines that night.[33]

★★★

In December the 3d Infantry Division temporarily organized a "Provisional Mounted Squadron" using some five hundred horses and mules that had been acquired in Sicily and Italy and put to use as pack animals in the mountains. The "squadron" had two mounted reconnaissance troops organized along old cavalry lines, a pack howitzer battery, a mule train, and a wire/communications platoon. Personnel were drawn from all over the division. The squadron performed well conducting reconnaissance to the enemy's flanks and rear, forming a counter-reconnaissance screen, and maintaining contact with friendly units to the flanks.[34] An observer who served with several outfits in II Corps in early 1944 recounted, "All cavalry officers and G-2s and S-2s questioned with one exception stated emphatically that horse cavalry would be extremely useful in the Italian theater."[35]

More generally, however, the infantry division reconnaissance troops in Italy during the winter were employed dismounted. The troopers manned outposts, filled gaps in the lines, and conducted contact and reconnaissance patrols.[36] Thus far, because the Germans had controlled the location of the battlefield along fortified lines of their choice, the cavalry in Italy—on foot, in vehicles, or a-horse—had probably fallen as far short of its envisioned mission as at any point in the war.

The Anzio Landings: Troopers Dismount

The Allies decided to bypass the bitter German resistance along the Gustav Line with amphibious landings at Anzio on 22 January 1944. The 3d Infantry

Division's reconnaissance troop contributed three combat patrols (later renamed "battle patrols") and three reconnaissance patrols to the assault wave on Red Beach. The squad-size combat patrols were made up entirely of volunteers, and the troop claimed that such groups, specially trained and equipped, could accomplish as much in battle as three times their number of average men with average training. Reaching shore at about 0300 hours, the recon men moved out for seven bridges across the Mussolini Canal, on the right flank of the division's sector. The men reached the objectives, blew the bridges that had been designated for destruction, and established defensive positions.

At Bridge Six, mechanized elements from the Hermann Göring Panzer Division counterattacked at 1800 hours, and three half-tracks crossed the span before the cavalrymen could blow it. The rest of the attacking force was stopped, and the Germans who had crossed were destroyed. The recon men held their positions until relieved by the 504th Parachute Infantry Regiment the night of 23 January, relying on salvos from a "provisional pack battery" (75mm guns) to fend off infantry assaults.[37]

Elements of the 1st Armored Division's Combat Command A began arriving at the beachhead three days after the VI Corps assault divisions went ashore. Corps commanding general Maj. Gen. John Lucas viewed his job as establishing and defending a beachhead at Anzio, not kicking open the door to Rome. He judged his initial assault force to be too weak to risk penetrating the Alban Hills, which dominated the landing site from a dozen miles inland, although by doing so he could have cut the main highway—and supply route— from Rome to the Gustav Line. The Germans responded to the landings with remarkable speed, and by the time CCA participated in VI Corps' first big attack on 30 January, the Germans were able to contain the breakout attempt. From the high ground, the Germans could see—and shoot—just about anything that moved in the beachhead. The tanks settled into a pine forest, where they were to spend months firing artillery missions.

The 81st Armored Reconnaissance Battalion joined CCA on 1 February 1944. The battalion's mission was to reconnoiter the road net for possible tank operations, after which it became a mobile reserve attached to the Canadian-American First Special Service Force (FSSF)—the famed "Devil's Brigade"—to prevent any enemy breakthrough at the extreme right end of the Allied line. The assault guns were separately attached to the field artillery to conduct fire missions.

The battalion saw little action in March and April, the exception being an intelligence-gathering raid conducted on Cerreto Alto on 15 April. The FSSF controlled the operation, which involved a battalion of its 2d Regiment, several medium tanks, and tank destroyers, as well as a reconnaissance and a light tank platoon from the 81st Battalion. The raid netted sixty-one prisoners and twenty counted enemy dead, but mines knocked out two medium tanks and an M8 armored car.[38]

On 1 May the battalion participated in a second raid on Cerreto Alto and a simultaneous one on a German-held gatehouse near the ocean's edge, which anchored the FSSF's right flank. The plan was for infantry and light tanks to enter Cerreto Alto under covering fire from tank destroyers, while infantry, light tanks, and M8 armored cars were to assault the gatehouse. German soldiers had been seen after the first raid planting mines in the road to Cerreto Alto, and a probable Mark IV tank had been spotted.

An account left by the acting commander of Company D (light tanks) provides a view into the fog of war and dubious real-world decisions in a small-unit action in which the cavalry supported the infantry in an assault role—all in a fight to obtain information that could not be gathered by stealthy reconnaissance. The officer was in his tank outside the headquarters of the FSSF battalion commander.

When radio silence lifted at 0530 hours, all stations began to net in at once, or rather I should say they tried to net in. There seemed to be no control, no [net control station—NCS]—only a senseless and wasteful cross-calling, stations canceling each others' messages. Confusion was not the exception, it was the rule. NCS would not acknowledge my call sign. I was worried about my platoons as I could hear them calling, did not hear any answer to their calls, and could already see tracers from the beach.

The platoon at the gatehouse called me, but I had shut down. He called again, and I went into the net to contact him and establish communication. I then tried to get the Cerreto Alto platoon (Lieutenant Davey). He did not answer. At this point, a messenger came from the CP to ask me to remain silent, as my signal was so strong that it ruled out that of NCS. I shut down again.

The platoon leader at the beach, after several unacknowledged calls to NCS, called me once more. I told him I had been ordered off the air. Soon he called once more, said he had been unable to contact NCS, and asked me to relay information that his tank had struck a mine, and that he needed the T2 [tank retriever] and ambulance. I relayed this information and shut down once more.

Then Colonel Moore [FSSF] and [Lieutenant] Colonel [Michael] Popowski [81st Armored Reconnaissance Battalion] came to my tank and ordered me to try to contact Lieutenant Davey and get him to move on in. I had heard only one transmission from him—to the [tank destroyers]—to "lift it up, you are too low." They did not answer. I did not hear him again and could not contact him. The [tank destroyers] were giving fire orders. I heard the infantry commander at Cerreto Alto say, "Where is our goddam support? Where are the tanks? Can't the tanks move in and make a path through the minefield?"

I called the secondary station of the tank platoon at Cerreto Alto and asked if he could relay to Lieutenant Davey; he tried, but there was no answer. I then asked his situation and why the platoon had not gone in as planned. He said he did not know why the advance had stopped, that the tanks were under artillery fire and were withdrawing, then that Lieutenant Davey had signaled them all not to fire. He (the platoon sergeant) said they had withdrawn and spread out wide in the fields by the road. I told him to contact Lieutenant Davey and tell him to move on in. . . .

At this point, the tank platoon at the gatehouse called, saying that his mission was completed, but that the beach was getting hot, and the ambulance and the T2 had not arrived. He requested orders. I again requested the ambulance and the T2. . . .

Next there were further calls from the CP, which gave orders to get Lieutenant Davey's platoon into Cerreto Alto as quickly as possible. . . . Colonel Popowski called from the [NCS] and said if things did not take an immediate turn for the better, I should go to Cerreto Alto myself. I called the infantry commander (Lieutenant Piette) and told him I would get the tanks through as soon as possible. He said that he needed them to cut a path through the minefield and that he needed ambulances. . . .

Lieutenant Davey came to Sergeant Kiddy's tank at this point, and I was able to speak to him for the first time. He said that his tanks had come under heavy artillery fire initially, and that he had been warned of mines by the infantry. I replied that his orders were to get into Cerreto Alto and to complete his mission. He mentioned mines again. I said, "To the best of my knowledge, that is a personnel minefield. Our friends want you to cut a path through it. Is this the only reason you can't get in? Have you had any tank or [antitank] direct fire?"

He said that he had not. I told him to go on in and get it finished. Lieutenant Davey said, "Wilco. I will go in regardless. . . ."

I hit the road for Cerreto Alto . . . at all the speed my tank and the roads would permit, so I did not hear, or rather was unable to read any transmissions during the period because of the interference that high-speed movement caused. As I cleared [crossroads] 12, I could see a pillar of black smoke rising from the yard beside the buildings at Cerreto Alto. . . .

I found three M5s of Lieutenant Davey's platoon spread out and facing Cerreto Alto. A fourth tank was burning furiously, its ammunition exploding. . . . Another tank was returning from Cerreto Alto. . . . Infantrymen . . . signaled me to slow down, then stop, waved me off the road and shouted, "Don't go up there—mines!"

I pulled to the right of the road, positioned my tank, and dismounted. As I did so, I saw Lieutenant Davey in the middle of the road being carried arm-chair fashion by three men. I called for more men from the nearest tank and lifted Lieutenant Davey to the back deck of my tank, where I gave him morphine, dressed his wounds, and put a tourniquet on his leg while questioning the crewmen present. . . .They said there were [Teller mines] in the road and the field beyond the culvert, that their tank had struck three mines, and that Private First Class Henry was still in the burning tank. [The infantry had suffered twenty-six casualties, all limbs blown off after walking into the minefield. The raid was a complete failure.][39]

Things had gone better down on the beach. One participant described the action:

Three light tanks of Company D with two M8s attached cleared Borgo Sabotino at 0500. Their mission was to give close support to a company of FSSF infantry troops attacking the gatehouse on Sunnyside Road and to capture any enemy in the area. . . . The three M5s went to the north of Sunnyside Road to clear a path through the antipersonnel minefield for the foot troops, and the M8s went south, opening up with direct fire on the jetty.

Lieutenant Hollis' own tank hit a single [antitank] mine on the north-south road before getting into the [antipersonnel] minefield. Lieutenant Hollis continued to give fire support from his disabled tank during the whole action. The other two tanks, with infantry in close support, assaulted house number 14.

After the infantry had reached house 14, the full firepower of the M8s was directed at the gatehouse, and the section of light tanks moved in on the gatehouse. Sergeant Robert's tank, on the left flank, knocked out an enemy [machine-gun] nest at a range of 100 to 150 yards. Sergeant Kugawa's tank, through fire and movement, got to within 50 yards of the wall in front of the gatehouse and covered the infantry approach from there.

At 0600 hours, the infantry started to withdraw under the cover of the armor. At 0615 hours, the battalion maintenance T2 arrived and hit an unseen Teller mine. [Both vehicles were disabled with thermite grenades when direct fire from self-propelled guns compelled a hasty withdrawal.][40]

★★★

Within the Anzio beachhead, infantry divisions used their reconnaissance troops differently. Still reflecting the aggressive approach shown during the landings, the 3d Infantry Division used its troop constantly to augment patrolling by subordinate units. The troop generally executed deeper missions conducted at night and on foot.[41] The 45th Infantry Division used its troop for some patrolling and to man OPs, but the troopers spent much of their time driving the coastal road at Anzio and securing the reserve line in the zones of the 179th and 180th Infantry regiments.[42]

The Breakout: The Cavalry Mounts Up Again
At 2300 hours on 11 May, II Corps, French Expeditionary Corps, and British 13 Corps attacked the German Gustav Line in full strength from the

Garigliano River to Cassino. The objectives were two: crack the German defenses and draw German divisions away from Anzio to ease the planned breakout there. The offensive succeeded on both counts.[43]

The second large cavalry outfit in Italy was now with II Corps. On 11 May the 91st Cavalry Reconnaissance Squadron was committed as light infantry supported by its own assault guns to provide flank protection for 88th Infantry Division operations around Monte Cianelli. This was the first in a series of reattachments of only a few days' duration that involved either dismounted flank protection duties or brief troop-size mounted reconnaissance forays.[44]

By 16 May, II Corps had broken through the Gustav Line and begun to pursue the beaten enemy, which withdrew to the Hitler Line by 18 May. "Victory was in the air," noted the Fifth Army history.[45]

★★★

At 0545 hours on 23 May, a tremendous artillery preparation rained down on German lines around the Anzio beachhead. At 0630 the breakout—Operation Buffalo—kicked off. The 3d Infantry and 1st Armored divisions made up the main assault force, supported by a limited advance by the 45th Infantry Division and by diversionary attacks by the British.

The 81st Armored Reconnaissance Battalion was split, with Company A attached to CCB and the rest of the battalion to CCA. The first day of the offensive, the squadron remained in reserve, but from that point on, at least some part of the outfit was in action.[46]

Likewise, the 3d Cavalry Reconnaissance Troop did not join the fight until 24 May, when it conducted its first real mounted reconnaissance since the day of the initial landings at Anzio. The reconnaissance platoons advanced ahead of the division to maintain contact with the rapidly retreating enemy and rolled up a hundred prisoners. Regarding the outfit's first use of M8 armored cars in battle, the after-action report noted, "Contrary to the expectations of some, the M8 armored car was found to be an excellent weapon for a reconnaissance platoon."[47]

By 25 May the 3d Infantry and 1st Armored divisions had cracked German resistance in the Cisterna-Valmontone corridor, and the initial phase could be counted a success. Lieutenant General Mark Clark, commanding Fifth Army, ordered VI Corps to attack below Colli Laziali, which would pry loose the southwestern corner of the last German defensive line before Rome.[48]

★★★

German resistance stiffened between 28 and 30 May as every available reserve rushed to the front, and by dusk on 30 May the Fifth Army drive on Rome appeared to have stalled. That night on the right wing of VI Corps, 36th Infantry Division GIs attacked up steep, wooded slopes near Velletri and broke through, which doomed the German position at Colli Laziali. Nevertheless, when the 1st Armored and 45th Infantry divisions renewed their push on 31 May, they continued to encounter strongpoints supported by tanks, self-propelled guns, and antiaircraft guns.[49]

Captain Raymond Baker, who had transferred from the 3d Infantry Division to take command of the 45th Cavalry Reconnaissance Troop in April, had formed his own battle patrol in early May modeled on those in his old division. Ten or so GIs from the infantry regiments joined the cavalrymen on "special assignment."[50] "The captain wanted recon to go into combat," observed Lt. Robert Flynn, who was included because he had trained as an infantry officer. "He cost recon a lot of boys' lives."

The night of 31 May, Baker ordered Flynn to take a patrol through the German lines to cut their line of withdrawal up a particular road. "It was dark, and we never did find the road. It must have been grenades or mortars. Something hit my right knee. I said, 'Follow me!' and we got the hell out of there. Baker wasn't very happy."

In what appears to be a reference to an unfolding mess along the road, Baker radioed the division headquarters at 0925 hours: "I have a platoon in trouble; pinned down at [map coordinates], in the crook of the road. I am sending the four M8s that I have. . . . I'd like to get a couple of tanks to come around the other way."

Light tanks from the 753d Tank Battalion soon arrived but found the fire to be too heavy to advance. By 1730 five men were still trapped, and two jeeps and an assault gun had been knocked out.[51]

That day, Flynn, wounded for the third time, was evacuated for combat exhaustion. "I just physically and mentally ran out of gas," he said later.[52]

★★★

II Corps during this time had continued driving north to link up with VI Corps. II Corps had assaulted the Hitler Line on 20 May and cut through it with relative ease, because the Germans had lacked time to get set and bring up reinforcements. By the time the 29th Panzergrenadier Division arrived on 21 May to strengthen the line, it was too late. II Corps hammered away relentlessly, and the night of 23–24 May the Germans abandoned Terracina, the last real strongpoint on the road to Anzio.[53]

On 24 May the 91st Cavalry Reconnaissance Squadron was unleashed to make contact with the Anzio beachhead forces. Troop A made first contact near Borgo Grappa on the morning of 25 May. At this point, the squadron underwent another series of rapid reattachments that lasted through early June, generally performing the mission of protecting the II Corps' right flank by seizing high ground through dismounted action and establishing OPs.[54]

★★★

A third battalion-size cavalry formation—the 117th Cavalry Reconnaissance Squadron—was just joining the battle with II Corps. The squadron had shipped to England as the 2d Squadron of the 102d Cavalry Regiment (Horse-Mechanized) in late September 1942. It had separated from the regiment and sailed in late December for North Africa, where it was assigned as the combat security element for Dwight Eisenhower. The assignment entailed reconnaissance missions in the area surrounding Ike's headquarters. At this time, the outfit consisted of Troops A and B mounted in scout cars and jeeps, and Troop F in M3 light tanks. The squadron also conducted training for newly organized French mechanized cavalry formations. It had finally reorganized as the 117th Cavalry Reconnaissance Squadron in late November 1943. On 3 May, Ordnance had painted white stars on all vehicles, in place of the yellow ones used in North Africa, and prepared them for shipment by sea. The squadron turned in its old light tanks for M5A1s and its diesel-powered T2 tank retrievers for one with a gasoline engine.

The 117th Squadron had arrived in Italy on 19 May 1944; it entered the line subordinated to II Corps on 24 May at Itri and Sperlonga. Before leaving Tunisia, the squadron had run every man through an intensive urban combat training course of its own design, which left it better prepared than many outfits for the realities of war in Europe. The 117th Squadron's first mission was to establish crossings over the Amaseno River and maintain contact with the enemy; the 117th Squadron was attached to the 91st Cavalry Reconnaissance Squadron. Taking a lesson from the battle-savvy men already in Italy, the squadron lined the floors of all of its wheeled vehicles with sandbags to protect against exploding mines, a practice it followed for the rest of the war.[55]

Staff Sergeant Philip Schriel, of Troop B, later recalled his baptism of fire. "I was walking point for recon when I came face to face with a German tanker with a Schmeisser [machine pistol]. I had a Tommy gun that misfired. He shot his whole clip, and it went all sides of me. Then we both backed away. I was sure I would be OK from then on."[56]

The squadron laid its own claim to having established the first link between the II Corps and the Anzio beachhead forces. On 25 May, Lt. Padraig O'Dea led his platoon through the flooded Pontine marshes and delivered a letter from Maj. Gen. Geoffrey Keyes, the commanding general of II Corps, to Maj. Gen. Lucian Truscott, commanding VI Corps at Anzio.

The squadron's first stand-up fight was that same day at Sezze. Troop A's commanding officer, Capt. Thomas Piddington, recalled, "Prior to crossing the [initial point] at 0300, the troops were fed eggs, any way you like them. . . . In the still dark early hours, Troop A, its 2d Platoon in the lead, took Terracina and advanced aggressively north against sporadic small-arms fire. Just south of the mountainous village of Sezze, near the Pontine marshes, the 3d Platoon was bogged down due to a bridge over a dry creek that was thought to be mined. I took a patrol forward to determine what was holding things up and to get them moving. While walking point with Maj. Bob McGarry, we were hit with a heavy concentration of machine-gun fire from the ridge beyond. Both McGarry and I were hit. We managed to work our way to cover, where we were able to bring assault-gun fire to bear on the ridge. In addition, we called up a platoon of [Company] F tanks, which then overran the enemy positions."

While this was going on, Major General Keyes dropped into the Troop A command post and asked where the commander was. Told that Captain Piddington was forward with the lead platoon, Keyes answered, "Good," and left.[57]

The troopers fought for two days to drive the elements of the 29th Panzergrenadier Division out of the mountain stronghold. It was grenade and Tommy gun work, supported by fire from the M8 assault guns. Troop B, tasked with establishing contact with the French, on the right, over terrain too rough for vehicles, borrowed some horses for the job, and the cavalry rode again.

On 1 June the squadron was attached to the FSSF, which then-Maj. Howard Samsel described as "a real cutthroat outfit." The mission was to cut off German forces still fighting delaying actions in the mountains, and the cavalrymen were to seize Collaferro. During the operation, a light tank accomplished a miracle when it set a Panther tank on fire after hitting it with six 37mm rounds.

As usual, the recon men were in front. "The half-track I was riding in was cut off by the Germans along with two other jeeps," Samsel recalled. "We drove into a deep washout and kept the German patrols pinned down with heavy .50-caliber machine-gun fire until dark. It was decided to make a break for it shortly after nightfall. One jeep stalled, and a hand grenade was dropped into it. I fired two bazooka rounds at the nearest German patrol, and we took off like a blast out of a sand pile. The 'fifties' kept firing [and] fortunately we escaped under heavy small-arms fire."[58]

The Liberation of Rome

Under constant pressure from VI Corps and threatened by II Corps' advance from the south, the Germans threw in the towel on 3 June, when it became apparent that they had begun a hasty withdrawal through Rome. On 4 June, Lieutenant General Clark issued orders for the drive on the capital. All units were ordered to be ready to push armored reconnaissance columns forward rapidly to seize and secure crossings over the Tiber River in their respective zones. The 1st Armored Division was to make the main thrust for VI Corps.[59]

As of 3 June, most of the 81st Armored Reconnaissance Battalion was in the line fighting as infantry near Campoleone between the British 1st Infantry Division and the U.S. 45th Infantry Division. Company A was "slugging it out" on Highway 6 with Task Force Howze (Col. Hamilton Howze commanding) a few miles from Rome.[60]

The next day the 81st Armored Reconnaissance Battalion received orders to protect the 1st Armored Division's left flank during the advance on Rome up Highway 7. Company B took the lead at 0500 hours, followed closely by Companies C and D. Progress was rapid at first because the Germans had pulled back overnight. The Germans had blown every bridge and culvert, cratered the road, and generally left a small rear guard to cover each obstruction. The forward platoon rolled up a number of these by catching the Germans unawares.

Dawn came, and the cavalrymen charged forward. One participant recalled the advance: "It was fun to watch Germans along the route as they came out of the farmhouses surprised to see such a formation traveling along the road. They could not understand how it had happened that they were prisoners so quickly."

Encountering a minefield south of the village of Falcognana, Company B set out cross-country to bypass it. Because of the quietness and speed of the armored cars, the company unwittingly bypassed several well-concealed antitank and machine-gun positions belonging to the German 362d Infantry Division. Both sides, therefore, were surprised when the advancing Americans ran into a strongpoint manned by about a hundred infantrymen. A fierce firefight erupted, and antitank fire tore into Company B's column.

"Before Lieutenant Fagan and Lieutenant Farr realized it," the battalion CO recalled, "they had overrun an antitank gun on the side of the road, and the point [M8 armored] car was in flames about 100 yards beyond. In the early confusion of the skirmish, it was difficult to make a good estimate of the situation. Tracers were everywhere. Four columns of black smoke spiraled skyward. Later, a quick inventory proved that two of the smoke columns were from the [battalion's] own armored cars and two were from German half-track personnel carriers, which apparently had been used as prime movers for antitank guns."

Two more M8s and a jeep were hit, and the recon men tried to extricate themselves.

At this point, Companies C and D arrived just like the cavalry. The assault guns from the two reconnaissance companies poured rounds into the German positions, as did 37mm cannons and .50-caliber machine guns. The light tanks, meanwhile, tried a flanking movement to the right. After suffering some forty men killed and wounded, the remaining German troops surrendered to Company B. The battalion charged onward and experienced no further losses despite a few more instances of antitank and small-arms fire. Twenty more German soldiers surrendered to the column.

The battalion's motorcycle platoon, meanwhile, advanced up a separate route accompanied by two armored cars. It encountered a roadblock, and the men dismounted. While the M8s laid down covering fire, the troopers moved forward, and the Germans scattered. Things went less well at the next road-block, which was manned by a German platoon with an antitank gun. German gunnery forced the motorcyclists to abandon their mounts, and the armored cars had to go into hull defilade, which left only their small turrets exposed to fire. This proved the end of the platoon's advance for the day.

The battalion received new orders to seize and guard a bridge over the Tiber River in Rome. At 1815 hours, Company B reported that it had established its CP at St. Peter's basilica, in the heart of Rome, joining the ranks of the many units that claimed to have been the first to enter the Eternal City. Overjoyed civilians greeted the men with flowers, wine, and sweets. Company C pressed on and after a brief fight established control over the Tiber bridge by 1900 hours, completing a classic cavalry task.[61]

Company A, meanwhile, was advancing up Highway 6 into Rome at the point of Task Force Howze. M10s from Company B, 636th Tank Destroyer Battalion, and a few tanks were with the recon men. The column plowed through several German delaying positions and entered Rome at 0715 hours, led by the M8 commanded by Company A's Sergeant Matthews. Company B's Charles Kessler recalled, "My tank destroyer rolled past a large 'Roma' sign marking the city limits and on into the capital. Ahead of me were five Sherman tanks and two [tank destroyers]. Behind were the entire Fifth and [British] Eighth armies. We had not gone 200 yards into the city when a monster 170mm German self-propelled gun opened fire. The lead M4 burst into flame, and the rest of us deployed off the road. The enemy gun was well hidden. . . ."

The recon men set out to find the gun. Having spotted both it and a good firing position, they returned and guided several M10s into position. The tank destroyer gunners took care of the problem, and the column rolled on into the city.[62]

★★★

On 4 June, II Corps had also established a task force under Lt. Col. Charles Ellis, the 91st Cavalry Reconnaissance Squadron commander, to enter Rome along one of its several routes of advance. Ellis had at his disposal two reconnaissance platoons, two platoons of medium tanks, one company each of infantry and engineers, two platoons of 105mm self-propelled howitzers, and medical personnel. Task Force Ellis moved out early in two columns and pushed aside resistance from rearguard elements. The task force entered Rome and subsequently claimed to be the first unit of "combat strength" to enter the Eternal City.[63] Fifth Army officially credited the 88th Cavalry Reconnaissance Troop, which had advanced along a different route, with being the first Allied element to cross the city limits, although the troop did not enter the city center until evening.[64]

"In the late afternoon of 4 June 1944," recorded the Fifth Army's history, "beaten elements of the German Tenth and Fourteenth armies, disorganized and torn apart by the twin drives of Fifth Army through the battered Gustav Line and out of the Anzio beachhead, were in full flight north of Rome. . . ."[65]

The 117th Cavalry Reconnaissance Squadron passed through Rome a day after its liberation. Then-Corp. Robert Lutz, who had been a horse soldier back in the 102d Cavalry, recalled, "I was on a little black-top road in the lead. About a quarter mile ahead, a little German car appeared and took off. We didn't shoot because we weren't supposed to be shooting." Greeted by deliriously happy civilians willing to share their drink and homes, the outfit briefly dissolved as a disciplined military organization. Troop C was assigned as security for Lt. Gen. Mark Clark and stayed there for several days.[66]

Back to the Grind

The cavalry charge ended north of Rome. Four fresh German divisions rushed to the front, and Field Marshal Albert Kesselring employed delaying tactics while he slid the 3d, 29th, and 90th Panzergrenadier and 26th Panzer divisions to block Fifth Army.[67] Of passing interest is the fact that the XIV Panzer Corps, which controlled most of those divisions and maneuvered northward from the Gustav Line at Cassino to fill a gap that had emerged between German Tenth and Fourteenth armies, was commanded at the corps and division levels by cavalrymen. *General der Kavallerie* Fridolin von Senger und Etterlin attributed his successful execution of a difficult operation requiring rapid moves and adjustments in part to the commonality of thought and language among the cavalrymen. He also used the excellent radio nets of his mechanized divisions' armored reconnaissance battalions to ensure perfect communications throughout.[68]

By mid-June, German resistance, lengthening American supply lines, and terrain combined to slow the advance dramatically.[69] The 81st Armored Reconnaissance Battalion's history recorded:

Terrain difficulties which hampered the actions of the battalion throughout the drive north toward the Florence-Pisa line started to show up around this time. Extremely rugged hills, deep ravines, and heavy underbrush growing on heavily wooded slopes often made the tanks stick to the highways and farm roads. The Italian peasant's idea of a road for a pair of oxen and a cart is hard for the uninitiated to realize. The grades are such that a jeep has to use low-range consistently, the slopes often are precarious, and rocks jutting up between the two ruts threaten to tear away the transmission or crankcase of a wheeled vehicle.

Jerry, of course, used every one of these features to the utmost. Small, innocent looking trails in the hills, as well as the main roads, were cleverly mined; bridges by the hundreds were blown. . . ; roads were cratered and blocked by large trees or buildings blown into the narrow streets of mountain towns; many fords or passes for blown bridges were mined. . . . S.O.P. were antitank and/or self-propelled guns sited to cover roadblocks, minefields, bypasses, and any obstacles that forced wheeled vehicles to slow down.[70]

The 81st Armored Reconnaissance Battalion, with elements of the 776th Tank Destroyer Battalion attached, worked on the division's right flank and maintained contact with French forces in the next zone. Fights were numerous but tiny, and frequently the men spent more time using pickaxes and shovels to get their vehicles through than they did performing actual reconnaissance. Still, by the end of June, Rome lay 150 miles to the rear, and Florence just 35 miles ahead.

The 117th Cavalry Reconnaissance Squadron spent the remainder of June variously attached to and spearheading the 85th, 36th, and 34th Infantry divisions and engaged in tough fighting north of Rome that resulted in heavy casualties, many of them from mines. Twice during the period, the troopers fought horse-mounted German cavalry. They encountered their first Tiger tanks and learned that they could defeat them, but only because the recon men could vector in fighter-bombers by radio! Daily operations reports reveal the evolution of new tactics that combined a reconnaissance platoon with a few medium tanks and tank destroyers to create a small combined-arms point element. This indicates that the troopers were having to fight for information, pure and simple. In mid-month, Troop C was detached for separate duty with Fifth Army, which precluded rotation of the troops in combat, and the squadron recorded the first signs of combat fatigue caused by the constant action.

On 29 June the squadron received orders to turn back to the south, and it drove to a staging area north of Naples. Already by 20 June it had advanced 210 miles and suffered 120 casualties, including 14 dead, in thirty-seven days. The squadron had captured 800 enemy soldiers and caused a large if unknown number of losses to the foe. A captured German report included the statement that the "117th Cavalry Squadron was the equivalent of two panzer divisions"— an excuse for failing to stop it perhaps, but the cavalrymen appreciated the compliment. The outfit had no idea what lay ahead, but its fighting days in Italy were over.[71]

A second Task Force Ellis similar to the earlier version at Rome but including all of the 91st Cavalry Reconnaissance Squadron also pushed northward, only to be subsumed by Task Force Raney, which filled the gap between American forces and the French, on their right. Late in June the squadron was attached to the 1st Armored Division to work with Combat Command B on the division's left.[72]

Progress in July was even slower than in late June, in large measure because the Allied push was easing off as it approached the Pisa-Florence line, where Kesselring planned to stand again along the partially completed Gothic Line. By mid-month the 81st Armored Reconnaissance Battalion stopped its forward movement and spread out to cover the extraction of the French division, to the right, for use in southern France. On 23 July it withdrew to a rest area near Bolgheri, where it remained through August.[73] The 91st Cavalry Reconnaissance Squadron was shuffled about during this period, serving under the 88th Infantry Division, the 34th Infantry Division, and the oddball 45th Anti-Aircraft Artillery Brigade.[74]

The Allied advance stopped on 4 August after covering 270 miles in sixty-four days, which for the cavalrymen meant a return to the ground-pounding life they had known so well south of Rome. The Americans, who viewed France as the decisive theater, had prevailed in a strategy debate with the British over whether to keep forces in Italy strong enough to drive into the Balkans. For now, the mission of 15th Army Group in Italy was to pin German forces in place so they could not shift to more critical fronts elsewhere, while VI Corps and the French divisions invaded southern France in Operation Dragoon.[75]

The 81st Armored Reconnaissance Battalion reentered the line on 1 September to maintain contact with the 6th South African Armored Division, on the right, and to maintain contact with the enemy. This familiar assignment changed on 16 September, when the battalion dismounted to fight northward as infantry. Patrols probed forward to identify German strongpoints in the mountainous terrain; the battalion then dumped artillery and small-arms fire onto the position until the Germans decided to pull back. There were no heavy firefights, and casualties were light on both sides.

The 91st Cavalry Reconnaissance Squadron, operating on II Corps' left flank, crossed the Arno River on 2 September and fought dismounted as infantry on the far side. Glen Norris kept a journal in which he recorded his experiences and thoughts once per week. On 17 September, while Fifth Army butted against the Gothic Line, Norris recorded, "From a broad plain below the mountains, the front is on top of you, somewhere on the near slopes. There is a line of smoke where our shells and mortars explode all day long. When the smoke line is near the top of the slopes, our men are advancing up. When the line [is] nearer the mountain's base, the Krauts are shoving us back. . . . Fighting was still going on yesterday not only for the two key mountains, but also for several lesser slopes. 'I never saw a front like this,' said Major Walter Ball Scronton. . . . 'Everybody has his own little piece of high ground and everybody is on everybody else's hill.' "[76]

Another entry described the fighting as September gave way to October:

We took several villages and mountains before we reached the [Arno] river. The river wasn't very wide. The Jerries was on one bank and we was on the other bank. We would go out on patrol and the Jerries would snipe at us as we crossed the river.

It was awful foggy and we couldn't hardly see where we were going. One of our boys walked up [within] ten feet of a Jerries' machine-gun nest before they seen him. The Jerries got him. A man never knows what he will run into. They are hiding and setting there waiting for you to come along.

They told us we would have to hold up there at the river until our left side caught up. The English was fighting on our left. We stayed up there and fought until 17 October.[77]

After a rest period, the 81st Armored Reconnaissance Battalion relieved the 91st Cavalry Reconnaissance Squadron. The mission was defensive and demanded mainly outposting and patrolling.[78]

When the 91st Squadron returned to the line, it once again held defensive positions as infantry. To Glen Norris, the scene was far too familiar: "They moved us . . . to the foxhole with machine guns to hold a defense line. We lay there in the mud for fourteen days. It sleeted, snowed, and cold rained on us all the time. We had a tough time. We lost some good men. We was laying in the mud and water like hogs. We couldn't get out of our holes, only at night. Then the Jerries' sniper would snipe at us. We would go out at night to see what we could find and see. We always find plenty. The Jerries would be hiding and waiting for us."[79]

More Lessons Learned

As the Italian front settled down into a stalemate until April 1945, mechanized cavalrymen had time to ponder what they had learned during the campaign. After the 117th Cavalry Reconnaissance Squadron had been pulled from the line, Lieutenant Colonel Hodge drafted a memorandum to the Cavalry School outlining his conclusions after service in North Africa and Italy. The squadron organization was sound, he deemed, making it a "very efficient, malleable, and maneuverable force." Hodge said the teachings of the Cavalry School were valid—but he had been overseas since the new doctrine for cavalry reconnaissance had been imposed, and he was probably referring to traditional cavalry doctrine. He thought both the M8 assault gun and M5 light tank were under-gunned. He advocated several changes, including expanding the medical detachment, adding flexible machine-gun mounts to the armored cars, and giving reconnaissance troops full training in artillery direction.

Hodge offered a couple of other pithy observations: "Those who neglect dismounted reconnaissance will be killed. . . . Mounted reconnaissance at night is impossible and is suicide."[80]

By the end of 1944, Lt. Col. Michael Popowski, who had just left his job commanding the 81st Cavalry Reconnaissance Squadron, could report, "Like all good cavalry, the 81st has fought dismounted, mounted, and in combinations of both. It has made rapid advances. It has fought delaying actions. It has performed security missions of flank and advanced guard. It has raided enemy positions in limited-objective action and harassing action." The outfit had accounted for at least its numerical strength in enemy dead and more than twice that figure in prisoners.[81] In other words, doctrine be damned; the mechanized cavalry was just cavalry with machines.

The Final Charge in the Mediterranean Theater

Fifth Army spent nearly five months with almost no forward movement, but it used that time wisely. Replacements joined the battle-thinned ranks, new vehicles replaced those that were worn out, and ammunition reserves piled up. By 1 April rehabilitation was complete.

The 81st Cavalry Reconnaissance Squadron held a narrow sector on the extreme right of the IV Corps line. Its parent, the 1st Armored Division, anchored the left wing of II Corps just across the Reno River, with the 91st Cavalry Reconnaissance Squadron attached. On a clear day, men could see Bologna a dozen miles from the closest American positions, bits of the broad Po River basin, and the towering heights of the Alps a hundred miles distant. If the Germans could be driven from the Genghis Khan Line, their last string of mountain fortifications, they had no hope of stopping an advance south of the Po.[82]

Could mechanized cavalry penetrate deeply into the enemy's rear and raise havoc? You bet.

At dawn on 14 April 1945, Fifth Army attacked all along its line. British Eighth Army, to the east, had launched five days before, and diversionary attacks by IV Corps near the western coast had begun even earlier. Troop A, 81st Cavalry Reconnaissance Squadron, advanced dismounted into the German stronghold of Vergato on the heels of a devastating artillery barrage. The Germans fought with determination, and the troopers, lacking tank support because mines blocked the road into town, battled from house to house. Troop C moved in to assist that night, but the men were unable to clear the town until 16 April, when three tanks and a bulldozer finally arrived to help.

Troop D and tanks from Company F pushed down the Reno River valley against scattered resistance, followed by the rest of the squadron and some tanks from the 13th Tank Battalion. The remainder of the division also thrust forward toward Bologna on 16 April and within two days reached their initial phase line. German defenses were crumbling across the IV Corps front.

The 1st Armored Division sideslipped westward and broke into the fertile Po River valley on 21 April, the same day that II Corps troops captured Bologna. IV and II corps burst loose, advancing abreast. The Fifth Army's history recorded, "The enemy had been dislodged, his disorganization had begun, but only our unrelenting pursuit, involving many stiff small-unit engagements and over-all coordination, turned his retreat into a rout. . . . The emphasis was placed on speed and more speed; for the first time in the Italian campaign we had an enemy falling back in terrain suitable for swift pursuit." In other words, this was ideal mechanized cavalry country.

By 24 April, much of Fifth Army had crossed the Po River and torn into the German rear. Soon after midnight on 26 April, near Brescia, reconnaissance elements operating with CCA and reinforced by Sherman tanks spotted a German column trying to escape to the north. The Americans pulled off the road and waited until the column was abreast of them, then a Sherman fired its main gun at the fourth vehicle in the line. At this signal, armored cars, tanks, machine guns, rifles, and Tommy guns raked the foe. When the ambush was over, 150 Germans lay dead and 200 surrendered. From them, the recon men learned that another column was due at about 0500 hours, and a second ambush was laid. This one resulted in the destruction of fifty vehicles and another substantial bag of prisoners.

By 0900 on 28 April, recon's armored cars reached Coma and shortly thereafter the Swiss border. CCB and the remainder of the 81st Cavalry Reconnaissance Squadron arrived and set up roadblocks to prevent German units from escaping. The next day the squadron raced westward, bypassing Milan, to the north, to reach the Ticino River, twenty-five miles distant. When the campaign was over, the cavalrymen liked to say that they had spent as much time behind enemy lines as most of the tankers had spent in front of them.[83]

The 91st Cavalry Reconnaissance Squadron operated for most of the offensive attached to the 10th Mountain Division or under direct IV Corps control. As part of Task Force Duff, the squadron spearheaded the mountain division's drive and reached the Po River on 23 April. The unit's history recorded, "Our advance continued swiftly and there was usually enemy to the rear and to the flanks of our elements as well as to the front. It must be admitted that while this swift exploitation of the breakthrough confused the enemy and often resulted in the capture of his artillery and the seizure of his ration trains moving to supply forces already behind us, all the confusion was not on his side. . . ."[84]

By 28 April, Allied forces controlled all of the Alpine passes, and German Army Group Southwest was out of options. The Germans capitulated effective 2 May, and the war in the Mediterranean was over.

CHAPTER 4

THE PACIFIC, PART I: WAR OF THE CAVALRY RECONNAISSANCE TROOPS

The employment of cavalry units in the jungle-clad islands and atolls of the Pacific has digressed many tactical furlongs from the horse-mechanized concept of the early 1940s.

—Lt. Col. Clay Bridgewater, Cavalry, 77th Infantry Division

Half a world away, the Allied counteroffensive against the Empire of Japan had begun even before Operation Torch in North Africa. The Pacific and Mediterranean theaters shared one overriding characteristic for mechanized cavalrymen: The terrain was generally hostile to vehicle-mounted men.

Because the jungle-clad islands of the Pacific theater were generally unsuitable for mechanized cavalry operations, no squadron-size formation participated in the Pacific war. Nevertheless, every infantry division had an organic cavalry reconnaissance troop, and these men were too useful to waste. This chapter will provide a look at the most typical employment of the cavalrymen—fighting dismounted as infantry reconnaissance units— and the early exceptions when the troops could fight as they were trained to do, atop steeds of steel.

The Japanese had swept across the Pacific after Pearl Harbor, seemingly unstoppable until checked by the naval engagement in the Coral Sea, 7 to 8 May 1942, then defeated in the Battle of Midway, 3 to 6 June 1942. It was time to recover the initiative, and the U.S. Joint Chiefs of Staff on 2 July 1942 ordered the re-conquest of the Solomon Islands in order to deny the Japanese the use of the huge naval and air base at Rabaul. The U.S. Marines took the first step when they landed at Guadalcanal on 7 August. The Japanese resisted fiercely, and a stalemate in the jungle ensued.[1]

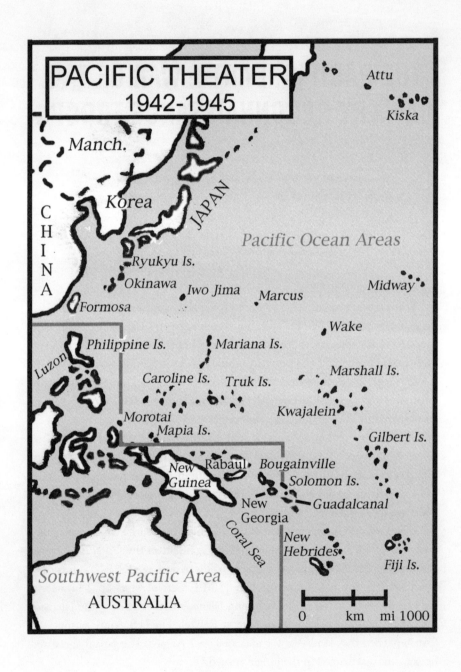

PACIFIC THEATER
1942-1945

Attu

Kiska

Manch.

C
H
I
N
A

Korea

JAPAN

Pacific Ocean Areas

Ryukyu Is.

Okinawa

Iwo Jima

Marcus

Midway

Formosa

Wake

Philippine Is.

Mariana Is.

Luzon

Caroline Is.

Truk Is.

Marshall Is.

Morotai

Mapia Is.

Kwajalein

Gilbert Is.

New
Guinea

Rabaul

Bougainville

Solomon Is.

New
Georgia

Guadalcanal

Coral Sea

New
Hebrides

Fiji Is.

Southwest Pacific Area

AUSTRALIA

0   km   mi 1000

Mechanized Cavalry in the Jungle

The challenges that cavalry would face in the theater were apparent from simple knowledge of geography. Colonel Harry Knight, Cavalry, an Army Ground Forces observer who visited the southwest Pacific area from October to December 1942, reported, "Neither New Guinea nor the majority of the islands in this theater where future combat may occur are suitable for the operations of either horse or mechanized cavalry. The majority of these islands are undeveloped and are virgin jungle except for small areas near the coast. . . . Should operations take place in the Philippines, Java, [or] Sumatra, both horse and mechanized cavalry could be profitably used." Knight spoke with the commanders of I Corps and the 32d and 41st Infantry divisions, and they all favored attaching a squadron of horse cavalry to each division to operate mounted and on foot as a reconnaissance element.[2] (One wonders. The Japanese, who fielded four horse cavalry reconnaissance regiments on Leyte and Luzon during the American re-conquest of the Philippines, wound up employing them almost entirely as foot soldiers.[3])

The first mechanized cavalry outfit to meet the Japanese enemy was the reconnaissance troop of the 25th Infantry Division, which debarked on Guadalcanal in December 1942. Conditions on the island precluded mechanized operations, so the cavalrymen fought dismounted. The other army infantry division on the island, the Americal Division, the forward elements of which had arrived in November, did not at this time have a mechanized cavalry reconnaissance troop, relying instead on its "Mobile Combat Reconnaissance Squadron," equipped with a few jeeps, towed 37mm antitank guns, and mortars.[4]

The 25th Cavalry Reconnaissance Troop entered battle on foot on 9 January 1943 attached to the 2d Battalion, 35th Infantry Regiment. Its M3A1 scout cars remained in the rear to provide security for the division CP. The troopers took up part of the battalion line on Mount Austen's Gifu.

At the urging of troop commanding officer Capt. Teddy Deese, who told his superiors that he was convinced that a light tank was capable of working in the mountainous terrain, part of the troop was mechanized for one critical if brief moment on 21 January 1943, during the battalion's final assault on the Gifu. Three Marine Corps light tanks—the Marines had the only American armor on the island—were delivered to the troop to support the battalion's attack on the Japanese defense line, which consisted of some 120 bunkers with interlocking fields of fire and had held off the infantry for a month. Reconnaissance patrols had failed to get through the line at any point.

The three tanks started up a jeep trail toward the 1,514-foot summit. Two broke down along the way, but the one commanded by Deese made it to the top. The GIs fired mortars and machine guns to mask the sound of the tank's final approach. Supported by fourteen riflemen, the tank rolled into the Japanese defenses at about 1040 hours. The gunner fired 37mm rounds into three pillboxes, then cut down the fleeing Japanese soldiers with canister rounds and his machine gun. The tank cut back through another portion of the Japanese line and returned in midafternoon to destroy five more pillboxes. The single cavalry tank had torn a two-hundred-yard hole in the defenses. After fending off a desperate "Banzai charge," the infantry surged forward to finish the kill. Deese and his driver were awarded the Distinguished Service Cross for their actions.[5]

The fighting on Guadalcanal set the pattern for what followed on most of the Pacific islands for both the infantry and cavalry fighting dismounted as infantry. Small, even patrol-size units did most of the fighting, which was often at very close range. Small arms claimed 32 percent of Americans killed in action in the southwest Pacific during the war, and artillery 17 percent. This represented a dramatic difference from the European theater, where the overall rates were 19.7 and 57.5 percent, respectively.[6]

It is not clear whether the troopers were any better or worse prepared for such combat than the GIs in a rifle company. The cavalrymen had not received equivalent training for small-unit ground action, but much of the training received by the infantry this early in the war had to be forgotten in the jungle.

More Islands, Cold and Hot

While fighting raged on Guadalcanal, Gen. Douglas MacArthur in November 1942 went on the offensive on Papua, New Guinea, where the Japanese threatened the strategic Australian base at Port Moresby. The cavalry reconnaissance troops of two outfits, the 32d and 41st Infantry divisions, fought through the jungles on Papua. The campaign concluded successfully in January 1943.[7]

Colonel Marion Carson, an observer, reported that divisional reconnaissance troops on New Guinea were used solely for reconnaissance and not for security duties. Frequently, they conducted platoon-size landing operations to scout small islands off the coast or beach areas on larger islands. Patrols sent to determine the enemy's battle lines usually consisted of seven to twelve men who operated on foot or in boats. Local boats were used so often that they received the informal designation landing craft, outrigger (LCO). Occasionally, "combat patrols" intended to fight rather than to scout were deployed to guard trails when the Japanese were nearby in force. Carson noted that the troopers preferred the short-barreled Tommy gun and the carbine for jungle work over the long-barreled M1 Garand.[8]

A five-month lull in ground operations in the South and southwest Pacific followed the capture of Guadalcanal in February 1943. The lessons learned thus far led most divisions destined for action in the Pacific to change the organization and training of their reconnaissance troops, a process that appears to have been unique to each division. The 77th Infantry Division, for example, eliminated all vehicles except for two 2 1/2-ton trucks and six jeeps; all of its .50-caliber machine guns; some of its light machine guns, bazookas, and mortars; and all of its authorized radios. It added seven-man and ten-man rubber rafts and fifteen hand-carried infantry radios. The men received infantry combat packs, sneakers, mechanics' caps, trench knives, grenade carriers, M1 rifles, and bayonets. The outfit trained to conduct nighttime amphibious assaults from destroyers.[9]

Mechanized Cavalry at Sea

Cavalry troops naturally had to accompany their divisions to the assault beaches on transports. Because the troopers were trained machine gunners, they at times helped man the air defense weapons on board. The 43d Reconnaissance Troop was one such unit; it found itself aboard the *President Hayes* in the waters of "Torpedo Junction," near Guadalcanal, the night of 16 February 1943. Troopers were crewing .50-caliber machine guns on each side of the bridge when the word went out that radar had picked up a large number of Japanese planes inbound.

Captain John Doll, the troop's commanding officer, recorded, "We didn't have long to wait before one of the enemy planes flew overhead and dropped a dozen flares, which illuminated the convoy with their brilliant light. General Quarters was sounded and the guns were warned to stand by to repel plane and torpedo attack. Then all hell broke loose as every gun in the convoy cut loose on the enemy torpedo planes as they roared to the attack. The planes could be clearly seen when the moonlight reflected from their silver wings. The ships were zig-zagging in a desperate attempt to avoid the torpedoes that were being dropped in our path. The noise of the battle was terrific, the *President Hayes* lurched as a torpedo exploded on impact with the water, enemy planes were burning in the water—this was our first baptism of fire . . . but not a single ship was hit."

The outfit soon thereafter became the first cavalry reconnaissance troop to conduct an amphibious assault in the Pacific theater. The 103d Regimental Combat Team with the two cavalry reconnaissance platoons attached off-loaded on Guadalcanal and, on the night of 20 February, proceeded by landing craft under heavy naval escort to assault the Russell Islands, tiny specks of land that lie off the northwest coast of Guadalcanal. The 3d Platoon men were the first Americans to set foot on Banika Island. Their landing was unopposed, and they quickly unloaded their jeeps and scout cars to conduct mounted reconnaissance of the island, which had a road through the interior. The Japanese, they found, had abandoned the island a few days earlier.[10]

The Cavalry's "Commandos"

The Japanese had seized several of Alaska's Aleutian Islands in June 1942, in part because they suspected that Lt. Col. James Doolittle's famous B-25 raid on Tokyo had launched from a secret airbase there. As the Americans in early 1943 readied to recapture the island chain, the Japanese had a garrison of four thousand on the island of Kiska and a garrison of one thousand on Attu. Because of shipping constraints, the smaller job of taking Attu was to come first.[11]

In April 1943 the 7th Reconnaissance Troop became perhaps the first mechanized cavalry to train for operations from submarines. Along with the 7th Scout Company, the troop conducted landings in ten-man rubber rafts at San Clemente, California, and Dutch Harbor, Alaska, from the *Narwhal* and the *Nautilus*. The commander of the *Nautilus* had worked with several marine raider battalions and had developed a new method for floating the rafts: The men would take their positions in the rafts on the rear deck, and the sub would then partially submerge.

The 7th Scout Company landed in the dark on 11 May on Scarlet Beach of Attu Island, which the Japanese had reinforced to the strength of some 2,500 men. After meeting no resistance, the scouts signaled their arrival to the subs by blinker lights, then moved inland. Several hours later, most of the 7th Reconnaissance Troop followed the scouts across the beach, while one platoon made a subsidiary landing at Alexai Point, on the far side of the island. The cavalrymen in the main body also proceeded inland to a bivouac about a mile and a half from the scout company. The 7th Division's 17th Infantry Regiment, meanwhile, after daybreak came ashore across several beaches in between the two recon landing sites.

Early the next morning, in coordination with infantry operations farther east, the "provisional battalion," consisting of the 7th Scouts and 7th Reconnaissance Troop, launched a two-pronged attack against the Japanese defenders. Descending from the snow-clad heights, the recon men met fire from antiaircraft guns, but they suffered no casualties, and the troop's 81mm mortar damaged one of the enemy guns.

The Japanese infantry had the advantage of prepared bunkers, and the fighting devolved into several days of close-quarters action. A single Japanese counterattack on 14 May broke down in a hail of machine-gun fire, which was a good thing because the shore fire-control party that was supposed to arrange for naval gunfire support could not contact the ships.

The Japanese pulled back on 16 May, leaving a large number of dead behind. The provisional battalion pushed off to link up with the infantry, troubled by nothing but snipers. By 1600 hours, its battle was over. The Japanese held out against the main infantry force until 30 May, expending their remaining strength in a suicide charge the night before their total collapse.

The provisional battalion had lost 11 men killed and 13 wounded, but most of the troops had suffered severe exposure of their feet because of the extreme cold. These losses compared favorably to those of the infantry, who had suffered 549 killed and 1,148 wounded, in addition to 2,100 non-battle losses due to the weather.[12]

The Tropics Get Hot Again

Admiral William Halsey's South Pacific forces landed on New Georgia on 20 and 21 June 1943. The Americans overran all key Japanese bases by late July, although the island was not fully secured until October.[13] MacArthur's forces, meanwhile, on 29 to 30 June conducted landings on New Guinea that were coordinated with Halsey's operation.[14] Reconnaissance troops do not appear to have played much of a role in these operations.

The reconnaissance troops began to reorganize when appropriate as standardized cavalry reconnaissance troops, mechanized, beginning in mid-November 1943, concurrent with the broader reorganization of the cavalry force into mechanized formations (excluding the cavalry divisions and two separate regiments). The single change about which the men seem to have had misgivings was the replacement of the well-liked 81mm mortar in each reconnaissance platoon by three 60mm mortars.

The Battle for Bougainville

The Marines launched the next major operation on 1 October 1943 when the 3d Marine Division landed in the Solomons on the west coast of Bougainville. On 8 November, the 37th Infantry Division's 148th Infantry Regiment arrived from Guadalcanal to relieve part of the Marine line, and most of the rest of the division came ashore over the next week. The men in the 37th Cavalry Reconnaissance Troop debarked during an air raid and rode to shore in Higgins boats, marveling at the dogfights taking place overhead, the many ships cluttering Empress Augusta Bay, and the two active volcanoes visible in the distance.

That night, torrential cold rains caused foxhole walls to cave in and gave the men a foretaste of the conditions they were going to face on the island. Indeed, although the 37th Reconnaissance Troop arrived mechanized with nine half-tracks and some jeeps, it fought the campaign in the wet jungles dismounted.[15] George Trentacosti—who had started as a horse cavalryman, converted to a mechanized cavalryman, and now found himself a jungle Scout—recalls that the men accepted this development philosophically. After all, the Americans held a small beachhead, and there was no room to use vehicles.[16]

The 37th Infantry Division viewed the roll of its reconnaissance troop as primarily distant reconnaissance beyond the limit of regimental patrols, generally from four thousand yards to thirty-five miles from the main line of resistance. The troop relied on shock-action weapons, and it increased the number of Tommy guns well above TO&E levels and added Browning automatic rifles to the mix.[17]

A Presidential Unit Citation gives a good overall picture of the outfit's actions on the island: "The 37th Cavalry Reconnaissance Troop, Mechanized, is cited for outstanding performance of duty in action against the enemy at Bougainville, Solomon Islands, during the period 16 November 1943 to 6 April 1944. Originally trained and equipped to perform motorized missions, this unit vigorously adapted itself to the exigencies of foot combat and patrolling in the jungle, and successfully completed many vitally important missions during the Bougainville operation. It undertook many hazardous long-distance reconnaissance patrols deep into enemy territory, where it gathered valuable military data [that] was immediately and effectively used for operations against the Japanese. The troops spent more than 60 days and nights in enemy country—one patrol trekked 68 miles over mountainous jungle terrain to accomplish its mission. Contacts with the enemy were numerous, but members of the troop exhibited high combat efficiency by uniformly inflicting severe losses on the enemy while sustaining only minor casualties themselves. Their success in skillfully reconnoitering and accurately mapping more than 270 miles of hitherto little-known trails, and in gathering a mass of intelligence data contributed materially to subsequent combat operations."

The first such long-distance patrol began on 16 November, when the seventy-four troopers boarded three jerky, noisy amphibian tractors to undertake a twenty-seven-mile beach reconnaissance from the Laruma River to Kuraio Mission. Orders specified that the patrol was to identify possible landing sites, scout trails, and locate enemy troops and facilities. The men carried only personal weapons augmented by three light machine guns. Amphibian tractors (amtracs) ferried the men across the mouth of the Laruma, where they off-loaded to proceed on foot. Ahead—the G-2 believed—was the 2d Battalion, 54th Regiment, Japanese 17th Infantry Division. The troopers set out, wading through swamps and following narrow jungle trails. At one point friendly aircraft appeared, and the patrol popped red smoke to alert the pilots to its presence. The day ended with a torrential downpour.

The patrol made its first contact with the enemy on 20 November, when a trooper spotted a lone Japanese who was looking intently at footprints that the patrol had left in the sand. The man spun and walked away. Shortly thereafter the man reappeared leading eight soldiers, seven of them carrying sniper rifles. The Japanese group passed within fifteen yards of one carefully concealed machine-gun position, but the troopers held their fire. Sergeant Leonard Daloia noted in his journal, "They learned well the rule that reconnaissance men, on an information gathering mission, must not seek to engage the enemy unless forced. General sadness resulted." The contact was reported by radio to the 148th Infantry Regiment, which sent out a combat patrol the next day to find and destroy whatever Japanese force was in the area.

The morning of 24 November, the patrol was only a few miles from the objective when a Japanese air strike on its bivouac revealed that it had been spotted. The patrol nevertheless continued cautiously to the Mission, which turned out to be little more than a cluster of ruined huts. Suddenly, the 3d Platoon point man, Technician 5th Grade Whitted, spotted three Japanese soldiers. He whipped up his carbine and downed the three with as many shots. Return fire zinged in from dense vegetation nearby. One round grazed Whitted's head, causing a gushing of blood, and another struck a trooper in the foot. The patrol withdrew under mortar fire to a more secure fighting position.

While the Japanese felt out the patrol's position, the radioman called the troop CP and reported the contact and casualties and requested that boats be sent immediately. As thirty men back at the beachhead piled aboard four boats, including an LCI (landing craft, infantry) gunboat, and set off to the rescue, a second message arrived: "Surrounded with enemy. Trail back blocked. Send boats immediately." Word arrived that Division had arranged for bombers and fighters to hit the Japanese around the stranded patrol.

Finally, at 2220 hours, the patrol waded to the rescue boats and roared back to the beachhead. The men were exhausted and grimy, but morale was high.

During subsequent long-range patrols, usually accompanied by native guides, the troopers covered terrain that one man likened to a sheet of paper after it has been crumpled into a ball, then spread out again. The patrols were supported by Piper Cubs that parachuted packets of supplies into drop zones cleared by the cavalrymen.[18]

★★★

The 21st Cavalry Reconnaissance Troop, Americal Division, arrived on Bougainville on 12 January 1944. The troop had been created in April 1943 mainly from personnel who had fought in the Mobile Combat Reconnaissance Squadron, which was disbanded at that time. The outfit's after-action reports indicate that it fought mainly dismounted, much like the 37th Reconnaissance Troop, but photographs show that it used half-tracks for some patrols, sometimes put in place from navy landing craft, and to provide fire support to foot patrols when practical.[19]

The troopers in the Solomons appear to have been spared the rigors of night patrolling into enemy territory. An informal report from XIV Corps noted, "There were no night operations of any consequence beyond resisting enemy attacks. . . . At night, all movement in forward areas was prohibited in order that Japanese making night attacks could be readily identified and destroyed. . . . In the rear, constant patrolling is necessary to protect against snipers and infiltrating patrols."[20] This pattern would emerge later on other islands, as well, until night patrols and attacks regained some favor in the more physically permissive environment of Saipan and Luzon.[21]

★★★

Even though the Japanese in the southeast area who were defending the strategic naval base at Rabaul had clearly been defeated by February 1944, Japanese commanders decided to stage a counterattack against XIV Corps on Bougainville. Two infantry divisions moved south beginning in mid-February to positions in the hills beyond the American perimeter. The Americans could see them coming. Patrols established the outlines of the Japanese positions, and captured documents revealed their plans and the general location of their artillery batteries.[22]

On 4 March the 37th Cavalry Reconnaissance Troop was pulled back from patrol work along the west coast and ordered to find the Japanese north of the division's pillbox line. Lieutenant Eugene Mowrer and fifteen men set off early in the morning from the outpost line, then worked cautiously up trails that faded into and out of existence. The point men stopped abruptly when they spotted footprints in the dirt. Technician 5th Grade Henry Lowther crept forward and spotted enemy troops dug in along the trail. A sentry stood nearby, staring stiffly in the wrong direction to see Lowther.

Mowrer crawled forward to determine what had stopped his men. After watching the Japanese for ten minutes, he withdrew the patrol seventy-five yards and tapped out a radio message to the troop CP. Mowrer and several troopers crawled forward again and established an OP within ten feet of the closest Japanese soldier. After further observation, the patrol returned to the outpost line and reported the location of the enemy position to Division artillery, which placed a barrage on the site.

Captain John McCurdy, troop commander, led a second patrol to determine the effect of the barrage. After advancing gingerly, McCurdy and the main body settled on a hillside while Mowrer led five men across the final distance with orders to observe for twenty minutes, then withdraw. Mowrer's men nearly ran into fifteen enemy soldiers drawing water from a creek. Twenty minutes came and went, and McCurdy became concerned. But Mowrer's team could not move without being spotted. When it finally looked safe, Mowrer made a dash for a slight depression near the creek. Shots rang out, and Mowrer crumpled, fatally wounded in the stomach. Despite continuing fire, the troopers grabbed the lieutenant and escaped to the main body.

The next day, Lt. Burt Winn and eighteen troopers were manning a defensive perimeter while other men scouted the area when a hundred Japanese infantrymen stumbled into the position. A blast of machine-gun fire killed two men in the Japanese point and wounded three others, but the enemy deployed to feel out the American line. The radiomen cranked their generator and signaled for help; the Japanese, who could hear the whirring of the generator, concentrated small-arms fire on their hideout. Naval aviation answered the call, and while aircraft strafed and bombed the Japanese force, Lieutenant Winn and his men slashed their way through the jungle to safety.

These and other skirmishes were but preliminary actions. By 7 March no patrol could depart the perimeter without drawing fire, and it was clear that the enemy would soon launch a major attack. The next day, Japanese artillery opened up on targets throughout the beachhead.[23]

The 145th Infantry Regiment held a 3,500-yard front anchored on Hill 700, which it had strengthened with pillboxes holding machine guns and 37mm antitank guns. Japanese ground attacks began against its line well before dawn on 9 March.[24] The 37th Reconnaissance Troop's half-tracks started a task that was to last the next few days, shuttling ammunition and supplies forward and bringing back the wounded. They were pestered by Japanese snipers who had infiltrated into the American rear and were able to disable four half-tracks temporarily with well-aimed shots to the radiators.

At 1815 hours on 10 March, orders came for the troop to go to the aid of 2d Battalion, 145th Infantry, which was being pressed hard by the Japanese 6th Infantry Division. Captain McCurdy gathered his 140 men and climbed into trucks; they reached the threatened sector at about 2330.

"Once there," wrote Sergeant Daloia in his journal, "the men were aware of the proportions of the battle. Flares seemed suspended in the sky. They illuminated the attacked area with brilliance. A conglomeration of the loudest noises man could muster, all converging over one locality, brought pain to the eardrums and dulled the brain." The troopers for the first time were frontline infantrymen.[25]

"We were up there, fully loaded, in eight or nine minutes," recalled then-S.Sgt. George Trentacosti, "and we knew we were going to face the enemy. There were thirty pillboxes strung across the hill, and we were summoned to fill the empty pillboxes. The Japanese were already coming up the hill."[26]

The aforementioned Presidential Unit Citation records, "The 37th Cavalry Reconnaissance Troop, Mechanized, further displayed its brilliant versatility during the attacks of the Japanese on the American perimeter atop Hill 700 in March 1944, when it functioned in a superior manner as an infantry company. Its assignments were many and varied: Two platoons executed a counterattack over a steep 50-foot slope, and ably defended the regained positions against bitter enemy attacks; one squad tenaciously held a strategic pillbox on the front line and killed scores of fanatic enemy threatening their position; one platoon efficiently manned front-line positions; and the armored vehicle section evacuated wounded and maintained supplies over a route exposed to constant enemy sniper and mortar fire. The troop's casualty rate of 51 percent during this action is indicative of the fierceness of the combat and the willingness of its soldiers to close with the enemy."

Sergeant Daloia described the fight at the pillbox line:

> The crawl to the pillboxes that each crew had to occupy was as dangerous as going through "no man's land." Mortar shells exploded all around them, and snipers added their bit to the difficulty. Sergeant [Melvin] Lucas occupied a pillbox that flanked a vital 37mm gun and several machine guns. This was one of the enemy's objectives. To his right was a pillbox whose Yank occupants had been wiped out. Further right was the installation that Sergeant [George] Trentacosti was to secure.
>
> The cause of all the trouble was a bare 25 yards away. A tremendous banyan tree, behind which the Japanese lodged four machine guns and a considerable number of soldiers, was the target. It was from this point that the Japanese sent waves and waves of their men in a desperate effort to reach the empty pillbox, occupy it, and from that point carry on their breakthrough.
>
> The enemy, in an effort to draw fire, held their dead in front of them, and the corpses were thus disintegrated by the resounding bursts from the front lines. Several times, by creeping slowly, the Japanese soldiers managed to get within 10 feet of Sergeant Lucas' installation. While his men fired from inside the box, Lucas passed into the communications trench nearby and tossed hand grenades at the enemy.[27]

George Trentacosti described his arrival at the pillbox line: "I positioned my men, and then I positioned myself and four other people. The guy ahead of me, R. G. Smith, took off 18 feet to a pillbox that wasn't firing. He got shot right in the chest. I took off quickly, figuring the Jap would have to reload, and cleared that [spot]. I crashed through the door and entered the pillbox, and there were two dead GIs and two BARs hanging in the window. That's what I fired for two hours."[28]

A Japanese survivor of the fight on Hill 700 wrote a poem in his diary:

"We have been discovered! Lie down!"
All at once a mortar shell comes.
One shell—two shells—four shells—five shells—
Boom! Boom!
Overhead the sound of metal—showers of sparks.
A change now to frightful concentrated fire.[29]

The fight lasted more than five hours, and when it was over, the men counted some ninety bodies to their front. The troop withdrew for rest and reorganization on 12 March.[30] The Japanese counterattack burned out by 24 March at the cost of five thousand dead and three thousand wounded.[31]

Amphibious Assault on Kwajalein

In January 1944, Adm. Chester Nimitz directed his Central Pacific forces to secure the Marshall Islands, and the 7th Infantry Division got the job of capturing the southern part of the Kwajalein atoll.[32] The 7th Cavalry Reconnaissance Troop was given responsibility for securing the two islands that flanked Gea Pass, which provided a deepwater route into the lagoon. It took pains after the fight to record what had transpired, leaving to posterity one of the most detailed accounts available of a reconnaissance troop fighting on foot in the jungle.

After paddling to shore on 1 February 1944 in darkness so total that the islets could not be seen until the men were upon them, the troopers handily took control over two islands, including Gea, just to the south of the pass. Unfortunately, the northern assault force had landed on the wrong islet in the dark, hitting Chauncey instead of Ninni. After a small firefight, the misplaced force moved to Ninni, under the impression that Chauncey was now unoccupied by any living Japanese. Ninni, in fact, was unoccupied, but a group left behind on Chauncey when its boat hung on the reef reported that it could now see two Japanese machine guns and a rising-sun flag.

At 2000 hours, Lt. Glenn Carr's platoon returned to Chauncey and confirmed the report of Japanese troops. Carr established a defensive perimeter and awaited the rest of the troop, which arrived at 0800 on 2 February.

The troop moved out, three platoons abreast. The men advanced by bounds, having learned that unless some of them remained in visual contact with the others, everyone tended to hit the dirt at the first enemy shot, and the formation lost its coherence. Scouts worked ten to fifteen yards ahead of the skirmish line.

After crossing three-quarters of the island, the troopers came upon an artificial dirt mound. The scouts flanked it, but there were no Japanese. A second probe around the mound drew sniper fire, and Capt. Paul Gritta, commanding, decided to deploy a light machine gun around each end to take out the snipers. The machine guns poured fire into the dense vegetation, and the troop bypassed the mound, joining flanks on the far side.

Almost immediately, rifle and automatic weapons fire pinned down the left end of the line, accompanied by squealing shouts from the Japanese, presumably intended to spook the enemy. Unable to see the foe, the troopers crawled to cover and fired back in the direction of the squealing. Return fire whipped the grass and trees around them and wounded several troopers.

Lieutenant Carr and Lt. Emmett Tiner crawled forward to spot the Japanese positions. Sergeant Earnest Fessenden poured machine-gun rounds over their heads and produced the first screams of pain—he had found the enemy position with reconnaissance by fire. Carr crawled forward another ten yards and finally identified the outlines of an oblong tent, camouflaged by palm fronds and covering an earthwork. Two more machine guns were moved forward to fire on the Japanese position, but return fire continued unabated.

The left end of the line was bleeding thin, now under the pounding of mortar shells being tossed from a tree. Lieutenant James Mahoney and his men were under attack from a submachine gun that sprayed them with dirt every time it fired. He finally realized that the gunner was hiding on the far side of the same tree that he was; a trooper took the man out from the flank.

Back at the mound, Gritta killed a Japanese soldier just as the other man shot him in the arm. More cavalrymen were moving forward. The Japanese parapet was growing higher as the defenders pushed their dead comrades to the top to absorb machine-gun bullets. Sergeant Fessenden realized that he was wasting ammunition, so he and the twelve riflemen nearby threw forty grenades into the earthwork, and Japanese fire petered out.

Just to make certain, Pfc. Emmanuel Fried launched a bazooka rocket into the fortification. Two Japanese stumbled out and were cut down. A second rocket exploded dead center and ended the fight. The troop had killed fifty-five of the enemy at the cost of fourteen men wounded.[33]

Amphibious Armored Cavalry

The 6th Cavalry Reconnaissance Troop appears to have been the first mechanized cavalry outfit in the Pacific to operate completely armored and tracked. Shortly after arriving on New Guinea in mid-June 1944, the troop was fully mounted in thirteen LVT(A)(1) amphibian tanks (amtanks) and four LVT(A)(2) amtracs.

The LVT(A)(2) Water Buffalo, directly descended from the unarmored Alligator, first used by the marines on Guadalcanal, outfitted the army's amtrac battalions. The LVT(A)(2) was made of armor plate and weighed sixteen tons. The vehicle had gun rails forward and to the sides and rear, which allowed machine guns to be mounted to fire in any direction. Twin forward-facing machine guns protected by shields were a common configuration. Thirty fully equipped infantrymen could be ferried to the beach; they had to exit by clambering over the sides, often under fire.

The sixteen-ton LVT(A)(1) was basically a covered amtrac with an M5 light tank turret mounted on top. As on the M5, the amtank had a 37mm main gun and a .30-caliber coaxial machine gun. The roomy vehicle carried 104 shells for the cannon and 6,000 machine-gun rounds. The turret had both hydraulic and manual traverse systems. Twin hatches on the rear deck had scarf mounts for .30-caliber machine guns. The six-man crew included commander, driver, assistant driver/radio operator, 37mm gunner, and two scarf machine gunners.

As of 23 June 1944, Japanese troops were strongly dug in on high ground dubbed Lone Tree Hill, where two battalions of the 20th Infantry Regiment were cut off and fighting for their lives. The 6th Infantry Division commanding general, Maj. Gen. Franklin Sibert, explained to Capt. Jean LaPlace that his troop, along with Company K, 1st Infantry, was to conduct an amphibious assault just west of the hill and clear out the resistance. At 0800 hours on 24 June, the troop's amphibians with the infantry aboard moved out by road and entered Maffin Bay at the Snaky River. The outfit performed a column left and "swam" along the shore until it reached a point a thousand yards off the landing point, where the vehicles performed a flank left and advanced toward shore in a line.

Japanese artillery opened up when the amphibians came within five hundred yards of the beach; the amtanks immediately replied with their 37mm guns. Tracks churning, the amphibians crawled up onto land and moved into hull-defilade positions behind a six-foot embankment. The infantry dismounted from the amtracs but immediately went to earth in the face of vicious machine-gun and sniper fire. Privates Donald Thompson and Harland Worra were awarded the Silver Star for dismounting from their tank and recovering wounded GIs under fire. Several of the armored vehicles began to operate as ad hoc ambulances.

As one LVT(A)(2) headed out to sea loaded with wounded men, a 77mm shell sank it, leaving the desperate men struggling in the water under machine-gun fire. Sergeant Harold Leake immediately directed his LVT(A)(1) to the site and banged away at the Japanese while his crewmen pulled three survivors from the drink. A 77mm round struck a scarf gun and killed one man and wounded another, but the armor fended off further damage.

By 1230 hours the tanks and infantry had finally suppressed the Japanese fire, and Company I, Infantry, landed aboard amtracs to help. Sherman tanks from the 3d Platoon of Company C, 44th Tank Battalion, were ferried to the beach by boat to take over the role of armored support. The troop's first amphibious mission had been a great success.

The outfit had been conducting "run of the mill" patrolling on New Guinea (one amtank had been lost to Japanese antitank fire) when it received orders on 15 July 1944 that the troop, reinforced by a 60mm mortar section and one and a half squads of riflemen, was to seize and secure Middleburg Island, off the coast of New Guinea. Once that was accomplished, it was to conduct an amphibious march and take Amsterdam Island.

On 26 July the troop loaded its vehicles aboard an LST and set off. Over the next three days, the LST traveled some five hundred miles. After a pre-combat breakfast at 0330 on 29 July, the troopers buttoned up, helmeted, loaded, and locked. The ramp dropped at 0730, and the cavalry flotilla churned to shore.

The results were anticlimactic. There were no Japanese on Middleburg Island, or on Amsterdam. The troop returned to the main island, where during August it conducted amphibious and land patrols on the Wewe, Table, and Wesan rivers and at the mouth of the Kor River, clashing occasionally with small Japanese detachments. The amtanks and amtracs were able to go where landing craft could not because they were able to crawl across coral reefs off-shore. At times, even they could not do the job, and the troopers reached shore by rubber raft from PT boats.

The outfit's after-action report describes one typical action:

> Tank #2 ... had left the Kor River 20 minutes [after Tank #3], ferrying an infantry patrol to Owl Creek. ... Approaching Owl Creek from the bay, seven of the enemy were observed on the beach. The tank delivered machine-gun fire. Tank #3 crewmen heard the fire [and] hurried to join the sister tank. ... Both tanks moved in on the beach. The crews dismounted, leaving only scarf gunners with the vehicles.
>
> Lieutenant Hill led one crew to the left [as] Sergeant Stoneking led his tank crew plus two of the infantrymen to the right, pursuing the enemy. Contact was made when one of the enemy, evidently an outpost, was seen behind a log and was killed. The patrol then secured high ground around a small clearing where enemy tents and shelters had been seen and placed fire upon the enemy. Moving into the attack, Sergeant Stoneking was potted by a sniper, and this enemy sniper was killed by an infantry [Browning automatic] rifleman. Counting seven of the enemy dead and 12 of the enemy probably dead and having lost contact with the enemy, the two tank crews withdrew. ...
>
> "The men are in fine spirits," reported Lieutenant Hill in a written message to the troop commander that night, "and really are looking for Nips. ... Putting many hours on these tank engines. ..."

At the end of the month, the troop reported, "LVT(A)(1)s and LVT(A)(2)s are excellent ferrying units in that they can deliver dismounted parties and remain close by in support."[34]

★★★

The 31st Cavalry Reconnaissance Squadron also was equipped with LVT(A)(1) amtanks to support the invasion of Morotai Island, Netherlands East Indies, by the 167th Infantry Regiment. The operation was a gamble, because a nearby garrison of fifty thousand Japanese troops could conceivably counterattack and cause quite a ruckus. The cavalry troop's twelve amtanks rolled off four LSTs at 0815 hours on 15 September 1944 on the heels of a naval bombardment, followed by LVTs and landing craft. The 31st Recon had experimented with a single amtank on Dutch New Guinea in July and evidently been pleased when the gunner had knocked out a Japanese machine-gun nest with six rounds of 37mm canister. The cavalrymen now were the first assault troops of Tradewinds Task Force to land. The tanks rolled two hundred yards through coconut groves and underbrush before they stopped to wait for the infantry. The landings, as it turned out, met no opposition, and PT boats interdicted piecemeal Japanese efforts to shift troops to Morotai.

A detachment of cavalry tankers saw a good deal more action when the troopers and two assault companies from the 2d Battalion, 167th Infantry, landed on Bras, in the Mapia Islands, just northwest of New Guinea, on 16 November. (This action is incorrectly placed in September by the army's official battle chronology of the division, and it merits but a passing reference in the official history.) Three cavalry amtanks and infantry-bearing LVTs approached Bras from Pegun Island, which had been captured the preceding day without a fight. A company of fanatical Japanese from the 226th Regiment, 36th Division, defended the beach, and machine-gun and rifle fire killed twelve and wounded ten of the debarking GIs. The reconnaissance troop's after-action report is missing, but Silver Star citations in the unit records provide snapshots of the assault.

"When the periscope was shot off the [amtank] which he was commanding as it approached the beach, Staff Sergeant [Clifford] Gonyea with complete disregard for his own safety opened the hatch and stood up in the turret exposing himself to heavy enemy fire in order to direct the movement and fire of his tank. Though hit by enemy fire, he held his position until the enemy position to his front had been knocked out."

"When the machine gun for which he was an assistant gunner on an [amtank] became jammed during an especially heavy fight with the enemy beach positions, Technician Fifth Grade [James] Smith . . . climbed outside of the tank and gave covering fire with his submachine gun while the first gunner cleared the stoppage. When, as a subsequent wave of infantrymen hit the beach [and] enemy machine guns opened fire, again he left the protecting armor of the tank, jumped down into the water, and under continuing enemy fire pulled a wounded soldier, who was still being fired on by the enemy, to a protected position. . . ."

"When an infantry rifle company was caught in a heavy crossfire from concealed enemy pillboxes, Sergeant [Clarence] Curb ordered the two [amtanks] of which he was in command to move in on the enemy from the flank. When it soon became apparent that, because of the heavy undergrowth and poor visibility, the tanks could not maneuver or fire effectively, he dismounted and under heavy enemy fire directed them to firing position. Having returned to his own tank, he directed the firing until the other tank became stalled and its radio inoperative. Once again he dismounted and under continuing heavy enemy machine-gun fire and rifle fire ran to the disabled tank and verbally directed its fire into the targets. Not only was he responsible for the annihilation of a superior enemy force as was evidenced by the approximately 100 enemy dead around his tanks but also prevented heavy casualties among our infantry."

"When the driver of his [amtank] was seriously wounded in the chest by a sniper as he attempted to repair the immobilized tank, Technician Fifth Grade [Robert] Licsauer . . . left the armored protection of the tank, exposing himself to sniper fire to help move the man out of the line of fire. After having accomplished this, he returned and succeeded in getting the stalled tank to run, but only in reverse. By skillfully maneuvering, he ran the tank over the enemy pillbox that was firing on them, crushing its occupants [and] thereby clearing a path for our advancing infantrymen."

The 31st Division's history recorded, "By noon of the 17th, the enemy had been encircled and could not withdraw from his prepared positions. Progress was slow, as it was necessary to destroy the Japanese position by position. . . . By displaying exceptional courage and skillfully employing tank landing craft which they manned, [the 31st Cavalry Reconnaissance Troop] made it possible to eliminate the last of the resistance." The total body count was 159. On 19 November two other cavalry amtanks spearheaded landings in the nearby Asia Islands, which proved to be unoccupied.[35]

CHAPTER 5

THE PACIFIC, PART II: THE MECHANIZED CAVALRY FINDS ROADS

After nearly three years slashing through the mud and slime of the South Sea jungles,
the men were going into a type of warfare they were trained to perform.

—History, 37th Cavalry Reconnaissance Troop

The campaigns in the Philippines and Ryukyu Islands took place on a scale similar to those in North Africa, Sicily, or Italy. For the cavalrymen, these Pacific battlegrounds, which physically approximated those in the Mediterranean in terms of economic development and infrastructure, meant one great thing: Roads!

The Philippines Invasion

The first major step in the re-conquest of the Philippines was the island of Leyte, where four divisions of the Sixth Army landed abreast on A-day, 20 October 1944, on the east side of the island. Jungle-covered mountains dominated the interior of Leyte, but two valleys and the coastal plain offered possibilities for mechanized warfare. X Corps (1st Cavalry and 24th Infantry divisions) was to clear the northern part of the island while XXIV Corps (7th and 96th Infantry divisions) seized the south. The two corps were then to converge at Ormoc, on the west side of the island. The 32d and 77th Infantry divisions formed the Sixth Army reserve. More than twenty thousand Japanese troops awaited the Americans.[1]

The 7th Cavalry Reconnaissance Troop, which had conducted the amphibious assaults on Attu and Kwajalein, received enough mechanized equipment in June 1944 to restore its 1942 skills. The outfit obtained permission to adapt its table of equipment to fit Pacific conditions. Each reconnaissance

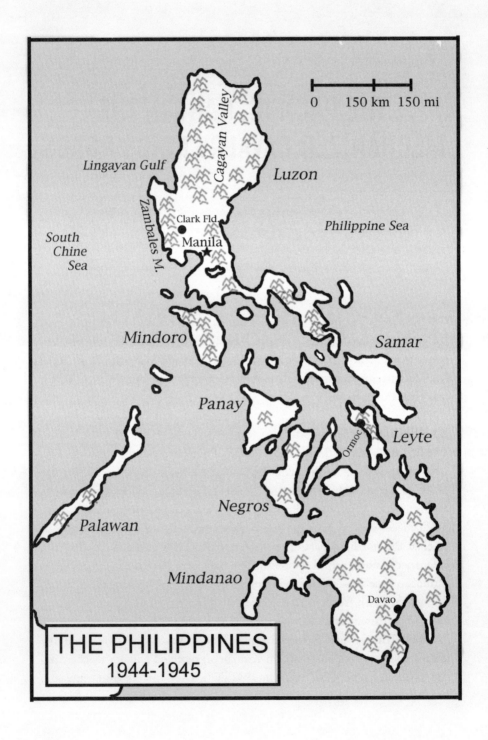

0   150 km 150 mi

Cagayan Valley

Lingayan Gulf

Luzon

Zambales M.

Clark Fld.

Manila

Philippine Sea

South
Chine
Sea

Mindoro

Samar

Panay

Leyte

Ormoc

Negros

Palawan

Mindanao

Davao

THE PHILIPPINES
1944-1945

platoon received two M8 armored cars, two fully tracked M29 Weasel carriers, and four jeeps. The headquarters platoon fielded two M8s, two M29s, a half-track, and three jeeps.

The troop went ashore in the fourth wave and gathered information on resistance and the initial progress of friendly forces. Preliminary reconnaissance indicated that the wheeled vehicles would be road-bound because of mud. The problem this posed became evident the next day, when the troop was unable to bypass a Japanese roadblock at the Daguitan River. The cavalrymen again dismounted for most patrol work.

By the end of the month, however, the Japanese were in retreat. On 28 October the troopers used M29s to cross the Bito River and enter Abuyog, where they contacted Filipino guerrilla forces. Over the next several days, the M29s did the trick, and the troop reached objectives at Bay Bay on the west coast of Leyte, on 3 November. The men spent the remainder of the month in the vicinity of Ormoc, patrolling and picking up Japanese prisoners captured by the guerrillas.[2]

★★★

The 24th Reconnaissance Troop landed on northern Leyte on 21 October and the next day conducted its first mounted patrols around Santa Cruz. Working to the division's front and flanks—much of the time on foot—the men encountered little but snipers until early December, when a concentration of six hundred Japanese was spotted near Dolores. The troop deployed to maintain contact, and one patrol was able to penetrate the Japanese perimeter and withdraw without being detected.[3]

★★★

The 32d Infantry Division joined the Leyte battle for the final phase of operations aimed at clearing the Ormoc valley. Its task, however, was to support the forces already committed by entering the daunting, mountainous interior.[4] For the mechanized cavalrymen, this spelled another round of fighting dismounted.

A unit citation provides a picture of the kind of war the outfit fought:

The 32d Cavalry Reconnaissance Troop is cited for outstanding performance of duty in action against the enemy from 20 November 1944 to 2 January 1945 during the Leyte, Philippine Islands campaign. Operating in the Ormoc Valley sector for a period of 43 days, the 32d Cavalry Reconnaissance Troop established a patrol base behind enemy lines and near his rear area installations. From this patrol base the troop conducted numerous reconnaissance patrols, harassing raids, and maintained observation posts [that] directed long-range artillery fire on these installations and activities with devastating result to the enemy.

Throughout the period operations were conducted under the most adverse conditions of weather and terrain. Heavy rains, with difficult mountainous jungle tracks and intermingled open valleys and forested mountains, made the movement of patrols ever subject to fire from enemy troops [who] occupied the area. The troop, operating with an average of 80 men from which its patrols and command posts were drawn, was attacked by enemy forces 14 times, but each attack was driven off and a total of 86 Japanese killed, with several hundred more being credited to artillery fire directed by the troop's observation posts.

Ambushes set by the troop resulted in the capture of 11 prisoners of war for intelligence interrogation. The harassing raids resulted in the destruction of three important bridges over which the enemy was moving supplies, and the reconnaissance patrols pinpointed three artillery positions upon which counter-battery fire was placed. Patrols also furnished information on troop movements and concentrations in the Ormoc Valley from Valencia to Lonoy and west to Palompon. This information, because of its timeliness and accuracy, permitted large-scale tactical planning which contributed greatly to the utter defeat of the Japanese troops resisting in the upper Ormoc Valley and the final collapse of all enemy resistance on Leyte.

The Cavalry Rides Seahorses

While the fighting on Leyte raged, the 33d Cavalry Reconnaissance Troop—dubbed Lewis Force—on 17 December landed on Morotai Island. The 136th Infantry Regiment's mission on Morotai was to clear the island, moving generally north and west. Lewis Force was given the mission of conducting amphibious "swims" to locations presumed to be enemy held and to reconnoiter inland, destroying the enemy where found. On 23 December troopers boarded LCTs (landing craft, tanks) to scout the first site on Raoe Island. For the next three weeks, the troopers deployed from place to place in amtracs and, on one occasion, DUKW amphibious trucks, tracking small Japanese parties with foot patrols. Firefights erupted with suddenness in the jungle; the foe was usually a group of twenty-five to fifty riflemen with one or two light machine guns. Working with field artillery liaison planes, the troopers were able to direct artillery concentrations against the larger enemy groups, which inevitably ended resistance.[5]

The Cavalry Mounts Up: The Fight for Luzon

Luzon was the heart of the Philippine Islands, the home of Manila. MacArthur intended to land on the northern part of the island at Lingayen Gulf, then drive south with a force that would grow to ten divisions and five independent regiments—the largest force to soldier in a Pacific campaign. Once ashore, Sixth Army's I Corps was to protect the beachhead's flanks while XIV Corps drove south to Clark Field, then Manila.[6]

General Tomoyuki Yamashita, the Japanese commanding general, did not intend to defend the Central Plains–Manila Bay area, where American superiority in armor and mobility would have its greatest advantage. Instead, he sought only to pin down MacArthur's forces in order to delay Allied progress to Japan.[7]

The reconnaissance troop of each assault division was mechanized, but there were some unusual twists. The 43d Cavalry Reconnaissance Troop was configured to regulation specs and had doctrine-perfect orders. It was to land on Beach White 2 and advance rapidly to the south and east to establish contact with the enemy in the Natangalan area.[8]

The 40th Cavalry Reconnaissance Troop had been an early participant in the theater's operations. The division's first mission was defense of the Hawaiian Islands, and while there the troop underwent ranger, amphibious, and jungle training.[9] The division deployed to Guadalcanal in December 1943, and the troopers trained and got their feet wet patrolling in the rain forest. In April 1944, the division moved to New Britain, where it had a defensive mission.

The 40th Reconnaissance Troop received nine battered, ancient LVT(A)(1) amtanks, the veterans of many landings. The outsides were scarred by bullets and shrapnel, and the floors were covered by an inch of slimy mud. Intercom cords were frayed, the radios were broken, and some walls were spotted with dried blood. The orders were to pick the best five and use the other four for spare parts.

The entire troop worked twenty-hour days to put the amtanks in working order because the lives of thirty men depended on it. Some radios had to be stripped from M8s that would land later, but the job was done on the eve of departure from New Britain for the Philippines and the island of Luzon.

Eighteen officers and men from the 37th Cavalry Reconnaissance Squadron had likewise been temporarily assigned to a "Provisional Amphibian Tank Company," which also included personnel from the 672d Amphibian Tractor Battalion, the 637th Tank Destroyer Battalion, and the 754th Tank Battalion.[10] The provisional company, attached to the 672d Amphibian Tractor Battalion during the initial assault, was to land at H hour minus one minute and clear a path for the infantry.[11] The troop had reacquainted itself with mechanized equipment on Bougainville back in November. Instead of the usual armored cars, the troop had received light tanks to work with its jeeps; it would not receive M8s until April 1945. On 11 December while at sea, the men learned their destination: Luzon Island.[12]

The 6th Cavalry Reconnaissance Troop had re-equipped as a standard mechanized cavalry troop only to be issued eight Marine Corps amtanks for this operation. The troop drew extra personnel from the rest of the division and formed a provisional platoon, which was placed under the operational control of the commander, Company B, 727th Amphibian Tractor Battalion, during the landing. Once ashore, four amtanks were to support the 1st Infantry and the other four the 20th Infantry. To compensate for the detachment, a platoon of light tanks from the 716th Tank Battalion had been attached to the troop for the landings. The rest of the troop had adopted the normal allocation of M8 armored cars and jeeps; it was attached to the 20th Infantry for the landings.[13]

No amphibian tank battalions had been assigned to the invasion force. Most of the amphibian tanks scheduled to storm the beaches beside the GIs were to be manned by cavalry troopers.

★★★

The invasion of Luzon began at 0700 hours on S-day, 9 January 1945, with a massive naval bombardment. One hour later, the 40th Infantry Division landed at Lingayan on the right wing near the town of that name, with the 37th, 6th, and 43d Infantry divisions strung out to the left.[14] The history of the 37th Cavalry Reconnaissance Troop recorded, "Through the still darkness of the night, the steady boom of the warships could be heard as they poured ton after ton of searing lead into the hostile shores, paving a protective road for our fighting soldiers. . . . As the infantry of the assault waves mounted their [amphibious] vehicles for the last leg of a 3,500-mile journey, their faces were sullen, yet confident."[15]

The 40th Cavalry Reconnaissance Troop's five LVT(A)(1) amtanks reached the beach with no difficulties and within fifteen minutes pushed inland with the infantry. Opposition was extremely light, a pattern that continued for the next three days that the amtanks worked with the infantry, after which the crews returned to their armored cars. The platoon commander claimed that the operation had just gone to show that the cavalrymen could ride anything with hair, wheels, or tracks.[16]

The amtank platoon from the 6th Cavalry Reconnaissance Troop crawled out of the surf at H+30. The cavalrymen were the first division troops to land on Luzon. Only one man was injured; he was shot in the arm by a comrade during the assault. "There was only one pillbox on the beach," recalled Robert Beutlich, who manned the radio in an LVT(A)(1), "and we bypassed it. The engineers brought up an armored bulldozer and covered it with sand. We had first, second, and third-day objectives. . . . We pushed on ahead and reached our third-day objective by 1100."

When the rest of the troop arrived thirty minutes later, the first jeeps drove off the ramps into water so deep that only the radio aerials could still be seen. The amtank crews were left behind when the division rolled toward Manila, and there was no plan for their operations after the third day. The two sergeants in charge eventually decided to abandon the vehicles outside a maintenance facility, and the men hitchhiked back to the outfit.[17]

Upon landing in its sector, the 37th Cavalry Reconnaissance Troop received orders to conduct a mechanized patrol to San Carlos. "A mechanized patrol," recorded the outfit's history. "The word mechanized left the men somewhat jubilant."[18]

★★★

The rest of the 40th Cavalry Reconnaissance Troop, meanwhile, followed the troop's amtanks ashore. The outfit split in two—half, led by troop commander Capt. John Robinson, to cut across the Bolinao Peninsula to the South China Sea, and the other half to head south.

The outfit's first clash occurred on 14 January in Alaminos, where a Japanese squad held the municipal building with ten men and two light machine guns. Captain Robinson sent two machine-gun jeeps to the back of the building to cut off escape, placed a machine gun opposite the building, then attacked the building frontally with an M8 supported by two machine-gun jeeps. The plan was immensely successful: The Japanese tried to run without bothering to fire their weapons.

There were other pockets of Japanese resistance in the vicinity. Serving in Captain Robinson's M8, S.Sgt. Paul Gerrish underwent his baptism of fire near Alaminos. Gerrish had been trained as a radio operator before he was "volunteered" to join the 40th Infantry Division's newly formed reconnaissance troop in early 1942. Already a one-year veteran at that time, Gerrish had had no wish to become a recon man, because he figured they probably suffered 100 percent casualties for every ten days of combat. As he later noted, "Fortunately by the middle of 1943 with better equipment and more intensive training, the life expectancy would be as good as that of other combat units."[19]

For Gerrish, the first fight took place in the midst of a classic fog of war. Some American troops had opened fire on the Japanese before everyone was in place, setting off a firefight. Filipino guerrillas, meanwhile, had advanced in front of the M8 armored cars, which interfered with fields of fire. After nearly killing some of their allies by mistake, the troopers told the guerrillas, who often wore captured Japanese clothing, to stay behind the armored cars.

The recon team pushed onward, encountering only small parties or delaying actions. The tactics were always the same. Rifle and machine-gun fire would pin down the Japanese, then either the M8s would fire high-explosive shells from the 37mm gun into their holdouts, or troopers would rush them with grenades.

After reaching the objective, the troop went into bivouac to wash up and replace uniforms that had been reduced to rags. They resupplied as well. "Just six rounds of canister for each 37mm," the ammunition corporal said. "You'll have to save it for Banzai charges." Indeed, enemy infantry was the main worry. The cavalrymen in the Pacific did not face the problem of heavy enemy armor, as did their comrades fighting the Germans, which led to a more upbeat view of the weaponry. "The 37mm cannon, .30-caliber machine gun, and carbine were excellent," Gerrish commented after the war.

★★★

The 40th Reconnaissance Troop reached Mabalacat Airfield 2, the most northeastern of the strips comprising Clark Air Center, on 23 January.[20] When the 160th Infantry Regiment encountered small-arms and mortar fire just south of the Bamban River, it became evident that the division had found the strong defenses that intelligence staffs had expected around the airbase, which was defended by the thirty-thousand-man-strong Kembu Group. The infantry advanced slowly through scrub, grinding down the outer line of resistance.[21]

Three days later, as the GIs continued their laborious advance, the 40th Reconnaissance Troop was ordered to a rendezvous point not far from the Clark Field complex. The 640th Tank Destroyer Battalion's Reconnaissance Company pulled in on the reconnaissance troop's left. Gerrish noted that it was also equipped with M8 armored cars and jeeps, and a platoon each of engineers, medium tanks, and M10s reinforced the company. Soon the 37th Reconnaissance Troop with its light tanks pulled in on the right. There had been rumors that Sixth Army was going to send its armor into Clark Field, and it dawned on the troopers that they were the "armor."

The ad hoc task force moved out in the early light and almost immediately ran into heavy small-arms, mortar, and artillery fire. The 640th Tank Destroyer Battalion's Reconnaissance Company encountered resistance at the end of Mabalacat Runway 1 and recorded in its history, "Observed many Jap foot troops and artillery and machine-gun installations on hill north of Dolores, in Clark Field area. Received Jap artillery fire and moved back under cover in line along Manila Railroad."

The 40th Recon Troop was ordered to try again farther to the left, but it met the same results. The 640th Tank Destroyer Battalion Recon Company directed artillery fire on the area and attacked again, but it, too, ran into a curtain of explosions. "Resumed mission and received heavy artillery fire. . . . We withdrew to the vicinity of the Manila Railroad; this was about 1600. Jap rifle and machine-gun fire was encountered throughout the day." The men had spotted Japanese tanks.

Now the three American units were told to spread out. Two pinned down the Japanese, while the 40th Reconnaissance Troop hooked far to the left to envelop the Japanese line.[22]

"Clark Field was *huge*," recalled George Trentacosti, of the 37th Recon Troop. "It was 2,000 feet in front of us. I'm in my tank ["Hombriago"], and artillery is going back and forth, left to right. We were told to get any Japs that tried to get away. . . . We did a lot of searching with our turrets open. Some of our troopers were on their feet to guard the tanks. We were along a two-lane highway.

"All at once, I saw on the road near Joe Ierardi's tank—a flatbed truck comes roaring out with four guys in the back with their rifles and two men up front. They were just trying to get away. The turret was operated by me, and the gunner could grab the control. I yelled out, 'Larson, get ready! We're going to fire a couple rounds. You've got to aim under the driver.' I tapped him on the shoulder. He put the shell right in there, and there was a huge explosion."

A Japanese soldier appeared and rammed a ten-foot pole charge into the track of Ierardi's tank. When it blew, it took part of the driver's foot with it. That was the end of Japanese activity in front of the 37th Recon Troop.[23]

The 40th Reconnaissance Troop found a soft spot and rolled through the Japanese outpost line with several minor skirmishes. Soon, Japanese light tanks were seeking out the 40th Reconnaissance Troop. The nearby foothills of the Zambales Mountains, ahead, were bristling with Japanese guns sited to fire on Bamban and Clark Field, and the decision was made to fall back. The 3d Platoon, at the head of the withdrawing column, ran into heavy fire near Bamban, which had been reported cleared. The platoon leader radioed back, "We have run into at least a regiment of Nips."

The 3d Platoon could lay down a lot of fire: three M8s with 37mm guns and .50-caliber machine guns, three jeeps with two .30-caliber machine guns mounted on each, three mortar jeeps with a .30-caliber each, plus miscellaneous rifles, carbines, and Tommy guns. The troopers opened up as the Japanese charged.

Captain John Robinson picked up the radio microphone and ordered all platoons to turn and head south at full speed. The 1st Platoon took the lead in a mad dash away from friendly lines. As its vehicles left the end of a runway, they plowed into a grass-covered swamp and sank up to their hubs.

Gerrish recalled, "Many commanders would have abandoned that platoon. Others would have taken the men into our remaining vehicles. However, we were not an ordinary unit. We were the elite 40th Recon. Furthermore, we had Captain Robinson, who could lead that proud recon troop right through the Devil's own back yard."

"Back 3d Platoon and fight the Nips off," roared Robinson into his mic. "In 2d Platoon and pull the 1st out; two M8s on an M8, and two jeeps on a jeep. All gunners protect our flank and front."

Men ran through a shower of bullets with winch lines to the stranded vehicles. Soon the 1st Platoon was back on solid ground. As the vehicles came free, Robinson deployed them to cover the 3d Platoon as it disengaged from the Japanese. The 3d Platoon took the lead, and the troop sprinted south for several miles through a gauntlet of Japanese.

Eventually the troop was able to turn east, then north back toward friendly lines. As darkness fell, the outfit came upon a river with a large sandbar. Worried that the Japanese would ambush the column in the dark, Robinson ordered the vehicles into a "covered wagon" circle for the night. When the engines were killed and quiet settled on the scene, a welcome American voice called out from the far bank, "What outfit is that? We would have fired, but we heard your . . . profanity."

The 40th Cavalry Reconnaissance Troop had made it home. The Japanese managed to hold out at Clark Field for two more weeks against determined efforts by the 40th and 37th Infantry divisions to capture the facility.[24]

★★★

The 6th Cavalry Reconnaissance Troop had been engaged with the enemy nearly constantly from its first firefight on 11 January, when its 1st Platoon, accompanied by a platoon of riflemen and some light tanks, ran into a reinforced Japanese battalion near Mapandan. Hostile fire immobilized one tank and disabled the gun on a second, and the force had to withdraw under covering fire from the M8s and 60mm mortars.

The 6th Division was driving nearly due east to cut the island in two, and the recon platoons often scouted fifteen to thirty miles ahead of the closest division elements. This created dangers unrelated to the enemy, as the troop learned on 13 January. A flight of Avengers and Hellcats, reasonably concluding that the 3d Platoon was the enemy, jumped the cavalrymen at Bayambang. Smoke signals and recognition panels did nothing to ward off the attack, so the patrol withdrew—"shaken and cursing mad," says the after-action report.

By 30 January the outfit recorded, "[The men] were tired physically and mentally. They were hungry, dirty, sleepy, and aching from abused muscles. The mental tension of day after day had piled up on them, and they noted a tendency to awaken at night and smoke innumerable cigarettes. Rifle stocks now had turned a bleached white from incessant rubbing against always sweaty clothing. Vehicles creaked, engines missed firing on cylinders, springs had been flattened by poundings of rough roads; gear boxes whined and complained. . . . In one enormous effort . . . they had sliced through the enemy's counter-reconnaissance screen to San Jose and Rizal. . . ."[25]

★★★

More divisions came ashore in the weeks after the assault wave, bringing their mechanized cavalry troops with them. The 25th Infantry Division, which had been the Sixth Army floating reserve, landed on 11 January.[26] The 25th Cavalry Reconnaissance Troop had been completely reorganized as a "jungle" unit after its experience on Guadalcanal, only to be ordered in October 1944 to convert to a standard cavalry reconnaissance troop. Because no M8s were available, it substituted M3 half-tracks, and its crews trained on infantry 37mm antitank guns and in light tanks so they would know how to use the cannons should any M8s show up.[27]

The troop conducted motor patrols around San Jacinto and Manoag, but its first firefight did not take place until 25 January, when a patrol encountered a Japanese reconnaissance party a thousand yards east of Santa Maria. The outgunned Japanese lost thirteen killed.

The 32d Cavalry Reconnaissance Troop shifted from Leyte to Luzon, arriving on 30 January, and for one exhilarating week conducted mounted patrols. By 7 February, however, the outfit was back to sending small patrols deep into the jungle along the Agno River.[28]

★★★

The dismounted 1st Cavalry Division, which had arrived at Luzon on 27 January to reinforce XIV Corps, took the laurels for capturing Manila after it formed a mechanized task force controlled by the 1st Cavalry Brigade. The task force consisted of two cavalry squadrons mounted in trucks, supported by armor and artillery, operating as separate "flying columns," one of which included the division's 302d Cavalry Reconnaissance Troop in its first major mounted action. Together with the headquarters and light tank company of the 44th Tank Battalion, the mechanized cavalry troop constituted the provisional reconnaissance squadron.

The provisional squadron made its key contribution to the advance on 1 February where a bridge at Gapan carries Route 5 across the Penaranda River. Japanese rifle fire from the south bank killed the provisional squadron commander. The 302d Troop commander, Capt. Don Walton, immediately took control and led a charge across the bridge, which prevented its destruction. One patrol drove half-tracks, armored cars, and jeeps down a railroad in the middle of the night, easing over flimsy trestles, to enter and secure the town of Penaranda.

The other "flying column" rushed into Manila on 3 February while the rest of the division mopped up pockets of bypassed resistance. The 302d Cavalry Reconnaissance Troop entered the city two days later.

Getting into Manila had been easy, but securing the capital proved difficult indeed. Strong Japanese forces, primarily naval, disregarded General Yamashita's plan to hold out in the mountains; instead, they fought for possession of the city. Nearly another month of brutal street fighting would be necessary to clear out last-ditch resistance, which left much of Manila in ruins.[29]

★★★

The 37th Infantry Division had also been on the road to Manila. The cavalry reconnaissance troop's light tanks were operating on point, the 1st Platoon probing a mile ahead of the infantry, when they ran into a Japanese roadblock near Angeles on 26 January. The lead tank hit a mine or was struck by an anti-tank round and slid into a ditch. Three Japanese soldiers threw hand grenades at the hatches and crept toward the vehicle. Corporal Joseph Ierardi, the tank commander, spotted the enemy infantry and tossed grenades at them from his turret. Meanwhile, Sgt. William Poitras, who was in a jeep yards behind Ierardi's tank, jumped out with his rifle and, despite a buzz of bullets around him, calmly picked off three of the enemy soldiers. A half-track raced forward, and the tank crew—the wounded driver carried by Ierardi—climbed aboard and withdrew to the rear.

The next day, two American P40s strafed the troop on the road to San Fernando, and the troopers took refuge in some nearby Japanese shelters. Commented Technician 5th Grade Bud Manion, "The Japs aren't bad enough, now we got this."[30]

The troop entered Manila on 3 February close behind the 1st Cavalry Division. Sergeant Dick Small recalled, "[The] 'Pearl of the Pacific,' the 'Gem of the Orient,' now lay in ruins and rubble; the stench of death was prevalent throughout the alleys, boulevards, and districts."[31] The troop provided security in the city for several days, then screened the division flank. During the middle of the month, the light tanks harassed Japanese positions on Engineer Island and sank barges in Manila Bay.

On 18 February the troop was assigned to protect the main highway into Manila from the west. At 0300 hours on 23 February, a Japanese infantry company attacked the troop's position. When Cpl. Albert Millheim realized that a large group of the enemy had infiltrated the position, he opened fire with his Tommy gun. The Japanese took cover behind a hedge on the far side of the road, so Millheim dashed to the center of the road until he could see them and tossed a grenade. He repeated this action fourteen times and killed at least nine of the enemy. Nearby, Pfc. Loal Tucker manned the machine gun on his jeep and fired at the enemy even after a grenade wounded him in the thigh. A second grenade set the jeep on fire, but Tucker stayed with his gun until he collapsed unconscious from blood loss.

The troop's light tanks had spotlights mounted on the turrets. One tank that pulled onto the road and illuminated another group of Japanese opened up with its main gun, wiping out fifteen of the foe. A crewman stood on the deck of a second tank and directed his spotlight into the ditches beside the road as his vehicle ground up and down the highway. The fight lasted until dawn.[32] Morning revealed the bodies of forty-three Japanese soldiers and three abandoned heavy machine guns.[33]

★★★

After the capture of Clark Field, the 40th Infantry Division was sent to drive the Japanese out of their stronghold in the Zambales Mountains. The recon troop was assigned the mission of harassing the Japanese flank during the day and forming a second line of defense behind the infantry at night because of the frequent Japanese counterattacks. One troop tactic was to roll into what the men nicknamed Death Valley and shell Japanese positions.

One day in the first week of February, the troopers spotted a Japanese tank moving along a ridge a great distance away. Captain John Robinson's driver, "Ack Ack," rested a 20-power sight on the hood of a jeep to spot rounds because Gerrish would be unable to see due to turret vibration after he fired the 37mm gun. Gerrish squeezed off a high-explosive round, which would be easy to spot. Low and to the right, reported Ack Ack. Gerrish took Kentucky windage, aimed the crosshairs high and left, and fired an armor piercing round. "Hit!" Ack Ack yelled. "The Japs are bailing out!"

Ack Ack climbed into the turret and shot a few more holes into their prize.[34]

★★★

The 6th Infantry Division joined the battle for the mountains on 15 February, driving to reach the Ipo Dam. The cavalrymen discovered nearly the same thing that their comrades in Italy had learned under somewhat similar circumstances, as recorded in the after-action report: "Feeling ahead for the division was no longer necessary. The enemy was in the hills of the mountains, close at hand, fighting from his caves and dying in his lair. Above one cave on the side of a hill was another cave, and behind one hill was another hill. The infantryman saw them and knew they were there; he needed no reconnaissance troop to beat him a path."

The troop engaged mainly in patrolling. In early March, attempts to use the armored cars' 37mm guns to fire into caves proved a failure.[35]

★★★

Beginning 22 February, Sixth Army's I Corps began a methodical, relentless drive to destroy the Japanese defenses blocking the approach to strongholds in the northern Luzon mountains and the Cagayan Valley. Some 110,000 Japanese troops were estimated to hold the area.[36]

While the 25th and 32d Infantry divisions clawed their way over rough, rain-soaked terrain toward Balete Pass beginning 6 March, the 33d Infantry Division operated along Kennon Road toward Baguio, on the corps' left.[37] The 33d Cavalry Reconnaissance Troop, which had landed with its division on 10 February, operated ahead of the infantry and at times formed the core of a combined-arms task force. The troop found that leading a column with a light tank followed by an armored car was the best formation because the free-swinging machine gun on the M8 could quickly engage enemy infantry to the flanks that the tank could not fire on immediately. At times the troop mounted four riflemen on the first four or five armored cars. The soldiers could rapidly dismount for foot reconnaissance, and they protected the formation against enemy grenade, pole charge, and satchel attacks.

On 20 March the 1st Platoon set off with a platoon of riflemen from the 130th Infantry Regiment attached, as well as two light tanks. The patrol found three large ammo dumps south of Buang and destroyed them, then continued toward Naguilian. The platoon spotted a like-size group of Japanese infantry on a ridge northeast of Bay-Lay and opened fire with 37mm, .50-caliber, and .30-caliber guns; it killed ten of the enemy and dispersed the rest.

The patrol pressed on until it neared a bridge across the Naguilian River, where it spotted another group of Japanese slipping to the other side. Fire again dispersed the enemy. The patrol found the bridge destroyed, but it was able to locate a ford nearby. The route to Naguilian and its airfield was open.[38]

★★★

The 37th Infantry Division also was assigned to liberate northern Luzon, and on 31 May it attacked through the 25th Infantry Division and up Highway 5. On 11 April the 37th Reconnaissance Troop had arrived at Buang, the "summer capital." There, a regiment of the Philippine Army was attached to the troop to form a Special Security Force. Foot patrols into the mountains began again. All but three of the M5 light tanks were traded in, and the troop finally drew its first thirteen M8 armored cars.

The troop then moved to San Isidro, where it became part of Task Force 59, which also controlled medium tanks from the 775th Tank Battalion, tank destroyers from the 637th Tank Destroyer Battalion, and some antiaircraft artillery. Dreamed up and commanded by the troop's own Capt. Roderick MacEachan, the task force was to sweep the Cagayan Valley.

Near Ilagan in early June, the troop fought one of the toughest scraps it ever faced. Lieutenant Beverly Mundy's 2d Platoon had rolled up Highway 5 to San Antonio Junction, where it was ordered to reconnoiter the San Antonio trail. Mundy took one look, spotted tank tracks in the soil, and said he would not budge without armor. Because cubs had spotted a sizable Japanese force along the trail, the 1st Platoon, five Sherman tanks, one of the troop's three remaining M5s, and four multiple .50-caliber antiaircraft half-tracks joined the 2d Platoon.

Sergeant Small described the action:

The first knowledge of the rear guard of an encounter with the enemy was when the lead medium [tank] radioed back that they had blasted one Nip tank to hell. Those in the rear were joyous, but their exhilaration was to be short-lived, for as the two rear 2d Platoon jeeps came to the spot where the Jap tank was knocked out, a hell of fire broke loose. A tree fell directly behind a 6x6 filled with the infantrymen, cutting the column in half. The infantry poured out to take positions on each side of the road.

The men in the two jeeps quickly dismounted and hit the good earth; the light tank [number 6, "Personality Plus"] and the two multiple half-tracks were blocked completely. The men inside the tank were without communication; they could see men running back toward the rear.

Then 37mm gunner Cpl. Ralph Coryell spotted two Jap tanks in the thick foliage lining the right of the road. He immediately issued the cry "Ambush!" and began firing into the tanks. . . .

Sergeant Joe Ierardi dismounted from his tank to gain an advantageous picture of the dramatic situation. In doing so, he exposed himself to the intense enemy fire; he was out no more than a minute when a battle-lull existed, so he called out Sgt. [Anthony] Tursi from the safety of his driver's position. As the two talked the situation over, hell broke loose again. Sergeant Tursi's hand was grazed with machine-gun bullets, Sergeant Ierardi's helmet was knocked off, and Sgt. Sandy Sandrin was hit in the abdomen. . . . Tank #6 found later that it had destroyed two Japanese tanks.

Two men died and three were seriously wounded, and an M8 was knocked out during the battle. Fighting along the trail eventually resulted in the destruction of eleven Japanese tanks and the infliction of many casualties, which prevented any counterattack against the flank of 37th Division formations battling along Highway 5.[39]

More Philippine Islands

By late March, American forces controlled all of Luzon that had any strategic significance, and some operations moved on to nearby islands. With only four days of "rest" to rehabilitate equipment, the 40th Cavalry Reconnaissance Troop landed on 18 March 1945 with the rest of the division on Panay, in the Visayan Islands. The troop immediately initiated reconnaissance to the north and northeast.

On 20 March, word arrived that some eight hundred Japanese troops had broken through a screen of Filipino guerrillas and was heading north. The troop received orders to establish contact with the enemy. Captain John Robinson organized a provisional reconnaissance team because his three platoons were away from the CP.

At Pavia the team, consisting of three M8 armored cars and three machine-gun jeeps, encountered the Japanese troops. The point vehicle radioed back that it had run into quite a few of the enemy, and Robinson ordered the small command to close up to the point and form for defense.

The platoon was on a narrow road with deep ditches to either side. The M8s opened fire on a group of charging enemy troops with canister and machine guns while the jeep crews bailed into the ditches. Soon the rattle of their Tommy guns, machine guns, and rifles joined the fusillade. Having learned respect for the canister fire, the Japanese drew off, peppered the cavalrymen with machine-gun fire, and worked around the flanks until the troopers were surrounded.

The cavalrymen held off the enemy for about two hours, constantly requesting reinforcement. In response they were told that there could not possibly be that many Japanese where they were. Staff Sergeant Gerrish began to wonder whether he was going to join the immortals of Custer's last stand.

At noon Captain Robinson called for his own 3d Platoon. Soon a report came in from the rescue party: "We ran into a Nip patrol, result twenty-seven dead Japs." Robinson replied to keep coming, because the ammunition was running out.

Soon the trapped men could hear heavy firing from the far side of Pavia and knew that the 3d Platoon was coming. The arriving cavalrymen charged through the Japanese line, all guns blazing. Even the drivers fired Tommy guns with one hand while steering with the other. Under the combined fire, the Japanese formation dispersed into small groups and escaped. Nobody stopped to count the piles of dead Japanese.[40]

★★★

The 40th Cavalry Reconnaissance Troop landed on yet another island, Negros, on 29 March. The next day the troop again encountered a large body of Japanese troops, reported by locals to number some three hundred, near Antipulian. The troop established the Japanese position in the usual way, by coming under small-arms and mortar fire from a thick three- to four-acre banana and coconut grove. (The recon troop had received only a one-day supply of C rations the day of the landing and were living off bananas.) The cavalrymen laid out three huge arrows with fluorescent panels and directed an air strike against the target by radio. Five A-20s might have dropped their bombs right on target, but it evidently was one they had selected a half mile from the grove. Complaints to Air Control produced two more A-20s that dropped eight bombs in the right place, but only one exploded.

After an attempt to enter the grove on foot resulted in nothing but four casualties, Capt. John Robinson deployed one platoon to cover possible escape routes and two platoons abreast to assault the Japanese position. Robinson organized the attacking force into a "tank-infantry team" using the armored cars as tanks. For once the troop had just received a large supply of canister rounds for the 37mm guns. Boxes of grenades were placed on the decks of the M8s, within reach of the turret crew and the men on the ground.

Blazing away, the cavalrymen advanced across a rice paddy under small-arms fire and into the grove, working together to blast bunkers and shoot snipers— who were trying to toss grenades into the open turrets of the M8s—out of the trees. The cavalrymen counted 114 enemy dead, plus 5 prisoners and an unknown number buried in destroyed bunkers, for the loss of 3 men wounded and 1 killed.[41]

★★★

X Corps' next stop, meanwhile, was the island of Mindanao, which still hosted a large Japanese garrison. The Japanese had constructed formidable beach defenses on the east side of the island, so X Corps planned to land on the undefended west side and take the Japanese from the rear.

The 24th Reconnaissance Troop landed on Mindanao on 17 April. The division hoped its speed and the availability of an all-weather highway across the island to Davao would open the door to a rapid campaign rather than a grueling slog. The troopers scouted the environs while the 24th Division built up its beachhead, and on 23 April the troop mounted up, passed through the lines of the 34th Infantry Regiment, and led a spectacular dash along Highway 1 to the far side of the island.

There, the recon men ran into elements of the Japanese 30th Division and took several prisoners. From this point on, the Japanese waged a vigorous delaying action and burned bridges, felled trees across the road, sniped, laid mines, and set up machine-gun positions. Assisted by engineers and the infantry, the troop was able to prevent the enemy from regaining his balance and establishing a coherent line. On 1 May the troop pushed northward, fanning out over secondary roads. Its quick overland thrust got behind Japanese beach defenses on this part of the island and forced the enemy to scramble back.

By 3 May, scouts were running into heavy fire and even infiltration attacks at night aimed at destroying the troop's vehicles. The war became the infantry-man's fight once more, and the troopers operated by platoon parceled out among the regiments. The troopers employed a new T18E6 knee mortar in lieu of the 60mm mortar and found it to be far superior because it could go into action almost immediately—as during an ambush—could shift targets rapidly, and could be used for direct fire into enemy installations. Heavy fighting continued until the troop was withdrawn to rest on 26 June.[42]

While the 24th Reconnaissance Troop was having a grand mechanized cavalry outing, the 31st Cavalry Reconnaissance Troop, which had traded in its amtanks for standard mechanized cavalry equipment, was spearheading the division advance northward through the center of the island. This route confronted the men with crossings of the Mindanao, Mulita, and Pulangi rivers, as well as smaller streams. The troopers discovered that the local wooden bridges would not support the weight of their M8 armored cars and that streams were impossible to ford. The M8s and jeeps, moreover, sank into the mud with annoying regularity, and platoons started to substitute half-tracks on missions.

The 2d Platoon from 25 to 30 April conducted reconnaissance missions from PT boats accompanied by local guerrillas. Japanese resistance was as fierce as any faced in the Pacific, and the 31st Reconnaissance Troop was still engaged in combat as late as 28 June.[43]

The Last Battle: Okinawa

The final battle on the road to Japan occurred on terrain that once again all but took the "mechanized" out of the cavalry mission after but a short period. American forces in the Pacific on 3 October received orders to plan Operation Iceberg, the invasion of the Ryukyu Islands, which constituted Japan's inner ring of defenses. Okinawa, the largest island in the group, is some sixty miles long and between two and eighteen miles wide. The northern two-thirds is mountainous and cloaked in pine forests. The southern third is covered by rolling hills studded with limestone ridges containing many natural caves. It is excellent defensive country, and some 66,000 Japanese troops were estimated to be on the island to exploit that terrain.

Three army and two marine infantry divisions under Tenth Army, reinforced by tank and amphibian tractor battalions—some 116,000 men—made the initial landings on 1 April after weeks of preparatory destruction by air and naval assets. The invasion beaches were located on the west coast roughly a third of the way up the island, and the vast American force charged ashore amidst an earthshaking bombardment, only to find that there were no Japanese troops there to resist them. Tenth Army quickly cut the island in two. The first signs of resistance began to emerge on 2 and 3 April after the 96th Infantry Division wheeled to advance southward into the rolling hills in conjunction with the 7th Infantry Division. The Japanese had concentrated their forces in the southern third of the island and were waiting for the Americans to come to them.[44]

The 96th Cavalry Reconnaissance Squadron had disembarked on Okinawa on L-Day shortly after the assault wave. The 1st Platoon operated dismounted and sealed caves around the landing site. The entire troop joined in the activity the next day, while vehicle crews de-waterproofed their "steeds." The troop had opted to substitute additional half-tracks for roughly a third of its armored cars because of their superior cross-country maneuverability.

The cavalrymen conducted their first mounted patrols through the infantry's lines on 3 April. The Japanese were still nowhere to be found. Preceding the 383d Infantry Regiment southward the next day, the troopers established contact with the enemy in the classic fashion. Captain Robert O'Neill that day led his 3d Platoon along the coast road, and all went well for more than an hour. Then, while the patrol was crossing a valley north of Uchitomari, Japanese troops concealed on a ridge some four hundred yards to the front opened up with antitank and machine guns. Mortars aimed with deadly accuracy chimed in from hills to the south and east. The barrage wounded six men, killed two more, and destroyed two half-tracks and a jeep.

One armored car found a hull-defilade position, and the commander directed artillery fire against the enemy. Finally the infantry arrived and relieved the battered platoon at 1500 hours. The division pulled the troop back to conduct security patrols in the rear. It spent the remainder of the campaign patrolling, clearing out bypassed pockets of resistance, and occasionally filling gaps in the lines between battalions.[45]

The 1st Platoon, 7th Cavalry Reconnaissance Troop, had also landed on Okinawa on 1 April; the remainder of the troop landed the next day. The troop had retained its modified table of equipment and its invaluable M29 Weasels after the Leyte experience, and each platoon consisted of five jeeps, two Weasels, two M8 armored cars, and a half-track. A Japanese plane had damaged the transport, and the cavalrymen could only off-load their Weasels and jeeps. Finally the armored cars arrived, and on 5 April one platoon led the 32d Infantry Regiment's advance in the vicinity of Ouki. It proved a slow operation because of numerous antitank ditches and frequent enemy fire. Able to contribute little to the grueling, high-intensity fight along the front, the troopers took up flank protection duties. On 4 May they spotted and destroyed with mortar and machine-gun fire a 250-man Japanese force attempting to flank the American lines by boat and land in the rear.[46]

The 77th Cavalry Reconnaissance Troop arrived on Okinawa on 24 April after having participated in the division's operation to clear nearby Ie Shima. This troop, too, found that there was little need for reconnaissance in the yard-by-yard campaign to root out the defenders, and the men wound up playing the role of assault infantry.

About noon on 5 May, the troop received orders to clear out a Japanese pocket in the Tanabaru sector. The division G-2 thought that there were only a few infiltrating soldiers there and the mission would demand perhaps half a day. The troop moved out, less the 1st Platoon, an hour later. At 1440 hours a patrol spotted about forty enemy infantrymen, but because the troopers could see several cave openings, they guessed that the news was even worse than that.

Machine-gun and rifle fire from the flank suddenly zinged through the American ranks, and the men dropped to the dirt. Lieutenant Simpson crawled forward to lead the patrol back to safety, but he, too, became pinned down by sniper fire and was killed. Firefights flared at two points, and the cavalrymen thought they accounted for nearly thirty of the foe before they extricated themselves for the night.

The troopers advanced cautiously early the next morning. Three of eight Japanese were eliminated in the first sharp engagement, and ten more plus a heavy machine gun in the second engagement. The 3d Platoon's Sergeant Thiele, covered by his squad, crawled with a satchel charge toward the first cave to be reached, only to come under grenade attack from a web of spider holes concealed near the entrance. The 2d Platoon had to join the fight before the resistance could be overcome.

On a ridge just above this action, another squad tried to slip up on a pillbox, but the Japanese spotted the movement; machine-gun bullets and grenades killed the squad leader and wounded another man. Private First Class Huber, the aid man, rushed to the downed soldier and was wounded while providing first aid. The troopers were able to recover their injured comrades but had to pull back. A tank came forward but was unable to get a line of fire. Finally, before nightfall, the troopers were able to slip around the pillbox and knock it out from the rear.

The troop mopped up during the third morning of the operation. Nearly seventy dead Japanese lay around the area. The cavalrymen blew the cave entrances closed and moved out. For the remainder of the fight for the island, the troop patrolled "secured" areas, keeping an eye out for infiltrators and bypassed enemy troops hidden in caves or on rough terrain.[47]

Although the mechanized cavalry had for practical purposes completed its service in World War II by May in both Europe and the Pacific except in the Philippines, the infantry soldiered on. On 18 June the Japanese commander ordered the remnants of his forces to go over to guerrilla warfare, and organized resistance came to an end. Only the atomic bomb blasts over Hiroshima and Nagasaki remained to end the war for everyone.

CHAPTER 6

NORMANDY: CAVALRY IN THE HEDGEROWS

During all our training in England, which amounted to almost two years, no one
thought that the troop would be used as an assault force. . . .

—Lt. Thomas Fernley, 29th Cavalry Reconnaissance Troop

The European theater of operations (ETO) was the main proving ground for the mechanized cavalry because the vast majority of that force fought there. Thirteen cavalry groups with twenty-six squadrons and one separate squadron fought in the ETO. So, too, did thirteen squadrons organic to "light" armored divisions, plus two armored reconnaissance battalions with the 2d and 3d "heavy" Armored divisions. Forty-two mechanized cavalry reconnaissance troops went into battle with their parent infantry divisions.[1]

The Cavalry on D-Day

Well before dawn on 6 June 1944, the men of the American 101st and 82d Airborne divisions leapt into the unknown near Ste. Mere-Eglise and Carentan. Their mission was to secure road junctions and exit routes from the invasion beaches on the coast of Normandy. When the sky brightened, gliders bearing more paratroopers landed in hedgerow-bounded fields, and Allied bombers and fighter-bombers began the first of the eleven thousand sorties they would fly that day against German emplacements, troop concentrations, and transportation nodes.[2]

Detachments of the 4th and 24th Cavalry Reconnaissance squadrons were among the first American troops to reach French soil by sea that morning. At 0430 hours, while the main assault force was still getting ready to board its landing craft, four cavalrymen armed with nothing but knives crept onto the

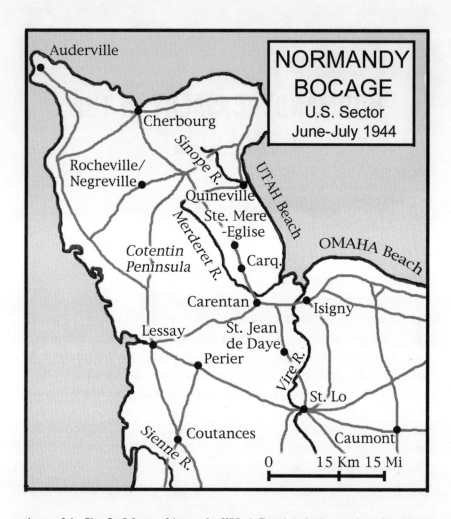

NORMANDY BOCAGE
U.S. Sector
June-July 1944

Auderville

Cherbourg

Rocheville/
Negreville

Sinope R.

UTAH Beach

Quineville

Ste. Mere
-Eglise

OMAHA Beach

Cotentin
Peninsula

Merderet R.

Carq.

Carentan

Isigny

Lessay

St. Jean
de Daye

Perier

Vire R.

St. Lo

Sienne R.

Coutances

Caumont

0   15 Km 15 Mi

shore of the Iles St. Marcouf, located off Utah Beach, which was thought to host a German strongpoint. Overhead, bombers and transports carrying more paratroopers filled the air with the humming sound of their engines. The men carefully marked the beach for the main body, including some sixty cavalrymen from Troop B, 24th Squadron, led by Lt. Col. E. C. Dunn. The island proved to be deserted but heavily mined, which caused nine casualties. By H-1 hour, the cavalrymen had secured the island and transmitted the first message to VII Corps headquarters to originate from ground troops in France.[3]

Some twenty minutes later, battlewagons, cruisers, and other warships in the vast Allied armada off Normandy unleashed a blizzard of shells onto the

German defenses along the American landing beaches, code-named Omaha and Utah. GIs clambered down rope nets into waiting landing craft, which then turned toward shore.

Cavalry in the Assault Wave

At 0630, the 4th Infantry Division and amphibious duplex drive (DD) Sherman tanks from the 70th Tank Battalion hit the beach at Utah, the VII Corps landing area. Within three hours, they had overwhelmed the defenses and were moving inland to link up with the airborne, all at a cost of only 197 ground-force casualties. The first of three landing craft carrying the 4th Cavalry Reconnaissance Troop had off-loaded its vehicles into deep water, and a second had not arrived due to engine trouble, so the troop was able to muster only two running vehicles when it attempted to reconnoiter to Ste. Mere-Eglise, which it found to be strongly held by the enemy.[4]

The V Corps landing at Omaha Beach, conducted by elements of the 1st and 29th Infantry divisions and the 741st and 743d Tank battalions, encountered heavy seas and a tough job. Most of the 741st Battalion's DD tanks sank, and, as Gen. Dwight Eisenhower had predicted in his message to the invasion force, the Germans along the beach fought savagely.

Eighteen troopers belonging to the 1st Platoon of the 29th Cavalry Reconnaissance Troop landed on Omaha Beach with the first wave from the 116th Infantry Regiment. The platoon was divided into seven teams, each carrying one SCR-300 walkie-talkie radio, and the troopers operated on the commanding general's radio voice net. Most of the infantry's radios were lost or damaged on the beach, and for some time the recon radios provided the division command with its only communications with the assault force.

By afternoon the infantry and tanks had clawed their way off the beach. They left 2,500 casualties in their wake. The 29th Recon troopers survived the 116th Infantry's bloody siege on the sand at the cost of eight casualties, and their net reported advances, locations, and resistance met by the assault companies until 0200 hours on 7 June.[5] The 1st Infantry Division did not include its reconnaissance troop in its D-Day landing force.[6]

Troopers Drive Inland

About three hours after the first men charged across Utah Beach, the lead elements of "Howell Force"—the seaborne component of the 82d Airborne Division—rolled out of their landing craft. Commanded by Col. Edson Raff, a daring veteran of the North Africa campaign, the force consisted of the 3d Platoon, Troop B, 4th Cavalry Reconnaissance Squadron; a company of medium tanks from the 746th Tank Battalion; and ninety riflemen from the 325th Glider Infantry Regiment. Lieutenant Gerald Penley commanded the troopers of the 3d Platoon. The 3d Battalion, 8th Infantry Regiment, followed the task force to shore. Together they were to drive inland to Ste. Mere-Eglise to link up with the 82d Airborne Division and secure the landing zone for the 325th Glider Infantry Regiment, due to land at 2100 hours.

As with many outfits on D-Day, the navy landed the task force a bit off target, and the M8 armored cars rolled off the LCT not onto firm sand but onto a mudflat. They promptly sank into the muck and drowned out, and it took nearly forty-five minutes to pull them onto solid ground. Artillery fire hitting the beach during this operation wounded four men and destroyed two platoon jeeps.

By noon the cavalry vehicles were de-waterproofed, the rest of the command had gotten ashore, and Penley's platoon set out to reconnoiter and to screen the advance. The column soon ran into Germans dug in on some high ground. A paratrooper from the 101st Airborne Division appeared and reported that there had been small-arms fire from the German positions, most likely held by *Landser*s of the 352d Infantry Division.

Penley was ordered to clear the obstruction, so he set out with an armored car followed by a tank and another M8, figuring that he was invulnerable to small-arms fire. Much to his dismay, direct fire from an antitank gun whizzed by. The column backed to safety.

The commander of the 2d Battalion was content to request artillery support and settle down until the next morning, but Raff was determined to try to break through to his airborne comrades. Infantry and tanks attacked the position twice but failed to break through. One Sherman tank was disabled in the first attempt and two were destroyed in the second.

The gliders swooped in to land as scheduled, and some came down in the uncleared German positions. Many others crashed, which resulted in high casualties. Raff ordered the cavalry troopers to form "glider rescue squads," and the men moved among the broken and sometimes burning aircraft giving first aid to the injured.[7]

★★★

Beyond the beaches was the Norman hedgerow country, or *bocage*, split into tiny battlefields by thick hedgerows that often could be penetrated only by tank dozers or explosives. Invasion planners had assumed that the Germans would withdraw to the Seine river after the Allies secured a beachhead, and they had devoted almost no attention to the tactics and equipment that the armies would need in the *bocage* should the Germans stand and fight.[8] The infantry and tankers hated the hedgerows; fighting was difficult and at close range, and losses were heavy. Cavalrymen initially had a different experience, because they could not really operate across the fields and were generally spared the worst of the fighting. The Germans, moreover, had poor fields of fire, and cavalry vehicles could get fairly close without exposing themselves.

One lieutenant from the 29th Reconnaissance Troop, looking back on the experience after the breakout in July, commented, "In Normandy we bitched about the hedgerows, but from experience in the open country since then, it is generally agreed that the hedgerows had their advantages for us as well as for the enemy. The M8 armored car is not an off-the-road vehicle, and in the open terrain it is sometimes very important to travel cross-country."[9]

★★★

Operations during the first two days after the landings were essentially a continuation of the assault phase, because few units had reached their D-Day objectives. VII Corps was to have moved immediately onto the Cotentin Peninsula but was directed instead to make contact first with V Corps in order to consolidate the American beachhead.[10]

On D+1 in the VII Corps zone, Lieutenant Penley's 3d Platoon, Troop B, 4th Cavalry Reconnaissance Squadron, received orders to move to a rendezvous point southwest of Ste. Mere-Eglise. The platoon set off in this order: two machine-gun jeeps, Penley's M8, the second M8, three mortar jeeps, the third M8, and the last machine-gun jeep. The platoon had to stay on the narrow roads because they were bounded on both sides by a ditch, then a wall of earth topped by an impenetrable hedgerow.[11] Asked how it felt to be driving the lead jeep toward the enemy through *bocage*, with no armor and a potential ambush on both sides, one veteran replied, "You just don't think about it. If something happens, you just roll out of the jeep. There was nothing else to do."[12]

Only occasional sniper fire troubled the column. The men quickly learned that speed was critical in such country because a sniper in a hedge or a tree had a great deal of trouble hitting a moving target but could generally hit a sitting duck. The platoon was shelled upon reaching the rendezvous point and was ordered to pull back.

The next day a report came in that fifty German troops had been spotted near Carquebut. Penley was told to take two M8s as an advance party for two companies of parachute infantry. They were to make a complete circle around the town, then wait for the paratroopers.

Penley and his platoon sergeant circled the village and took only a bit of rifle fire. A civilian appeared and flagged down the armored cars. There were 150 Germans, he reported, in a nearby barracks.

When the paratroopers arrived, the commander evidently did not like the odds and ordered Penley to attack the barracks. The M8s worked their way down a narrow trail, and the platoon sergeant raked the second-story windows with his .50-caliber antiaircraft machine gun. Five officers and 120 men emerged to surrender.

The next day, D+3, Penley's platoon moved into a bridgehead the paratroopers had established across the Merderet River. There he was ordered to check out a report of a large German truck column driving toward Ste. Mere-Eglise. Moving out with his three M8 armored cars, Penley encountered 150 Germans about a half mile down the road. The German riflemen dove into the ditches along the roadsides, and Penley could see three antitank guns in position farther down the road. He fired canister at the guns and killed or dispersed the crews. Then his M8 and the other cars crawled slowly up the road, sweeping the ditches with their .50-calibers and wiping out the German infantry. Six *Kettenkrad* half-track motorcycles turned out of a side road, and the cavalrymen finished them off, too. With the report "checked out," the detachment pulled back to the river.

On 10 June, ground forces of V and VII corps finally made contact near Carentan. The remainder of Troop B, 4th Cavalry Reconnaissance Squadron, arrived that day at Ste. Mere-Eglise, and Penley's men drove to join it. The platoon had lost not a single man since the four wounded on the beach.[13] The new arrivals were not so fortunate; on 11 June the 2d Platoon was trapped while on patrol and all were killed or captured except for two lucky troopers who escaped in a jeep.[14]

★★★

The remainder of the 29th Reconnaissance Troop in the V Corps zone, meanwhile, had landed on 8 June and blazed a new path in cavalry action the following day. The 175th Infantry Regiment was attacking westward from Omaha Beach in an attempt to link up with the 101st Airborne Division, which was pushing to meet it in the vicinity of Carentan.[15] Company K was stalled before the Vire River because of heavy fire from the other side at Auville. The troop collected odd bits of lumber and built numerous rafts, then used the M8s to carry them forward to the riverbank. The troop then deployed its eleven M8s for direct fire and nine 60mm mortars for indirect fire and placed a barrage on the German positions. Under the cover from this shelling, the infantry advanced to the river and established a bridgehead, with only minor losses.

The next day the troop contacted paratroopers from the 101st Airborne Division who had been fighting alone in the Cotentin Peninsula since D-Day. "I never saw a group of men as happy to see us as they were that day," remembered Lt. Thomas "Jim" Fernley.[16]

A short while later a patrol captured a Russian who had been a Red Army tanker before being taken prisoner and winding up in a labor battalion under the Todt organization. He supplied information on German positions that proved so accurate that the troop put him in an American uniform and sent him out with patrols. He was a good soldier, but the troop eventually had to turn him over to a prisoner-of-war stockade.[17]

★★★

The cavalry squadrons were generally spared the worst of the hedgerow war during June and early July, a pattern that characterized later periods of high-intensity ground combat as well. Indeed, a post-war study of three infantry divisions, three armored divisions, and three cavalry groups that arrived in Europe at about the same time revealed that during the European campaign the infantry for every thirty days of combat suffered 105 combat losses per thousand men on average, the armored divisions experienced a rate of 47 men per thousand, and the cavalry outfits only 16 men per thousand. The percentage of days spent in combat was generally similar, ranging from 73 percent for armored divisions to 85 percent for cavalry groups. One side effect of the lower attrition rate was that cavalry units retained more combat-seasoned junior officers and senior noncommissioned officers, which in turn helped reduce losses further.[18]

The 102d Cavalry Group's experience in Normandy illustrates the case. The 38th Cavalry Reconnaissance Squadron disembarked with dry wheels across Omaha Beach on 12 June. Troop A was ordered to reconnoiter the three main routes out of Caumont for the 1st Infantry Division, but it became clear immediately that the Germans were well positioned in strength. The squadron spent the period from then until the breakout in late July filling the gap between the 16th and 18th Infantry regiments, and later the gap between the 1st and 2d Infantry divisions.[19]

Similarly, the 102d Cavalry Reconnaissance Squadron participated in the Caumont operation, then spent most of its time in the *bocage* holding a stretch of the static line between the 1st and 2d Infantry divisions adjacent to the 38th Squadron.[20] The 106th Cavalry Group, which arrived beginning 3 July, conducted defensive and mopping-up missions. It called Normandy its "experimental lab," where it learned how to fight.[21]

The cavalry reconnaissance troops in the infantry divisions often played a similar role once the combat settled down to hard slogging. The 9th Infantry Division, for example, entered the line on 14 June and deployed its troop to maintain contact with the adjacent 82d Airborne Division. It subsequently used the troop for similar missions and flank protection.[22] The 2d Infantry Division, which joined the battle at about the same time, used its reconnaissance troop for similar tasks, as well as to provide radio liaison between the infantry regiments and division headquarters.[23]

Seeing the *bocage* for the first time often came as a shock, because the mechanized cavalry had undergone no preparation for such conditions. "[The situation] was static and one in which our troops were unable to close with the enemy," recorded the 4th Armored Division's 25th Cavalry Reconnaissance Squadron, which entered the line on 17 July. "Being shelled and not being able to return fire was dragging on morale. It was a type of warfare totally different than all previous training. The troops were very excited and scared on first contact and had a tendency to fire at unseen snipers."[24]

★★★

The first major American objective outside the beachhead was the port of Cherbourg. Between 14 and 18 June, Maj. Gen. J. Lawton Collins' VII Corps wheeled from Utah Beach and cut across the Cotentin Peninsula, on which the city is located. By this time, Maj. Gen. Troy Middleton's VIII Corps had become active and taken responsibility for protecting the south flank. The remnants of five German divisions defended Cherbourg; they had orders from Hitler to fight to the last man.[25]

The 24th Cavalry Reconnaissance Squadron on 16 June relieved elements of the 4th Infantry Division's 22d Infantry Regiment, which was committed to the drive on Cherbourg. The squadron established a counter-reconnaissance screen along high ground west of Quineville and conducted patrols along the

Sinope River, all to make sure that German troops being cut off at the tip of the peninsula caused no trouble. For three days the squadron line along the high ground suffered constant harassing fire from enemy artillery and heavy mortars directed from Bourg de Lestre, on the far side of the river.

The squadron was going to have to mount a "reconnaissance" to try to drive the Germans out of the village, and there were no two ways about it. By now, as one unnamed squadron officer recorded, the troopers were figuring out that "reconnaissance had to become more and more aggressive, and strong-points had to be reduced instead of merely reported and bypassed. In fact, bypassing would have been impractical, if not impossible, because of the terrain and the extension of enemy installations."

Fortunately, the Germans for some reason had left the bridge on the Bourg road intact. Thus, at about 0300 hours on 19 June, two foot patrols from Troop C crossed the bridge and reached a crossroads, where they heard the sounds of digging nearby and spotted a house that appeared to contain a machine-gun nest. The Germans noticed the patrol and attacked, and the troop commanding officer ordered the men back across the river. The patrol estimated that a reinforced company held the crossroads, but it had seen no antitank guns.

At 1400 the next day, the tankers in Company F received orders to attack the crossroads under supporting fire from the Troop E assault guns. Lieutenant Sam Mitchell and his 2d Platoon's M5A1s crossed the bridge in column twenty-five minutes later. The tanks roared up the road as a five-minute preparation of 75mm howitzer rounds sped overhead to the objective, followed by two rounds of smoke that exploded just south of the crossroads. Breaking through the smoke, the lead tank spotted an antitank gun only a hundred yards away.

The American gunner was the faster, and three rounds of HE dispatched the German gun and its crew. The rest of the platoon arrived and spread out to secure the site. The 1st Platoon was ordered to move through the 2d Platoon and advance to a railroad station.

As these five tanks approached the crossroads, someone noticed another antitank gun that had been in the thick of the smoke screen and been driven past unseen by Mitchell's platoon. The Germans had just wheeled the gun around to engage the 1st Platoon as soon as the smoke cleared, and one round of HE from an M5A1 ensured that they never got the chance.

Upon reaching the station, one tank commander saw a cave opening and fired into it. A tremendous secondary explosion revealed the presence of an ammo dump. A second M5A1, meanwhile, engaged a column of German infantry attempting to enter town. By now heavy artillery was crashing around the light tanks, which were ordered to withdraw. The cavalrymen had learned another important lesson: any show of tank strength would provoke the enemy to open up with everything he had.[26]

★★★

The 4th Cavalry Reconnaissance Squadron (less Troop B) participated in the drive across the Cotentin Peninsula, during which it filled the gap between the 9th and 79th Infantry divisions directly under the control of the 4th Cavalry Group. On 19 June the squadron rolled down narrow roads between hedgerows. After a brief firefight with a company of enemy infantry in Negreville, the squadron pushed on to Rocheville, where Troop A ran into heavy small-arms and artillery fire. The troop pulled back to organize an assault.

In what may have been the first tank-mounted American cavalry assault of the war, Troop A and a platoon from Troop C climbed aboard the light tanks of Company F. The assault guns laid down a covering barrage, and the cavalrymen charged into the village and quickly eliminated all resistance. Two men were killed and eleven wounded during the fight. "Considering it was the first pitched battle for the assault troops," noted the 4th Cavalry Group in its after-action report, "they conducted themselves exceptionally well, fighting from building to building, wiping out all enemy encountered. Lieutenant Harrison, Company F, led and directed the employment of his tank platoons, standing in the open turret of his tank, spraying enemy-occupied buildings and positions with the anti-aircraft .30-cal machine gun mounted on the turret. . . ."

The next day the squadron was attached to the 9th Infantry Division and ordered to protect the division's right flank. With the tanks in the lead, the squadron set out for Les Flagues. The terrain opened up near the village, and Jerry had taken full advantage of the fields of fire. Antitank rounds from a roadblock destroyed two light tanks, including that of Lieutenant Harrison, who was killed. This time a dismounted attack was in order. After the assault guns and division artillery had worked over the roadblock, Troops A and C overran the position.

The squadron subsequently shifted to protect the division's left and rear during the attack on Cherbourg. Dismounted patrols penetrated enemy lines and operated in his rear for up to three days, gathering intelligence on German strongpoints and artillery and troop concentrations that was fed back to squadron and division artillery for fire missions.[27]

★★★

The 29th Reconnaissance Troop at this time was outposting a ridge south of La Meauf, mainly in the 175th Infantry Regiment's zone. The night of 21–22 June, Lt. Edward Jones took a ten-man patrol out to capture prisoners. The troop had spent a week in the UK working only at night to get a feel for conditions. Jones described the patrol in his memoirs:

> We moved out about 2030 hours and got onto the road in front of the infantry position, then moved south toward what had appeared to us previously as a strongpoint. Artillery and air strikes had knocked down the communications lines and concrete poles used by the French for this purpose. The Germans had tied cans to some of those wires—we jingled some of them, but no activity. We moved on in and entered an ambush.
>
> Approaching a corner of a hedgerow, I heard a bolt close on a rifle (unmistakable). I literally dove to the side of the road and called out to take cover—I was leading the patrol—landing in a ditch at the edge of the road just as the man with the rifle fired. Then they gave it to us in spades, machine pistols, rifles, handguns, grenades, etc. I lay as I had fallen, face up, and watched as tracer bullets plowed into the dirt hedgerow over me. . . .
>
> [A]fter about 10 minutes, the firing stopped, and I suppose they thought they had hit me good, as well as some of the other men. A grenade thrown just ahead of me away from my helmet created some concussion, but one or two thrown near my legs did do some damage. . . .
>
> I was determined not to be captured. . . . I backed down the ditch as quietly as possible—an occasional shot or machine-gun burst helped in this effort. At a wide place in the ditch, I turned snake-like and was pointed the way I wanted to go. I came to a gate opening in the hedgerow going into a field. My patrol had of course scattered—I had no idea where any of them might be. . . .[28]

Jones made his way back toward friendly lines until he was challenged in a low voice, "That you, Jones?" The troop did not refer to rank in combat because officers tended to attract sniper fire. Jones, it turned out, was the only man wounded.

★★★

With the capture of Cherbourg on 26 June, Lt. Gen. Omar Bradley on 3 July turned his First Army south to drive inland through the heart of the *bocage*. The troops encountered stiff resistance at every turn, and casualties mounted alarmingly for little gain in territory. Indeed, the next three weeks would cause senior Allied commanders to worry that they were falling into a stalemate similar to that of trench warfare during World War I.[29]

Amidst the near stalemate, the inventive men of Troop B, 4th Cavalry Reconnaissance Squadron, found one way to briefly restore movement to the operation. Attached to 9th Division's 39th Infantry Regiment on 30 June, the troop was ordered to reconnoiter the regiment's advance to Auderville. The problem was that the Germans manned an unbroken line. Under cover of darkness, the cavalrymen drove their vehicles to the top of a hill behind friendly lines, then one-by-one the jeeps and armored cars coasted down the highway with engines off and passed unnoticed through German lines. When the enemy awoke to the situation, he evidently realized that his position was untenable and slipped away. By the time the GIs advanced the next morning, they encountered almost no resistance. The cavalrymen, meanwhile, raced into Auderville and quickly neutralized the surprised garrison.

The squadron moved into reserve to rebuild for the planned breakout. Its experience in the *bocage* had defied its expectations and training. As the outfit's informal history recorded, "The missions had been consistently dismounted, and the fighting at times confused, but though new in combat [and] organized, equipped, and trained for mounted action, the men had tackled every mission with determination. . . . The squadron's first campaign had been tiring and costly: 138 casualties, including 24 officers and men killed in action."[30]

★★★

The veteran 2d and untested 3d Armored divisions arrived in Normandy during June and got a first taste of action, though their true coming out would await the great cotillion of the breakout from Normandy. The 2d Armored Division began landing on 11 June, and its two combat commands were ashore within three days. The tires and tracks of the 82d Armored Reconnaissance Battalion were hardly dry before V Corps on 11 June ordered it to send patrols to establish contact with friendly forces to the front and flanks.[31]

The 3d Armored Division disembarked less than two weeks later, and the 83d Armored Reconnaissance Battalion saw its first action on 7 July, when

Company D was attached to Combat Command B to perform reconnaissance in the area of Ariel. On 9 July, Company A less one platoon but plus a platoon of light tanks was attached to the 125th Cavalry Reconnaissance Squadron for an attack near St. Jean de Daye. This appears to have been the first time that an armored division's reconnaissance troops fought with a separate mechanized cavalry squadron.[32]

The 125th Squadron's running mate in the 11th Cavalry Group, the 113th Cavalry Reconnaissance Squadron, was fighting nearby at Goucherie.[33] The outfit's after-action report recorded the troopers' baptism of fire along a secondary road in the *bocage* on 7 July:

> First contact was made by the 3d Platoon, Troop A, acting as advance guard. . . . The platoon formation was built around an armored point. Line up, front to rear, was as follows: Light tank, assault gun, platoon leader's armored car, light tank, followed by the two remaining armored cars and six 1/4-ton vehicles. Dismounted men from the scout sections followed closely behind the point tank. The tank drew rifle fire from the hedgerow and returned the fire with its coaxial .30-caliber machine gun. One German unteroffizier and a private were flushed. Approximately three hundred yards farther down the road, the lead tank was again fired upon by two machine guns emplaced along the side of the road. Returning the fire with bow and coaxial machine guns, the tank commander moved his tank forward and crushed the machine guns into the road. The enemy crews left their guns and escaped.
>
> Pushing on to the junction of the unimproved road and the Goucherie–St. Jean de Daye highway, Lieutenant Gundrum sent a dismounted party forward to reconnoiter the road junction, revealing a 57mm antitank gun concealed and in position, covering both avenues of approach. The dismounted party moved in and killed the crew with small-arms fire and occupied the position.[34]

★★★

Capturing St. Lo was the last necessary preparatory step that Bradley needed to stage a massive breakout. By 18 July, at a horrendous cost in casualties, the 29th Infantry Division had come within a couple thousand yards of the city. Major General Charles Gerhardt, commanding, a day earlier had created Task Force C, a reference to its commander, Gerhardt's deputy Brig. Gen. Norman Cota. The task force consisted of the 3d Platoon, 29th Reconnaissance Troop; five M4 Shermans from the 747th Tank Battalion; and ten M10s from the 821st Tank Destroyer Battalion. By this time, recalled Lt. Edward Jones, who had just taken command of the troop, "most of the unit had more or less reached a point of not caring from one day to the next what might happen, just so long as we did not let the others down. We had been in constant operations for over 40 days, suffered heavy casualties, been operational both night and day. . . ."[35]

The infantry attack was going so well on 18 July that Gerhardt before noon ordered the task force to advance along the Isigny–St. Lo road, followed by a battalion of infantry. The task force moved out early in the afternoon, with the cavalry in the lead. "We moved very fast," recalled Jones. "We were sniped at by Germans and by some elements of the 115th [Infantry] when we passed through their zone. We had casualties right away. . . . I radioed, lay them beside the road, let the medical detachment which was to follow up take care of them. . . ."[36]

Lieutenant Thomas Fernley commanded the 3d Platoon and was one of the army's "90-day wonders," a young man of about twenty.[37] Fernley described the entry into St. Lo:

> We reached the outskirts of the city before we encountered any real resistance. . . . As the column started up the long hill leading into the city, it came under strong small-arms fire from entrenched infantry at the top. There was nothing to do but go ahead and hope they didn't have any antitank guns. Luckily, they did not, and the M8s started to grind up the shell-pocked road to their destination. Half a dozen times we stopped and used our .50-caliber machine guns and 37s with devastating effect. . . .
>
> Firing all the time, we gradually approached within 20 yards of the main enemy positions at St. Lo. Then suddenly, the German resistance broke.
>
> We entered the city proper. It was the most thoroughly devastated, ruined city that I have ever seen.[38]

The troopers helped repel a counterattack, then patrolled through the deep rubble on foot. Late that night, the green 125th Cavalry Reconnaissance Squadron arrived to relieve the 29th Recon Troop. The exhausted veterans told them about antitank guns they had spotted. "They sent out armored groups who went right down the road into the muzzles of the [antitank guns] we had told them about," recalled Lt. Edward Jones. "They lost several jeeps and armored cars—I suppose they thought they would scare the enemy to death. . . . Their funeral—not mine."[39]

CHAPTER 7

THE BREAKOUT FROM NORMANDY

*Mechanized cavalry was designed and created to perform the type of missions which
were assigned to the squadron during the month of September. . . .*

—AAR, 38th Cavalry Reconnaissance Squadron

Lieutenant General Omar Bradley's plan to break out of the Normandy
stalemate with his First Army was dubbed Operation Cobra. Major General
J. Lawton Collins' VII Corps was to make the main effort in the American
center immediately west of St. Lo, with the 83d and 9th Infantry divisions on
the left, the 30th Infantry Division in the center, and the 29th Infantry Division
on the right to protect the flank. Once a penetration had been achieved, the
motorized 1st Infantry Division, with Combat Command B from the 3d
Armored Division attached, was to exploit four miles southward to Marigny,
then turn west ten miles to Coutances, on the coast, to cut off the German left
wing. The remainder of the 3d Armored Division, with a 1st Infantry Division
rifle battalion attached, was to secure the southern exits from Coutances. The
2d Armored Division, with the motorized 22d Infantry Regiment attached,
was to drive through the gap and establish more blocking positions. XIX and V
corps were to launch smaller attacks to pin the Germans in place along their
fronts east of VII Corps, while VIII Corps pushed southward down the coast
to the west to destroy the German left wing after delaying just long enough for
VII Corps' action to be felt.[1] To the rear, Lt. Gen. George S. Patton Jr.'s Third
Army bided its time, ready to explode into France.

The Germans had also suffered terrible losses during the hedgerow
fighting, and those losses were not nearly being replaced. The Germans were
stretched thin and were vulnerable to Bradley's concentration of his forces.
Moreover, Gen. Bernard Montgomery's Operation Goodwood around Caen,
initiated on 18 July, had drawn off most of the German armored strength to

face the Commonwealth troops, leaving only a much-weakened Panzer Lehr Division facing VII Corps and the 2d SS Panzer and 17th SS Panzergrenadier divisions opposite VIII Corps.

Cavalry Ingenuity

The brainchild of a cavalry trooper has gone into popular lore as giving American armor a decisive edge in mobility through the *bocage* during the

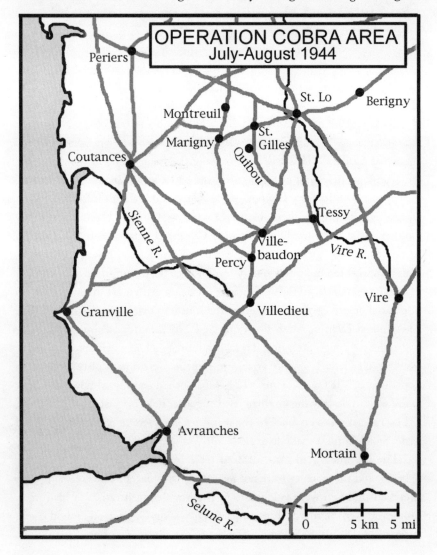

breakout in late July, although similar devices were designed by others in Normandy even earlier. Sergeant Curtis Culin, of the 102d Cavalry Reconnaissance Squadron, designed a contraption made from steel girders from German beach defenses. It amounted to a set of steel teeth protruding from the nose of the tank and could be mounted on tanks or tank destroyers. The teeth allowed the vehicle to grip and plow through a hedgerow up to six to seven feet deep with hardly any loss of speed. Vehicles outfitted with the Culin device were called Rhinos. After seeing one in action, Lt. Gen. Omar Bradley ordered that all tanks be fitted with them for the upcoming offensive.[2]

Tank battalions and cavalry squadrons hurriedly installed the devices during the second half of July in preparation for Operation Cobra. The use of the Rhino in combat was barred until the big attack in order to maintain tactical surprise.[3] By the time the breakout began, 60 percent of the tanks involved had been fitted with Culin devices.[4] In the 6th Cavalry Reconnaissance Squadron, every tank received the attachment.[5]

Escape from the Hedgerows

Following an abortive attempt to launch Cobra on 24 July that resulted in the bombing of American lines by Allied aircraft, VII Corps kicked into gear the next day, disregarding additional "friendly" bombings of its line. Fifteen hundred B-17 and B-24 heavy bombers from the U.S. Eighth Air Force dropped more than 3,300 tons of bombs in a 2,500-yard by 6,000-yard box in front of VII Corps. More than 550 fighter-bombers from the IX Tactical Air Command (TAC) dropped more than 200 tons of bombs and a large amount of napalm, while 396 B-26 medium bombers unloaded more than 650 tons of high explosive and fragmentation bombs.[6]

Carpet-bombing had a devastating impact on the Panzer Lehr Division, which stood in the way of VII Corps. *Generalleutnant* (two stars) Fritz Bayerlein, commanding, recalled, "The digging in of the infantry was useless and did not protect against bombing as the bombed area had been turned into a terrain pitted with craters. Dugouts and foxholes were smashed, the men buried, and we were unable to save them. The same happened to guns and tanks. . . . For me, who during this war was in every theater committed at the points of the main effort, this was the worst I ever saw."[7]

Despite the fact that most of the carpet-bombing hit its intended targets, the Germans fought stubbornly, and for the first day and a half progress was glacially slow. Collins decided on 26 July to commit his mobile forces, despite the failure to capture objectives that he had originally deemed necessary to permit use of his exploitation force. His timing was impeccable because the German fabric had begun to tear.[8]

Ripping the Hole Wide Open

Collins sent two armored columns driving south into the guts of the disintegrating German defenses on the afternoon of 26 July. On the right, Maj. Gen. Clarence Huebner's 1st Infantry Division (motorized) with Combat Command B, 3d Armored Division, attached, was to pass through the 9th Infantry Division and capture Marigny. Major General Edward "Ted" Brooks' 2d Armored Division, with the 4th Infantry Division's 22d Infantry Regiment attached, was to drive south and east on the left, passing through the 30th Infantry Division to seize St. Gilles.[9] The reader will recall that the 2d and 3d Armored divisions had not reorganized into "light" armored divisions, and with an infantry regiment attached, each of the heavy divisions wielded a combat power nearly twice that of a light one.

★★★

The 4th Cavalry Reconnaissance Squadron was to screen the advance of the 1st Infantry Division toward Marigny, maintain contact with the 9th Infantry Division on the right, and establish communication with the 3d Armored Division's CCB to the south. The squadron, less Troop C, rolled out as planned and linked up with the 39th Infantry Regiment, but it was unable to locate the armored combat command, which was advancing faster than expected. Indeed, CCB had outpaced the infantry and was rolling south on a front no wider than the hedgerow to each side of the main road, and the Germans filled in the hole when the last vehicles had passed.

The 1st Platoon of the Reconnaissance Company, 33d Armored Regiment, led CCB's advance on 26 July. The two heavy armored divisions, the reader will recall, included a reconnaissance company within each armored regiment, which operated separately from the armored reconnaissance battalions. Lieutenant K. M. Rothmeyer's platoon set off at the point at about 0700 hours, equipped with four jeeps, four M8 armored cars, two trucks, and one ammunition carrier. The recon men raced through occasional small-arms fire until reaching Montreuil, where they spotted a self-propelled gun on one side of the road and a Mark IV on the other.

For the first time in the war, the armored divisions had established a fairly well-oiled method for working with their tactical air support, and the recon men put the capability to good use. Responding to a radio summons, a flight of P-47s pounced on and destroyed the self-propelled gun. The demonstration evidently was frightening enough that the panzer crew bailed out and took off.

After scooping up a mixed bag of prisoners, including paratroopers and SS, the platoon rolled southward toward Marigny. Per instructions, the point cut cross-country to bypass Marigny to the west, and by 2000 hours Rothmeyer's men had reached Gruchy, where they encountered mortar and artillery fire. The lieutenant turned around to retrace his path and reestablish contact with the main column; German infantry ambushed the platoon and destroyed two jeeps with panzerfausts, but the remainder of the patrol made it through.

The 2d Platoon, on hearing of Rothmeyer's plight over the radio, raced forward at full speed to help, raking the hedgerows on both sides of the road with machine-gun fire, but the platoon ran into a second ambuscade. Mines planted after Rothmeyer's command had passed destroyed one jeep and an assault gun, and the 2d Platoon fought for its life from ditches and hedgerows. At the critical moment, the 1st Platoon arrived and took the Germans from the rear. Rothmeyer was wounded in the fight. The arrival of friendly medium tanks effectively ended the struggle, although mortar concentrations continued to drop on the recon men for some time.

The following morning, Troop A, 4th Cavalry Reconnaissance Squadron, also bypassed Marigny, which was still defended by the Germans, and attempted to push south on the main road to find CCB. One platoon encountered small-arms, mortar, and antitank fire from a group of buildings west of Marigny and called up the assault guns to help out. Because the strongpoint looked like a tough one, the remainder of the troop concentrated south of the buildings, and all but the 3d Platoon dismounted for the attack. When the troopers advanced on foot supported by the light tanks, a Mark IV appeared between two buildings and opened fire. The German gunner was good: He destroyed two M5A1s, two jeeps, and every other vehicle in the 3d Platoon except three armored cars. Five troopers were killed, eight were wounded, and four went missing. The squadron turned over the job to a reinforced infantry battalion from the 1st Infantry Division.

That same morning, 27 July, at 0700, Company D of the 83d Armored Reconnaissance Battalion, reinforced by a platoon of medium tanks, joined the 3d Armored Division's spearhead on the road to Coutances. Progress was rapid despite small-arms fire from all sides. A flight of P-47s was assigned to assist the spearhead, and at about 0800 the airmen spotted eight panzers near Marigny and went to work on them. At about 1000, the reconnaissance company encountered two self-propelled and two towed 75mm guns. "With cool deliberation," the combat command recorded in its after-action report, "they outflanked the guns, knocked them out, took 12 prisoners, and pressed forward again." The column used tank dozers to fill the bomb craters that occasionally held it up. As dusk approached, the combat command ordered a halt to allow the infantry to catch up.[10]

On 28 and 29 July, the Germans succeeded in building a masterful ad hoc defensive line running north to south parallel to the coast. The line denied the 1st Infantry and 3d Armored divisions—even with the commitment of CCA on 28 July—their objective at Coutances. This allowed the bulk of the units north of the town to slip the noose and escape to man a ramshackle east-west line that was thrown together about ten miles to the south.[11]

★★★

Brigadier General Maurice Rose's CCA led the 2d Armored Division advance as the second column punched south toward St. Gilles on 26 July against sporadic resistance. The combat command rolled through St. Gilles by midafternoon, and therewith the breakout from Normandy was guaranteed.[12]

The 24th Cavalry Reconnaissance Squadron was attached to the 2d Armored Division on 27 July. To reach the command, it had to drive through the area that had been carpet-bombed. The troopers slipped around Mark IV and Mark V tanks, some of them still burning, from the hapless Panzer Lehr Division. Half-tracks and trucks were strewn along the roads, and craters slowed the squadron's progress. Late in the day, the squadron was split among two task forces to reconnoiter in force toward Tessy sur Vire and Villebaudon. Both task forces encountered vigorous German delaying actions, and the squadron spent the next several days operating in that area.[13]

During the afternoon of 27 July, Maj. Gen. Edward Brooks issued orders to his Combat Command B to swing to the coast well south of Coutances, an order destined to compensate for the Germans' success over the next two days in holding back the 1st Infantry and 3d Armored divisions. The combat command set off in two columns, the 82d Armored Reconnaissance Battalion in the lead.[14] For battalion commander Lt. Col. Wheeler Merriam, this mission was just the type that he and his troopers relished: a high-speed reconnaissance in and behind the enemy with many opportunities to disorganize the enemy's rear.[15]

The armored reconnaissance battalion staged a classic envelopment at this point. Merriam ordered his men to avoid pitched battles and to disengage from fights as quickly as they could, for the aim was speed. Company B took the lead, and on the road out of Laisney toward Quibou it spotted four Panther tanks. Because 37mm rounds bounced harmlessly off the panzers, the company raced by them at full speed, a nerve-racking ploy that cost one assault gun. Company A, following, spent two hours scouting with bazookas trying to find the Panther that had fired the killing shot because the rest of the column would soon be coming down the same road. Failing to find it, the company set off again. As the lead jeep rounded a blind turn, it nearly ran into the Panther. The cavalrymen bailed out, and the Mark V backed away and eventually disappeared to the east under fire from the company.

At Quibou, the armored reconnaissance troopers ran into a roadblock. Part of the advance guard pinned the Germans in place, and other elements worked their way around the flank. Self-propelled howitzers attached to the spearhead opened up, while fighter-bombers dive-bombed a German-held ridge nearby. Resistance collapsed under this combined-arms assault.

The reconnaissance troops soon charged through Dangy. In one building a few yards off the road *Generalleutnant* Fritz Bayerlein was holding a staff meeting in the joint headquarters of his Panzer Lehr and the 275th Infantry divisions. Upon witnessing the mechanized cavalry race by, Bayerlein reported that his division had been completely annihilated.

Combat Command B early on 28 July received orders to advance only as far as the Sienne River to avoid overextension. Once again the mechanized cavalrymen took the lead. The troopers sped by surprised German troops at fifty miles per hour and by evening had captured five bridges across the Sienne. Soon the rest of CCB thundered into the sector. The division had successfully trapped much of German LXXXIV Corps, which was destroyed over the next few days by air strikes and the closing jaws of VII and VIII corps.[16]

Earl Mazo was a correspondent for the *Stars and Stripes* who rode with the 82d Armored Reconnaissance Battalion during its dash. He reported on 30 July:

> Our recon unit, which raced to the Sienne [River] in advance of a heavy armored column, fought every inch of the way against tanks, assault guns, and pockets of infantry, but always moving towards the sea. Advanced patrols reached the Sienne earlier but had to pull back because of the weight of the large number of German Tiger tanks [sic—there were no Tigers] fleeing in their direction from the north. Scores of those tanks are now out of the war, pounded to pieces by the Air Force. . . .
>
> Although contact with friendly armored units was made, fighting is going on today all along the western half of the line this division is holding, like a drawn noose around a sack. . . .
>
> Overhead, little Cub planes, known as the 2d Armored Stukas, were the reconnaissance for the reconnaissance. These Cubs, radioed into action from the command half-tracks, spotted enemy tanks, guns, and infantry as close as 200 yards from our forward armored cars. Their aid was invaluable.[17]

The breakdown of German resistance became evident in front of the 3d Armored Division on 30 August as well, when Companies A and B, 83d Armored Reconnaissance Battalion, advanced easily to bridges over the Sienne and captured some five hundred prisoners.[18]

★★★

VIII Corps, meanwhile, had been pushing directly down the coast. The 106th Cavalry Group had been deployed between the 90th and 83d Infantry divisions in the VIII Corps line when it kicked off on 25 July. Part of the 106th Cavalry Reconnaissance Squadron got its first taste of operating in the assault role in the hedgerows when a platoon from Company F was attached to the 330th Infantry Regiment. The outfit's informal history recorded:

> It was to be our first job, and everybody was a little uneasy.
>
> The engineers blew a hole in the hedgerow, and Lt. [John] Carruthers led us through. The platoon fanned out beautifully and streaked for the next bank with the company of infantry strung out

behind. It was amazing how far the guns could be depressed. We literally dug the enemy out of each hole. After the first row was cleared we didn't stop but continued on to the next and next barrier until we were on the battalion objective.

The platoon was very successful and was credited with killing 60 enemy, destroying 12 machine-gun nests and one antitank gun.[19]

The 4th and 6th Armored divisions took the lead on 28 August, and 4th Armored Division elements established rolling contact with the VII Corps formations along the Sienne. The 121st Cavalry Reconnaissance Squadron operated on the right flank along the coast, while the 106th Cavalry Reconnaissance Squadron fought attached to the 83d Infantry Division on the corps' left. The VIII Corps drive continued toward Avranches, the capture of which would open central France and Brittany to exploitation.[20]

The 6th Armored Division employed its 86th Cavalry Reconnaissance Squadron in classic fashion ahead of the combat commands. The recon men were the first in the division to engage the enemy in combat on 28 July while reconnoitering the routes to the Sienne River.[21]

The 4th Armored Division's 25th Cavalry Reconnaissance Squadron trailed the combat commands during the fighting advance. But near Avranches, Troop D on 31 July received orders to take and outpost the area southwest of the city. "This was the first offensive action our troops had seen," the squadron recorded, "and it was reconnaissance in force. They advanced by firing on all probable targets." At one point, Company F light tanks ran into bigger, tougher panzers and infantry with panzerfausts, but timely intervention by P-47 Thunderbolts knocked out the tanks and scattered the enemy. In Avranches itself, Capt. Murray Farmer found his light tank suddenly face-to-face with a Panther. The quick-thinking captain ordered his driver to charge until the two tanks rammed, which prevented the panzer from annihilating the M5A1 with its 75mm gun. The Panther tried to back away but slipped off the road and rolled over, and the confounded German crew bailed out and escaped.[22]

The 4th Armored Division cleared Avranches that day, and the lead elements of the 6th Armored Division filled in behind them. Patton's Third Army was to become operational the next morning and absorb VIII Corps. The stage was set for one of the greatest episodes in modern mechanized warfare.

★★★

On 1 August, on the left shoulder of the breakout, the 4th Cavalry Reconnaissance Squadron, still attached to the 4th Infantry Division, captured the strategic
road hub of Villedieu, which the German commanders viewed along with
Avranches as the keys to any American success.[23] Troop B hooked around
the end of friendly lines and rolled into Villedieu against scattered resistance. The
troop reported that the roads from the west and south were open, so Troops A
and C followed the same route. Anticipating a German counterattack to recoup
this loss, Lt. Col. John Rhoades, the squadron commander, deployed Troops A
and B, supported by light tanks and assault guns, in defensive positions on high
ground to the west and in the northern and eastern outskirts of town.

The Germans hit Troop A's positions in eastern Villedieu in company
strength during the evening. The M8 assault guns engaged panzers for the first
time in the squadron's experience and knocked out one Mark IV, an armored car,
and a half-track in exchange for the loss of one assault gun. The German infantry
fell back, but renewed attacks hit the cavalry lines three more times. At 2330
hours, the 4th Infantry Division relieved the squadron with a reinforced infantry
battalion.[24] The cavalry had taken and held a strategic objective until relieved.

A Pure Assault Role

The breakout was costly for the cavalry outfits that were committed to V
Corps' subsidiary attack to pin the Germans in place while VII Corps tore
through their line farther west.

The 102d Cavalry Reconnaissance Squadron was attached to the 2d
Infantry Division, which on 26 July kicked off as part of V Corps' attack. The
day started well enough, with Company F's light tanks participating in a "sortie"
adjacent to the 741st Tank Battalion. The after-action report of the 741st Tank
Battalion described the operation:

> With the new [Rhino] device, it was felt that the unit would be
> enabled to operate with more freedom, as the hedges were much less
> an obstacle than they had been before. . . .
>
> The Commanding General, 2d Infantry Division, after confer-
> ring with Lieutenant Colonel Skaggs, conceived a plan for the use of
> tanks in the next attack that would very nearly approximate the
> manner of using tanks in open country suited for tank combat. This
> plan, which came to be called a sortie, involved the maximum number of

tanks, equipped with the Rhino device, that could be brought into position, allowing for the variation of the terrain. In most cases the full number of tanks could be used. The tanks would be placed in position at the line of departure and the infantry elements withdrawn several hundred yards [to the] rear, for safety purposes. At H hour a barrage of timed fire would be laid down over an area from 300 to 500 yards in depth past the [line of departure]. The tanks would advance rapidly under the airbursts, smashing hedges and uprooting enemy emplacements in the zone of action, at the same time placing a maximum amount of direct cannon and machine gun fire on the enemy. After breaking the enemy defenses the tanks would return to the line of departure, establish contact with supporting infantry, and resume the attack with the infantry-tank team.

On 26 July, 1944, at 0600, this battalion attacked in support of the 38th and 23d Infantry regiments, with the line of departure south of the St. Lo–Berigny road. . . .

The attack started on schedule and the tanks smashed through the hedges on the tank sortie. With their cannons blasting and machine guns stuttering, the tanks were an awe-inspiring spectacle as they churned their way through the enemy positions after a crashing barrage of timed fire. The enemy was obviously stunned by the ferocity of the attack, as not a single tank was lost on the initial sortie. Hundreds of German infantrymen were killed as they lay in their foxholes, and then ground under the tracks of the onrushing tanks. Machine gun emplacements were ripped out of the hedges by the impact of the Rhino devices, and the enemy lines, to a distance of 300 to 500 yards, were a shambles.

At H+20 [minutes] the tanks returned from the sortie, joined the infantry half of the team and resumed the onslaught at H+30.[25]

Troop E's assault guns participated in the covering barrage for the sortie.

After the sortie, the squadron pushed off with the infantry, and despite the damage inflicted in the tank raid, the Germans mounted a ferocious resistance. Troop A lost four of its five officers in the dismounted hedgerow fight over the next two days, and both the squadron commander and his executive officer were wounded.

The 2d Division's reconnaissance troop during these encounters operated in the gap between the attacking regiments and rooted out pockets of bypassed resistance. "The men in this organization," recorded the troop's executive officer, "are very aggressive in their work, not slow in returning enemy fire, and are not afraid to use [the] firepower that we have to the fullest advantage."[26]

By 31 July, V Corps had reached the Vire River, where German infantry held strong positions on the far bank. The 102d Squadron was given Hill 204 as its objective for 2 August. Troop B, supported by light tanks and assault guns, crossed the river first; it was to swing to the left, and Troop A was to follow, swing right, and attack the German flank.

Troop B's advance stalled three-quarters of the way up the hill in the face of intense fire. Three M5A1s were destroyed, and many other vehicles were either knocked out or immobilized. Troop A's flanking move pried the Germans off the height, but by the time the action was over, the troopers had lost thirty-three men, and some platoons had to be completely re-equipped.[27]

★★★

The 38th Cavalry Reconnaissance Squadron (less Troop B), also attached to the 2d Infantry Division, participated in the tank sortie on 26 July before pushing off across the St. Lo road. Despite the crushing impact of bombardment and tank sortie, the Germans fought for the very first hedgerow. Squadron commander Lt. Col. John Lee was wounded within the first thirty minutes of action. The troopers took the hedgerow, but almost immediately a powerful artillery and mortar barrage dropped on them. Casualties were heavy, and a German counterattack drove the cavalrymen back to their starting positions. Troop A, 102d Cavalry Reconnaissance Squadron, was attached, and the dogged cavalrymen crossed the same ground and retook the hedgerow. The squadron had lost 108 men during the fight, and only four of the seventeen light tanks were still in action, the remainder having been hit or become stuck in the hedgerows. Troop B in the meantime had accomplished the difficult task of storming a town in the 5th Infantry Division's zone.

The squadron advanced in the direction of Vire as the Germans withdrew, and on 3 August conducted a pursuit to reestablish contact with the enemy. The troopers did so at Optive, where a dug-in force engaged the point with small arms and artillery. Troop C sought to circle around the enemy, but the nut was too tough to crack, and the troopers were recalled to allow the 2d Division's infantry and medium tanks to clear the way.[28]

Mechanized Correspondents
Anticipating fast-moving operations over wide spaces in the near future, Patton gave the 6th Cavalry Group an unusual assignment, code-named Operation Unicorn, effective 1 August. The group was to function as Third Army's "Army Information Service," its mission being to field a system of radio-equipped liaison patrols to report to the Third Army G-3 the dispositions of and opposition to

forward regiments, battalions, and combat commands across the entire front, bypassing all command channels. The 6th Cavalry Reconnaissance Squadron, for example, attached small units to XX Corps, the 5th Armored and French 2d Armored divisions, and the 35th Infantry Division.[29]

The 6th Cavalry Group rotated its two squadrons so that each performed information services every other month. This left a squadron available for ad hoc reconnaissance and security duties.[30] The group's role earned it the nickname "Patton's Household Cavalry."

The Great Race

Cobra had opened the door for the mechanized cavalry to gallop. Even though the next six weeks would be the test under laboratory-perfect conditions for the new cavalry doctrine, the idea that mechanized cavalry should conduct reconnaissance by stealth and not force of arms looked suspect at the end of the race.

The Conquest of Brittany

Patton on 1 August ordered VIII Corps to make a sharp right turn onto the Brittany Peninsula in accordance with Operation Overlord plans that anticipated using captured Breton ports to supply the Allied armies. Patton intended first to drive through Rennes to Quiberon Bay to cut the peninsula at its base, then drive up the central plateau and pen German forces into coastal fortresses. VIII Corps' wide-open left flank was to be screened by patrols from the 106th Cavalry Group.

A three-pronged mechanized force, trailed by infantry divisions as quickly as they could move, surged onto the peninsula. The 4th Armored Division led the advance on Rennes, the 6th Armored Division slashed up the middle toward Brest, and the provisional Task Force A rolled toward Brest along the rail line that generally follows the north coast. Other divisions followed through the Avranches choke point, ready to strike eastward toward the Seine river.[31]

★★★

The 4th Armored Division pushed off first on 1 August and covered the forty miles to Rennes' northern outskirts by evening.[32] The 25th Cavalry Reconnaissance Squadron operated between the combat commands instead of in front of them and acted as a communications hub to keep the far-flung elements in contact.

Upon reaching the city, the 4th Armored Division employed the squadron in blocking positions southwest of Rennes to destroy any enemy force attempting to flee during its capture.[33] The combat commands left the assault on the city to the attached 13th Infantry Regiment, 8th Infantry Division—which was hustling forward in trucks—and swept around Rennes to the west, ultimately setting up blocking positions to the southeast. The 13th Infantry stormed the city late on 3 August. Surrounded and their lines penetrated, the defenders exfiltrated along secondary roads toward St. Nazaire that night. On 5 August the 4th Armored Division—its orders relayed directly from Patton by the Household Cavalry, and somewhat delayed by gasoline shortages—reached the coast at Vannes.[34]

The 8th Reconnaissance Troop, meanwhile, must have thought it had taken a wrong turn toward heaven. An informal history of the outfit recorded, "[T]he Troop had the mission of protecting the right flank of the division until at Rennes, France, the best mission was assigned the troop. It was there we were given the mission of going to Chateaubriant to block all roads and keep tab on some eighteen thousand Germans who had been reported massing along the Loire River. Being some forty miles from the nearest help made the situation uncomfortable, but it had its advantages. For seven days the troop enjoyed the hospitality of the French population, especially the girls. It was there that some fifty thousand cases of cognac, wines, and other spiritous drinks were uncovered in a warehouse abandoned by the Germans."[35]

★★★

The 6th Armored Division, in the center, passed through the Avranches bottleneck on 1 August and advanced fifteen miles to the Cousenon River. There it successfully established a bridgehead, which it expanded the next day.[36] Patton on 1 August had concisely told Maj. Gen. Robert Grow, commanding, "Take Brest." In five days, Patton added. Grow delighted that he had been given a cavalry mission by a cavalryman.[37]

The 86th Cavalry Reconnaissance Squadron had landed in France on 24 July, been committed to action four days later, and had not until now operated in a true reconnaissance role. There were teething problems, and they showed up in the first few days. Radios had not been tested, and in once case no frequencies were assigned. The squadron had no maps. Coordination with CCB was excellent, but it was almost nonexistent with CCA. All of these problems had to be sorted out during an advance so rapid that the cavalrymen were unable to conduct what they considered to be thorough reconnaissance.

With German forces on the peninsula trying to get to the fortress ports along the coast, the 86th Cavalry Reconnaissance Squadron encountered only scattered resistance, though occasionally the resulting fight was intense. By 8 August the 6th Armored Division was in position to attack Brest. In only ten days, the 86th Cavalry Reconnaissance Squadron and the rest of the division had covered 250 miles.[38] The cavalrymen were assigned to patrol the perimeters that had been established around Brest and Lorient, on the south coast, while VIII Corps readied to assault the former.[39] Brest would withstand concerted assault by several divisions until 19 September.

★★★

Troop C, followed by the rest of the 17th Cavalry Reconnaissance Squadron, set off on 1 August at 0100 hours through the streets of Avranches, then swung west along the coast road into Brittany, its armored cars and jeeps harassed occasionally by strafing German aircraft. The 15th Cavalry Reconnaissance Squadron followed close behind. The 15th Cavalry Group that morning formed the spearhead of Task Force A, commanded by Brig. Gen. Herbert Earnest, which was to drive toward St. Malo and secure key railroad bridges along the coast. The task force, under the control of the 1st Tank Destroyer Brigade, consisted of the 15th Cavalry Group, the 705th Tank Destroyer Battalion, and a company of engineers.

The cavalry made first contact with the enemy at a roadblock east of Dol at 0710 hours in the worst possible way; the Germans destroyed most of the lead platoon's vehicles and caused many casualties. The cavalry group commander, who was riding with the point, went missing, and the platoon commander was killed. The 15th Squadron swung ahead to the left and found a bypass route, and the advance got under way again. By evening the task force had reached St. Malo, which the Germans clearly intended to hold. Artillery and mortar fire disorganized the cavalrymen, radios failed at crucial moments, and commanders lost control of their units. The new group commander, Col. Logan Berry, called a halt at 2100 hours and ordered his squadrons to reorganize.

The cavalry, supported closely by tank destroyers and engineers, failed to make much headway the next day against German troops backed by shore batteries, mobile 88s, and river gunboats. That evening the lead elements of the 83d Infantry Division arrived to deal with the defenses. Before Task Force A backed off, the 17th Squadron, with the help of fire from the tank destroyers, on 5 August finally managed to eject the Germans from Chateauneuf, which they had defended stoutly.

On 6 August the task force slipped away from St. Malo and headed west. The mechanized cavalry's first job was to capture three bridges at St. Brieuc, including a crucial railroad span. The 15th Cavalry Reconnaissance Squadron reached Brieuc after fighting a series of skirmishes with scattered German formations that appeared to be trying to withdraw to St. Malo.

At Brieuc, the troopers discovered that the Resistance, organized by British officers, had cleared the town and secured the bridges. A hostile force estimated at a thousand men was holed up in some nearby woods. On 7 August, after calling in air strikes, Colonel Berry used the 15th Squadron to apply pressure to the Germans from the front while the 17th Squadron enveloped them to the south, an operation that killed or captured most of the defending force. The following day, Task Force A secured the last crucial railroad bridge at Morlaix, and its job of exploitation was done. The task force then turned back to help eliminate pockets of bypassed resistance along the coast.[40]

★★★

With action on the peninsula settling down to siege warfare, the 4th Armored Division in mid-month headed east to join Third Army's charge to the German border. The 15th Cavalry Group also headed east in mid-September to screen Third Army's long open flank along the Loire River, but it would return to Brittany in January 1945 to contain St. Nazaire.

Charge!

Commanders on both sides knew that the game had changed, producing disaster or almost unimagined opportunity, depending on one's perspective. Twelve hours after the American capture of Avranches, Field Marshal Günther von Kluge signaled Berlin from the German Seventh Army headquarters, "As a result of the breakthrough of the enemy armored spearheads, the whole Western front has been ripped open. . . . The left flank has collapsed." On 2 August, VII Corps captured Mortain, which was to be the pivot point for a sweep through northern France. Bradley, who had taken charge of the newly activated 12th Army Group on 1 August, ordered Patton on 3 August to leave the minimum necessary force in Brittany and to throw the weight of Third Army toward Le Mans. Montgomery, who still commanded all Allied ground forces in France, issued a bold order the next day: "Once a gap appears in the enemy front, we must press into it and beyond it into the enemy's rear areas. Everyone must go all out all day and every day. The broad strategy of the

Allied forces is to swing the right flank towards Paris and to force the enemy back to the Seine."[41]

★★★

While First Army dealt with a German counterattack early on 6 August at Mortain, aimed at closing the hole at Avranches, Patton's Third Army took the lead in driving deep into the German rear. Patton, on the night of 3–4 August, ordered Maj. Gen. Wade Haislip's XV Corps, which had been activated on 31 July, to race to Mayenne, there to be ready to move north or northeast on army order.[42]

Conditions for exploitation were perfect: German Seventh Army had prepared no security measures in its rear areas, which were covered by under-strength guard troops of the Military Commander Southwestern France. Static battalions consisting mainly of overage personnel protected bridges, headquarters, and communications centers. Remnants of Panzer Lehr had pulled back to the Alencon area, east of Mayenne, for rehabilitation, although that was prevented by unforeseen events. Otherwise, only a few "Ostbattalions"manned by former Soviet troops near Mayenne and an antiaircraft division spread from Mortain to Domfront posed the only speed bumps in the road. The 9th Panzer and 708th Infantry divisions were allocated to cover Seventh Army's southern wing, but they were still en route to the area. Moreover, as late as 4 August, German commanders misinterpreted XV Corps' role, thinking the Corps was going to screen operations in Brittany.[43]

XV Corps drove south out of Normandy, then turned toward Paris. The 106th Cavalry Group, which had been screening VIII Corps' left flank until it was attached to XV Corps on 3 August, peeled off on 5 August to lead the XV Corps advance. That day, Patton learned from Bradley's staff that XV Corps was to continue its drive past Mayenne to Le Mans.[44] A task force spearheaded by the 2d Platoon, 90th Cavalry Reconnaissance Troop, easily reached Mayenne on 5 August. Only fifty yards from the city limits, antitank guns destroyed two armored cars and killed five men, but the task force eliminated the problem and established a bridgehead across the river. The neighboring 79th Infantry Division ran into German tanks near Laval and was unable to quite keep the pace.[45]

The 106th Cavalry Group advanced within both division zones. The troopers encountered small delaying forces armed with a few antitank guns, mortars, or machine guns. At Gorron, however, Troop A, 106th Cavalry Reconnaissance

Squadron, encountered a panzer that forced a hasty withdrawal by the lead jeep. So much for stealth. Captain John Winkler called forward a section of assault guns to deal with the problem. The outfit's informal history recorded:

> Sergeant Cecil Hitt carefully selected his position behind a thick hedgerow and beside a tree whose low-hanging branches afforded good concealment. It was necessary to cut away some of the branches to secure a good field of fire, and while Hitt was doing this, the German tank rolled into full view on the road leading into the town. Corporal Upton Staudinger, gunner in the section, waited only long enough to get the Jerry vehicle in his sights before firing the first round, and the muzzle blast blew Hitt to the other side of the hedgerow. . . .
>
> The entire fight lasted some 15 minutes, with Hitt and his crew coming out the victor. The E Troopers fired a total of 23 rounds at the Jerry tank and drew only three rounds in return. . . . Unfortunately, the German vehicle was not knocked out, although Staudinger's marksmanship forced its withdrawal, and Troop A moved into Garron unmolested. . . .[46]

On 7 August, XV Corps reached Le Mans, led by elements of the 106th Cavalry Group, which entered the city but were driven out after capturing a hundred prisoners. The 79th Division's 313th Infantry moved in that evening and cleared out the resistance the next day.

The just-disembarked 80th Infantry Division's reconnaissance troop arrived near Le Mans at the head of the division early on 9 April. It recorded in its history, "We went busting down the road to Le Mans damn confident of ourselves until we began passing burning tanks and freshly killed Krauts. Upon reaching the outskirts of the city and finding a battle still in progress, we pulled off the road and laid around watching elements of the 90th Division flushing hordes of enemy out of nearby bushes without realizing we were lounging around almost in the midst of a heavy battle."[47]

Patton ordered the corps to turn north on 9 August, a maneuver that would lead to the creation of the Falaise Pocket and, with First Army pressure from the south and Canadian attacks from the north, the destruction of most of the encircled German Seventh Army. The 106th Cavalry Group screened the corps' right flank and faced no real opposition during the decisive advance to Argentan, which cavalry elements reached on 12 August. On 14 August, XV Corps received orders to continue its push eastward with half its divisions.[48]

★★★

XX Corps, executing orders issued on 6 August, slid in on XV Corps' right and directed its efforts at the Seine river just south of Paris. The corps captured Angers on 9–10 August and pivoted eastward, at which time it took control of the 3d Cavalry Group.[49]

That race across France was sometimes quite dangerous for the men in the very first vehicles to enter every new mile of heretofore enemy-held territory. The wild ride of the 43d Cavalry Reconnaissance Squadron is representative of the experiences of many mechanized cavalry outfits.

Colonel Frederick Drury, commanding the 3d Cavalry Group, noted with relief during the drive to the corps headquarters on 10 August that the terrain was changing from hedgerows to wide-open spaces broken by occasional patches of woods. It looked ideal for mechanized cavalry, though the maps showed many rivers and streams farther east.

The group's first assignment was to establish contact between XX Corps and First Army, to the north. First Army was swinging northeastward to help trap the German Seventh Army. XX Corps was to provide flank protection for the encirclement. That part was easy, relatively speaking. A scrap with German 88s at Jublain on 12 August cost the squadron its first light tank, but fighting through traffic jams was perhaps the greatest hindrance to accomplishing the mission.

XX Corps on 14 August received a new mission: to pivot on Le Mans and strike northeastward to the Seine river near Paris. At 1830 hours, Lt. Col. Leslie Cross, commanding the 43d Cavalry Reconnaissance Squadron, was told that his outfit would conduct reconnaissance across the entire corps front in a box roughly seventy-seven miles wide and some seventy miles deep. The 3d Cavalry Reconnaissance Squadron, the 48th Squadron's running mate in the cavalry group, was being sent to XII Corps to lead the 4th Armored Division's drive on Orleans.

Cross called his troop leaders together in the dark to issue his orders. The squadron was to roll the next morning three troops abreast: B on the left, A in the center, and C on the right. Troop B officers described how the troop advanced: "The troop moved in patrol formation . . . , that is, two jeeps out in front, followed by a light scout car, then a jeep, then three armored cars, and the rear brought up by two jeeps, in staggered formation of from 50- to 75-yard intervals between vehicles, the two front jeeps being about 200 yards apart but at all times remaining within eyesight. The distance and the formation of the vehicles varied according to the leader, who directed movements and formations by signal. The radio was not used during scouting, but when a message was to be sent back, one vehicle or radio jeep would drop back several miles covered by an armored car and send the message. . . . Usual movement was by leaps and bounds. The scout cars or advance jeeps would go ahead and reconnoiter, signal by arm movement for half the column to come forward while being covered by the remaining half, and then after the safe arrival of the first half of the column the remainder would follow. When information on the enemy was lacking, the [platoon] of approximately 40 men and two officers would split into two or sometimes, but rarely, three patrols and would advance in two or three columns with a rendezvous point never over three or four miles away. . . ."

Departing at 0700 hours, Troop B was surprised to be overtaken by the 87th Cavalry Reconnaissance Squadron of the 7th Armored Division, which pushed by and entered northern Chartres. That night the 3d Platoon watched the fighting from a bivouac on high ground nearby while Combat Command B stormed the city.

Troop B's 2d Platoon encountered the first enemy troops, about seventy-five men flushed from Chartres by the 7th Armored Division, at Gallardon. The Germans showed considerable fight, so the platoon lobbed 37mm shells at them and called for backup. The assault gun platoon arrived at about 1730 hours, and a pitched battle ensued, with the Germans trapped between the two forces. The 3d Platoon heard the shooting and joined the fray from a third direction, and soon thirty-seven of the enemy lay dead and seventeen were prisoners.

In the meantime, a section commanded by S.Sgt. Donald Krueger had charged toward Rambouillet. The troopers picked up a lost First Army 2 1/2-ton truck carrying engineers, and entered the town with Krueger's armored car in the lead, followed by the truck, a machine-gun jeep, and a mortar jeep.

Just as Krueger entered town, the enemy felled logs across the road, creating a barricade a foot and a half high. The column stopped, and a heavy machine gun at the roadblock opened fire. At the same time, a civilian car dashed up behind, slammed on its brakes, and ended up crossways on the road; the German driver jumped out and sprinted into nearby woods. Ambush!

Another heavy machine gun opened up from the left flank and sprayed the column with slugs. The mortar crew jumped out and tried to set up the tube, but three of the four men were killed. The engineers were jumping to the sides of the road, the lieutenant commanding falling mortally wounded. Grenades or panzerfausts were sure to follow soon; the key to surviving an ambush is to get out of the kill zone. Krueger engaged the flank machine gun and ordered his driver, Technician 5th Grade Ralph Schroeder, to floor it and smash the barrier.

Schroeder had the throttle wide open and the M8 moving at thirty-five miles per hour when the M8 hit the logs. The car went four feet into the air, tipped, and landed heavily, then careened down the street. An antitank round hit the armor, and shrapnel struck Schroeder's back, but he continued driving. He turned at the first corner.

Two Mark III tanks were coming straight at the troopers. Krueger fired his 37mm gun at the first one, and the German driver was so surprised that he turned sideways into a brick wall and blocked the second panzer.

Schroeder found a safer route, and the M8 raced onward. A German motorcyclist was the next victim, followed by a truck full of soldiers who lost an unequal fight with the .50-caliber. At this point, a Frenchman offered to show the crew a way out of town.

The M8 exited heading west, which was why the 88mm gun crew on the main highway had the weapon pointing the wrong way when the M8 approached. Krueger hit them with the 37mm, then the .50 caliber; the loss of two men spurred the remainder to vanish. Krueger dealt with three more emplaced guns in the same fashion as Schroeder drove down Highway N191. The crew made it back to troop headquarters, but the accounts do not reveal the fate of the lost engineers.

Troop A's day started badly when four P-47s strafed the rear guard and destroyed two jeeps and an armored car. The 1st Platoon ran into 20mm and 88mm guns at Illiers and was unable to get past until the next day. Troop C had its own problems, and progress was slow.

Lieutenant Colonel Cross was summoned to corps headquarters at 1800 hours. The chief of staff, Brig. Gen. William Collier, told Cross, "I want patrols on the Seine River by [tomorrow] night. This is not a reconnaissance mission. I want you to get there. It is over 60 miles into enemy territory, and we want to know what bridges or fords are available to us over the Seine."

The 2d and 3d platoons of Troop A reached the Seine at Ponthierry on the evening of 17 August. The troopers were 25 miles ahead of troop headquarters, which was in turn 12 miles in front of the closest ground combat unit. Since 10 August, the 43d Cavalry Reconnaissance Squadron had advanced 254 miles; it proudly recorded in a document produced for the theater historian, "In seven days, the 43d covered distances that would have won admiration in peacetime maneuvers, covering areas considered by all the manuals to be beyond the capabilities of the cavalry."[50]

★★★

Even the continuing nightmare of hedgerow fighting in the V Corps zone was coming to an end. German resistance gave way in front of the 2d Infantry Division, and on 15 August Lt. Col. Robert O'Brien, who had just taken charge of the 38th Cavalry Reconnaissance Squadron, ordered his men to seize the corps objective of Tinchebray, which lay five miles ahead and astride the boundary line between the American and British sectors. Troops C and E drove straight down the road that marked the inter-army group boundary, closely followed by British recce and a battalion of Coldstream Guard Churchill tanks, which had been ordered to attack down the same route. Troops B and F, meanwhile, rolled cross-country using their Rhinos to bust through the hedgerows, while Troop A used a secondary road.

Troops A and B moved with reckless abandon, heedless of the risk of ambush, scooting out from under artillery barrages directed at them by German observers. The two troops raced into town and found the enemy a mile beyond. The success was a salve to morale sapped by heavy losses in the *bocage* and earned the squadron a new nickname—the "Lucky 38th."[51]

★★★

The "rat race" opened the door to use mechanized cavalry differently. The armored divisions, which in the *bocage* had typically parceled out their reconnaissance battalions and cavalry squadrons by company or troop to the combat commands, began to use them at times as complete maneuver units. Indeed, when Brig. Gen. Maurice Rose took command of the 3d Armored Division in early August, he announced that he intended to keep the entire 83d Armored Reconnaissance Battalion under division control.[52] Nevertheless, even in the 3d Armored Division, the actual employment of the reconnaissance element in mass or in packets varied for the remainder of the war as circumstances demanded.

In some cases, infantry divisions used their cavalry reconnaissance troops to reinforce squadrons working with the division. The 4th Infantry Division, for example, attached its reconnaissance troop to the 4th Cavalry Reconnaissance Squadron during the initial breakout in late July, to the 24th Squadron in mid-August, and to the 102d Squadron in late August. The division would follow the same practice later in the Hürtgen Forest with the 38th and 24th Cavalry Reconnaissance squadrons.[53] Similarly, the 84th Infantry Division routinely attached its troop to the squadrons of the 113th Cavalry Group on the Roer River front.[54]

The Liberation of Paris

Eisenhower had hoped to bypass and surround Paris, in part because logistical planners recoiled from having to take responsibility for meeting the basic needs of the city's huge population. The French Resistance, however, in mid-August launched a rebellion that quickly got into trouble, and Resistance leaders called for help. Free French leader Gen. Charles de Gaulle insisted on intervention, and he and the French 2d Armored Division commander, Maj. Gen. Jacque Leclerc, gave every indication that French troops under U.S. First Army command would disobey orders not to take the city. Eisenhower gave in and ordered Bradley to enter the capital.

Major General Leonard Gerow's V Corps got the assignment on 22 August. Gerow put together a truly Allied force consisting of the 102d Cavalry Group, which had been in corps reserve, with the 4th Cavalry Reconnaissance Troop attached; the 2d French Armored Division; the U.S. 4th Infantry Division; a 12th Army Group technical intelligence unit; and a British contingent. Leclerc, accompanied by American cavalry and the British, was to enter Paris first flying the three national flags.

Fortunately for the Allies, *General der Infanterie* (four star) Dietrich von Choltitz, the Military Commander Paris, had already decided to abandon the capital despite orders from Hitler to defend the city even if that meant its destruction. By the time the Allied columns got under way, intelligence reports indicated that the Germans were evacuating Paris.[55]

The 102d Cavalry Reconnaissance Squadron, which had reached Sees on an administrative march, received its orders on 22 August to screen the advance into Paris. Troop B was to work with the French 2d Armored Division, while the remainder of the squadron was attached to the 4th Infantry Division. All troops pushed off on 23 August and reached the outskirts of the city by the evening of the following day. Troop B and the French 2d Armored Division entered the metropolis in force at first light on 25 August, encountering only sniper and sporadic mortar fire. By 1530 hours, the cavalrymen had gathered at the Arc de Triomphe.[56]

Frustrated by seemingly slow French progress against modest German resistance, Bradley had meanwhile ordered that the 4th Infantry Division accelerate its attack regardless of French prestige.[57] The "Lucky 38th," as a result, also got tapped to enter Paris, receiving its orders at 0530 on 25 August. The squadron advanced quickly, screening the movement of the 12th Infantry Regiment, and by 0830 Troop A had pushed its way through mobs of hysterically joyful Frenchmen to reach Notre Dame cathedral. The troop claimed to be the first Allied formation to enter the city as a unit. Be that as it may, the rest of the squadron was close behind, and the troopers quickly secured the bridges across the Seine river, operating at times with the local Resistance. That evening the squadron was assigned to "Task Force Paris," a 12th Army Group detachment charged with securing sites of intelligence interest.[58]

Three days later, the 102d Cavalry Reconnaissance Squadron formed the honor guard for a parade celebrating the liberation of Paris. Troop C provided the escort for Omar Bradley and General de Gaulle.[59] As for the 38th Cavalry Reconnaissance Squadron, its informal history recorded, "The squadron was assembled in a park between the Place de la Concorde and the Petit Palais along Champs Elysees. Here the squadron spent the happiest week in its history as it received uninhibited and enthusiastic greetings of the Parisienes and the Parisiennes. . . . Morale was never higher . . . and the 'Lucky' tradition grew stronger."[60]

★★★

The 106th Cavalry Group had led the XV Corps advance to the Seine, some days logging between fifty and sixty miles. Troop A's 2d Platoon in the 106th Cavalry Reconnaissance Squadron got as close as any of the men would to Paris. From a little town on the southern outskirts, the troopers could just make out the Eiffel Tower.[61] On 26 August the group, having been in constant contact with the enemy since 1 August, withdrew to the vicinity of Thoiry to refit and perform maintenance.[62]

Lieutenant Colonel J. F. Homefield, commanding the 121st Cavalry Squadron in the 106th Cavalry Group, wrote in a letter about this time, "We were fortunate to be leading the pack in the big chase. We know how it feels to be cut off with Jerries all around. It's an all-gone feeling, but we got out by always going forward. We have by-passed many of them, and it's a queer feeling to know they are behind you, but reconnaissance runs to that. . . ."[63]

Pushing to the Limits

The 125th Cavalry Reconnaissance Squadron on 1 September set off from just north of Paris as the advance guard of First Army's XIX Corps, which was pushing northeastward toward Brussels on the left wing of the American zone. The cavalry troops advanced quickly under conditions much like those troopers had faced west of Paris. Captain Reuben Trant, commanding Troop C, described the situation this way: "[S]mall-scale battles continued throughout the day. Every town was defended by a small number of Germans, most of whom were either killed or captured. The American forces were moving so fast that as many Germans were bypassed as were met. After the first attempt to send prisoners to the rear, which nearly resulted in the capture of the escort party, all prisoners were delivered to the [Resistance], who were armed with weapons captured from the Germans. . . . Many times, after delivering captured arms to the French, the troop moved forward while the French were left to mop up the remaining Germans."

Supply difficulties were such that the squadron sent a fuel truck along with the troop headquarters so that vehicles could be refueled without the need to wait for supply from far to the rear. In two days, the troop covered 150 miles and secured the 30th Infantry Division's concentration area just east of Lille.[64]

On 5 September the 125th Cavalry Group set off from Tournai for the Albert Canal with orders from XIX Corps to bypass all resistance. The 125th and 113th Cavalry Reconnaissance squadrons rolled out abreast, liberating village after village. "The Belgians would rush out, armed to the teeth," recalled the group's operations officer, "and tell us that the Germans were here or there, and we would just smile and wave and pass right on through." At times the squadrons were so far ahead of the rest of the corps that they could not be contacted by radio, and Cub planes were used to deliver messages.

The group covered sixty-seven miles the first day, forty the next, and the remainder on the third. On the second day at St. Trond, heavy small-arms fire from dug-in infantry greeted the 113th Cavalry Reconnaissance Squadron's 1st Platoon, Troop A, as it approached the town. Sergeant Allen Goemer led his section in a flanking move that allowed them to kill twenty of the enemy, and the rest of the point pressed forward.

Two cleverly concealed Panthers, meanwhile, waited until most of the column had passed, then knocked out two M10 tank destroyers bringing up the rear. They then destroyed an armored car and two jeeps commanded by Goemer that had turned back to investigate; the sergeant was wounded in the chest and eventually evacuated. The squadron turned its back on the problem and raced ahead on its mission.

It was only on the third day that the cavalry group ran into fighting along the Albert Canal that it could not bypass. The advance culminated in the first American attack on Fort Eben Emael, though—as one trooper admitted—that consisted of rolling a tank destroyer up and firing a few rounds that bounced off the fortress like hail. The challenge of capturing the fortress was left to the 30th Infantry Division when it could catch up.

After this operation, Col. William Biddle, the cavalry group commander, opined that the cavalry needed to have speedy M18 tank destroyers issued as organic equipment. The M10s, he said, had not been able to keep up with the fast-moving spearheads.[65]

★★★

Advancing with First Army's VII Corps, the 4th Cavalry Reconnaissance Squadron recorded in its informal history, "The entire Western front had become a turmoil of armor racing across France as tank and infantry columns stretching for miles rumbled over every passable road leading to Germany. These were the days of ringing church bells and wildly cheering crowds . . . flowing champagne and mademoiselles . . . candy-hungry kids who tossed apples, flowers, and what have you as the tide of war swept dizzily past their homes and villages."[66]

The 38th Cavalry Reconnaissance Squadron had been resubordinated to the 102d Cavalry Group on 1 September and was racing eastward on the southern wing of First Army, reaching the Meuse River on 3 September. The troopers found the bridges at Vireux and Fumay destroyed. Troop B engaged German forces on the far bank at Fumay, and some of the men crossed the river in assault boats. The 2d Platoon found a spot where it could ford the Meuse through three feet of water and did so, followed by Troop A. The current was so swift that the armored cars had to tow the jeeps across.

The troopers cleared Fumay and drove on. Under this cover, 4th Infantry Division engineers quickly installed a bridge so the big advance could continue.[67]

The cavalry and infantry repeated this approach time and again over the coming days; the squadron's after-action report at month's end summarized: "The squadron was determined to give the 4th Infantry Division an efficient and fast-moving screen that would enable the infantry to advance as rapidly as they could march. . . . By fording and securing bridgeheads over the Meuse and the Ourthe, and by like actions at Fumay, Haybes, [and 10 other named places], the platoons and troops of the squadron, reinforced by infantry and medium tanks [in one case], had pushed back delaying forces, which enabled the infantry to march without interruption. By the action at Rienne, Haut-Fays, [and six other named places], the aggressive action of the small-unit leaders on the spot had developed the enemy forces so precisely that the infantry was able to march into the attack without hesitation or delay."[68]

★★★

To the south in the Third Army's zone, fuel shortages were starting to constrain the surge toward Germany by the beginning of September. XX Corps' 7th Armored Division reached Verdun and the end of its gasoline supplies on 1 September. The 87th Cavalry Reconnaissance Squadron gathered all its fuel to keep Troops A and B on the road and sat down with the rest of the division to await resupply, which took two more days. The mobile troops had to cut the size of patrols during the day, but frequent reports of German infiltration meant that full-size groups patrolled at night.[69] In XII Corps, the 4th Armored Division's 25th Cavalry Reconnaissance Squadron as of 2 September had enough fuel for only a twenty-mile march, and it had to save that for an emergency. The 25th Squadron, too, cut patrols to a minimum for the next two days.[70] The 121st Cavalry Reconnaissance Squadron, at the far right flank of Third Army, was immobilized due to lack of fuel from 2 to 7 September.[71]

Patton wanted to push on and seize Metz before the Germans could regain their footing, and on his orders XX Corps began planning the operation on 1 September. The 3d Cavalry Group was the most mobile formation in the corps, having captured four thousand gallons of high-octane gasoline from the Luftwaffe.[72] Colonel Frederick Drury, commanding the 3d Cavalry Group, that day called on Lieutenant Colonel Cross at the 43d Cavalry Reconnaissance Squadron CP. "Who is your best platoon leader? I really need a good one. I want [him] to take some men and go to the Moselle River, set up OPs, and report on activities and bridges on the Moselle."

Lieutenant Robert Downs was the man, and he set off at noon the next day in his armored car, accompanied by three machine-gun jeeps and Monica Storrs, a French volunteer translator. The patrol stayed on secondary roads and trails and encountered no Germans except for six Luftwaffe personnel and three riflemen guarding a Russian work detail, all of whom surrendered without a fight. The French in every village greeted the column joyfully, but the cavalrymen fervently wished they would stop ringing the church bells in celebration because the Germans might become curious. After traversing forty-three miles, the patrol reached high ground near Haut Kontz, about eight miles north of Metz. From there the troopers watched Germans digging trenches and repairing rail lines damaged by bombing on the far bank of the river; they reported it back by radio.

The only way to power the radio was to run the M8's engine, and by 5 September fuel was running dangerously low. Downs received orders to return to the squadron but found that German combat troops, some with antitank guns, occupied roads they had used to reach the river. In Mairy, the patrol ran into SS soldiers and barreled past them, firing away; two of the enemy were seen to fall. Fortunately, it was raining heavily, and the column drove through several other villages past parked German vehicles, their owners staying dry inside. On several occasions when enemy vehicles were clustered, Downs blasted them with 37mm shells, then departed at full speed. Eventually the cavalrymen made their way back to squadron headquarters, having suffered not a single casualty.

Things had not been going well there. The squadron CP had been shelled that day by the 90th Infantry Division's artillery. When an officer showed up the next morning to express his regrets, Lieutenant Colonel Cross had to be forcibly restrained. Colonel Drury, in the meantime, had accompanied a 3d Cavalry Reconnaissance Squadron patrol that had driven into ambush near Rezonville. Drury and the occupants of four jeeps were taken prisoner, and a rescue attempt resulted only in the loss of two light tanks.

The 3d Cavalry Group, as it turned out, had just encountered the outer defenses of Metz. Repeated attempts by the group over the next several days to capture a bridge across the Moselle came to naught. The Third Army would stay stuck here for the next two months. Initially the 43d Cavalry Reconnaissance Squadron was assigned to maintain contact with First Army's V Corps on the left, while the 3d Cavalry Reconnaissance Squadron filled the gap between the 90th Infantry and 5th Armored divisions in XX Corps.

One of the more unusual combat experiences of the mechanized cavalry took place in Murville, entered hastily on 7 September by Second Lieutenant Diercks and a section of his 3d Platoon, Troop B, 43d Cavalry Reconnaissance Squadron. His patrol had just come under fire from suspected 88s, and the lieutenant was seeking cover. Diercks noticed that the 90th Infantry Division doughboys there were patrolling the street armed with bazookas. Just as Diercks stopped to ask what was up, the answer became apparent as two panzers (said to be Tigers) roared around the corner and headed straight for the column.

Diercks' gunner, Pvt. Joseph Side, instinctively fired the 37mm HE round he had in the chamber at the first panzer, which was only twenty-five yards away. The round entered the muzzle of the German gun, peeling it back as it traveled the length of the barrel to enter the tank, where it exploded, killed the crew, and set the tank on fire. The tank scraped to a stop beside the M8, and the intense heat and fire set the M8 ablaze as well.

The second tank drove by the crippled armored car and ground over the two jeeps behind the burning M8; the troopers bailed out in time to save their skins. A GI hit a bogey wheel with a bazooka round while the tank was atop the jeeps, and it limped off to the north, pursued by infantrymen with more bazookas. They later returned to report that they had bagged it. The patrol's only casualty was a crewman in the armored car who had suffered severe burns.[73]

★★★

The 2d Cavalry Group, which had joined XII Corps in late August, also on 3 September reached the Moselle River, where it found the bridges blown and German resistance stouter than it had been in weeks. The cavalry spent the next week working along the west bank of the river, and the story was always the same. One troop of the 42d Cavalry Reconnaissance Squadron finally slipped across the river on 12 September.[74]

A Sudden End to the Race

Over the course of a few days in mid-September, mechanized cavalry formations along with the rest of the U.S. Army in northwestern Europe ran into renewed and determined German resistance from the First Army's left, in Holland, to the Third Army's right, south of Metz.

On 14 September the 102d Cavalry Group's 38th Cavalry Reconnaissance Squadron received orders to secure an objective on the Kyle River, which happened to lie on the far side of the German frontier fortifications known to the defenders as the West Wall and to the Allies as the Siegfried Line. The Germans had been in headlong retreat for so long that nobody anticipated that the enemy would give the cavalry much trouble, so Troop B—along with Troop B of the 102d Squadron, which was attached—set out toward the Kyle River.

The latter troop was stopped cold almost instantly; the former made it two miles before running into machine-gun, mortar, and artillery fire near Krewinkel, Germany. The cavalrymen drove the Germans out of Krewinkel by using light tanks to physically crush several points of resistance, but this time the foe did not run far. The troopers could see pillboxes and dragon's teeth antitank obstacles on the high ground just beyond.[75] The outfit's after-action report noted that, "at Krewinkel, Troop B determined, by its gallant fight in that town, that the Siegfried Line was very much occupied, and that the long march was over."[76]

Likewise, Troop B, 4th Cavalry Reconnaissance Squadron, on 14 September reached high ground just west of the German border, from where the men could see Germans moving around in a stubble field a thousand yards to the east. The troop called up an artillery barrage, and the Germans disappeared into holes in the ground. Further reconnaissance of the position provoked intense machine-gun and mortar fire.

The 4th Cavalry Group on 15 September received orders to screen the VII Corps' right flank during its attack on Aachen. The group had been reinforced beginning 3 September by tanks, tank destroyers, and briefly an infantry battalion, to give it staying power in combat. At the time it moved into the area around Büllingen and Bütgenbach, Belgium, the 4th Cavalry Group controlled its own 4th and 24th Cavalry Reconnaissance squadrons, the 759th Light Tank Battalion (less one company), the 87th Field Artillery Battalion, the 635th Tank Destroyer Battalion (3-inch, towed), and two companies of the 297th Engineer Combat Battalion. The group headquarters thus served one purpose foreseen for it by Lt. Gen. Leslie McNair—it had become the center of an ad hoc combat command.

Dense woods made vehicular patrolling impossible, so the squadrons sent out aggressive foot patrols to the east. The troopers encountered the Siegfried Line fortifications the very first day, which ended forward progress. "German patrols were fully as active as friendly patrols in the sector," related an officer from the

24th Cavalry Reconnaissance Squadron. "Enemy patrols consisted of from eight to 20 men, depending upon the mission assigned. Numerous skirmishes resulted as friendly and enemy patrols met in the woods."

The cavalrymen flattered themselves that they were able to create the illusion of greater strength by moving tanks around and firing interdictory missions using artillery howitzers, assault guns, and tank destroyers.[77] The German LXXIV Corps, however, quickly discerned that only scattered armored reconnaissance elements faced the southern end of its sector, and the corps could focus its efforts on fighting in the northern third of its line near Aachen.[78]

In Third Army's zone, elements of the 2d Cavalry Group near Luneville were rolled over by a German armored counterattack aimed at the 4th Armored Division in the hope of stopping Third Army's rapid progress. The group's commanding officer, his operations officer, and the commander of the 42d Cavalry Reconnaissance Squadron were killed in the course of the day. The 4th Armored Division smashed the German force over the next several days, but the stop-thrust had achieved its aim—the unfettered advance was over.[79]

On the right wing of Third Army, XV Corps' 106th Cavalry Group reported that by 13 September the 121st Cavalry Reconnaissance Squadron was held up by roadblocks manned in anywhere from company to battalion strength and employing artillery, mortars, and small arms. The squadron also experienced local counterattacks by panzers. By 15 September the cavalry group was no longer advancing and had turned to patrolling. From here on, XV Corps noted, the enemy tenaciously resisted every advance.[80]

Medical Care in Combat

For the GI or the tanker, it was natural that a wounded man would be evacuated to the rear fairly quickly, but there was no handy rear for cavalry troops operating well in advance of the main body. The cavalry reconnaissance squadron's medical detachment consisted of two officers and twelve enlisted men equipped with four half-track ambulances, a jeep, and a one-ton trailer. One half-track normally worked with each troop, and the medical officers would typically accompany the two most active troops. Casualties would at some point be turned over to an infantry aid station.[81] Helping the wounded under combat conditions was a hazardous enterprise, and medical corpsmen sometimes numbered among the casualties themselves.

Captain Lawrence Loewinthan, a medical corpsman with the 125th Cavalry Reconnaissance Squadron, offered a look at the medical support available to cavalrymen in combat:

> The nature of work performed by a medical detachment of a reconnaissance unit in actual combat presents problems of evacuation and medical care under fluid conditions that are not covered by any standard procedure or field manual. . . . The plan to have an ambulance accompany each troop necessitated intense training in map reading, evacuation under various tactical situations, and the development of individual initiative and self-reliance in all medical matters.
>
> On 7 July, the squadron was attached to the 30th Infantry Division and went into action across the Vire Canal in the vicinity of St. Jean de Daye and Goucherie. This was an assault mission on which the squadron encountered well-established antitank weapons and well-dug-in infantry positions, protected by high hedgerows. Although casualties were high, the evacuation system worked satisfactorily. The armor protection of the halftrack ambulances saved the aid men on numerous occasions when small-arms fire hit the ambulances. . . . [T]he medical detachment lacked sufficient personnel to allow one aid man per platoon, as does the infantry. . . .
>
> Beginning 1 September, the squadron drove north . . . and into Belgium just south of Tournai. Because of the speed of the advance, there was never time to set up an aid station; patients were examined and treated in one of the halftrack ambulances, redesignated into a mobile aid station. . . . Despite the fact that the second echelon of evacuation was 95 miles behind, the three collecting company ambulances kept the flow of casualties running smoothly. . . .
>
> [On] 30 September, the squadron once again went into a defensive position, this time on the left flank of XIX Corps. For the first time since the squadron was committed to action, the medical detachment moved its aid station indoors—in a factory north of Sittard. . . . The squadron unit had been in constant action for a tremendously long period of time, and the reaction began to appear in the form of nervous disorders and combat fatigue.

While attached to the 84th Division on 26 November, the squadron was given a dismounted holding mission at Prummern and Beeck, Germany. The medical men went dismounted and once again the lack of sufficient personnel and litter bearers caused the treatment and evacuation to be extremely difficult. The mission further proved that a halftrack ambulance with its two men works well for all types of cavalry missions, but if the aid men are dismounted, the personnel is insufficient.[82]

CHAPTER 8

SOUTHERN FRANCE: THE STRATEGIC CAVALRY CHARGE

The wearers of the yellow cord of the mechanized cavalry led the Queens into battle.

—History, 117th Cavalry Reconnaissance Squadron, Mechanized

On 15 August 1944, Maj. Gen. Lucian Truscott's VI Corps, now part of Lt. Gen. Alexander "Sandy" Patch's Seventh Army, launched Operation Dragoon and invaded southern France along a forty-five-mile section of the Cote d'Azur near St. Tropez. Truscott had been allowed to choose the divisions he wanted, and he selected some of the best available in Italy: the 3d, 36th, and 45th Infantry divisions.

The battle patrol of the 3d Cavalry Reconnaissance Troop landed at Yellow Beach in the assault wave. The troopers swept down the beach, crossed a small peninsula, and linked up with another 3d Division battle patrol that had landed on Red Beach. En route, it cleaned out numerous strongpoints and captured, killed, or wounded 150 enemy soldiers.[1] The 36th and 45th Cavalry Reconnaissance troops landed after the assault wave and conducted typical road reconnaissance missions.

The 117th Cavalry Reconnaissance Squadron also landed in the assault wave, with one recon troop (plus a platoon of light tanks and a section of assault guns) attached to each of the three divisions. This was the first time that mechanized cavalry troops with vehicles hit the beach alongside the infantry. Indeed, a foul-up with the landing schedule caused the Troop A trains to come ashore before the assault infantry—the "queens of battle"—near Frejus, and the surprised troopers immediately scrambled for cover.

The recon elements were patched into the overall communications net with which they were able to direct naval gunfire onto German targets. The remainder of the squadron landed a short while later, and the cavalry operated in advance of the corps front all along the line.[2]

French II Corps, which was temporarily subordinated to Seventh Army, landed in the secured beachhead and struck westward to capture Toulon and Marseille while VI Corps pushed inland. Another French corps was to come ashore as transportation from North Africa became available.

Operation Dragoon had produced sharp disagreements between the Americans, who gave top priority to operations in northwestern Europe, and the British, who wanted to keep VI Corps in Italy to participate in a drive northward into Austria. Eisenhower backed the landings in large measure because he expected to need the logistic pipeline up the Rhone valley to support operations along the German frontier.

★★★

Truscott had no American armored division available despite his mission to mount a mobile offensive deep into enemy territory, and he knew he would not be able to use the French armored divisions scheduled to land shortly after D-Day for his own needs.

Truscott decided instead to improvise an armored-division-style combat command; on 1 August he had created a "provisional armored group" led by his assistant corps commander, Brig. Gen. Frederic Butler. Born in 1896, Butler was an engineer who had previously served as assistant commander of the 34th Infantry Division. The formation generally referred to as Butler Task Force consisted of the 117th Cavalry Reconnaissance Squadron; the 2d Battalion, 143d Infantry Regiment; two companies of medium tanks from the 753d Tank Battalion; Company C, 636th Tank Destroyer Battalion; the 59th Armored Field Artillery Battalion; and assorted other units. Butler Task Force in strength closely approximated an American combat command, which was usually built around a battalion each of tanks and armored infantry. The command was to form at Le Muy on order once VI Corps was established ashore. Butler and his hastily gathered staff had set to work planning for various contingencies, including an advance up the Route Napoleon toward Grenoble to block roads east of the Rhone River near Montelimar.[3]

By late on D-Day, Truscott knew that his forces had successfully established a foothold in France. Truscott was certain that the Air Corps could bring down every bridge along the Rhone and prevent the Germans from escaping westward. The Seventh Army's plan called for an advance westward with two corps

This experimental Dodge light armored car fielded by Troop A, 1st Armored Car Squadron, appears to be one of those built by the troopers themselves in 1928. *U.S. Army photo*

Mechanized cavalry assemble during First Army maneuvers in August 1939 as war looms in Europe. The M3A1 scout cars in the foreground have just entered service, and the M1A1 "combat cars" behind are obsolete. *Signal Corps photo*

A scout car operates with horse cavalry during pre-war maneuvers. The Cavalry branch thought it could still rely primarily on the horse. *Signal Corps photo*

Troopers exercise at the Cavalry Replacement Training Center in April 1942. *Signal Corps photo*

Motorcycle cavalrymen dismount for action during maneuvers. This ill-fated concept did not survive under the standardized mechanized cavalry organization of 1943. *Signal Corps photo*

The Philippine Scouts, seen here with an M3 light tank from the 192d Tank Battalion, were the only horse-mounted outfit to face the enemy. They were unable to avoid or contend with Japanese armor. *Signal Corps photo*

An M3A1 scout car rolls toward Mateur, Tunisia, on 26 April 1943. The final phase of the Tunisia campaign allowed the mechanized cavalry to run the way it had been trained to do. *Signal Corps photo*

A T30 assault gun belonging to the 82d Reconnaissance Battalion rolls through Ribera, Sicily, on 25 July 1943. The battalion spearheaded Patton's charge into Palermo. *Signal Corps photo*

A dismounted patrol from the 37th Reconnaissance Troop moves through the jungle on New Georgia on 29 July 1943. Terrain such as this characterized the early Pacific campaigns. The M3 light tank belongs to the Marine Corps. *Signal Corps photo*

A 91st Cavalry Reconnaissance Squadron M8 fires near Cassino, Italy, on 20 February 1944. The daunting terrain made mounted action a rarity. *Signal Corps photo*

A 21st Cavalry Reconnaissance Troop mounted patrol in M2 half-tracks nears the mouth of the Tekessi River, on Bougainville, on 26 May 1944. The half-track was the standard-issue cavalry vehicle most likely to get through the Pacific mud. *Records, Americal Division*

91st Cavalry Reconnaissance Squadron vehicles halt just outside Rome on 4 June 1944, the day that Fifth Army liberated the city. A self-propelled gun has just knocked out the Sherman tank seen burning ahead. *Signal Corps photo*

The LVT(A)(1) amtank (this one belonging to the 708th Amphibian Tank Battalion) was used by several cavalry troops in the Pacific. The 6th Reconnaissance Troop was the first to do so on New Guinea in June 1944. *Signal Corps photo*

Armored cars belonging to the 29th Cavalry Reconnaissance Troop navigate through the ruins of St. Lo, France, on 20 July 1944. Note the field-expedient .50-caliber antiaircraft gun. *Signal Corps photo*

The Reconnaissance Company, 67th Armored Regiment, 2d Armored Division, halts briefly near Barenton during the Normandy breakout in August 1944. *Signal Corps photo*

Elements of the 4th Armored Division, led by 25th Cavalry Reconnaissance Squadron M8s, head into Brittany on 2 August. *Signal Corps photo*

Butler Task Force's 117th Cavalry Reconnaissance Squadron races toward Riez on 18 August 1944. Shortly after the vehicles were under cover in the village, a flight of German bombers roared overhead. *NARA, Signal Corps photo*

An M8 belonging to the 87th Cavalry Reconnaissance Squadron, 7th Armored Division, engages the enemy near Eparnay, France, on 27 August 1944. *Signal Corps photo*

Cavalrymen clear an unidentified village during the advance across France in early September 1944. *U.S. Army photo*

M8 HMC assault guns belonging to the 113th Cavalry Reconnaissance Squadron prepare to fire in Belgium on 9 September 1944, near the end of the "rat race" to the German frontier. The nearest vehicle sports a hedgerow cutter. *Signal Corps photo*

An M5A1 light tank crew from the 2d Cavalry Group takes a break in Beauzemont, France, in October 1944. This tank has a hedgerow cutter variant still attached. *Signal Corps photo*

4th Cavalry Group troopers pause while on patrol on 25 November 1945. Static conditions along the Siegfried Line and in the Vosges Mountains forced the cavalry to dismount again. *Signal Corps photo*

An M5A1 light tank working with Troop B, 106th Cavalry Reconnaissance Squadron, fires its main gun during street fighting near the Maginot Line on 29 December 1944. *Signal Corps photo*

Cavalry reconnaissance amtanks land at Lingayan, Luzon Island, on 9 January 1945. The troopers manned most of the amtanks to join the GIs in the assault wave. *U.S. Army photo*

An armored car crew from Troop A, 41st Cavalry Reconnaissance Squadron, meets 84th Infantry Division GIs near Houffalize on 16 January 1945. Cavalry action brought the First and Third armies into contact as the Battle of the Bulge wound down. *Signal Corps photo*

A reconnaissance jeep belonging to the 94th Cavalry Reconnaissance Squadron sports .30-caliber machine guns mounted on the rear pedestal and in front of the passenger, which appears to have been a fairly common field expedient. *Courtesy of Vernon Brown*

Trooper Vernon Brown mans the .50-caliber machine gun on his jeep in the Vosges Mountains. Note the log-covered foxhole to the rear. *Courtesy of Vernon Brown*

New M24 light tanks were issued to the 18th Cavalry Reconnaissance Squadron in January 1945. The M24 enabled the troopers to fight German tanks on more equal terms. *Signal Corps photo*

The 71st Reconnaissance Troop awaits orders in Essen, Germany, on 11 April 1945. Less than a month later, it brokered the surrender of Army Group South. *Signal Corps photo*

The 81st Cavalry Reconnaissance Squadron, still equipped with M5A1 tanks, crosses the Po River, in Italy, on 25 April 1945. The squadron ran riot in the German rear and reached the Swiss border. *Signal Corps photo*

Private John Lyons and Technician 5th Grade Alfred Weilend, 125th Cavalry Reconnaissance Squadron, are pictured with some of the Soviet soldiers they met in Apollensdorf on 30 April 1945 during the first contact between the Ninth and Red armies. *Signal Corps photo*

37th Reconnaissance troopers take a roadside break in the Cagayan Valley, on Luzon, in June 1945. The mechanized cavalry remained in action in the Philippines until Japan surrendered. *Records, 37th Infantry Division*

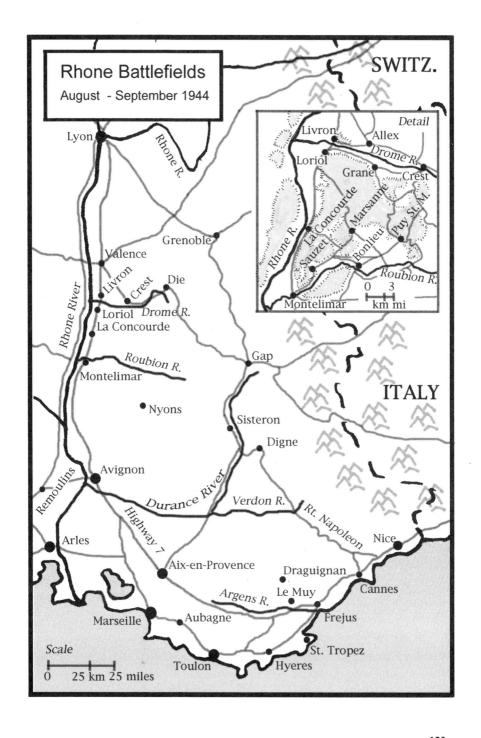

Rhone Battlefields
August - September 1944

SWITZ.

Lyon

Rhone R.

Detail

Livron
Allex
Loriol
Drome R.
Grane
Crest
La Concourde
Marsanne
Puy St. M.
Rhone R.
Sauzet
Bonlieu

Grenoble

Roubion R.

Montelimar

0   3
km mi

Valence
Livron
Crest
Die

Rhone River

Loriol
Drome R.
La Concourde

Roubion R.

Gap

Montelimar

ITALY

Nyons

Sisteron

Digne

Avignon

Remoulins

Durance River
Verdon R.
Rt. Napoleon

Nice

Arles

Highway 7

Aix-en-Provence
Draguignan
Le Muy
Cannes

Argens R.

Marseille
Aubagne
Frejus

St. Tropez

Scale

Toulon
Hyeres

0   25 km 25 miles

abreast to capture the major ports before driving up the Rhone valley, with which Truscott was in full accord. But there was a spot some hundred miles northward where high ground east of the Rhone created a bottleneck near the town of Montelimar. The Germans, Truscutt expected, would concentrate their forces to stop the Seventh Army's push westward. Truscott saw an opening to send a strike force toward Grenoble and from there to the high ground just upstream from Montelimar. No army plan had foreseen such an early exploitation, but Truscott had. This was exactly why he had created Butler Task Force.[4]

On 17 August, Hitler instructed Army Group G, which controlled all German forces in southern France, to disengage from the enemy except for units occupying Marseille and Toulon and to retreat northward to link up with the southern wing of Army Group B, retreating before the Normandy landing forces. An initial order to withdraw elements not committed to the battle reached Army Group G that day, and instructions for a total withdrawal arrived the next day. The 11th Panzer Division, at that very moment trying to reach the battle zone from west of the Rhone River, was to protect the Rhone valley and serve as rear guard for the German Nineteenth Army, which commanded the formations opposite Seventh Army.[5]

Butler Task Force Charges North

The same day that Hitler ordered Army Group G's withdrawal, Truscott gave Butler oral instructions to push off at 0600 hours the next morning with Sisteron, on the Durance River, as his first objective. After some discussion on the subject, Truscott left it to Butler to choose his route. Butler and his staff had carefully studied the maps and concluded that the Route Napoleon, which ran through Digne to Sisteron, traversed such mountainous terrain that a handful of determined men could stop the advance. Butler instead decided to start westward out of Draguignan toward Riez, then swing north to Sisteron. Asked by Truscott how long it would take him to reach Sisteron, Butler replied that he would certainly make it in three days and possibly in two. Furthermore, he told the seemingly incredulous corps commander that he would reach Riez, forty-five miles distant, the first night.[6]

Hitler and Truscott issued their orders. It was going to be a race to see whether Butler's task force could cut off the Germans before they slipped away. Even if Butler's command succeeded, the question remained as to whether the task force could hold the pass.

★★★

Troop C, reinforced by several light tanks and assault guns, slipped away at 0600 and motored north through Draguignan toward North Castellane, which left the route west of town clear for the main body. The 142d Infantry, 36th Infantry Division, had run into determined resistance in North Castellane the evening before, and Butler worried that trouble might arise from that direction.

The remainder of the task force cleared its bivouac on schedule, and Butler raced forward to catch up to the point. He was looking forward to a "rat race." Just outside of Draguignan, Butler found the column stalled. He tracked down Lt. Col. Charles Hodge, commanding the 117th Cavalry Reconnaissance Squadron, who was in his radio-equipped command vehicle—the communications nerve center of the task force. The point, Hodge reported, was stopped at the first bridge west of town. Butler continued his race forward.

At the bridge, Butler was astonished to see a roadblock, painstakingly constructed by 36th Infantry Division engineers despite his efforts to coordinate his movement with the division staff. Steel rails and cables, posts, boulders, antitank mines, and two hundred pounds of explosives blocked the route. Butler hounded his men to clear the obstruction; after a half hour of frenzied labor, one lane was clear and the main column started to move.

The column soon stalled again, and Butler once more tracked down Lieutenant Colonel Hodge to find out why. After concluding that only caution was slowing the point, Butler charged off to find it and explain a few things about aggressive route reconnaissance. Having done so and satisfied himself that his point was doing a better job, Butler headed back toward the command center. He took comfort that communications within the task force were excellent. One reason was that the squadron had managed to wangle extra short-range FM and long-range AM radios so that every jeep in the outfit had one or the other, and each troop CP had a command half-track mounting both. The column hooked northward, fanning out over subsidiary roads toward the day's objective.

Troop C, on the right flank, encountered antitank guns, and it dismounted men to scout them out while maneuvering its supporting assault guns into firing positions. The squadron had somehow obtained permission to replace its six standard-issue M8 HMC assault guns with M7 Priest 105mm self-propelled howitzers, which delivered a much heftier punch and were capable of knocking out a Tiger tank. After destroying several antitank guns, the cavalrymen chanced upon LXII Reserve Corps commander *Generalleutnant* Ferdinand Neuling, along with much of his staff and brandy reserve. Three German officers with a white flag approached the M8 armored car commanded by Sgt. Robert Lutz and told him that their general wanted to surrender to an American officer. Lutz summoned his platoon commander forward and accompanied him and the Germans to a cave, where Neuling handed over his pistol.

Hodge came barreling up in a jeep to tell Butler the good news. Butler returned to Draguignan, where the prisoners had been taken, and found Neuling sitting on a park bench guarded by a cavalry corporal and having a good weep. After accepting the general's formal surrender and sending him to the rear, Butler headed forward.

The advance was getting into gear. The field artillery battalion's Cub spotter plane was aloft and giving real-time reconnaissance information to the cavalry point. Soon, the artilleryman noticed that a bridge in one village on the route of advance had been blown, and he directed the column along a winding bypass through the hills. (After this experience, the squadron made certain that it always had one or two Cubs assigned or attached for the remainder of the campaign in Europe.) The Resistance, or *maquis*, by and by reported that a German delaying force had occupied said village, and Butler—who had a Seventh Army *maquis* liaison officer with him—left the job of ejecting the enemy to the Resistance. This was only the first of many such small instances: Butler lacked the manpower to protect his line of communication and relied entirely on the Resistance to secure it for him.

The column rolled onward through Salernes and Montemeyan, meeting nothing but the occasional German motorcycle or staff car. The artillery aircraft proved invaluable; it could sweep down a road and report either "all clear," which gave the reconnaissance troop the confidence to pelt ahead at full speed, or sound a warning, which enabled the cavalrymen to respond quickly. At every halt, vehicles moved under cover as protection against possible German air attack.

One reconnaissance platoon reinforced by tank destroyers scouted southwestward off the main route to the road hub at Barjols. The tank destroyers provided over-watch from outside the town, and the cavalry's M8s had just rolled into the village when sniper fire rang off the armored sides. The commander and gunner worked in an open-topped turret, so snipers posed a deadly threat. As if that were not enough, two self-propelled guns clanked into view with the clear intention of doing the recon men no good. The little 37mm guns on the M8s barked first, and the rounds penetrated the thin armor on the German guns. Still, the odds looked bad, and the platoon retreated out of town and exchanged fire with the Germans from there. Butler arranged for help from the 45th Infantry Division, and elements of the 179th Infantry Regiment arrived just in time at dusk; German infantry were pressing an attack toward the recon men, who were almost out of ammunition. The 179th Infantry fought for two days to secure Barjols.

At Quinson, on the Verdon River some ten miles short of the day's objective, the *maquis* again made a crucial contribution. The Cub reported that the bridge was out, and the first jeeps to reach the scene had difficulty fording the stream. The Resistance pressed the citizenry into service to cover the riverbed with flag-stones and to help push vehicles to the far bank. There was a certain irony in the situation: Allied bombers had unsuccessfully tried to destroy the bridge, and the *maquis*, concluding that its removal must be important, had, in fact, blown up the span. Indeed, Butler would soon learn that bridges knocked down by the Resistance were the greatest impediment to the task force's speedy progress. Butler also contacted the VI Corps air officer to request that he cancel all bridge bombing missions in the Durance valley because they were hindering his advance.

The point reached Riez with four hours of daylight remaining. Butler decided to halt and refuel when the supply trucks caught up after dark rather than press on. No sooner had the vehicles moved under cover than a flight of German bombers with fighter escorts roared overhead toward the landing beaches, a stroke of fortune for the task force. At this point, only cavalry elements with three attached infantry platoons and a few tanks, tank destroyers, and artillery pieces were in Riez; the rest of the task force was stretched out between ten and forty miles to the rear. Troop A outposted nearby Valensole, and Troop B set up outposts north of Riez.

That evening, Butler was delighted when an American captain from one of the Office of Strategic Services (OSS) action teams reported to him with a tough French World War I veteran in full uniform. Butler decided that he could make good use of them on the morrow. The Resistance, meanwhile, reported that retreating Germans might pass through Quinson to the rear, and a light tank platoon from Company F was sent back to secure the ford. The squadron was thus providing security for the spearhead on most routes of approach open to the enemy.

★★★

Butler decided to reach Sisteron on 19 August and ordered Troop B to protect his right by advancing through Digne, Troop A to proceed up the Durance River, and Troop C, which had rejoined the spearhead, to protect his left west of the Durance. He placed the local *maquis* forces under his OSS captain and assigned them and some light tanks and assault guns to reinforce the Digne mission because several hundred Germans were reported to be stationed there.

Troop B ran into resistance at Mezel, eight miles outside Digne, but the Germans gave way after a two-hour skirmish and fought small rearguard actions all the way back to Digne. American scouts slipped into town but retreated under fire, so the command commenced pounding Digne with fire from light tanks and armored cars preparatory to an assault by the *maquis* infantry, which failed. Butler later commented that "small arms and machine guns together with an abundance of grenades was all the enemy was showing. Grenades thrown from upper floor windows somewhat restrict the effectiveness of light armor. Put yourself in a sardine can and close the lid and see how it is for yourself."

The other task force elements rolled ahead with but minor encounters with the enemy. Troop A found a damaged bridge across the Durance River that was capable of bearing armored cars and tanks. This was good news because the task force's engineers had not yet appeared, and there was not a single piece of hasty bridging equipment in all of Seventh Army. Planners had dropped the equipment from the shipping lists because it had not been used in North Africa or Italy, despite southern France being one of the best-watered spots in Europe.

The troop ran into resistance backed by armored cars in Malijai and another group of 150 defiant Germans in Chateau Arnoux. In Malijai, the Germans had dug in on high ground above town on the far bank of the little Bleone River. The cavalrymen destroyed the armored cars, cleared the near bank, and prevented the Germans from blowing the bridge. Nevertheless, the hostile fire was too hot to risk a crossing.

Butler sent a second column, including a company each of medium tanks and infantry, to clear up both Malijai and Digne. The Germans folded in Malijai after a few rounds of 75mm gunfire. The Digne garrison ran up the white flag before the tanks and assault guns even cut loose, and the cavalrymen captured their first brigadier general. In Chateau Arnoux, a pounding by assault guns had sufficed to induce the defenders to surrender.

By nightfall, the bulk of Butler Task Force was at Sisteron. The command had run off the edge of its army-supplied maps and turned to locally acquired Michelin maps. Butler's supply line already stretched 125 miles back to the dumps.

Butler commented regarding this point in time, "The 117th from the beginning functioned perfectly in communications, and to me this was 90 percent of the problem. They were perfect now in the technique of reconnaissance, and they certainly could carry on a persuasive conversation! Their personnel was still of the old swank Essex Troop of the New Jersey National Guard and was plenty courageous and daring. And, too, they had learned to live in the field."

★★★

On the morning of 20 August, Truscott instructed Butler to reconnoiter to the north and west to establish whether he could move to Montelimar. Truscott told him to be prepared as well to move on Grenoble instead and promised definitive word later in the day. In the meantime, Truscott suggested that he would order the 36th Infantry Division to Sisteron by the next day. Indeed, Lieutenant General Patch the preceding day had instructed Truscott to alert one infantry division to move on Grenoble upon Seventh Army orders.[7]

Truscott was already thinking that it was time to turn the rest of his corps northward and give a push to the Germans east of the Rhone and south of Montelimar. Truscott called Patch and got the green light to send Butler to Montelimar and push the entire 36th Infantry Division in behind him.[8] He also met with Maj. Gen. William Eagles, who said he would have two regiments of his 45th Infantry Division across the Durance River that night—a step that Dragoon planners had not expected to occur until 15 October! Truscott told him to send the 179th Infantry Regiment north along the river, which would bring it into contact with the forces in the area of Sisteron.[9]

Butler during all this time had received none of Truscott's instructions because of the unreliable communications setup back to corps, so he acted on his own in response to reports of German forces moving south from Grenoble. He pushed his outpost line closer to Grenoble and sent Troop A supported by light tanks and assault guns to the road nexus at Gap—said to house a large German garrison—to protect his right flank. The command picked up some *maquis* along the way, and a small task force of the 2d Battalion, 143d Infantry, arrived separately after getting lost because of a damaged radio, lack of maps, and misleading road signs switched around by the *maquis* to confuse the Germans.

The reconnaissance elements spotted German outposts before Gap early in the afternoon. Spearheaded by the M5A1 light tanks, the troop overran the German trenches so quickly that the surprised defenders evidently were unable to communicate with the garrison.

The Americans quickly moved into position to assault the town, which sits in a bowl surrounded by hills. The town was fairly large, and even with the help of the Resistance, a fight in its streets was going to be tough and bloody. Captain Omer Brown, commanding Troop E (assault guns), decided to try diplomacy, and he hopped into a jeep and drove to the German garrison at about 1500 hours. He told the German commander that he was surrounded by a superior force and would be shelled immediately, and that sixty B-17 Flying Fortresses were ready to bomb him at 1700. The Germans, worried that they would be turned over to the Resistance, haggled with Brown, but he would have none of it.

Brown returned to his command and ordered the assault guns to drop twenty-five rounds in rapid fire on a radio station just outside of town. Perhaps the Germans thought the B17s had arrived: White flags sprouted all over the place. Brown returned to accept the surrender of 1,100 German troops. Faced with this huge bag of prisoners, the troop detailed a half-track and two jeeps as guards—supplemented by some freed Polish prisoners—and marched the Germans to the rear. After Butler appeared in Gap, the Americans were able to turn security of the town over to the Resistance.

That evening, Truscott signaled Butler, "You will move at first light 21 August with all possible speed to Montelimar. Block all routes of withdrawal up the Rhone valley in that vicinity. Thirty-sixth Division follows you." (This message didn't reach Butler until 0400 hours the next day by courier.[10])

★★★

German defenses along Butler's route of advance were catastrophically disorganized. Army Group G commanding general *Generaloberst* (three star) Johannes Blaskowitz, moreover, as of 20 August was operating in an intelligence vacuum, but he could imagine what the enemy ought to do. He told Nineteenth Army to reckon with an American advance through Digne toward Valence, on the Rhone River, or to Grenoble and ordered the dispatch of a mobile group to secure Valence against that eventuality.[11]

Generalleutnant Wend von Wietersheim, meanwhile, gathered all elements of his 11th Panzer Division—and enough fuel to enable his tanks to fight—on the east bank of the Rhone. The general had already received orders two days earlier to screen the withdrawal of Nineteenth Army up the Rhone (an order soon amended to simultaneously spearheading the withdrawal and securing all entrances to Highway 7 from the east).[12]

★★★

While Butler Task Force was swinging around Nineteenth Army, the 3d Infantry Division was pushing toward the Rhone valley, where it was to turn north and pressure the rear of the retreating enemy. The 3d Cavalry Reconnaissance Troop could not provide all of the scouting that the division needed in the increasingly fluid operational environment, so the division created a "provisional reconnaissance squadron" by adding the reconnaissance company of the 601st Tank Destroyer Battalion and the light tank company of the 756th Tank Battalion. The provisional squadron conducted three types of missions: contact, straight reconnaissance, and aggressive reconnaissance.

Indeed, the last category was the most common mission. A light tank platoon, a squad or a section of the battle patrol, and at times a platoon or a company of infantry were attached to one of the reconnaissance platoons. The small command often worked in unison with an artillery observation plane, which enabled it to rapidly place fire on a target. This package had the manpower and firepower to overwhelm enemy roadblocks without waiting for the infantry to come forward. The troop commanding officer nevertheless in September recommended that such outfits be issued assault guns because, in reality, aggressive reconnaissance and fighting for information were expected of them.[13]

Race to the Choke Point

"We were attempting to set the stage," wrote Truscott in his memoirs, "for a classic—a 'Cannae'—in which we would encircle the enemy against an impassable barrier or obstacle and destroy him."[14] The Rhone valley offered several points at which such a maneuver was possible, one of them north of Montelimar. The town sits on the east bank of the Rhone on a ten-mile-long plain, north of which is the narrow Cruas Gorge, known as the "Gate of Montelimar." From this point north, the valley is generally narrow, save only for a plain in the area of Valence. Highway 7 runs along the east bank of the Rhone; Highway 86 matches its course along the west bank, and railroads run parallel to both roadways. Two hill masses (designated 294 and 300 after their heights in meters) dominate the valley on the eastern bank just north of Montelimar. Hill 430, northeast of Montelimar, overlooks the small Roubion River, which flows into the Rhone at that point, as well as a road net along the north bank of the Roubion that offered a potential bypass around the choke point on the Rhone.[15]

Butler had overextended himself toward Grenoble, in the north, and now had to shift his command rapidly at least seventy miles westward to reach the Rhone—close to twice the average daily advance to date. Fortunately, enough fuel had caught up with the task force that it could make the race, and ammunition was in ample supply. Leaving Troops A and E backed by medium tanks and tank destroyers as a holding force at Gap, Butler ordered his point to be on the road by daybreak.

Early on 21 August, Lt. Col. Joseph Felber, commanding the 753d Tank Battalion and the main column of armor and infantry, received orders to pass through Die and then, operating behind a cavalry screen, to occupy the high ground overlooking the Rhone approximately three miles south of Livron. Troops B and C, 117th Cavalry Reconnaissance Squadron, each with a platoon of light tanks attached, received the mission to seize and hold that high ground.

Working their way along a twisting road cut at times into the sides of cliffs, the lead elements of Troop B reached the high ground by midafternoon. Two platoons probed south to the outskirts of Montelimar. Armored cars and light tanks fired on German vehicles moving north along Highway 7 and at aircraft taking off from a nearby airfield. Their arrival clearly caused confusion and consternation below.

Troop C, meanwhile, advanced westward from Crest down the north bank of the Drome River, which flows into the Rhone north of the hill masses above Montelimar. Troop C took the high ground east of Loriol, and cut Highway 7 near Livron. A patrol advanced to within two hundred yards of the highway bridge across the Drome; then a fifteen-man demolition squad crept to the span and set charges. The first hint that the Germans had of trouble was when the bridge blew under the very wheels of their column. Once the main bridge had been knocked down, the cavalrymen spotted German forces crossing at a ford closer to the Rhone. One platoon charged to the ford, shot up the German column, and blocked the crossing. Another platoon rolled north up the highway and fell upon the tail of another German column. Threading its way through the vehicles with all guns firing, the platoon destroyed fifty trucks.

Truscott had for the moment achieved his bold desire and cut Nineteenth Army's escape route. But only two platoons of cavalry troops held the choke point, and the Germans immediately realized their danger. Shortly before dark, German counterattacks pushed Troops B and C back from their advanced positions, which left only one platoon overlooking the highway near Loriol.

Felber Force, meanwhile, rolled toward its objective over steep and winding roads, dropping elements here and there along the route to secure key junctions, and closed on Condillac at about 2145 hours. After examining the terrain, Felber concluded that he lacked the manpower to hold all of the high ground and decided to occupy hill masses to the north and south of the road running from Condillac down to La Concourde, where it intersected Highway 7 near the Rhone. Felber had only a rifle company (less one squad), a heavy weapons company, a few antitank guns, a company of fourteen medium tanks, a handful of tank destroyers, an armored field artillery battalion (less one battery), and a company of non-combat engineers. Felber deployed his limited resources on the high ground and at a few strategic roadblocks, positioning four tank destroyers to command the Rhone road by fire. M7 Priests clanked into firing positions while forward observers made themselves comfortable, peering down on the German Nineteenth Army snaking northward below them. Felber obtained Butler's permission to outpost several more hills with Troop B, 117th Cavalry Reconnaissance Squadron, and met with the local Resistance commander, who supplied two hundred men to assist in manning outposts and roadblocks.

By 2300, Felber Force was in position. Troop A, 117th Cavalry Reconnaissance Squadron, arrived that night from Gap after being relieved by the 36th Infantry Division, but the medium tanks and tank destroyers lagged behind.[16]

★★★

The sky gradually lightened enough on the morning of 22 August that the gunners of Felber Force could see a target-rich environment of German vehicles below them crawling past hulks destroyed by shelling during the night. Cannons barked, shells flew true, and soon so much additional wreckage clogged the route that it became temporarily blocked.[17] There were many smaller paths parallel to the highway, however, so that German movement never ceased entirely.

Slowly, the ranks of Butler Task Force were swelled by additional formations: the missing armored field artillery battery, plus another column including a half-dozen more tank destroyers. But, as Butler later observed, "the Germans were building up against me faster than were our own forces building up."[18]

Armored cars, artillery, tanks, tank destroyers, and even the infantry's 57mm antitank guns rained death on Highway 7 during the long daylight hours. The 59th Armored Field Artillery Battalion smashed several trains, which blocked the rail line on the east bank of the river. Two trains carrying munitions put on an impressive display of pyrotechnics as they burned.

Troop C, manning the right flank along the Drome, had a turkey shoot, and the entire assault gun troop had arrived to join it. The M7s hammered the German columns, trying to move north, from a 2,500-yard range with high explosives and white phosphorus. The armored cars were closer and laid down punishing machine-gun fire. By dusk, hundreds of vehicles were burning.

Butler's main concern that day turned out not to be the Rhone highway but rather German efforts to advance from Montelimar along the north bank of the Roubion River and thence northeastward across his rear, which Felber now protected with a small reserve force. Five Panthers supported by panzergrenadiers smashed a roadblock at Cleon manned by Troop A of the 117th Squadron. Sergeant Mike Aun's armored car section took up concealed positions on the Germans' right flank in hit-and-run fashion and picked off eighteen support vehicles without being spotted. In Cleon itself, Lt. Carl Ellison raced down a street mounted in the back of a jeep and gripping the .30-caliber machine gun. Spotting the German column, Ellison fired at it, then turned and roared off to another street, where he did the same, creating the impression of a larger force that appeared to confuse the enemy. Ellison then directed artillery fire onto the German column. The cavalrymen fought skillfully, but the Germans knocked out two armored cars and three jeeps and cut off the troop.

The attackers rolled toward St. Martin, where Felber had his CP. Felber had only a few tank destroyers at hand, which engaged the Germans; the Shermans and tank destroyers on the road from Gap—which were to form the core of his reserve—had not yet arrived. A Cub artillery plane was dispatched to drop a message of dire need to the column. Butler described what happened next: "[O]ur rescue column arrived for a movie finish. The German tanks that had crossed the Roubion were destroyed, the infantry were driven back, and on the south bank several fires burned merrily where our guns had found trucks and light vehicles. It was a good honest fight. The reserves had arrived in the nick of time."

The arrival of Panthers and panzergrenadiers was a sure sign that the 11th Panzer Division was joining the battle. Butler assured Felber that he would soon have help for his overextended reserve. But after the day's slugfest, Butler Task Force was down to twenty-five rounds of artillery ammunition per tube, half Butler's desired minimum. Fire ceased until supplies arrived after dark.[19]

The Battle of Montelimar

Truscott called the 36th Infantry Division's CP at 0200 hours on 23 August. "I want to get word to Butler or to [division commanding general] Dahlquist, if he is over there, to interrupt by demolitions that main road. Do you understand? In the Rhone valley. I don't want a single vehicle to get up that road!"[20]

Butler Task Force troops were doing their best to block the Rhone highway with direct and artillery fire, which added steadily to the wreckage along the roadway. But Butler still faced a sticky situation to his rear early on 23 August. Another crucial roadblock had collapsed at Sauzet on the road that passed east of Butler's main positions after some *maquis* attached to Troop A had mistakenly allowed panzers and grenadiers into town, thinking they were Americans. In the early dawn light, the panzer crews spotted a Sherman tank outposting the hill just north of town and a little more than a mile from the American CP. Long-barreled 75mm cannons roared and smashed the M4.

Just as things looked rather dire, the first trucks bearing the 2d Battalion, 141st Infantry Regiment, arrived. Backed by several Shermans, the reinforcements attacked Sauzet and restored the situation.[21] Troop B, 117th Cavalry Reconnaissance Squadron, arrived to strengthen the 2d Battalion's defenses.

Other German probes followed, and tanks and tank destroyers engaged panzers at several points east of Condillac. Troop A, on the Roubion, was hit again. The squadron's executive officer described it this way: "A superior force of German armor was engaged by our light tanks and armored cars, but by superior marksmanship and determination of purpose, the enemy was forced to withdraw."[22]

Butler Task Force dissolved as of 0900 hours, although Butler for the time being continued to direct the action. The 36th Infantry Division took command of all its elements.[23] By evening, two infantry battalions were on the high ground along the choke point. The cavalry had seized the strategic objective and held until reinforced by the infantry, just as the old cavalry doctrine had anticipated.

★★★

The 2d Battalion, 141st Infantry, attacked Montelimar at 1630 hours. Troop B now supported the infantry through battle reconnaissance and found the

German defenses about a thousand yards northeast of town. The Germans struck back at the cavalry and penetrated its thin line in several places. The cavalrymen claim to have destroyed two Mark IV tanks and several self-propelled guns during the battle, and they rolled up some prisoners.

The main American attack, meanwhile, appeared doomed from the start, despite support from newly arrived 155mm Long Tom guns. The tanks and tank destroyers failed to appear on time, and a group of *maquis* who were to have supported the operation dispersed when they were hit by a German counter-attack.[24] Butler, who observed the operation, thought the Germans were having the better of it. He obtained Major General Dahlquist's permission to stop the attack and withdraw the cavalry screen, which had been bypassed by the enemy assault elements, through the friendly infantry line. The battalion dug in on high ground roughly two thousand yards northeast of Montelimar.[25]

Meanwhile, along the Drome, American forces had withdrawn four miles east of the Rhone, where Troop C, reinforced by the 141st Infantry Regiment's antitank and cannon companies, manned a roadblock north of the river.[26]

★★★

As reports from reconnaissance units arrived at the 11th Panzer Division CP confirming the American bid to cut off the Nineteenth Army's retreat, the Germans threw the division's armored reconnaissance battalion, strengthened by some panzers and an artillery battery, forward toward Loriol and Crest. The battalion's mission was to prevent at all costs any renewed American push westward down the Drome River to the Rhone. Von Wietersheim also raced his non-combat elements north past the bottleneck into the area of Valence.[27] He now had orders to extricate his delaying forces from the south and send them forward as well.[28]

Moving to the Flank

With the 36th Infantry Division taking charge of the fight, the 117th Cavalry Reconnaissance Squadron pulled back into reserve on 24 August. Butler was already looking at his possible routes north after the battle in Montelimar, and Capt. Thomas Piddington's Troop A was dispatched with a small task force to reconnoiter the route toward Briancon and to protect the 45th Infantry Division's right flank as it swung by the 36th Division, to the latter's east. The armored cars crawled over alpine roads above sheer drops to rocks below. Lieutenant Dan Lee kept communications working by re-positioning his M8 to the highest local point to act as a relay station. Much of the task force command group came to grief on 27 August when it was overrun by the Germans near Col du Lautaret, but Troop A had almost all of its elements out on patrols and escaped the disaster.[29]

Most of the squadron returned to the Drome valley on 25 August in response to advances there by the 11th Panzer Division's reconnaissance battalion. Battle flared along the east shoulder of the German escape route on 26 August. Before dawn, Dahlquist ordered the re-formed Task Force Butler's 143d Infantry Regiment, which was at battalion strength because of detachments, to attack through the Condillac pass toward La Concourde at 1300 hours to establish a roadblock on the Rhone River road. The light tanks of Company F, 117th Cavalry Reconnaissance Squadron, were attached for the action. The 3d Battalion pushed off nearly as scheduled but by 1800 was still fighting to establish itself along the ridgeline overlooking the highway. Because of these difficulties, the next morning the 3d Battalion of the 45th Infantry Division's 157th Infantry Regiment was brought forward to the vicinity of Condillac to press the attack.[30]

To do the job, Butler Task Force's Lt. Col. Joseph Felber was given Company A, 191st Tank Battalion; the assault gun troop and light tank company from the 117th Cavalry Reconnaissance Squadron; and the 3d Battalion, 157th Infantry Regiment. The attack collapsed in the face of fierce small-arms fire and sharp gunnery by Panther tanks, but the cavalry assault guns had a field day smashing up vehicles below them with direct fire.[31]

Butler Task Force was ordered to disengage and move to the Drome valley to attack Loriol.[32] On 28 August, Felber Force, including Troops B and E and Company F, tangled with Panthers from the 11th Panzer Division's rear guard near Loriol. Panthers firing from hull-down positions claimed three Shermans and two tank destroyers.[33] Butler Task Force nevertheless by late afternoon pushed to the outskirts of Loriol and cut Highway 7 with two roadblocks. Just before midnight, German infantry supported by panzers launched a vigorous attack, which drove the Americans reeling back out of town.[34]

The Americans effectively cut the escape route for good on 29 August. Much of Nineteenth Army had wriggled through Truscott's chokehold, but it did so at tremendous cost. Estimated German casualties amounted to 11,000 men, and some 2,100 vehicles, 1,500 horses, and numerous artillery pieces were destroyed.[35]

Summing up after the battle, Maj. Harold Samsel, the 117th Squadron's executive officer, said, "The purpose of a reconnaissance squadron is to hit the enemy hard and often at different points, giving him the impression that it is a much larger force attacking him and giving him no rest at any time."[36] It was not doctrine, but it was true.

★★★

Truscott's VI Corps drove northward again, striving to cut off the German retreat once more. Truscott was keen to push the lead elements of the 117th Cavalry Reconnaissance Squadron north of Bourg, but Troop B had ground to a halt under heavy artillery fire. Truscott applied heat to the 45th Infantry Division: "Put the steam on and barge right in there. You haven't anything in front of you except scattered elements of the 11th Panzer Division. . . ."[37]

Late on 2 September, the 117th Cavalry Reconnaissance Squadron received orders to seize and hold Montreval, which sat astride the road from Bourg that the 11th Panzer Division intended to use for the next stage of its fighting withdrawal. The squadron was badly strung out, and Lieutenant Colonel Hodge protested the order. Troop A had just arrived after a grueling road march from near the Swiss border, and the outfit's armored cars had expended all of the high-explosive ammunition for the 37mm guns. Troop C, the tanks, and the assault guns were still well to the south of Montreval in Meximieux.

Nevertheless, Troop B attacked Montreval on 3 September and by noon had cut all roads to the north, taking about seventy rear-area troops prisoner and knocking out a few armored cars. The lead elements of Troop A arrived by noon. The advance had unknowingly put the small command in a sensitive position ten miles behind the German line.

The 11th Panzer Division's armored reconnaissance battalion, supported by six Panthers, artillery, and engineers, struck back from Bourg and the south-west. The attack had isolated Montreval and evolved into a pitched battle when the first platoon of M5A1s arrived from Meximieux. They were unable to break through the German ring, and the platoon commander was badly injured in the attempt.

Technician 5th Grade George Scruggs and his armored car crew were defending a roadblock at Montreval when a Mark V Panther tank lumbered into view at about 1100 hours. Scruggs' gunner engaged the monster and managed to cripple it by hitting a track. Three hours later the cavalrymen spotted a self-propelled 88mm gun nosing forward with the presumed intention of doing them harm. The gunner opened up again, and the third round penetrated the final drive and set the panzer ablaze.

Inside the town, the cavalrymen spotted another Panther tank on the road to the east. Captain Piddington ordered two armored cars to advance abreast, firing their 37mm guns as fast as they could at the massive panzer's tracks—the only point reliably vulnerable to the light guns. The desperate plan worked, and the Panther halted in a spot where it could not bring its powerful main gun to bear. Captain John Wood, commanding Troop B, shot the panzer commander as he tried to climb out of the turret.

At about 1500 hours a second attempt to reach the men in Montreval, using a platoon of tanks, three armored cars, and one half-track, failed, at the cost of two light tanks and one M8. One section of tanks ran into a roadblock covered by antitank guns, and the lead M5A1 was destroyed by direct fire. The second section also ran into a hailstorm of hostile shells.

Back in town, Lt. Dan Lee took action for which he was later to be awarded the Medal of Honor. His citation described his deeds:

"After the fight had raged for hours and our forces had withstood heavy shelling and armor-supported infantry attacks, 2nd Lieutenant Lee organized a patrol to knock out mortars which were inflicting heavy casualties on the beleaguered reconnaissance troops. He led the small group to the edge of the town, sweeping enemy riflemen out of position on a ridge from which he observed seven Germans manning two large mortars near an armored half-track about a hundred yards down the reverse slope. Armed with a rifle and grenades, he left his men on the high ground and crawled to within thirty yards of the mortars, where the enemy discovered him and unleashed machine-pistol fire that shattered his right thigh. Scorning retreat, bleeding and suffering intense pain, he dragged himself relentlessly forward. He killed five of the enemy with rifle fire, and the others fled before he reached their position. Fired on by an armored car, he took cover behind the German half-track and there found a panzerfaust with which to neutralize this threat. Despite his wounds, he inched his way toward the car through withering machine-gun fire, maneuvering into range, and blasted the vehicle with a round from the rocket launcher, forcing it to withdraw. Having cleared the slope of hostile troops, he struggled back to his men, where he collapsed from pain and loss of blood."

Troop C and the rest of Company F, plus a battalion from the 179th Infantry Regiment, rushed to the scene, but the enemy's grip on Montreval was firm. VI Corps ordered the force not to attack, despite continuing resistance by the troopers in town. The last transmission out of Montreval from Captain Wood reported that the remaining troopers could not withdraw under any circumstances because there were too many wounded men. Wood and Piddington decided to surrender when a panzer pulled up in front of the building housing the CP and the wounded and fired its main gun through the wall.

When the Germans withdrew eastward the next day, they left behind twelve of the most seriously wounded, including Lieutenant Lee, with a squadron doctor. When squadron elements reentered the town, they found only four bodies. Indeed, 102 men—a third of them wounded—had been taken into captivity. Realizing that comrades feared dead were in fact prisoners, the squadron S-3 recorded that the disaster could have been worse. The doctor passed to Hodge compliments from von Wietersheim for the gallant fight that his men had waged in Montreval.

The Cavalry Stops Riding

The 117th Squadron was reduced to Troop C and a provisional Troop A, soon rejiggered into the usual three troops with only two platoons apiece. By the time the squadron rebuilt itself, the rat race had ended in the face of determined German resistance west of the Vosges Mountains. Optimism in the squadron ranks that the war would soon be over quickly faded away.[38]

Indeed, by 15 September the 3d Infantry Division's reconnaissance troop reported that it was receiving artillery fire at almost every roadblock it encountered and on several occasions had successfully directed counter-battery fire. Booby-trapped minefields slowed the advance. On 22 September the troop's lead elements reached the Moselle River only to find that the Germans had destroyed almost all of the bridges. The 3d Division was able to cross the river, but on 30 September the troop recorded, "[T]he enemy held high ground and woods east of the Moselle River and was fighting savagely for every foot of ground." The enemy was even infiltrating company-size elements behind the American front line, and reconnaissance platoons and the battle patrol had to be diverted to conducting nighttime security patrols to contain the menace.[39] The cavalry's charge was over.

★★★

Not far away, the 45th Infantry Division on 21 September was trying to identify river crossings because all of the bridges had been blown except in German-held Epinal. The 117th Cavalry Reconnaissance Squadron was helping out the division.

Early that morning, Brig. Gen. Frederic Butler, at VI Corps, ordered that Recon's battle patrol infiltrate across the Moselle at Archettes to seize the high ground around Hill 412. French forces to the division's right reported that there were four hundred German troops in Archettes, and patrols from the 117th Squadron identified five machine-gun nests there at hundred-yard intervals that were positioned to sweep the road on the west bank. At 1715 hours the battle patrol reported that it was still on the west bank and was receiving considerable small-arms and machine-gun fire from the far bank. It could see five German armored cars. Nonetheless, it had laid on an artillery preparation and would cross when the shelling ended.

The 1st Platoon tried to cross the river but found the current too swift at the chosen spot. Another place was found, and sometime after 1850 hours the battle patrol made it across.[40]

According to veterans, the members of the patrol were caught in a machine-gun kill zone when they tried to climb the east bank of the Moselle.[41] By 2108 the patrol had pulled back. Captain Raymond Baker contacted the division headquarters shortly after midnight, sounding shocked. "Our known casualties are 27, two dead, and seven missing. It is utterly impossible to cross the river at that point. I would like to know, what am I supposed to do?" He had only twelve men still standing.

The battle patrol was authorized to stand down, get dry clothes, and warm up.[42] It had paid a crushing price for Baker's success at turning cavalrymen into special assault troops.

CHAPTER 9

THE REICH'S TOUGH HIDE

Oh, we're the suicide unit of the fighting 44th
First to sight the enemy and strike with lighting force
With eyes of an eagle, we watch his every move
Report it to the proper ones; the enemy is through.

—44th Cavalry Reconnaissance Troop Song

The battle along Germany's western border most sharply highlighted the mismatch between a doctrine of non-combat reconnaissance and real-world conditions when mobile warfare was impossible. Everybody knew where the Germans were: To the north, they were in the Siegfried Line bunkers and trenches, and in the forests, cities, and stoutly constructed villages along the border that served as ready-made fortresses. From roughly Metz south, where the West Wall still lay well behind the front lines, the Germans held the forested approaches to the Vosges Mountains and the daunting heights themselves. If reconnaissance was not exactly suicide, it was a very tough prospect.

The Germans had few fresh first-rate troops to defend the border, but they had troops good enough to fight in prepared positions. Division and regimental staffs were generally intact as they reached the frontier from France, and they were able to take control over the disorganized rabble as it arrived in Germany and put the men into the line. Moreover, static or fortress battalions from inside the Reich were available to man the bunkers, and a few fresh formations, such as the 12th Infantry Division, in the Aachen sector, intervened at the critical moment to drain the Allied momentum. In this, the Germans were greatly abetted by the mounting Allied supply shortages, especially of fuel and ammunition, which had to be moved by truck all the way from the invasion beaches in Normandy and the Cote d'Azur.

The Cavalry Finds Its Limits

Operations against the static German defenses surpassed the cavalry's capabilities and doctrine and generally left the troopers to screen and secure against an enemy who had no interest in striking back on a large scale . . . yet. Indeed, conditions for most purposes resembled those of static trench warfare during the Great War, which had left the cavalry in all armies on the western front with little role to play. The story was pretty much the same along almost the entire American front; a few examples will suffice to capture the whole.

South of Aachen, the "Lucky 38th" Cavalry Reconnaissance Squadron could see the change immediately upon reaching the West Wall. As noted in the outfit's history, "The balance of September was spent defending the eight miles of squadron front against patrol action on the part of the Germans. . . . It was heartbreaking to see the strength build up in the Siegfried Line daily as the enemy became stronger."

On 1 October the squadron took over a three-mile stretch near Monschau from the 102d Cavalry Reconnaissance Squadron, adjacent to the 28th Infantry Division's zone in the Hürtgen Forest. Although the reduced frontage enabled the cavalrymen to patrol more aggressively, rifle strength was so low that it held its line primarily through establishing interlocking and grazing fields of fire for its machine guns, further covered by pre-plotted artillery fire plans. The men sowed antipersonnel mines liberally in all routes of approach from the fortifications a mile to the east. This was to be the squadron's home until late January.[1]

In the zone of XV Corps, which was transferred to Seventh Army in late September, the 106th Cavalry Group became engaged in and around the Foret de Parroy in support of the 79th Infantry Division. The outfit's informal history recorded, "Here we learned the bitterness of the infantryman without rest. Our forward pace was almost imperceptible: In 43 days, we advanced eight kilometers. There seemed to be only one way to escape the brush, the mud, the stunted trees—to be carried out. . . . [O]ver the entire period in Parroy, we lost more men than we had lost in the drive across France."[2]

After a month of near static warfare in the VI Corps area in Seventh Army, the 117th Cavalry Reconnaissance Squadron recorded in October, "Because of our long stay in this area, the enemy has complete knowledge of our positions, and the heavy vehicles are no longer moved. When a troop is relieved, the vehicles remain in place and the crews are changed." The squadron busied itself with vigorous dismounted patrolling, including going behind enemy lines to find German artillery emplacements and directing friendly fire onto them.[3]

★★★

One exception to the general pattern occurred in the Netherlands, where elements under the command of XIX Corps—the 7th Armored Division, the 113th Cavalry Group, and the Belgian Brigade—on 29 September began operations to clear the Peel marshes astride the boundary between 21st and 12th Army groups. Not only was the going tough for the cavalrymen involved, the troopers also found themselves in the path of one of the few armored counterstrokes that the Germans were willing to make while they hoarded panzers and other resources for a major counteroffensive in the Ardennes, currently planned for late November.

The 113th Cavalry Group and the Belgian Brigade attacked the German 176th Infantry Division across flat, marshy ground cut by innumerable streams and drainage ditches. The cavalry suffered so many losses in men and vehicles that, on 4 October, Col. William Biddle asked and received permission to halt the group's attack.[4]

The 7th Armored Division, which had arrived only the preceding day from Third Army's sector near Metz, kicked off on 30 September. The same streams, ditches, and swamps that afflicted the 113th Cavalry Group forced the tanks to stay on the roads, which were thoroughly mined and covered by fire from concealed tanks from the 107th Panzer Brigade, antitank guns, and

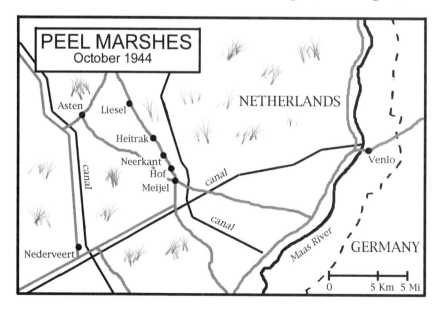

panzerfausts. On 2 October the Germans launched the first of a string of localized counterattacks that were to torment the 7th Armored Division continuously. The division's attack sputtered out by 5 October. During these operations, the 87th Cavalry Reconnaissance Squadron protected the division's flanks.

British 8 Corps took over the offensive effort on 12 October while the U.S. XIX Corps elements manned a thirty-mile defensive line and staged a mock attack to keep the Germans there in place. The British had made no more rapid progress than had the Americans by the time they stood down on 17 October.

Field Marshal Walter Model, who commanded Army Group B, about this time was looking for a way to ease pressure on the Fifteenth Army, which was defending the Shelde estuary against 21st Army Group assaults aimed at opening the shipping route into Antwerp. Model had available the XLVII Panzer Corps, which consisted of the 9th Panzer and 15th Panzergrenadier divisions, and his target was the 7th Armored Division positions in the Peel marshes, west of Venlo. The two divisions were not up to strength, but the 9th Panzer Division nonetheless fielded twenty-two Panthers, and the 15th Panzergrenadier Division could scrape together a half-dozen Mark IV tanks. (References to "Tigers" in American accounts are cases of misidentification.) The attack at 0615 hours on 27 October caught the Americans completely by surprise.[5]

The 87th Cavalry Reconnaissance Squadron sat athwart the main axis of attack, as recorded in its after-action report:

The town of Meijel was lightly held by the headquarters platoon of Troop C plus one platoon of assault guns from Troop E—a total of 43 men. Visibility was limited to about 50 yards because of a heavy morning mist. Then a few minutes after the [German] artillery stopped, a German officer suddenly stood up about 40 yards from the defensive position, shouting orders. Immediately about 200 enemy soldiers stood up all around him and behind him, and began to attack. They came in three waves, standing up, and they appeared to be drunk or doped. The defenders held their fire until the first wave was within 30 yards, and then opened up with every available weapon. The two assault guns were in the line, blasting away at ranges of 60, 50, and even 40 yards. All of the first and second wave were either killed or wounded excepting a few who filtered around the flanks, but the third wave came in throwing hand grenades, and they over-ran the position and gained the houses, from which they opened fire.

Meanwhile, the flank platoon had been called in to support, but as the enemy attack continued the position became untenable and at 0830 it was decided to withdraw and try to save the vehicles.

About a quarter of a mile out of town, the troop was met by [squadron executive officer] Major [Charles] Cannon, followed closely by Troop B. The reserve troop formed a defensive line through which Troop C withdrew, and then both troops parked their vehicles and organized for a counter-attack. At 0930, [squadron commanding officer] Lieutenant Colonel [Vincent] Boylan arrived and took command, pushing the attack off at 1010, with the two troops astride the road— C on the North and B on the South—and all four assault guns in support. The two troops pushed ahead side by side until Troop B reached the eastern edge of the woods just west of Meijel. Here, at the edge of a 500-yard open field, Troop B was stopped by automatic weapons, small arms, artillery, and mortars. They held at the edge of the woods, and Troop C pushed some distance farther, but was forced back to a point on line with Troop B.

With the arrival of the light tank company, Troop C organized for another attack along the same 200-yard front north of the Asten-Meijel road. On this attack, the 1st Platoon of the tank company swung wide to the left, protecting the left flank, while the 2d Platoon proceeded down the road, peeling off to the left in direct support, and the 3d Platoon followed down the road in local reserve. The flanking platoon took some prisoners, and one tank from the 2d Platoon was sent over to take them back. On the way across, it was hit by bazooka fire from the rear and knocked out. One after another, three tanks from the 1st Platoon were knocked out in the same way, so that only the platoon leader, Lt. Albert Bryant, and one other tank were left. These two pushed on into the woods [in the] vicinity [of] Hof and never came back. Meanwhile, two of the remaining tanks of the 2d Platoon were knocked out in rapid succession by an antitank weapon, and the attack again fell back to the line from which it started. . . . [An armored infantry battalion arrived at about 1300, and the troopers on foot were able to withdraw.]

The remaining light tanks from Company F resisted briefly, the company commander's gunner bouncing four rounds of 37mm AP off the leading tank, but Lieutenant Good's tank was promptly knocked out and further resistance was clearly useless. . . .

In the northern zone, held by Troop D, enemy infantry attacked at 0700 in the vicinity of Heitrack; Troop Headquarters was moved up in support of this section of the line, and the attack angled off to the south toward Neerkant, where a simultaneous attack was in progress. At this point the line was seriously threatened, but prompt artillery support plus intensive use of small arms stopped the enemy 100 yards in front of the defensive positions. In answer to a call for support, Lt. Col. John P. Wemple arrived at 0830 with one company of medium tanks, one of light, and one of tank destroyers. Troop D was then attached to this force, which in turn was a part of CCB. . . .

About noon, a Troop D M8 armored car was hidden behind haystacks and buildings at the Hoogebrug road junction, when three Tiger tanks moved slowly down the road, about 300–400 yards apart. The armored car allowed the first Tiger to pass, and then from a range of approximately 15 yards, pumped six rounds of 37mm AP into the rear of the tank. The tank was ditched, and the crew abandoned it. At least one member of the crew was killed as he fled. Meanwhile, the second Tiger continued up the road toward the junction, and the third swung off to the North to flank the armored car. The armored car escaped when the Tiger was within 200 yards. Later in the afternoon three [tank destroyers] and one medium were sent to get a Tiger; three [tank destroyers] and one medium were lost.[6]

The German spearheads made substantial progress on 27 and 28 October, despite the commitment of two 7th Armored Division combat commands. The cavalrymen were particularly hard-pressed in the Meijel sector, as recorded in the after-action report:

Troop C held its positions under this fire until 1000, when about 65 enemy came up in front of the 1st Platoon. These were blasted back by artillery fire and assault guns. At 1600 the enemy made a determined attack along this whole front. The line held, except the 2d

Platoon, which, being pushed forward, was flanked on both sides. Moreover, heavy mortar fire caved in foxholes and filled carbines with dirt so that they failed to function. The platoon leader, Lt. Charles Robertson Jr., ordered his men to withdraw to a ditch between the 1st and 3d platoons, while he personally covered their withdrawal with a machine gun. He was wounded at least once but continued firing; he was left behind and never got back. The platoon (2d) continued back past the ditch, and the 3d extended south to close the gap. Enemy tanks and infantry over-ran this line, but the troops held their positions and remained through the night although some enemy had got through behind them.

In the northern zone, the 1st Platoon of Troop D had repelled an aggressive enemy patrol during the night, with casualties on both sides. At daylight, the platoon leader's light tank (substitute for M8 armored car) was knocked out by an 88, and when a section from the 2d Platoon arrived to support, the armored car of the platoon sergeant who was leading the section was also hit by 88mm fire and burned. Enemy tanks and infantry continued to advance, and Troop D was driven back to the vicinity of Liesel. . . .[7]

Model called off the attack on 29 October rather than risk grave damage to the 9th Panzer and 15th Panzergrenadier divisions. He had nevertheless succeeded in drawing some British infantry from the Fifteenth Army's front to the threatened sector.[8]

This was the first time in northwestern Europe that the mechanized cavalry had confronted an organized and substantial armored attack. Events foreshadowed some of those during the Battle of the Bulge. Mechanized cavalry on its own could not withstand such pounding for a sustained period, and its ability to hold ground at all depended heavily on being able to call on supporting artillery fires. On the other hand, the troopers in the 87th Squadron learned invaluable lessons about fighting as infantry that they would put to use only six weeks later in the Ardennes.[9]

The November Offensive

Eisenhower, determined to keep pressure on the Germans all along the front, ordered the 21st, 12th, and 6th Army groups to mount an offensive in mid-November. For the first time, Ike shifted the main effort from 21st Army Group to 12th Army Group.[10]

At the northern end of the 12th Army Group's zone, the Ninth Army, which had taken responsibility for the northernmost stretch of the American sector, and First Army's VII Corps kicked off on 16 November, fully intending to reach the Rhine River in December. Instead, a muddy, grueling slugfest ensued, and the Americans had to fight hard just to advance the twenty miles to the west bank of the Roer River by the time Hitler's Ardennes counterstroke ended offensive operations on the Roer plain.

The 29th Cavalry Reconnaissance Troop was engaged in the brutal fight on the plain west of the Roer River. In a lessons-learned report, the troop concluded, "Mounted reconnaissance in terrain such as this is virtually impossible, and costly. Quarter-tons can be used to some extent, but use of the M8 in the forward areas is not advisable. For communications, the M8s have to be brought forward. We got around this by picking suitable locations during the day and moving the large vehicles up under cover of darkness."[11]

Harold Smith, who often accompanied his platoon commander, Lt. Thomas Fernley, on patrols, recalled, "They were usually two-man patrols with a lot of creeping and crawling. The less men you had with you, the better it was for stealth."[12]

The fighting on the Roer plain was smash-mouth, straight-ahead stuff, and even the far better protected tankers in the Shermans suffered high attrition rates. The 3d Armored Division, recognizing this reality, employed the 83d Armored Reconnaissance Battalion mainly to mop up behind the main advance, establish contact with neighboring units, and destroy abandoned German equipment.[13]

The 24th Cavalry Reconnaissance Squadron was attached to the 4th Infantry Division, which was the rightmost element in the offensive and faced perhaps the toughest conditions along the front as it battled through the Hürtgen Forest. This was no fight for the cavalry, and the troopers were used to man outposts along a counter-reconnaissance screen between the division's scattered regiments. This did not spare them constant bashing by German artillery.[14]

★★★

The 3d Cavalry Group was still attached to XX Corps with Patton's Third Army, which on 9 November kicked off a drive that Patton hoped would get him to the Rhine. While the infantry divisions struggled through torrential rains and mud to capture the fortress city of Metz, the cavalry group operated on the corps' left wing along a twenty-plus-mile front adjacent to the 90th Infantry Division north of Metz. The group was dubbed Task Force Polk, named for commanding officer Col. James Polk; it had been formed on 19 September when it had become apparent that forward movement was over for some time. Once again per Leslie McNair's vision, the group operated as the controlling headquarters for an ad hoc, combined-arms command. In addition to the 3d and 43d Cavalry Reconnaissance squadrons, Polk initially had under command the 689th Field Artillery Battalion (155mm), the 241st Field Artillery Battalion (105mm), the 705th and 807th Tank Destroyer battalions, and the 135th Engineer Combat Battalion. The task force was badly unbalanced, however, because it lacked rifle strength.

The task force nevertheless conducted limited-objective attacks during the November offensive, pushing in the direction of Saarburg. Polk used a consistent approach: All artillery, assault guns, and tank destroyers would fire on an objective. Reconnaissance teams probed; then the remainder of the reconnaissance troops attacked—mounted or dismounted, depending on circumstances. All towns were assaulted mounted.

When only one battalion of artillery was available, Polk used his squadrons in "seesaw" fashion. All artillery worked with one squadron until it had taken its objective, then switched to enable the second squadron to kick off.[15]

The XX Corps' history put it this way: "Task Force Polk, though lightly armored, used armored tactics whenever possible. . . . The cavalry, by a series of dashes, lightning changes of direction, and sometimes plain, ordinary bluffing, ran the gauntlet of enemy strongpoints. . . . Instead of barging head-on into centers of resistance, the XX Corps cavalry preferred more startling entrances from the flanks and rear, coming through farmyards, barns, or even stone walls. This unit made such frequent use of secondary roads that it was sometimes called the "Cowpath Spearhead."[16]

★★★

The 42d Cavalry Reconnaissance Squadron, along with the rest of the 2d Cavalry Group, was working on the right wing of Third Army's XII Corps southeast of Metz. In theory, the cavalry group's mission was merely to screen the corps' south flank.[17] James Stuckey and the rest of Troop C were in reserve in Coincourt on 12 November when Capt. "Buck" Harris learned that his men were to reconnoiter Ley, accompanied by a platoon of light tanks from Company F.

Troop A patrols had worked out that Ley was a strongpoint, and Squadron wanted to know how strong it was.

Harris led a dismounted party down a concealing draw to a spot about six hundred yards west of Ley while engineers cleared friendly mines outside Moncourt for the tanks. A German outpost evidently noticed the men on foot, and mortar shells started dropping around the troopers. Seeing that, Lieutenant Kraatz ordered his M5A1s forward toward the village.

Stuckey later described the "reconnaissance in force":

Now we moved forward to the attack, leaving our machine guns on the rise as a base of fire. That's when I think T/5 Dave Fearer was hit, because some heavy stuff started coming in and small arms and machine-gun fire laced into us from the town. We reached the road the tanks were on, about 300 yards from Ley where it turned east to enter town, and found it heavily mined. The tankers saw that too, and pulled up on our right, pumping their cannon and machine guns into town like holy hell.

It was getting pretty hot, and we could see the bridge blown out over the stream about 100 yards from town. We were ordered forward and gained the creek in a rush. Some Kraut machine gun in the church steeple was particularly obnoxious. Lynch and McDonald were both hit. Then Lt. Kraatz' boys really laid into that steeple. That stopped his water!

Now we ran into barbed wire and trenches. The grenades came in handy then, but with the mines we had seen along the creek bottom, and with the mud that was about four feet deep, we couldn't use the tanks in a rush. A couple of guys got into town, but they had us. The wounded were helped back. The tanks smothered the Krauts' small-arms positions until we got back to the ridge, but they couldn't stop those 150s from coming in![18]

★★★

The going was no easier for the mechanized cavalry in the armored divisions. The newly arrived 10th Armored Division was committed to the XX Corps offensive south of Metz on 16 November. Two reconnaissance troops from the 41st Cavalry Reconnaissance Squadron took the lead for Combat Command A, but resistance almost immediately proved too tough for the lightly armed cavalry. The troops shifted to secondary roads, but the story was the same. At Haute-Sierck, a reconnaissance platoon worked its way through a minefield and entered the village, only to become pinned down by fire from the second stories of the brick and stone houses that lined the road. The Sherman tanks behind the platoon could not fire their 75mm guns to full effect for fear of hitting the troopers. Once the situation was finally wrapped up, the reconnaissance troops were pulled back and employed for flank security.[19]

The infantry and armored divisions took Metz the hard way—with head-on attacks, for which the cavalry was unsuited. The city fell to this unremitting pressure on 22 November.

★★★

The 6th Army Group, at the extreme south of the front, made the most significant Allied gains in November. On 13 November, Seventh Army launched an offensive through the Vosges Mountains toward Strasbourg. XV Corps during this time employed its mechanized cavalry to screen its left flank during the advance, including the 106th and 121st Cavalry Reconnaissance squadrons and, for a period in mid-November, the 45th Cavalry Reconnaissance Troop. The corps on 21 November attached the 45th Recon to the 44th Infantry Division to guard its north flank. A counterattack aimed at the corps' flank by the Panzer Lehr Division on 23 November briefly discomfited the 106th Cavalry Group, but the advance of Third Army troops north of the XV Corps' zone compelled the Germans to withdraw several days later. Despite Panzer Lehr's counterstroke, the French 2d Armored Division liberated the city on 23 November. The corps pivoted northward over the next few days to advance astride the Vosges Mountains toward the German border.[20]

The 117th Cavalry Reconnaissance Squadron entered Strasbourg on 27 November with VI Corps' 3d Infantry Division shortly after its liberation by the French 2d Armored Division. The squadron then pushed north along the west bank of the Rhine as far as Gambsheim. Its job was to outpost the river line, and it obtained some DUKW amphibious trucks for its patrols. The Germans patrolled aggressively from the far bank, and there were many small clashes.[21]

Vernon Brown manned a recon jeep in the 14th Armored Division's Troop D, 94th Cavalry Reconnaissance Squadron, which had just arrived at the front and on 1 December relieved elements of the 117th Squadron in Weyersheim. Brown recalled, "Whereas our vehicles were shiny and new, theirs showed the signs of heavy wear and scars that must have come from flying shrapnel. Our jeep windshields were folded down flat and neatly encased in canvas covers; theirs had simply been discarded and machine-gun mounts welded to the right side of the vehicle. We also noticed their weapons. Many of the troopers wore captured German pistols, and the vehicles themselves contained a large collection of rifles and submachine guns, many more than the standard issue. They explained that on day patrols they liked to carry the long-range M1 rifles, while on night patrols the weapon of choice was the short-range, rapid-firing sub-machine gun, hence they picked up any stray weapons any place they found them. . . . These were a jaunty, dirty, ragged bunch, who seemed to be constantly listening or watching like animals might for the slightest sign of danger, and it gave us a sobering glance into our own future."22

CHAPTER 10

THE BATTLE OF THE BULGE

Between 0750 and 0815, all front line positions were attacked by enemy infantry supported by tanks or [self-propelled] guns.

—AAR, 14th Cavalry Group, 16 December 1944

E arly on 16 December, Hitler launched a three-pronged offensive along a seventy-five-mile front in the Ardennes that caught the defending First Army completely by surprise. In the north, the SS-heavy Sixth Panzer Army struck toward the Meuse River and Antwerp. In the center, the Fifth Panzer Army attacked toward Brussels. The Seventh Army pushed forward in the south to reel out a line of infantry divisions to protect the flank of the operation.

Good Luck at Monschau

The 38th Cavalry Reconnaissance Squadron held positions near Monschau, along what would become the northernmost shoulder of the Bulge. The "Lucky 38th" enjoyed about the most advantageous circumstances that a group of cavalrymen forced to hold ground could have.

The squadron held an unbroken main line of resistance studded with positions for its dismounted .50- and .30-caliber machine guns, which were laid in for grazing cross fire on the final protective line. The machine-gun positions included dug-in firing points from which light tanks could employ their coaxial machine guns. Barbed wire and flare trip wires covered the entire front. At night and during periods of poor visibility, troopers manned listening posts well forward.

The terrain consisted of high ground cut by a series of deep, rocky draws and overlooking fields bounded by hedgerows that offered some concealment but no cover. Behind the center of the line was one patch of dense woods.

Behind the squadron positions, a battalion each of the 9th and 1st Infantry divisions manned a secondary defense line. A platoon of M10s from the 893d

Tank Destroyer Battalion was attached, and the 62d Armored Field Artillery Battalion provided support. The squadron had substituted 81mm mortars for its 60mm mortars on a basis of two for three and trained intensively on them. The 102d Cavalry Reconnaissance Squadron held adjacent positions to the north, and the 99th and 2d Infantry divisions held the line to the south.

At 0525 hours on 16 December, a terrific artillery, mortar, and rocket barrage struck the 38th Squadron; a series of time-on-target concentrations first shook the main line of resistance, then rolled toward the artillery positions in the rear. The initial barrage lasted thirty-five minutes and was followed by heavy interdictory and harassing fire.

All telephone lines were broken; but even before the shelling eased, volunteer crews were out repairing the damage. At 0605, a tanker reported the first sounds of enemy activity, and ten minutes later Troop A reported that a radio transmission indicated the 78th Division was under assault at Kesternich.

Staff Sergeant Bielicki commanded the 2d Platoon of Company F, which was the first squadron element to be hit by the 751st Regiment of the 326th Volksgrenadier Division. Knowing that the barrage portended immediate

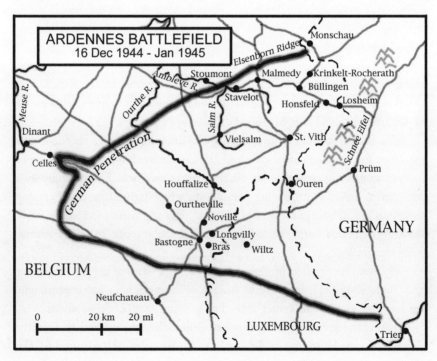

action and thinking quickly, Bielicki ordered all his tanks to load canister and open up when he fired his own gun. As it happened, an unlucky volksgrenadier tripped a flare, and his unit received what must have resembled a nineteenth-century grapeshot cannonade. All five 37mm guns disgorged a cloud of vicious steel pellets into the face of the enemy. As a mortar popped an illumination round, the tankers were overjoyed to see German troops running away in headlong retreat, leaving a carpet of bodies behind them.

Troop C opened up on the fleeing enemy with 81mm mortars, then directed artillery fire on that area until daylight. An ad hoc group from Company F headquarters arrived to reinforce the platoon.

The volksgrenadiers tried again at 0745 hours, and one group managed to work its way along the bed of the Roer River (still but a stream near its head-waters) and between two sections of tanks. Tank commander Sergeant Messano grabbed a .30-caliber machine gun and went into action to close the gap. Others joined him, and the enemy retreated with losses.

Troop C spotted the next German move and smeared a company of infantry with artillery. When another group revealed itself in some buildings, an M10 rolled up and pummeled the walls with 3-inch rounds. A secondary explosion blew out the walls of one house. Finally, sixty Germans trying to occupy some pillboxes received a barrage of 105mm fire, and the spark seemed to go out of the foe. Snipers became the main irritant for the remainder of the day.

On 17 December the Germans attacked repeatedly in platoon strength during the early morning hours and were driven off each time by artillery and machine-gun fire. A single self-propelled gun appeared, but Troop E's assault guns spotted it and knocked it out before it could do any harm.

The most dangerous attack, in battalion strength, struck Troop B at 0900. Infiltrators penetrated the line in one spot, and two artillery observers had to abandon their positions. A section of light tanks arrived, and Troop C observers were able to continue to provide artillery support. The squadron asked the 102d Cavalry Reconnaissance Squadron, which had experienced no enemy action except a few artillery rounds, for help.

A platoon of engineers arrived by truck at the critical moment and counter-attacked behind Sergeant Oxenham's M8 armored car. Oxenham stood in his turret and fired his .50-caliber machine gun as his driver charged straight at the enemy. Two observers from Troop E had also appeared and spotted German

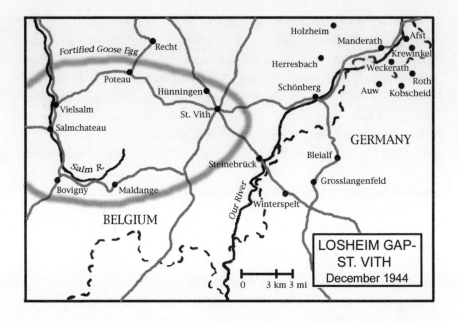

reinforcements emerging from one of the draws. The observers immediately called down fire on the group, and the 75mm shells killed more than fifty of the volksgrenadiers, the largest loss they suffered at any one point that day. The personnel at the Troop B command post, meanwhile, successfully beat off an infantry assault on the hedgerow that concealed the CP.

At 1023 hours the 102d Squadron reported that a company of armored infantry was on the way to help. By the time the men of Company A, 47th Armored Infantry Battalion, arrived at 1100, the squadron had fended off two more attacks in company strength or greater. Twenty minutes later, the squadron "borrowed" two passing platoons of medium tanks, and the crisis had passed. More than two hundred of the enemy by actual count lay strewn about the squadron's lines, but the troopers miraculously lost only two men.[1]

No Luck at All: The 14th Cavalry Group

The 14th Cavalry Group was deployed not far to the south of the 38th Squadron, defending the northernmost part of the VIII Corps zone astride the Losheim Gap, twenty miles northeast of the key road junction at St. Vith. The 18th Cavalry Reconnaissance Squadron (less Troop B) had moved into the area in late November, relieving elements of the 2d Infantry Division, and it now manned a series of strongpoints across a six-mile sector. The towed 3-inch guns from Company A, 820th Tank Destroyer Battalion, plus two of that outfit's reconnaissance platoons, anchored the left flank, and the untested 106th Infantry Division's 422d Infantry held the area just to the south. The group headquarters had arrived on 11 December to take charge of the 18th Squadron. Its second assigned squadron, the 32d Cavalry Reconnaissance Squadron, was refitting at Vielsalm after prior action with the 28th Infantry Division. Many of its vehicles and much of its equipment had been disassembled for maintenance and repair as of 16 December.

The terrain in the gap was hilly and covered by pine, so the strongpoints were generally located in small villages at crossroads. The skeptical troopers called them "sugar bowls" because they were "sugar" to any enemy that occupied the high ground that surrounded these settlements on all sides.

The squadron had made the best of the bad situation. It had deployed one or two armored cars, a like number of .50-caliber machine guns, and two or three 60mm mortars at each strongpoint. Barbed wire was strung for all-around protection. More than two hundred pre-plotted fire patterns involving all likely routes of advance had been worked out and were covered by the 105mm howitzers of the 275th Armored Field Artillery Battalion. All the squadron's assault guns had prepared positions for direct and indirect fire.

Colonel Mark Devine, the cavalry group commander, was concerned that there was little coordination with the 106th Infantry Division, to which the group was attached. He and his staff had just finished working out a contingency plan of their own should the Germans attack in force; he intended to circulate the plan on 16 December. Devine conceived of two fallback positions to which the 18th Cavalry Reconnaissance Squadron could withdraw under pressure, and he intended to bring the 32d Cavalry Reconnaissance Squadron forward to counterattack.

It just so happened that the boundary between the Sixth and Fifth Panzer armies ran right down the middle of the 18th Cavalry Reconnaissance Squadron's zone. The German 3d Airborne Division was to attack through the positions held by the tank destroyer detachment and cavalry strongpoints in Krewinkel, Afst, and Manderfeld (all in Belgium), while the 18th Volksgrenadier Division was to roll over the rest of the cavalry's strongpoints, all of which lay on the German side of the frontier. Indeed, the main weight of the 18th Division's attack was on its right, which had been reinforced by an assault gun brigade.

The only warning the troopers had of the attack, had they understood its significance, was that German flare activity to their front ended mysteriously on 14 December. One patrol stumbled onto a group of thirty riflemen the night of 15 December; it was the largest group the squadron had yet encountered in the area, but nobody thought much of it.

Freezing troopers were huddled in their weapons pits when, at 0525 hours on 16 December, the eerie stillness gave way to the sputtering sound of a buzz bomb approaching from inside Germany. Then the high ground of the Schnee Eifel, to the east, was suddenly backlit by a brightness, the meaning of which soon became apparent as shells of all sizes crashed into the squadron's positions. The light was a combination formed by artillery flashes and spotlights intended to prevent flash detection for counter-battery fire. Artillery concentrations dropped everyplace the Germans thought it was logical for the Americans to have established defenses, including unoccupied hills. "It was intense, stunned all of us a little," recalled one lieutenant.

The barrage lasted twenty minutes. Expecting the worst, the men readied their battle positions, but only the strongpoint at Roth—held by a reconnaissance platoon, Troop A headquarters personnel, and two towed tank destroyers—found itself under immediate attack by a company of infantry from the 18th Volksgrenadier Division, supported by a few assault guns. Defensive fire by the 105mm howitzers dealt with the threat for the moment.

Things changed as weak gray light began to illuminate the battlefield. Between 0750 and 0815 hours, German infantry—supported by armor and advancing in suicidal mass formations while singing and shouting—hit at every point along the cavalry front. At Krewinkel, German paratroopers marched in parade formation almost to the barbed wire line before the cavalrymen opened fire. Despite taking heavy casualties, the Germans got into town, and fighting raged among the buildings. The troopers in nearby Afst also waited until the Germans had reached the wire—the troopers ironically could see their silhouettes because of the backlighting intended to hide German artillery positions—before cutting loose; in that case the enemy pulled back immediately after losing thirty men killed.

At Kobscheid, Troop A's Pvt. Joseph Gallo manned a machine gun. "I wouldn't have noticed them, except some of them screamed," he recalled a short while after the battle. "It was not quite light, just about daybreak when I saw them. They were only twenty-five yards away from my position, about fifty of them all in one bunch. I let go and they dropped. A lot of them were yelling as if they were hurt bad." Soon, the Kobscheid position was taking fire from all directions and was ringed by defensive fires from the field artillery. One mortarman had removed the base from his weapon so he could drop shells as close as twenty-five yards away.

A platoon of Company F's M5A1s tried to reach the men at Roth at 0930 but found the way blocked by heavy German armor. At the north end of the sector, the Germans by this time were into the tank destroyer positions, and the squadron ordered the guns to pull back at 1000. Only two guns were able to get away.

The cavalry group attempted to implement its brand-new contingency plan, and a general order for withdrawal to the first fallback line at Manderfeld reached troop commanders at 1100 hours. Devine also instructed the 32d Cavalry Reconnaissance Squadron to move forward. Here, Clausewitz's "friction" in war reared its ugly head. Hotly engaged strongpoints were unable to comply, and the 32d Cavalry Reconnaissance Squadron, with many of its vehicles partially disassembled for maintenance, was in no condition to mount a counterattack.

Troop A's Capt. Stanley Porche, in Roth, replied that his positions were surrounded and withdrawal was inadvisable. In that he was right: At 1100 Porche radioed the Kobscheid garrison and indicated that the squadron was pulling back. "Advise you to withdraw on foot," Porche said, but his besieged troopers there were no more able to move during daylight. The last transmission from Porche at about 1600 hours reported, "Tanks 75 yards from CP, firing direct fire. Out." Only one man escaped Roth to reach friendly lines.

Troop C's CP, meanwhile, was in Weckerath, theoretically protected by the 3d Platoon in a strongpoint not far to the east. The 3d Platoon fended off the advancing enemy during the early morning hours with machine guns, mortars, and artillery fire, but the volksgrenadiers swarmed around each flank and entered the village. At 0900, Lt. James Miller and his 3d Platoon, Company F, rolled into Weckerath to cover the withdrawal of the reconnaissance platoon and headquarters. Small-arms fire rattled off the armor like rain on a tin roof. Miller shuttled his tanks through town as turrets rotated to the left and right and guns blasted the enemy. "[They] bunched together, just egging us to hit them with canister," Miller recalled.

In response to the withdrawal order at 1100 hours, the Troop C garrisons in Krewinkel and Afst clambered aboard every vehicle that would run; they pulled to the rear, blazing away at the Germans to keep their heads down. The Germans had only light reconnaissance elements in the immediate area. Only a single man was wounded during the escape to Manderfeld, the location of Devine's group CP.

The cavalrymen in Weckerath also pulled back under covering fire from the assault guns to the rear and from Miller's tanks, which fought as a rear guard. The weather was so cold that drivers had to stand on the clutch pedals to get the armored cars in gear, and the vehicles could manage only about ten miles per hour. Just five minutes after the troopers cleared Weckerath, a German time-on-target barrage leveled the village.

The Troop A garrison at Kobscheid waited until dark, then destroyed its vehicles and withdrew on foot. At that moment, the 14th Cavalry Group was pulling back from Manderfeld toward the second fallback position. The troopers at Manderfeld had been under no enemy pressure, but it had been clear that the 3d Airborne Division was sweeping by the north flank, and it looked very much like the 18th Volksgrenadier Division was about to do the same on the south flank. The remnants of the 18th Squadron joined the gradually arriving 32d Squadron along a delaying line running from Herresbach to Holzheim. (At this time, the 18th Cavalry Reconnaissance Squadron's Troop B was on detached service with the 106th Infantry Division, where more than half its personnel went missing in action between 16 and 22 December.)

The 18th Squadron's withdrawal had dire consequences for the 106th Infantry Division, because it allowed the volksgrenadiers to envelop the 422d Infantry Regiment's north flank. The 18th Volksgrenadier Division's southern pincer arm at the same time was breaking through and turning the right flank of the neighboring 423d Infantry Regiment, and within four days both regiments surrendered. Still, the cavalry group had kept the division command fully informed of its actions during the day, and the responsibility for the failure to take remedial action must rest there. Indeed, Maj. Gen. Alan Jones, commanding the 106th Infantry Division, during the evening fended off first a warning from VIII Corps about his exposed flank, then a suggestion that he pull back his two exposed regiments. The cavalry had delayed the advance of an enemy overwhelmingly superior in numbers and firepower, which was all that even the robust doctrine for pre-war horse cavalry had asked of the troopers.

Pecked at by German attacks, on 17 December the cavalry group fell back again nearly ten miles and established its headquarters at Poteau. Some historians, such as Charles MacDonald, have implied that the outfit's will to fight had badly weakened by this point. It is worth recalling the conditions under which all cavalry units along the Siegfried Line that autumn had been expected to be able to fight off large-scale infantry attacks for more than an hour or two: Positions for automatic weapons were carefully constructed to create fields of overlapping fire, barbed wire was strung, pre-plotted artillery fire patterns were worked out, and mines were often laid. The cavalry group, once driven from its initial positions, had none of these conditions working for it and had no reserve, and the Germans were steadily bypassing its flanks. Perhaps the inclination to withdraw is more understandable from this perspective, although better leadership might have produced a somewhat different outcome.

That evening, while returning from the 106th Division CP in St. Vith, Col. Mark Devine's column drove into an ambush, but the colonel managed to escape on foot. By the time he had trudged nine miles through the snow to his CP, he had evidently "cracked" and told Lt. Col. William Damon, commanding the 18th Squadron, to take over. Damon, however, was almost immediately summoned to St. Vith, and the eventual appearance of Devine's executive officer, Lt. Col. Augustine Dugan—who had also escaped the encounter with the Germans—resulted in his taking command in Poteau.[2]

★★★

While all this was happening, the 106th Infantry Division's cavalry reconnaissance troop was fighting in the village of Grosslangenfeld, not far from—but out of sight of—Troop B, 18th Cavalry Reconnaissance Squadron. The division had provided the troop with no artillery fire plan. In other words, the troop was unable to prepare even the artillery-backed strongpoints that the cavalrymen had constructed farther north. A single telephone wire ran to the 424th Infantry Regiment, and radio silence was mandatory.

Then-Lt. Joseph Haines, who gathered the accounts of more than thirty men who were there, described the untried troop's struggle:

> At approximately 0530 on 16 December 1944, we came under attack by German artillery, rockets, and mortars. This attack set fire to several buildings in the village, including my command post. The barn where our ammunition trailer had been hidden took a direct hit during the night of 16–17 December, and our ammunition supply was destroyed except for the small amounts we had placed at various platoon positions.

Shortly after the initial shelling ceased, German infantry began to advance toward our positions in Grosslangenfeld. We were successful in repulsing them with small arms, machine guns, and 60mm mortar fire; the mortar ammunition was soon exhausted. Later in the morning, another attack was mounted, and again repulsed, with heavy losses to the Germans. . . .

Shortly after the German attack began early on 16 December, our telephone lines were cut to the 424th Infantry Regiment. We were now out of communication with anyone. The troop commander sent out mounted patrols to both flanks in an attempt to make contact with adjacent units (Cannon Company of the 424th and Troop B, 18th Cavalry Reconnaissance Squadron). The patrol to the left flank returned to report they had made contact with Troop B, 18th Cavalry Reconnaissance Squadron, and were told, "We thought you guys were wiped out!" Heavy firing was heard on our right flank during this period, and the patrol we sent to the right flank (Cannon Company) did not return; nor did we receive a report from them since we were forbidden to use our radios.

Once the fighting started on the 16th, we uncovered our armored cars and began firing the 37mm cannon at the attacking German troops. Since these guns were received new in England, we had never had an opportunity to "bore sight" or fire the guns—we accomplished the "bore sighting" firing at the enemy! The ground attacks and shelling continued off and on throughout the day of the 16th, but tapered off that night.

Early on the morning of 17 December, the enemy ground attacks and shelling resumed. We were successful in repulsing the ground attacks, but were running critically short of ammunition. Around noon on the 17th, the troop commander, Capt. Paul Million, called an officer's meeting at his command post to discuss the situation and determine a plan of action. After reviewing the situation, it was determined that only two courses of action were available: One, to continue to hold our position until all ammunition was exhausted and be killed or captured; or, two, to break contact with the enemy and attempt to fall back to Schönberg where it was believed the division reserve was located. It was believed if we could get back to contact Division, we could get updated on the situation, get supplied with food and ammunition, and receive new orders.

Course of action two was adopted and orders (verbal) were issued that on a given signal we would break contact, one position at a time, and attempt to reach Schönberg to the north. . . . Our withdrawal began shortly after 1300 with the 1st Platoon successfully breaking contact and withdrawing as planned. Headquarters and part of Headquarters Platoon then fell in line behind the 1st Platoon and began their withdrawal. The 2d Platoon managed to break contact with two-thirds of the platoon intact and joined the withdrawal (the third section of the 2d Platoon was cut off by advancing German troops and unable to complete the withdrawal). The 3d Platoon leader had arrived late to the officer's meeting and either misunderstood the direction of withdrawal or discovered the planned route was now blocked by the enemy (I believe the latter to be the case); he attempted to withdraw back the way we had initially entered Grosslangenfeld— from Winterspelt to the west and the area of the 424th Infantry Regiment. Their first vehicle in line was struck and disabled by a mortar or artillery shell thereby blocking the road (possibly by "friendly fire," since it had been reported to others in our sector that "Grosslangenfeld had fallen" the previous day). Lt. Johnstone was "slightly" wounded when a mortar shell exploded on the rail of his half-track. The enemy was then able to quickly overrun those still remaining in Grosslangenfeld— which included the 3d Platoon, parts of Headquarters Platoon, and the third section of the 2d Platoon. During this brief encounter of intensive fighting, several members of the troop were killed or wounded. The wounded and other survivors were quickly taken prisoner and marched to the rear into Germany.

The sections of the troop that managed to withdraw proceeded in a northerly direction on the paved road that ran through Grosslangenfeld toward Bleialf. However, attempting to avoid contact with the enemy, we decided to leave this major roadway and travel cross-country, with the hopes of making contact with friendly forces. Shortly after leaving the paved road, we entered a deserted village (Winterscheid, in the 423rd Infantry Regiment area) where we stopped to put tire chains on our vehicles. Resuming our trek, we met up with elements of Troop B, 18th Cavalry Reconnaissance Squadron, at a crossroads just outside Winterscheid. They were really surprised to see us—they thought we had been "eliminated" the day before (16 December). It was decided we would join them in the attempt to reach Schönberg. Troop B, 18th Cavalry Reconnaissance Squadron, attached to the 423rd, had been given approval by radio to withdraw the day before—16 December! We were not aware of this decision, which left our left flank completely exposed.

We fell in behind Troop B, 18th Cavalry Reconnaissance Squadron, and continued northward on secondary roads toward Schönberg. During our journey, we were under occasional artillery fire, including some tree bursts, until it began to get dark. We stopped on a wooded knoll just short of Schönberg to confer with the officers of Troop B. . . . After a short conference, it was decided we would break up into small groups and attempt to infiltrate the lines west toward St. Vith and get back to what we hoped would be American territory.

We disabled our vehicles, guns, and radios, then walked a short distance into the woods to what appeared to be a woodcutter's shack. It was then decided we would spend the night here and see what the situation was in the morning. Just after daylight on 18 December 1944, we were nudged awake by German troops holding submachine guns and rifles and told we were now prisoners of war and the war was over for us![3]

Delaying Action at St. Vith

Field Marshal Walter Model, commanding Army Group B, believed that the Ardennes offensive would become a battle for road junctions because of the restrictive terrain.[4] The Sixth Panzer Army was tangled on the northern shoulder of the penetration by the tenacious defense offered by the 99th and 2d Infantry divisions and the "Lucky 38th," and the German Seventh Army was making slow progress on the southern shoulder. The Fifth Panzer Army, in the center, badly needed the road junction at St. Vith, and it expected to capture the objective by 17 December.[5]

Combat Command B, 9th Armored Division, which had been attached to V Corps and was released at 1120 hours, was the first reinforcing element to reach St. Vith on 16 December, passing through the town with orders to destroy enemy forces at Winterspelt. The 27th Armored Infantry Battalion with Troop D, 89th Cavalry Reconnaissance Squadron, attached was sent ahead to hold the high ground south of the Our River at Steinebrück and to take Winterspelt on division order. The 62d Volksgrenadier Division's 2d Battalion, 164th Grenadier Regiment, reached Steinebrück just about the same time, and there the advance came to a halt.[6]

★★★

By 17 December, VIII Corps' analysis of the German attacks led it to the same conclusion as Model: The Germans needed more roads than they had available. Therefore, the corps would concentrate on building defenses before the key road centers of St. Vith, Bastogne, Houffalize, and Luxembourg City.[7]

St. Vith was still in the hands of what was left of the 106th Infantry Division when the 87th Cavalry Reconnaissance Squadron led the 7th Armored Division into town late on 17 December after a sixty-mile march over clogged and slippery roads. The division had been transferred to VIII Corps the preceding day. Major General Jones, 106th Infantry Division, passed command to Brig. Gen. Bruce Clarke of Combat Command B. Clarke set about organizing a horseshoe-shaped defensive perimeter around the town, supported by CCB, 9th Armored Division, and the remnants of a regiment each from the 106th and 28th Infantry divisions. Clarke found the 14th Cavalry Group's situation to be "one of confusion and extremely hazy," and he deployed the 87th Cavalry Reconnaissance Squadron to the northeast to link up with the 14th Cavalry Group and screen the left flank. He fed each new battalion into the perimeter as it arrived.

Clarke's goal was to delay the Germans as long as possible, not to hold St. Vith indefinitely. Indeed, his division commanding officer, Brig. Gen. Robert Hasbrouck, commented shortly after the battle, "I don't think we ever got any orders to hold St. Vith. We just came and defended." The Germans were preoccupied with reducing the two surrounded regiments of the 106th Infantry Division and would first attack the defenses at St. Vith in any strength on 20 December.[8]

Hasbrouck, upon arriving on the scene, ordered Lt. Col. Augustine Dugan in Poteau to retake ground abandoned the previous day. Dugan rallied his troops and attempted to mount a counterattack with an ad hoc task force drawn from men of both squadrons early on 18 December, the initial objective being high ground near Recht. Unfortunately, the 1st SS Panzergrenadier

Regiment was at that very same time moving against Poteau from Recht. A bazooka round struck an assault gun, which was the second vehicle in the column, after the task force had moved less than two hundred yards, and enemy infantry closed from both sides. All vehicles opened fire, and the column backed down the road into Poteau. Captain Henry Williams, the squadron's assistant S-2 (operations), later conceded that "the men were tired and discouraged, and when no assistance was given them, they gave the job up."

The cavalrymen held onto the town, but just barely. A panzer inside of ten minutes destroyed two assault guns and an armored car. And one of two light tanks supporting a patrol that attempted to clear some woods on high ground overlooking Poteau was disabled by artillery fire. At noon the cavalry group fell back once more. That afternoon the 7th Armored Division took charge of the remnants and ordered the group to reorganize as a single squadron. Hasbrouck clearly was not happy, and of the reorganization said, "[We] got rid of the lame, halt, and blind." Dugan was relieved of command. The 14th Cavalry Group had lost 28 percent of its manpower (some later reappeared after wandering through the forest) and 35 percent of its vehicles.[9]

★★★

Action came quickly for Troop A, 87th Cavalry Reconnaissance Squadron, which deployed several hundred yards from Hünningen. At 0800 hours on 18 December, a hundred German infantry supported by a platoon of Mark IVs approached the line. The cavalrymen fired at the infantry, who went to ground, but the approach of the panzers left the troopers, bereft of antitank defenses, little choice but to draw back toward St. Vith.

At 1100 the "cavalry" arrived to save the cavalry in the form of a column from the 811th Tank Destroyer Battalion, which engaged the Mark IVs and forced them to pull back. This fortuitous event transpired because CCB, 9th Armored Division, had just moved in force into the area to engage the 1st SS Panzer Division. The Germans evidently gave up on this route, and the troop was left in relative peace for the remainder of the operations at St. Vith.[10]

★★★

The 62d Volksgrenadier Division, meanwhile, made a determined effort on 18 December to capture Steinebrück from the 9th Armored Division's CCB. Troop D, 89th Cavalry Reconnaissance Squadron, underwent a pounding from artillery and panzers on the far bank of the Our. The Germans smoked the stone bridge across the river, and patrols infiltrated the village. As the action became fiercer, a provisional company of infantry from the 106th Division evacuated without orders. A handful of courageous engineers planted explosives and rendered the bridge unusable by vehicles, but the Germans hit Troop D in better than company strength and overran the 2d Platoon. Only five troopers fought their way free. By midafternoon it was clear that the rest of the troop was about to be encircled, and after as many men as could do so clambered aboard the armored cars and remaining jeeps, the troop moved out toward safety.[11]

Corporal Charles Raney recalled the action from his perspective:

> We . . . were sent into another break in the line at a railroad depot and stream just a few miles from St. Vith. . . . Here we fought a long-range battle, 500 to 5,000 yards, with the Germans. One of our platoons to our left, a ways up the tracks, was entrenched and overrun. . . .
>
> [W]e set up a machine gun on the hillside directly behind the station building. From there we could see what we were shooting at and give better protection to the armored cars below us with their 37mm guns. . . . [A]ll the vehicles pulled out while we were on the hill. We couldn't cross the road to where our jeep was parked, as there was a direct line of fire down this road at the retreating vehicles.
>
> A year later at a reunion we found out what happened. Our troop was put into this hole . . . to hold the advance at this road to St. Vith as long as possible giving the rest . . . time to move back and set up new defenses, dig in, and get all the commands working together again after being surprised and scattered. This we did till our troop commander, Captain Dow, found that the enemy had broken through on our left and was surrounding us. Thinking, I suppose, that we were of no more use where we were, he gave orders over the radios to pull out as we could. This is when the vehicles all pulled out, forgetting us on the hill. They had to fight a running battle for about two miles, and some vehicles were lost and three men were shot off the armored cars. . . .[12]

Raney was captured a short while later while trying to find his way to American lines.

★★★

A heavy artillery barrage slammed into St. Vith at about 1400 hours on 21 December, and infantry probed the lines of Troop B, 87th Cavalry Reconnaissance Squadron, east of the village at about 1800 hours. At 2030, the sound of enemy tanks and heavy firing carried from the Schönberg road. Sergeant Leonard Ladd headed back to St. Vith to find the 23d Armored Infantry Battalion CP. Just as he reached the outskirts, a panzer took up a position on a railroad bridge and opened fire on the town. Two tank destroyers engaged the tank but were unable to knock it out, and they pulled back.

Ladd found Germans crawling all over St. Vith and headed instead for the CCB headquarters, where he personally spoke to Brigadier General Clarke to explain the situation. Clarke told him that he had ordered a withdrawal over four or five radio channels. The reconnaissance troop clearly had not received the message.

Back at St. Vith, thirty-five Troop B men at the outfit's motor park realized they were cut off, and they headed for safety through pitch black and swirling snow. Soon they spotted another clump of men and, after a few nervous moments, identified them as Americans. The enlarged group trudged on and soon encountered a band of men from Troop C, and the now the hundred soldiers made their way to safety. Nothing further was heard from the remainder of Troop B, which had been overrun.[13]

Some Redemption for the 14th Cavalry Group

The American forces around St. Vith were under steadily growing pressure from five German divisions, and Hasbrouck was increasingly worried that the 2d SS Panzer Division, advancing to his south, would cut his only remaining line of supply. On 22 December, Hasbrouck told a representative sent by Field Marshal "Monty" Montgomery, who had taken charge of the Allied forces on the north side of the Bulge on 20 December, that he did not want to stay in the area west of St. Vith unless it was viewed as critical terrain. Hasbrouck also wrote to Maj. Gen. Maxwell Ridgeway, commanding XVIII Corps (which had taken control over the St. Vith forces on 20 December), "In my opinion, if we don't get out of here and up north of the 82d [Airborne Division] before night, we will not have a 7th Armored Division left." Monty authorized a pullback, despite misgivings on Ridgeway's part.

CCB of the 9th Armored Division had to slip away first, covered by the 7th Armored Division. At 0500 hours on 23 December, Hasbrouck informed CCB that because it was uncertain that the 82d Airborne Division could hold open the escape route across the Salm River, immediate disengagement was necessary. The operation began at 0700, and CCB tanks and half-tracks picked up and carried the dismounted GIs from the 106th Infantry Division's 424th Infantry as they went. The combat command had cleared the area by noon.[14]

The 14th Cavalry Group, operating as a single squadron incorporating the remnants of the 18th and 32d squadrons, was split among the three task forces that Hasbrouck had established to cover his withdrawal from the area west of St. Vith.

Captain Willard Wamke commanded provisional Troop A, made up of about a hundred men from the 32d Squadron, which was part of Task Force Navaho (mainly Combat Command Reserve [CCR], 7th Armored Division), on the northern and eastern rim of the "fortified goose egg," as the positions at St. Vith came to be known. The troop had reported to the task force commander on 19 December with four M8s, an M20 utility armored car, three half-tracks, and 2 1/2-ton truck, and it was ordered to dig in. The sector remained surprisingly quiet until shortly before daylight on 23 December, the day of the withdrawal, when a man ran into the CP to report that his outpost had been overrun.

The outposts were important because the cavalry's job was to screen the task force's retreat westward through Vielsalm. Lieutenant Joseph Mezga piled seventeen men into a half-track and set out to recapture the outpost. The troopers spotted a burning M8 armored car and a dozen German soldiers as they approached, but by the time the troopers had dismounted, the Germans had disappeared. They or their comrades, however, signaled their presence by shooting anytime a man exposed himself. Mezga's command stayed under cover while—to the rear—tanks, tank destroyers, and other vehicles pulled out as engineers prepared the last bridge east of Vielsalm for demolition.

Mezga's team was the last to go. The Germans showed themselves again as the troopers clambered into their half-track and raced off. The half-track quickly left the enemy behind and roared down the road to the bridge. Two engineers tried to detonate their explosive charges, but the plunger failed. Mezga stopped the half-track and spent twenty nerve-racking minutes covering the engineers, who struggled to find another way to destroy the bridge. Finally, the explosives went off, and the relieved troopers slipped away across the Salm River to the new defensive line being set up by the 82d Airborne Division and remnants of the 106th and 28th Infantry divisions.

★★★

Captain Franklin Lindsey Jr. commanded a special task force made up entirely of about 120 cavalrymen from Troop B, 32d Cavalry Reconnaissance Squadron. In Hasbrouck's words, "They backed up the 424th Infantry, which I never had any faith in because they were so pooped. . . ." The troop had almost its normal complement of armored cars available, and from 19 to 23 December fought a series of delaying actions along the southeastern edge of the goose egg alongside some riflemen who had been separated from their units. Early on 23 December, orders arrived that the 7th Armored Division would pull back from that area beginning at 0700 hours. The task force was to hold in place until 1300 to cover the column.

Lindsey ordered his platoons to fall back in stages beginning at 1245, but the plan nearly came undone when German infantry, supported by artillery and assault guns, hit the troopers holding the road junction at Maldange at about 1225. The cavalrymen managed to hold until 1259, when they opened up their throttles and ran through a gauntlet of interdictory fire toward Salmchateau. That evening at the 7th Armored Division CP, Brigadier General Clarke called this "one damn good job of delaying action—a job well done."

★★★

Captain Charles Martin commanded provisional Troop C, reinforced by three M8 assault guns and a platoon of light tanks. The troop on 20 December had reported to Lt. Col. Robert Jones, 814th Tank Destroyer Battalion, in charge of a task force of the 7th Armored Division's CCR at Bovigny. Jones instructed Martin to deploy a counter-reconnaissance screen of three mini task forces along the southwestern rim of the goose egg, and he provided a few tank destroyers and engineers to help out. The troopers found that they definitely did not man a quiet stretch of the line but were engaged in close-range firefights from the first moments. Fortunately, the Germans had no tanks, so the M5A1 light tanks and M8 armored cars were the kings of the battlefield.

Task Force Jones ran into German tanks and infantry south of Salmchateau when it pulled back on 23 December. The 2d SS Panzer Division had worked its way to the west side of the Salm from the south, and Task Force Jones had to fight for every mile toward the safety of the 82d Airborne Division lines. The command broke up into small groups, and Troop C had to abandon and cripple its vehicles so the men could escape through wooded hills to the west.

★★★

Troop D, 87th Cavalry Reconnaissance Squadron, was deployed at Baraque de Fraiture, which lies nearly due west of Vielsalm, on 23 December when the southwestern wall of the deflating fortified goose egg collapsed. Major Arthur Parker, 589th Field Artillery Battalion, 106th Infantry Division, had established an ad hoc blocking position there on 19 December with a pair of his remaining 105mm guns, gradually adding the cavalry troop and assorted odds and ends. The defenders were strong enough to drive off infantry probes, but on 23 December the 2d SS Panzer Division arrived, and the roof caved in at what became known as Parker's Crossroads (although Parker had been wounded and evacuated).

During the morning, Lt. Arthur Olsen, of Troop D, told an interviewer, the SS cut the road to the rear, completing the isolation of the roadblock. At about 1700 hours, a heavy artillery concentration began falling on the crossroads, and shortly thereafter an estimated two battalions of infantry and two companies of enemy tanks came at the block from three directions.

The panzers knocked out several American tanks and all of the cavalry's armored cars. The defenders fled for their lives, some of the troopers clawing free only after hand-to-hand combat. The troopers drifted back to friendly lines over the next four days. When all was said and done, forty-four men remained unaccounted for.[15]

★★★

After a week of battle, the 14th Cavalry Group had lost 20 percent of its officers, 33 percent of its enlisted personnel, and 53 percent of its vehicles. The group's headquarters estimated that the troopers had killed some four thousand of the enemy in turn, half of them by directing artillery fire against the attackers on the first day of the battle.[16] On 24 December, much of the cavalry group was temporarily incorporated into the 87th Cavalry Reconnaissance Squadron, which had lost two reconnaissance troops during the engagement at St. Vith.[17] Troop B, 32d Cavalry Reconnaissance Squadron, became provisional Troop D of the 87th Squadron, and Troop C, 32d Squadron, provisionally replaced Troop B, 87th Squadron.[18]

The Stand at Bastogne

The stubborn defense at St. Vith, combined with determined stands farther north at Rocherath-Krinkelt, limited the Sixth Panzer Army to a twenty-mile-deep but only five-mile-wide salient carved out by the 1st SS Panzer Division spearhead. To the south, meanwhile, the Fifth Panzer Army had sent the 2d Panzer and Panzer Lehr divisions racing for a second key road junction at Bastogne.

The 10th Armored Division was attached to VIII Corps as its third armored division on 16 December and was assigned assembly areas near Luxembourg.[19] On 18 December, Troop D, 90th Cavalry Reconnaissance Squadron, assembled with Combat Command B, 10th Armored Division, at Arlon, Belgium. The troop rolled out at the head of the armored column to lead the way to Nothum; but, while on the road, new orders arrived—head for Bastogne. That the situation there was "fluid and obscure" was all the division had learned from VIII Corps. Major General Troy Middleton had ordered, "Move with the utmost speed. Hold [those] positions at all costs."[20]

The lead elements arrived in Bastogne about dusk, pressing by stragglers who jammed the roads trying to escape to the south and west. Confusion bordered on panic in some cases. CCB, which was placed under direct corps control, formed a screen consisting of three small task forces east of town, each of which had a reconnaissance platoon attached to it. Those task forces had to delay the enemy onslaught long enough for the just arriving 101st Airborne Division to dig in to hold the vital town.

The 1st Platoon joined the fifteen Shermans and four hundred soldiers, mostly armored infantrymen, of Maj. William Desobry's team in Noville, where at about 1400 hours on 19 December German tanks and infantry first probed the American positions. The platoon had taken up positions at the south end of town and organized for close-in defense. Most of the action during the morning took place northeast of the village, where Shermans and a platoon of tank destroyers that had arrived at an opportune moment engaged tanks of the 2d Panzer Division. That afternoon, when the first German tank appeared in front of the cavalrymen, Technician 5th Grade George Coward Jr. set it ablaze with an armor-piercing round from his M8 armored car at a distance of nine hundred yards. Platoon gunners during the course of the afternoon convinced three other panzers to draw off by peppering them with ineffective but apparently alarming 37mm fire.

The 3d Platoon, attached to Team O'Hara, had been given the mission of outposting Bras. The troop's after-action report described the scene: "About 0800, civilians who were entering Bras reported enemy tanks approaching from north and east. The platoon leader, 2d Lt. Hubert Schietinger, took a [machine-gun] jeep and started to check the report. . . . When he reached about 800 yards north of Bras, he could hear the tanks approaching from the east. He returned to the platoon and ordered it to withdraw to Team O'Hara's position immediately, with the jeeps first and the two armored cars covering the withdrawal. The platoon leader with his jeep remained with the last armored car, and before they could leave, the first tank came into view out of the fog at about 100 yards range. The tank was unbuttoned, and the armored car opened up with .50-caliber machine-gun fire and six rounds of 37mm AP and got away before a return shot was fired." The platoon joined Team O'Hara's position and warned the task force, which was able to hold most of its ground until pulling back early in the evening.

The 2d Platoon, attached to Team Cherry at Longvilly, had by far the worst luck that day. The Germans enveloped the town while cutting the only escape route by fire. Lieutenant Colonel Henry Cherry radioed the CCB command post, "We're not driven out, we're burned out! We are not withdrawing, we are moving!" Nevertheless, the troopers had to abandon their vehicles and make their way to safety on foot.

The next morning, 20 December, in Noville, three panzers managed to drive into the village despite the efforts of the 1st Platoon. One panzer struck a mine, but two others forced passage and headed toward Bastogne. Technician 5th Grade George Coward managed to disable both with 37mm fire aimed at their more vulnerable rear armor. Once the panzers were stopped, medium tanks and tank destroyers were summoned to destroy them. Artillery rounds and gunfire from panzers on nearby high ground pounded Noville during the day, and Coward fired his last rounds.

Major Charles Hustead, who had taken over from a badly wounded Desobry, ordered the 1st Platoon to scout the route to Foy to determine whether it would be possible to withdraw, and Coward led a team of five other men toward the rear. About five hundred yards from Foy, the troopers saw Germans; the battered command was surrounded. The situation in Noville was nevertheless untenable, and the task force set off through the fog toward the 101st Airborne Division's lines. At the very spot identified by Coward's patrol, enemy fire knocked out the lead tank. The platoon leader dismounted all men except the vehicle drivers, and the cavalrymen participated in a desperate but successful assault that cleared the way to safety.[21]

Team Desobry had lost about half its men, eleven Shermans, and five tank destroyers, but it had held up the German advance on Bastogne for two critical days and claimed to have destroyed thirty-one panzers.[22] The defense of that town by the 101st Airborne Division, CCB, and other formations would join the ranks of the greatest feats of arms in American history. The men of Troop D conducted numerous patrols and served as a mobile reserve during those days of desperate courage.

Squashing the Bulge

Beginning on 18 December, Patton turned the weight of Third Army more than ninety degrees and tore into the southern flank of the Bulge. His men moved 125 miles through a blizzard to accomplish this feat. Through 23 December, 133,178 motor vehicles traversed a total of 1,654,042 miles. III Corps, including the 4th Armored and 80th and 26th Infantry divisions, attacked on 22 December to relieve the surrounded "Battling Bastards of Bastogne," a mission accomplished on 26 December.[23] By then, the 2d Armored Division had arrived from the north and destroyed the German armored spearhead at Celles, and Hitler's offensive was a spent force. Nonetheless, the Bulge still had to be eliminated.

The cavalry was in on the kill on 16 January 1945, the day that by most reckonings the Americans destroyed the Bulge when Third Army's 11th Armored Division linked up with First Army's 2d Armored Division in Houffalize, about halfway from the base to the tip of the penetration at its maximum extent. The 11th Armored Division had just raced to the front on a forced road march that covered 345 miles over four days. Its first day of battle, 1 January, had been costly to the tune of forty-nine medium and fifteen light tanks.

"Up until the moment that the lead armored car fell into a tank trap, I had firmly believed that the task force could sneak into Houffalize undetected," recalled then-Maj. Michael Greene, commanding a task force of the 11th Armored Division's 41st Cavalry Reconnaissance Squadron. The task force on 15 January had begun an arduous journey over treacherous ice-covered trails to sneak ten miles behind enemy lines and make contact with the 2d Armored Division, which Patton wanted accomplished right away. Now it was just past 0630 hours the following morning, and the trapped M8 was only two hundred yards short of the objective. Greene dismounted from his own armored car—his command half-track had struck a mine under way—and, accompanied by a lieutenant, walked to the town limits sign. The men congratulated each other on having reached Houffalize.

The lieutenant spotted a couple of soldiers in a foxhole on a nearby hill, and the cavalrymen, assuming them to be from the 2d Armored Division, walked toward them, covered by the command M8. The German soldiers waited until their targets were within twenty feet, then stood, pointing a machine gun at them and yelling for them to raise their hands.

"This is a German up here—fire at him!" Greene yelled to Sergeant Till, in the command M8, and the good sergeant immediately cut loose with the antiaircraft machine gun. Rather than shooting, the Germans dove for cover, and the cavalrymen skidded down the hill as fast as they could. The cavalry had established contact with the enemy.

The alerted defenders opened up with small arms, mortars, and antitank guns, and the American column beat a hasty retreat to the cover of a nearby mill. Greene decided to contain the Germans with assault-gun fire while Troop D moved to high ground to try to determine whether elements of the 2d Armored Division had arrived. Troop D moved into position while two assault guns laid direct fire into Houffalize and the remaining four guns fired indirectly.

The first sign of friendly troops was a barrage of shells that dropped on Troop D. Greene realized that they had originated in the presumed 2d Armored Division sector. He ordered the troop to withdraw, and he passed a request up the line that First Army be told to cease the shelling.

At about 0900 hours, the troopers spotted figures advancing some 1,500 yards away. Judging them to be Americans, Greene sent a patrol forward to establish contact. In the meantime, he ordered the light tank company to conduct a lightning raid on Houffalize to establish the enemy's strength.

"Company F," Greene recalled, "had little difficulty getting across the open ground, receiving only small-arms and mortar fire as it advanced. There was no opposition to its move to the high ground because troops in the town had no good fields of fire. The tanks then moved into the town firing 37mm and machine guns, setting fire to buildings, flushing several Germans from houses, and then withdrawing to their previously designated positions."

At 1000 hours, the patrol reported back that it had made contact with the 41st Armored Infantry Battalion, 2d Armored Division. A platoon of Troop A, meanwhile, had met patrols from the 334th Infantry Regiment and the 82d Armored Reconnaissance Battalion along the Ourthe River. The cavalry had given the final pinch to close the Bulge.[24] The squadron's AAR recorded, "On every side, we saw abandoned Jerry equipment, from bullets to

Tiger tanks and the 'good' Jerries, the frozen stiffs. The cold of winter does have its advantages."[25]

Operation *Nordwind*

Six days into the Ardennes offensive, the German High Command ordered Army Group G to exploit the thinning out of American lines along the southern end of the western front by retaking the Saverne Gap and cutting off much of U.S. Seventh Army. Code-named Operation *Nordwind* (North Wind), the attack was to take the form of two pincers, the first formed by General Obstfelder's First Army driving southward from the area of Bitche, and the second by a northward thrust out of the Colmar Pocket by elements of Nineteenth Army. The anticipated meeting point was Sarrebourg, just west of the gap.[26] As it turned out, the Colmar Pocket operation never amounted to much, and most of the fighting occurred south of the Franco-German border where it cuts west from the Rhine River.

The Seventh Army by late December held an eighty-four-mile-long front from its junction with Third Army, a few miles west of Saarbrücken, to the Rhine, as well as the west bank of the river down to Strasbourg. XV Corps held the left wing, and the 106th Cavalry Group screened its left flank. Major General Edward Brooks's VI Corps manned the ten-mile-long line in the lower Vosges abutting XV Corps with the brigade-size Task Force Hudelson. The 45th and 79th Infantry divisions, backed by the 14th Armored Division less one combat command, held the stretch to the Rhine.[27]

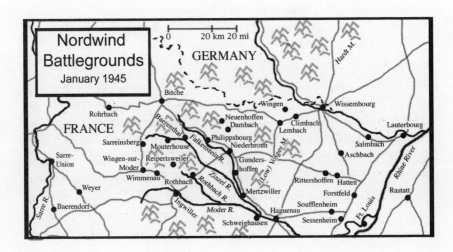

Colonel D. H. Hudelson's command was doomed to a mismatch from the start. The task force was built around CCR, 14th Armored Division, less the tank battalion that would normally give CCR its main punch. Instead, the light armored vehicles of the armored division's 94th and the 117th Cavalry Reconnaissance squadrons (the former attached to the latter), backed by Company B, 645th Tank Destroyer Battalion, were supposed to be sufficient. Other than the cavalry, Hudelson had but the 62d Armored Infantry Battalion to hold ground and a single company of chemical mortars for extra indirect-fire support.[28] Late on 31 December, the 1st Battalion, 540th Engineer Regiment, was attached to the task force to fight as infantry.[29] For the veterans of Task Force Butler in the 117th Cavalry Reconnaissance Squadron, the mix looked somewhat familiar. But instead of a mission to exploit against a disorganized foe, Task Force Hudelson was supposed to stop a thoroughly prepared enemy.

The 117th Cavalry Reconnaissance Squadron had arrived on 22 December and energetically set about constructing defenses consisting of mines, booby traps, flare trip wires and grenades, and both concertina and apron-style barbed wire. The light tanks and armored cars were dug into hull defilade, leaving only the turrets exposed. The assistant battalion S-3 organized a set of secondary defenses to which the troopers could fall back if necessary.

As New Year's approached, at least some of the men probably pondered the fact that since landing at St. Tropez the outfit had lost 36 men killed and more than 350 wounded—close to half the squadron's authorized strength. Certainly every man was aware that not one platoon was up to strength. Indeed, there was no continuous "line" but rather a string of strongpoints.[30]

The German LXXXIX Corps' 361st and 256th Volksgrenadier divisions struck southeastward from Bitche without a preparatory barrage as the new year began. Because of the broken and forested terrain, the Germans needed to quickly reach the north-south roads behind the American lines in order to approach their objectives. They intended to bypass strongpoints and had received a few assault guns to support the infantry.[31]

At 0015 hours the 2d Platoon of Troop B, 117th Cavalry Reconnaissance Squadron, reported large numbers of enemy soldiers outside its wire, and the German attack developed rapidly from there. By 0100, most of the squadron was heavily engaged, and the German volksgrenadiers, screaming and shouting, pressed forward with no apparent concern for the minefields and wire entanglements in their path. At 0300, Lieutenant Colonel Hodge, the squadron commanding officer, asked the task force CP to order forward Troop A, which had been held in reserve, only to learn that it had already been committed to aid the hard-pressed 62d Armored Infantry Battalion, which had also been hit around midnight.

Despite supporting artillery fire called down to within twenty-five yards of the American line, the cavalrymen gave way under the crushing pressure, and the squadron ordered a general withdrawal to the secondary line on a ridge 1,500 yards toward the rear at about 0330 hours. Crews in Troop B had to remove the breechblocks from many of the M5A1s and M8s because the vehicles were dug in and could not be driven out. The 3d Platoon, Troop C, was overrun before the withdrawal could be accomplished. Platoon sergeant Robert Lutz recalled:

> We were in mountains, in very dense forest. Troop B was down along a road to our left. We had 10-inch logs over our foxholes. We had eight or 10 guys where I was, and we were so far spread apart that we couldn't see the next group. The Germans had infiltration opportunities everywhere.
>
> I had set up a machine gun 50 or 75 yards forward. About midnight, my machine gunner came back and said, "They're coming!" I told him to go back and open up. He went.
>
> I picked up my Tommy gun with two 32-round clips taped together. I got out and ran for a tree. All of a sudden, I sensed things around me and behind me. I couldn't actually see them, but I opened fire. I emptied one clip and turned it around, but I dropped it in the snow and couldn't find it.
>
> My officer was still in the foxhole, and nobody in the foxholes had opened fire. I think they were already overrun. Only the machine gun was firing. I knew they were behind us now. I headed cross-country to headquarters, probably a quarter of a mile away. They had heard nothing over the phone line. After the war I heard that the Germans had thrown a grenade into the [command] foxhole, but it didn't explode. Then came pistol shots, and the Germans took the men in the command foxhole prisoner.[32]

Private First Class Arnold Lasner, in the 2d Platoon of Troop B, manned a .30-caliber machine gun in a forward position. Lasner blazed away at the attacking infantry, even as shells exploded around his position, two of them close enough to knock over his gun. Each time, Lasner righted the weapon and fired on. His action covered the platoon's withdrawal, and he pulled back himself only when he had run out of ammunition.[33]

The troopers in some cases had to fight their way out because German infantry had already bypassed them. Five M5A1s from Company F that covered the withdrawal fired eighteen thousand rounds of .30-caliber ammunition.

When Lieutenant Colonel Hodge contacted Hudelson to report the critical situation, he was told that the 19th Armored Infantry Battalion had been assigned and would come to his aid. By the time the armored infantrymen arrived at about 1000 hours, German infiltration of the cavalry's positions was so advanced that they could do little but plug some of the holes in the line.

In the cold morning light, the 117th Cavalry Reconnaissance Squadron, reinforced by four tank destroyers from the 645th Tank Destroyer Battalion and some engineers, beat off one attack supported by panzers.

★★★

To the west of the 117th Cavalry Reconnaissance Squadron's zone, the 14th Armored Division's 94th Cavalry Reconnaissance Squadron held defensive positions north of Mouterhouse. About midnight, a heavy artillery barrage crashed down on the cavalry line. The CP by 0120 hours had picked up word from the 117th Squadron that it was under attack. About that time, Troop D evidently received the word to pull back, and it did so by bounds, leaving a delaying force each time to engage the German infantry following close on its heels. It was pitch black and bitterly cold, and each side could do little but fire into the darkness where it thought the enemy to be.[34]

At 0527 hours, Troop D radioed that it was engaged in a terrific fire-fight, and it sounded as though Troop B had been hit as well. Three minutes later, Troop B confirmed that it was in danger of being surrounded and asked permission to pull back its vehicles.

The squadron's unofficial history recorded: "2d Lt. David Compton's platoon of [Troop B] was forced to pull out in its sector; the attack had started when there was a blast from a burp gun; the men heard the guns firing up and down the line, and when the burp gun fired, the .30-calibers opened up on the muzzle flashes in the same instant. Compton was given 10 minutes to pull out, but by the time the order was given, two of his outposts had already been cut off. The telephone line was out; by that time, both American and German artillery was landing on his position."

The situation was similar elsewhere along the squadron line. By 0630, both Troops B and D were reeling back to their secondary positions, fighting German infantry as close as a hundred yards away, and reports had arrived that German tanks could be heard. Several armored vehicles had to be abandoned because they could not get through the snow-choked woods, and troopers dismounted the machine guns and carried them.[35]

★★★

Once Hudelson realized the gravity of the situation, he ordered the entire task force to fall back on a prepared delaying line around Sarreinsberg and Reipertswiller—where his troops subsequently held firm until relieved. His withdrawal order nonetheless opened the door for the Germans to press toward Baerenthal and Phillipsbourg.

Lieutenant Colonel Hodge had lost contact with the task force headquarters in Baerenthal (which by noon was surrounded) and did not receive Hudelson's instructions. But it was clear that his flanks were open and the Germans were advancing, so he issued his own withdrawal order. The entire command exfiltrated down a single dirt road by 1600 hours. Major Samsel, the S-3, abandoned the CP with the last six troopers in a half-track under fire from German riflemen only two hundred yards away.

"Our feelings were distraught," Samsel recalled, "as this was the first time in combat the squadron had ever taken a backward step." The squadron fell back toward new positions near Lemberg and Sarreinsberg and suffered the indignity of being strafed by American P-47s en route. The 117th Cavalry Reconnaissance Squadron lost so many of its vehicles during the initial attack and retreat—including twelve M8 armored cars, six light tanks, and thirty-eight jeeps—that VI Corps conducted an investigation of the unit's conduct.[36]

The situation was more promising in the 94th Cavalry Reconnaissance Squadron zone. By 1330 the 19th Armored Infantry Battalion had arrived to help, and Troops B and E were able to pull back behind its protecting line. By the next day, friendly armor had arrived in force, and the danger of penetration in the squadron's sector dissipated.[37]

★★★

The German pressure was so intense that VI Corps by 21 January had withdrawn behind the Moder River, surrendering all of northern Alsace. There, VI Corps held fast. The fighting was bitter and casualties were high on both sides, but Operation *Nordwind* blew itself out by the end of January.

CHAPTER 11

ON TO VICTORY

Go on to Berlin. There is nothing to stop you between here and there that I know of.

—German officer captured by the
43d Cavalry Reconnaissance Squadron, 30 March 1945

Even as the fighting surrounding Operation *Nordwind* wound down in late January 1945, the Allies readied themselves for their last offensive, the one that was to continue with but brief fits and starts until the collapse of the Third Reich.

Upgrading the Force

As hard as many found it to believe, the U.S. Army was a learning organization, and it was taking steps to help the mechanized cavalry fight more effectively, no matter what the doctrine said.

One big step was to field the new M24 light tank to replace the M5A1s in cavalry squadrons. The first M24s reached forward depots in December 1944, but deliveries in quantity began only in 1945, and most cavalry squadrons and armored reconnaissance battalions received their full allotments by February.

The 117th Cavalry Reconnaissance Squadron received its first M24s in January. Captain Paul Seidel, who had been fighting in the M3 and M5 light tanks since North Africa, was delighted. "Always was convinced our M5 light tanks were of little combat value," he observed later.[1]

The 38th Cavalry Reconnaissance Squadron received enough M24s to equip Company F in early February, while the Ninth and First armies waited for the Roer River flooding to subside enough to attack across it. Demonstrating yet again the cavalry's penchant for modifying official tables of organization and equipment, the squadron replaced nine of its M8 armored cars with M5A1s and trained the reconnaissance crews to use them.[2] As far as gunnery went, of course, there was almost no difference at all.

M24s also reached the 4th Cavalry Reconnaissance Squadron, which was refitting west of the Roer River in early February as well. The squadron judged that the tank "put it on a more equal footing against the heavier German armor."[3] The cavalry reconnaissance squadrons in the armored divisions also received allotments of the M24 during this period, though the first four M24s did not reach the 4th Armored Division's 25th Cavalry Reconnaissance Squadron until late March.[4]

The replacement of 60mm mortars with 81mm mortars undertaken by the "Lucky 38th" during the static autumn months along the Siegfried Line became generalized in the First and Third armies before the end of hostilities. The availability of a jeep to transport each tube meant that weight was not an issue, and the cavalrymen welcomed the return of the more powerful weapon with which they had started the war.[5]

The message from cavalry units in the field regarding their lack of adequate rifle strength had by February worked its way up through the War Department, and plans were afoot to correct the problem. In February a new TO&E was formulated to apply to divisions that were to be transferred to the Pacific upon completion of the European campaign. Headquarters, Army Ground Forces, added a rifle platoon to each cavalry reconnaissance troop. It also authorized the squadron an air section with two light aircraft and formally re-adopted the 81mm mortar in place of the 60mm mortar. Personnel strength in each reconnaissance troop increased by nearly 60 percent, to 14 officers and 235 enlisted men from 6 officers and 143 enlisted men.[6] None of these changes actually took place before the end of hostilities upon Japan's surrender.

Push to the Rhine

The Canadian First Army on 8 February kicked off Operation Veritable, the first step in a cascading series of offensives along the entire western front that were to achieve Eisenhower's goal of destroying the German armed forces west of the Rhine River. This would leave nothing of any great menace east of that barrier to prevent the final drive into the heart of the Third Reich.

Ninth and First Armies

At the north end of the American zone, Lt. Gen. William Simpson's Ninth Army had bided its time preparing for Operation Grenade, which was to be the southern jaw of a crushing operation in tandem with Operation Veritable. The Germans had sabotaged dams near the headwaters of the Roer River on 6 February and created an artificial flood downstream that Simpson preferred not to cross. Supported on its right by First Army's VII Corps, Ninth Army crossed the subsiding but still swollen river on 23 February under the cover of the largest artillery barrage ever fired on the western front.

Operation Veritable had drawn most of the German armor away to that sector, and the defenses east of the Roer shredded quickly. The 2d, 3d, and 5th Armored divisions charged into the Germans on 26 February to exploit the infantry's gains. The S-3 of the 36th Cavalry Reconnaissance Squadron, operating on the far American left adjacent to the Commonwealth forces, recorded: "The morning of 27 February found all of the 'Red Devils' 'tugging at the bit' and like a young colt kicking up his heels in pasture—raring to go!" Go they did, reaching the Rhine at Homberg on 4 March, only to find the bridge there blown by the Germans.[7]

Major General "Lightning Joe" Collins' VII Corps faced the toughest fight of the Roer offensive, and the mechanized cavalry was in the thick of it. Collins had ordered the 3d Armored Division to punch to the Rhine, while the 99th Infantry Division and 4th Cavalry Group cleared the ground to its left.

The 83d Armored Reconnaissance Battalion crossed the Roer on 26 February in the vicinity of Düren in VII Corps' zone, where the German 9th Panzer Division was still putting up a fight. The action probably did not at first look much like exploitation to the cavalrymen. The battalion attacked near Lamberishof as a unit, divided into two "battle groups." Major Richard Bradley commanded one battle group consisting of two dismounted reconnaissance companies (B and D) supported by two platoons of M24 tanks, plus a section of tank destroyers and two squads of engineers. The second battle group, under the command of Capt. Spencer Wilson, included Company B, dismounted, plus a platoon of light tanks, a tank destroyer section, and a squad of engineers.

Ironically, at first the U.S. Army proved more of a hindrance than the German army. The battalion pushed forward and swept aside the defenders in its path, but "friendly" artillery "overs" from an adjacent task force dropped onto the men as they entered Mannheim, and twelve A26 bombers narrowly missed the command group when they dropped their payloads.

The next day, the reconnaissance troopers "got the book thrown at them" by the Germans, the after-action report recorded. At Barrendorf, on the road to the objective at Grouven, small-arms, mortar, and artillery fire pinned down the dismounted cavalrymen, and panzers appeared nearby. A bid to flank the Germans seemed in order, so a concentration of HE and smoke was laid on Elsdorf, and Company B attacked from the south. The M24s churned across the muddy fields followed by the troopers and reached Grouven. This success allowed the remainder of the battalion to move forward, and in the tough house-to-house fighting that followed, twenty-three men were wounded.[8]

★★★

The 24th Cavalry Reconnaissance Squadron, 4th Cavalry Group, meanwhile operated in the gap adjacent to Ninth Army. On 26 February the squadron crossed the Roer and tried to clear some woods short of Elsdorf. All troops ran into enemy rifle positions, and Troop C fell back four hundred yards under fire from two panzers. Bazooka patrols went forward to destroy the tanks but could not find them.

On 27 February, Company F got a chance to try out its new M24 tanks at Esch, where Troop C encountered surprisingly spirited resistance early in the morning from two hundred counterattacking German infantry backed by three Tiger tanks. Called to help the lightly armed reconnaissance troopers, a platoon of four M24s raced into town. Two struck mines and were disabled, and two entered the melee, blasting away with 75mm and machine guns at the enemy troops and tanks. Although the M24 was more lethal than the M5A1, it was no match for a Tiger, and the tankers were fortunate that several towed 3-inch guns from the 635th Tank Destroyer Battalion were already in Esch. One gun hit a panzer, which plowed into a house, upon which the German attack broke down. Seventy German riflemen chose to surrender.

By evening on 2 March, VII Corps had established a three-mile-deep bridgehead across the Erft River, and from that point the Germans were capable only of delaying actions west of the Rhine River. VII Corps had the dual responsibility of continuing to protect Ninth Army's flank and reaching the Rhine north of Cologne. On 3 March the 24th Cavalry Reconnaissance Squadron received orders to advance to the Rhine in tandem with the 83d Armored Reconnaissance Battalion, on its right. The next day, Company F was rolling en masse toward Worringen, the objective on the banks of the Rhine, when antitank fire knocked out five of its new M24s. The remaining tanks turned northwest and raced for cover in Hackenbroich, leaving the Troop B members following the tanks pinned down under fire that killed three men.

The following morning, the squadron conducted a pre-dawn attack to seize a textile factory just outside Hackenbroich. The troop commanders requested that no artillery preparation be fired, and the cavalrymen caught the German defenders asleep in the buildings. Only a few were able to get off some shots before they were subdued.

The firing was enough to attract two Panther tanks, which rumbled into the complex to investigate. The M24s accompanying the assault force maneuvered to the flank and knocked out both Mark Vs as well as a Mark IV that they spotted following the duo, claiming some revenge for the previous day's losses.[9]

The 83d Armored Reconnaissance Battalion, meanwhile, had changed its tactics to attacking mainly at night to reduce losses. The battalion marked each "check point" on the route of advance with white phosphorus, and the troopers were able to find their way in the dark without becoming disorganized. At 0400 hours on 5 March, Company B ran into two Panthers at Langel. A bazooka man was able to see well enough to destroy one panzer, and the other panzer drew off. About the same time, Company D encountered three Panthers near the Forst Benrath. An M24 maneuvered into place to kill one with a shot into the thin rear armor plate. A tank destroyer dispatched a second Mark V, and when the third drew away, an M24 working with Company B dispatched it with a shot through the side of the turret. The 88s in Langel—all subsequently captured—knocked out three M24s in return, but, miraculously, not a single crewman was hurt. Two officers and twenty-seven enlisted men became casualties fighting their way into town, most of them victims of vicious fire from four 20mm guns that were also taken. At about 1200 hours, Company B won a case of champagne offered by 3d Armored Division commanding officer Maj. Gen. Maurice Rose back in Belgium to the first outfit to sink a boat on the Rhine River.[10]

★★★

Lieutenant General Omar Bradley designed Operation Lumberjack to employ the remainder of First Army in a pincer operation with Third Army to trap and destroy German forces in the Schnee Eifel. III Corps was to make the main effort just to the south of VII Corps, and it crossed the swollen Roer River using the latter's bridges before kicking off on 25 February.[11]

The 9th Armored Division's bold dash to Remagen, where it captured the Ludendorff railroad bridge across the Rhine, was perhaps the most dramatic episode in Allied operations to clear the west bank of the river, but the mechanized cavalry played only a supporting role. The 14th Cavalry Group screened the corps' north flank adjacent to the 1st Infantry Division, but there was nothing really to screen against. Likewise, the 89th Cavalry Reconnaissance Squadron screened the left flank during the armored division's unmolested charge into Remagen.[12]

Third and Seventh Armies

After supporting First Army's initial push toward the Rhine in late February, Third Army attacked into the Palatinate on 1 March. Patton's divisions quickly reached the Rhine at Koblenz, from where they could cut off the Germans manning the Siegfried Line north of Seventh Army if they turned southeastward across the Moselle River and advanced down the west bank of the Rhine. On 13 March, Third Army kicked off to do just that.

That day, XX Corps sent the 316th Provisional Mechanized Cavalry Brigade into action in the gap between its right flank and XII Corps. Patton had attached a second cavalry group, the 16th, to the corps. Because the group had never seen action, Col. James Polk, 3d Cavalry Group, was placed in command of a provisional brigade to provide seasoned leadership. Attached to the command were the 241st Field Artillery Battalion, the 245th Engineer Combat Battalion, Company A of the 818th Tank Destroyer Battalion, and an air-support party. The brigade could count on support from an artillery battalion and an artillery group.

The brigade, which covered a seven-mile front stretching south from the Moselle, attacked initially dismounted. The light tanks and tank destroyers supported the troopers by fire from defilade, and the assault guns were kept back to fire support indirectly in battery. The engineers worked with the cavalrymen to remove roadblocks, while the air support parties directed strikes against villages before the ground forces assaulted them. The brigade organized tank-infantry teams for the actual attack into a town, with the troopers riding on the back decks.

Within a day, the troopers had reached the Ruwer River, only to find all the bridges destroyed, but the 19th Cavalry Reconnaissance Squadron was able to get tanks across the river using a ford discovered by 94th Infantry Division GIs near Geizberg. The 49th Cavalry Reconnaissance Squadron mounted up and crossed, using the same ford, on 16 March, then struck northward through the difficult terrain of the Hunnsbruck Mountains foothills.

By 18 March, the enemy was in headlong retreat across the corps' front, and the brigade's short history came to an end. The 3d Cavalry Group, having been in the line without a break for three months, went into Supreme Headquarters Allied Expeditionary Force (SHAEF) reserve, and the now-tested 16th Cavalry Group assumed responsibility for the sector.[13]

★★★

To the south, in the 6th Army Group's zone, the 117th Cavalry Reconnaissance Squadron on 18 February was operating along the Moder River as Seventh Army pushed north to reclaim ground lost during the *Nordwind* offensive. Sergeant Robert Lutz, Troop C, received an order to lead a patrol across the river that night. He later recalled:

> The night was clear. The river crossing in rubber boats was uneventful. . . .
>
> I decided first to try to locate the enemy positions. They were not too difficult to spot. They talked and smoked with no apparent concern

that they might be observed. . . . I selected Sgt. Bill Foster and three men to accompany me and left the other 10 near the river crossing to form a base of fire, which was to cover our return should we get into trouble.

We crawled up the furrows in a line, abreast of each other. We froze in position, frequently, under the light of flares until they faded. In that way, we made our way up to a barbed wire fence. . . . We could hear the Germans talking up ahead, and we crawled under the fence. We inched our way up toward their position, each man moving up when the guy on his left did so. I recall asking myself, am I really going to go through with this as I again moved forward.

It was fortunate that I understood the German language for we were about 50 feet from them when one of the Germans, who had been talking, said he was going to walk down the fence line. I had hardly signaled a stand fast when the man walked right into Bill and me. We stood, in a crouch, and I ordered him quietly (with a Thompson submachine gun to his nose) to keep quiet, put his hands on his head, and come with us.[14]

On the night of 22 February, Troop B and the 36th Reconnaissance Troop sent patrols across the Moder preparatory to the 36th Infantry Division's attack the next day. The Troop B patrol ran into heavy small-arms and machine-gun fire, reinforced by artillery and mortar rounds. The 117th Cavalry Reconnaissance Squadron's daily report noted, "In directing our artillery on the enemy machine-gun positions, the patrol leader sighted a four-man enemy patrol silhouetted by the flash of a shell burst. The patrol leader brought his artillery down closer behind the [enemy] patrol, herding them toward himself. Two enemy were wounded, one killed, and one taken prisoner. . . ."[15]

By the first half of March, the 36th Infantry Division and other elements of Seventh Army had pushed within striking distance of the Siegfried Line once again. In anticipation that Patton's marauding Third Army would soon force the Germans to withdraw from the Siegfried Line in front of Seventh Army, the 101st Cavalry Group and 70th Infantry Division patrols energetically felt out the enemy at the left end of the XXI Corps line, which now faced northward toward the Palatinate adjacent to Third Army's sector. Already on the morning of 13 March, the patrols detected the first signs that German activity had decreased sharply.

The 6th Army Group launched Operation Undertone on 15 March, and the Germans really did not stand much of a chance. Haislip's XV Corps struck first. At 0100 hours, the 45th and 3d Infantry divisions moved out silently through the lines of the 44th Infantry Division and easily overran the forward German defenses. The 106th Cavalry Group moved forward to protect the 3d Division's right flank and got to use its brand-new M24 tanks on 16 March when a recon troop each from the 106th and 121st Cavalry Reconnaissance squadrons were ordered to capture Briedenbach. The outfit's informal history recounted the experience of Company F, 121st Squadron: "You might say we attacked in three waves: First the tanks, then the armored cars, and lastly the half-tracks. All three overran the dug-in positions. One half-track dismounted its personnel to clean up, while the others went into the town. Major [Joseph] McCarthy and Capt. [Herbert] Benecke were in this half-track. Major McCarthy was seen with a pistol in one hand and a grenade in the other making a clean sweep of one dugout. Captain Benecke did the same job on another dugout with three hand grenades."[16]

The two assault divisions pushed on deeper into Germany, bypassing strongpoints as they went, and reached the main West Wall defenses around Zweibrücken by 17 March—an advance of between five and ten miles. That gain was through what had been an impenetrable barrier for five months.

XXI Corps attacked with only its 63d Infantry Division at 0100 hours on 15 March. The 70th Infantry Division and 101st Cavalry Group, on the left wing, had only to hold the enemy in place around Saarbrücken, while the 12th Armored Division waited to exploit any hole the assault division might create.[17]

Seventh Army continued to grind forward. By 20 March, Third Army's 4th Armored Division had reached the Rhine at Worms, and German resistance in front of Third and Seventh armies imploded. On 21 March, the 106th Cavalry Reconnaissance Squadron, still working with XV Corps, recorded, "No definite front lines. Enemy continued to defend towns in area with weak Volksturm [militia] units; no artillery." The squadron advanced quickly that day and lost not a single man in action.[18] By 25 March there was no more meaningful German resistance west of the Rhine.

Across the Rhine

Montgomery's assault across the Rhine on 23 March was to have been the first Allied crossing, but it was almost the last. Not only had First Army jumped the river at Remagen, Patton sneaked the 5th Infantry Division across at Oppen-heim the night of 22 March, then quickly carved out two more bridgeheads on the east bank at Boppard and St. Goar on 24 and 25 March. Seventh Army crossed at Worms on 26 March.

As April got under way and the Allies rolled eastward, cavalry action for the most part came to resemble the model of open pursuit of a beaten enemy, the main exception being the Ruhr industrial basin in the north, where the mechanized cavalry left the heavy lifting to the infantry and tanks. The 113th Cavalry Reconnaissance Squadron, operating with Ninth Army's 83d Infantry Division north of the Ruhr, contributed to creating the pocket when it contacted elements of First Army's 3d Armored Division near Paderborn on 4 April. The 3d Armored Division had had a nasty scrap with King Tiger tanks from an armor training school in the area a few days earlier, and Troop B encountered one of the massive panzers that evening. Two M24 light tanks outflanked the Tiger and destroyed it with shots into the thinner side and rear armor.[19]

South of the Ruhr, the experience of XV Corps was more typical. The corps' after-action report at the beginning of April observed: "XV Corps, with three infantry divisions abreast, was advancing rapidly to the northeast in a zone approximately 40 kilometers in width. . . . Resistance, except in defended towns, was conducted principally by ineffective, hastily formed battle groups. Towns were defended tenaciously. . . ."[20]

Fortunately, it was not the cavalry's job to storm well-defended towns, such as Aschaffenburg and Heilbronn. The 121st Cavalry Reconnaissance Squadron, which reconnoitered and screened the XV Corps surge to Nürnberg, then south into Austria, recorded a typical summary in its after-action report: "Throughout the movement, the troops encountered road blocks, craters, and blown bridges prepared by the enemy to slow the advance of our units. Although no strongly organized enemy resistance was encountered, troops were constantly in contact with small delaying forces who were, at times, supported by artillery."[21] The daily report from the 36th Cavalry Reconnaissance Squadron, on the American left wing, noted on 10 April, "Enemy Front Lines: Non-existent as such."[22]

The 14th Armored Division had joined XV Corps east of the Rhine and formed one spearhead. Corporal Vernon Brown was now a gunner in an armored car in the 94th Cavalry Reconnaissance Squadron's Troop D. He recalled, "[W]e were now operating as cavalry was meant to, moving swiftly behind German lines, tearing up Jerries' supply lines and cutting off his reinforcements to prevent them from consolidating any possible strongpoints. This called for a bold change in tactics. Whereas on dismounted patrols stealth and watchfulness were the key, we now used speed and surprise to catch the enemy off guard, especially as we were often operating well in advance of the main body of troops. We had also learned to come in shooting, it didn't matter at what, just create as much noise and confusion as possible. . . ."[23]

Cavalry squadrons and armored reconnaissance battalions usually operated in front and to the flanks of the advancing divisions and corps, sometimes as complete units and at other times parceled out by troop or company. "An armored division on the move is vulnerable," recalled one 11th Armored Division officer. "It stretches out about 30 miles when all the units are rolling. We kept running our 41st Recon Squadron up and down the roads leading north to the mountains looking for signs of enemy units coming south out of the passes."[24] Reconnaissance troops also were often employed to maintain communications across widely spread corps fronts as the advance got into gear. VIII Corps was one exception, for during early April it employed the 6th Cavalry Group to mop up bypassed pockets of resistance behind its infantry divisions.[25]

The race across Germany resembled the one that had taken place across France except for the absence of welcoming crowds. Armored divisions rolled along multiple parallel routes, and communications often frayed. The 9th Armored Division adopted a typical policy and split one troop of the 89th Cavalry Reconnaissance Squadron into radio relay teams so that the division could stay in touch with its wide-flung subordinate elements.[26]

★★★

The 43d Cavalry Reconnaissance Squadron set out on 29 March to screen the XX Corps advance northeast of Frankfurt along with its group running mate, the 3d Cavalry Reconnaissance Squadron. By afternoon the advance had turned into a dash. Three disgusted captured German officers said resistance was impossible when the soldiers refused to shoot at the advancing Americans. The squadron raced over an excellent road net, two troops abreast. German resistance along the Fulda River stopped the 3d Cavalry Group for a few days, but then XX Corps—having gathered its strength—exploded eastward. The 4th and 6th Armored divisions rolled out on 11 April with orders to get to Dresden as fast as possible, bypassing centers of resistance, and to stop only if they ran into the Red Army.

In each town, the population was told to gather all firearms in a public place. One of the M24s then ground them into fragments, and the charge continued. When it looked as though the Germans might put up a stiff fight for a town or city, the cavalry bypassed the obstruction, left it to the infantry, and rolled onward. Small pockets of resistance could be dealt with. When Troop C encountered SS troops in Blankenheim on 1 April, the troopers dismounted, and the M24s moved slowly through the town, pumping 75mm shells into each house, while the cavalrymen riddled them with Tommy-gun fire.[27]

★★★

Occasionally, as at Fulda, German resistance would consolidate for a few days, normally along a river or in a city. The 101st Cavalry Reconnaissance Squadron was advancing on the 4th Infantry Division's right flank on 8 April when it ran into a determined group including SS troops. The squadron had been fighting to join its running mate in the 101st Cavalry Group, the 116th Cavalry Reconnaissance Squadron, on the Tauber River line for a week and had finally reached it. The outfit's after-action report recorded, "[Troop C] encountered a strong enemy defensive position along the line of the Tauber and Gallach Rivers. During 9 April, Troop C was unable to overcome or bypass this resistance, but Troop B, aided by the attack of elements of the 4th Infantry Division on its left flank, attacked across [a ford] in the face of determined small-arms and mortar fire and gained the high ground beyond. . . . There the troop met heavy antitank and mortar fire and was forced to withdraw . . . to await reinforcements."

The next day, the squadron protected the flanks of CCR, 12th Armored Division, which cracked the defensive line and made a broad swoop to catch the enemy from the rear. When CCR made its turn on 12 April, the squadron peeled off to exploit in the original direction of the attack.[28] As XXI Corps drove southward in its wake to grab the rumored "national redoubt" in the Alps before the Nazis could, the 101st Cavalry Reconnaissance Squadron was attached to the 4th Infantry Division, while the armored division's 92d Cavalry Reconnaissance Squadron was attached to the 101st Cavalry Group. Resistance flared in many small towns, and if the cavalrymen could not dispatch it quickly, the armored division stepped in to crush the defenders. The 101st Squadron reverted to the group by 19 April, and for most of the remainder of the war, the 101st Cavalry Group operated as a powerful three-squadron force.[29]

The fluid battlefront meant that small groups of enemy troops were moving about as well, and a town that offered no trouble to the lead elements could cause problems for those that followed. Captain Stuart Seborer, who commanded the 113th Cavalry Squadron's Troop B during the early April advance east of the Weser River before XIX Corps, recalled one such instance: "Headquarters moved into Lithorst. As the first sergeant's [jeep] turned a corner in the center of town, it was confronted by five 'diehards' armed with at least two panzerfausts. One fired a rifle and another a panzerfaust at a range no greater than 20 yards. Both occupants piled out of the [jeep], which was hit and immediately began to burn. An SS captain five yards away suddenly rose and aimed his Luger at the sergeant's back. [My] driver, who was racing around the corner, came to a sliding halt and fired a full clip from a .45-caliber Thompson submachine gun at the SS captain, who ran about 50 yards with at least five bullets in his chest before he fell dead. The others escaped. An armored car then sprayed nearby doorways with .30-caliber machine-gun fire. . . ."[30]

Yet the fluid battle also played to the mechanized cavalry's strengths. The after-action report for the "Lucky 38th" Cavalry Reconnaissance Squadron observed: "The month of April 1945 saw the squadron being used extensively in two primary cavalry missions of flank security and mopping-up operations. It was a period of constant movement in which the squadron zig-zagged its way across Germany and finally ended the month a stone's throw from the Czechoslovakian border. The necessity for quick and repeated movement, and to get to a destination ready to operate, made the missions ideally suited to cavalry."[31]

★★★

As the 4th Cavalry Group approached the Harz Mountains, east of the Ruhr industrial basin, in mid-April, it had developed a technique that approached the ideal of mechanized cavalry riding steeds of steel from which they could fight mounted or dismounted. When the 4th Cavalry Reconnaissance Squadron encountered small-arms and panzerfaust fire at Sievershausen on 10 April, for example, Troop A spread out to attack, while attached Shermans from the 759th Tank Battalion and M10s from the 634th Tank Destroyer Battalion laid down covering fire from the flanks. A platoon of M24s carrying troopers on the decks took the center, and the armored cars and jeeps with .50-caliber machine guns deployed on the wings. The formation rolled toward town, all guns firing. When small-arms fire endangered the troopers on the M24s, they rolled off and accompanied the armored vehicles into town in classic tank-infantry style.

In Bad Grund a few days later, Lt. Charles McKeand led two platoons of M24s into the seemingly deserted town. He parked on the eastern edge with his main gun pointing at a farmhouse door. The door opened, and German major general Gorbig, who was responsible for defense of the western Harz Mountains, walked out and surrendered himself and his staff to the surprised cavalry tankers. McKeand sent Gorbig toward the rear in front of a machine-gun-equipped jeep. As they walked through the silent town, more doors opened, and 175 German soldiers walked into the street to join their commanding officer.[32]

★★★

The infantry division reconnaissance troops experienced the same general rapid movement as the squadrons and armored reconnaissance battalions, and flexibility was just as crucial, as highlighted by the "Lucky 38th" Cavalry Reconnaissance Squadron. The informal history of the 99th Cavalry Reconnaissance Troop, for example, noted: "The front had finally cracked! Thus having to mop up the loose ends left in the wake of the fast-moving heavier armored outfits found the lighter cavalry units in front of the infantry, yet behind the front. As the heavy armor of the Allies fanned out in a wild race with the Russians to crush the German armies, now already reeling and tottering back, reconnaissance outfits again and again changed their tactical employment. Like the feet of a boxer, where they are you can tell what he is doing, so it was with the Reconnaissance. . . . Sometimes the cavalrymen were bringing up reserve armor to the rear of the front (their most dangerous assignment), other times they were policing up and catching stray [prisoners of war] even behind the infantry, other times they were just a security guard for a town or even an entire area somewhere along the fluid front. . . . Assignments of the complex nature were thrown up overnight and may be changed by morning. It was a tremendous experience only made possible by the team work, coordination, and adaptability of all the units involved."[33]

The infantry division reconnaissance troops could not count on backup from organic tanks or assault guns that were readily at hand in the armored divisions. The problem was that when one was moving fast with little expectation of organized resistance, the small pockets of resistance could take one by surprise. The 69th Cavalry Reconnaissance Troop's history offers one example:

On Tuesday [3 April], the 2d Platoon had a skirmish at Weimar. The Heinies let Paradine's car slip by and opened up on it from the right rear flank. A slug hit the jacket of the .50-cal., and a piece of shrapnel from it injured Snyder in the forehead. (He returned the next morning.) They shot four Heinies near the railroad tracks there.

The other two teams ran into a roadblock outside the town. A panzerfaust was fired at Viguet's armored car, but it hit a tree and exploded between Dugaw's jeep and the armored car. Dugaw got two Krauts with his M3 [submachine gun] as they fled into the woods. The vehicles withdrew to a hill behind them quickly, because the roadblock was defended by an antitank gun, firing as they went. Abbott, Elliget, and Lieutenant Viguet fired furiously while the vehicles maneuvered, pinning [the Germans] down. They scattered like flies.[34]

Lieutenant Thomas Fernley, who had led the 29th Reconnaissance Troop's advance into St. Lo, died in just such an ambush two weeks before the end of the war. His 3d Platoon had just reached the Elbe River in advance of the 116th Infantry Regiment, where it encountered a sizable enemy force in Lasse on 24 April. The lieutenant was seeking out the enemy using his binoculars and exposed himself above the turret of his M8 when a slug fired by a sniper claimed his life. Remarkably, Fernley was the only troop officer killed during the European campaign.[35]

★★★

XX Corps never did make it to Dresden because it received a stop order and was turned south into Bavaria on 17 April.[36] As the war neared its end, the 3d Cavalry Group executed a classic offensive operation while preceding the XX Corps advance to seize a crossing on the Danube river. The 43d and 3d Cavalry Reconnaissance squadrons as of 22 April were deployed abreast southeast of Nürnberg at Neumarkt and pointed southeast toward Regensburg. The group had attached to it Companies A and C, 811th Tank Destroyer Battalion; Company A, 245th Engineer Combat Battalion; the 5th Ranger Battalion; and the 274th Armored Field Artillery Battalion. The 65th and 71st Infantry divisions were to advance abreast behind the cavalry and cross the bridges to be captured at Regensburg.

The 3d Cavalry Reconnaissance Squadron, on the left wing, organized three task forces, each with a company of rangers mounted on tanks and half-tracks, a platoon of tank destroyers, and a platoon of engineers. A battalion of self-propelled 105mm howitzers supported one of the task forces.

The group set out at 0600 hours through rain and snow. The terrain was mountainous and wooded, and the secondary routes that the cavalry chose in order to avoid probable roadblocks were in generally poor condition. The engineers proved useful for repairing roads that were beaten to impassable muck by vehicles, and for pulling mired vehicles loose. Resistance consisted of scattered roadblocks, most often manned only by infantry but at times supported by 20mm or 88mm guns.

The 3d Squadron's Task Force Baldwin ran into the tail of a German column at Eglee. Informed by a prisoner that his outfit was headed for a bridge across the Naab River at Burglengenfeld, which would be blown once crossed, Capt. Clark Baldwin sent a reconnaissance platoon over a fairly decent road at forty miles per hour to seize the bridge. The platoon crested a hill just outside of town and surprised the German column, which was just starting to cross. The cavalrymen opened up with all weapons, and even though the Germans possessed several 75mm guns, their confusion was so complete that no return shots were fired.

The troopers raced by the scattering foe and across the stone and steel bridge, where they stopped two soldiers trying to hook wires to explosives under the span. The 71st Infantry Division was following close behind, and it organized a task force that exploited across the bridge and rolled toward Regensburg.

By the afternoon of the third day, the cavalry had arrived within striking distance of Regensburg, where reconnaissance showed that all of the bridges had already been destroyed. The infantry moved up to assault the city anyway, and the demoralized garrison surrendered on 27 April.[37]

The End of the Charge

Old cavalrymen may have taken some solace from the way the western allies and Soviets first met after slicing clear through the heart of the Third Reich to the Elbe River. An infantry patrol from First Army's 69th Infantry Division established first contact with the Red Army in the form of horse-mounted Cossack cavalry near Torgau on 25 April.[38]

Soon, the Soviets were meeting American cavalry mounted on steeds of steel. The 125th Cavalry Reconnaissance Squadron in late April was farther east than any other Allied element in northern Germany, and on 30 April it contacted the Soviet 121st Infantry Division east of the Elbe River, the second recorded linkup between East and West. A Troop A patrol first detected the Soviets when it came under Soviet fire near Cobbelsdorf and withdrew. Troop

C sent a Russian-speaking civilian into Apollensdorf to tell the Soviets that American troops were trying to establish contact, but the Soviets did not believe the man and threatened to shoot him. The 3d Platoon then sent two jeeps forward, one of which detonated a Soviet mine that killed two troopers. Sergeant Raymond Gard and two privates pressed on and contacted the 1st Battalion, 320th Infantry Regiment.[39]

By early May 1945, mechanized cavalry units had reached the limitations of Eisenhower's planned advance, from the Elbe River in the north to Czechoslovakia in the south. Yet men still bled and fell in small fights against a few diehards at roadblocks and villages at many points where the western allies had not linked up with the Soviets. The troopers were tired. It was time to end this war.

Colonel Charles Graydon described the 101st Cavalry Group at this stage: "After three months of constant movement our column had taken on a less military but much more interesting appearance. [Displaced persons] of all nationalities often hitched rides atop the vehicles. Now and then a black top hat or a spiked old type German helmet appeared from a tank or armored car turret, adding a touch of GI humor. Various types of captured German vehicles were scattered along the column. For a while one troop had adopted a life-sized female manikin wearing nothing but a fancy lady's hat as she rode jauntily along in a jeep."[40]

The 101st Cavalry Group had rolled far into southern Germany with the 12th Armored Division, then shifted to reconnoiter routes for the 101st Airborne Division in the vicinity of Hitler's once-beloved Berchtesgaden. At 1710 hours on 5 May, the cavalry group operations officer appeared at the 116th Cavalry Reconnaissance Squadron CP to announce that German Army Group G had agreed to surrender all forces in the area, and that all offensive operations were to cease. The end was near.

The following day, the squadron sent out parties with interpreters under flags of truce to inform German commanders of the surrender and its terms. The squadron staff set about organizing for military government duties.

At 1050 hours, a verbal order arrived from cavalry group headquarters that sealed the victory: "Alert one complete platoon for immediate movement." The platoon was to take into "protective custody" Field Marshal Albert Kesselring, Germany's last supreme commander in the West, and the Third Reich's longtime number-two man, Hermann Göring, with their families. Major Edward French and Troop A did so.[41]

★★★

The 71st Infantry Division's reconnaissance troop netted itself perhaps an even bigger haul. On 6 May it received orders to cross the Enns River, in Austria, into the Soviet zone to establish contact with the Red Army, known to be somewhere west of Vienna. Lieutenant Edward Samuell's 1st Platoon instead found itself passing by thousands of non-belligerent German troops trudging west toward American lines. Technician 5th Grade Charles Staudinger, in search of fuel with an obliging German soldier, found himself at a German headquarters, where he boldly demanded that the Germans surrender. Samuell, then the rest of the platoon, were eventually brought to the headquarters, where Samuell managed to broker the surrender of German Army Group South. The surrender was effective at one minute past midnight on 8 May. At that time, the army group was still a coherent fighting force in control of 800,000 men.[42]

★★★

The 6th Cavalry Reconnaissance Squadron's after-action report recorded the outfit's colorful way of ending the war in Europe: "A field message . . . announcing the capitulation of German armed forces effective midnight, 8–9 May 1945, was received by the squadron at approximately [1000 hours]. . . . The squadron commander [Lt. Col. Samuel Goodwin], riding in an armored car proudly flying the squadron national standard, entered the packed square [of Erlbach] and delivered a brief statement in the name of the Supreme Commander to the people explaining that Germany had unconditionally surrendered its army, its navy, and its air force to the allied armies of the United States, the British Empire, and the Union of Soviet Socialist Republics. This message was immediately translated into German to the silent, disciplined, motionless people. Beginning at 2350, Company F fired a 101-gun salute; the target was a wooded hillside near company billets, the ammunition was high explosive, and the [aim] was celebration."[43]

CHAPTER 12

A BRILLIANT LEGACY

Maj. Gen. Wade Haislip: "Why do you give the cavalry a job you know they can't do?"

G-3: "We have given them jobs before we knew they couldn't do, but they not only did what we wanted, they did more."

—History, 106th Cavalry Group

The 117th Cavalry Reconnaissance Squadron's journal contains a manuscript history that well sums up the mechanized cavalry: "These are no ordinary fighting soldiers, but the most highly trained specialists and versatile fighting men of the ground forces today. They are proficient tank and armored car drivers; expert gunners; skilled radio operators; artillerymen with heavy-caliber assault weapons; highly trained as engineers in removing enemy minefields and booby traps, preparing demolitions, and building improvised bridges. Their auxiliary weapons include mortars, light and heavy; antitank guns; bazookas; anti-aircraft guns; and all types of automatic machine guns. Every type of personal arms, from pistols, Thompson submachine guns, rifles, carbines, rifle and carbine grenades, and entrenching knives are carried by the individuals."

Those mechanized cavalrymen served in a bona fide combat arm. An Army General Board set up after V-E Day to review the use of mechanized cavalry in the ETO concluded that it had performed a vital role that nonetheless bore no relationship to that anticipated by doctrine. Squadrons in cavalry groups, the board's survey showed, had spent 33 percent of their time in defensive combat, 29 percent in "special operations" (mobile reserve, rear-area security, and operating an army information service), 25 percent conducting security missions (screening, protecting flanks, and filling gaps between other units), 10 percent in offensive combat, and only 3 percent conducting the theoretically primary mission of reconnaissance. The board noted that security and reconnaissance missions often involved offensive combat, and dismounted action was nearly two times as frequent as mounted action. Interestingly, a similar British study showed that its Reconnaissance Corps had spent only 12 percent of its time conducting pure reconnaissance and 79 percent engaged in standard combat operations.

Squadrons in armored divisions spent somewhat more time both conducting reconnaissance (13 percent) and in reserve. Cavalry reconnaissance troops in infantry divisions spent a disproportionate amount of time—50 percent—engaged in security missions.[1]

This should have come as no surprise; any mechanized cavalryman on almost any front could have offered the same general view of how things really worked in battle. No such survey exits for the Pacific theater, but one probably would have shown that troops spent more time engaged in reconnaissance than in Europe, and dismounted action accounted for an even greater proportion of combat time.

"[M]echanized cavalry units," the General Board concluded, "executed, generally with creditable success, most of the traditional combat missions of the cavalry—namely, to quote paragraph 34 of Field Manual 100-5: 'Offensive combat; exploitation and pursuit; seizing and holding important terrain until . . . arrival of . . . main forces; ground reconnaissance; . . . screening; . . . security for . . . other forces; . . . delaying action; covering . . . retrograde movements of other forces; combat liaison between large units; acting as . . . mobile reserve for other forces; harassing action; and surprise action against designated objectives deep in hostile rear areas.'"

The fact that periods of fluid movement had proved the exception rather than the rule, the board noted, had forced reconnaissance elements to fight for information most of the time. Indeed, its number-one combat lesson was, "Mechanized cavalry must be organized and equipped for combat and must fight to gain information." Ready availability of air reconnaissance assets, meanwhile, had generally made anything but close-range ground reconnaissance superfluous, so most combat commanders had given their cavalry assets combat missions instead. In the Pacific, of course, jungle had conserved the cavalry mission of long-range reconnaissance, because pilots could not see the ground.

The board condemned the transformation of cavalry regiments into groups and argued that each regiment-size formation should have a third squadron. This would allow rotation and relief when the cavalry had to man a defensive line for long periods. "[E]limination of the regiment," the board intoned, "removed those elements of unity, esprit-de-corps, history, and morale which concern the preponderant part of the soldier's life. . . ." To underscore the point, perhaps, the board wanted to give regiments back their bands.[2]

The mechanized cavalrymen of World War II shaped what became the armored cavalry in ways that strongly influence how American cavalrymen fight to the present day. In 1948 the troopers regained their beloved regimental structure with the re-creation of the 3d Cavalry Regiment at Fort Meade, Maryland. As the 3d Cavalry Group, this storied formation dating back to 1846 had in Europe covered three thousand miles in 265 days, 117 of those in combat. Lessons learned during the war took on substance as the new structure added heavier assault guns, organic infantry squads, light tanks in every company, and medium tanks at the battalion level.

Doctrine caught up with the way the troopers had actually fought the war in practice. Now reconnaissance formations were to "engage in offensive or defensive combat, either mounted, dismounted, or a combination of both, primarily in execution of security and reconnaissance missions."

In 1950 Congress passed the Army Organization Act, and the Cavalry branch was absorbed by the Armor branch.[3] In ten years, the cavaliers had been wiped from the organization chart.

★★★

The armored cavalry was absent from the Korean conflict but served extensively in Vietnam, where the same adaptability that the mechanized cavalry had shown in the Pacific theater convinced Gen. William Westmoreland that he had been wrong in thinking that the armored troopers were unsuitable for his war.[4] As of 1968, the army had deployed nine armored cavalry squadrons in Vietnam, the first to arrive being the 1st Squadron, 4th Cavalry, which accompanied the 1st Infantry Division to Vietnam in 1965.

The 11th Armored Cavalry Regiment arrived in September 1966, and each of its three squadrons looked suspiciously similar to its World War II counterpart, fielding three reconnaissance troops, a tank company, and a howitzer battery (155mm). The recon troop included three armored reconnaissance platoons (mounted in M113 armored personnel carriers), plus a mortar squad. Much like their predecessors, the squadrons usually fought attached to a division. An air cavalry troop rounded out the regiment.

The cavalry's most frequent missions were reconnaissance in force, counterattack, defense, cordon and search, sweeps, and security—much like the World

War II mechanized cavalry. Its chief strengths were mobility, firepower, and protection against small-arms fire.[5] Little had changed in a quarter century.

In a monograph on the core competencies of the modern cavalry, Maj. J. Bryan Mullins observes with apparent disapproval that the cavalry in Vietnam generally discovered the enemy by running into his ambushes and rarely found him before being fired upon.[6] Lieutenant Colonel Charles Hoy had learned back in the North African desert that the cavalryman's job in reconnaissance boiled down to finding someone to shoot at him.

★★★

When the 2d Armored Cavalry Regiment led the VII Corps envelopment of the Iraqi Army in February 1991, the spirits of the men who had done the same to Hitler's Nineteenth Army surely rode by its side. The 3d Armored Cavalry Regiment spearheaded the XVIII Airborne Corps advance, carrying on the tradition established by the mechanized cavalry in North Africa, Sicily, Italy, western Europe, and the Pacific. A decade later, the 3d Squadron, 7th Cavalry Regiment (3-7 Cavalry) led the 3d Infantry Division's charge toward Baghdad during Operation Iraqi Freedom.

But the army had gone schizophrenic and had split the cavalry into light formations mounted mainly in Humvees (HMMWVs)—at best lightly armored—and heavy formations fielding tanks and Bradley infantry fighting vehicles. It has continued to "complexify" the cavalry with the creation of Stryker brigades and of Reconnaissance, Surveillance, and Target Acquisition (RSTA) formations, which are supposed to be as passive as possible on the battlefield, letting the information come to them through means such as radar and remotely piloted aircraft. Now, the army has to hope that it has the *right kind* of cavalry on the scene when the unexpected happens. Perhaps there was some wisdom to the World War II approach that created a standard cavalry organization capable of performing a broad range of jobs and that tailored the cavalry to particular local needs by providing specialized training and equipment.

★★★

Remarkably, the army has again been debating essentially the same question that it did in the early days of mechanization: Should cavalry doctrine and organization favor reconnaissance at the expense of combat? The trend in recent years has been toward light cavalry emphasizing speed and stealth.[7]

History suggests that the cavalry will not always get to choose the conditions under which it will operate, and it had better be able to fight. The stories from America's more recent wars sound very similar to those of the World War II cavalrymen.

Consider the surprises that life could spring on cavalrymen in Southeast Asia. On 12 November 1965, Troop A, 1st Squadron, 4th Cavalry, newly arrived in Vietnam, took up defensive positions with Company A, 2d Battalion, 2d Infantry, south of Ap Bau Bang, in the III Corps' zone. The enemy attacked at dawn and hit the American line repeatedly through the morning. At one point, the cavalry's armored personnel carriers sallied forward, raked the foe with machine-gun fire, and drove the enemy into retreat.[8] Nobody said it was a cavalry mission, but that is how the war came to the cavalry.

Reconnaissance is dangerous work—combat work when the enemy makes it so. In May 1967 a mounted patrol from Troop K, 11th Armored Cavalry Regiment, was conducting a route reconnaissance when it ran into an ambush. Eight vehicles were destroyed and forty-four men were killed or wounded in a matter of minutes. In December the Vietcong ambushed two platoons of the 3d Squadron, 5th Cavalry, destroyed nine of eleven vehicles, and caused forty-one casualties.[9]

Consider the 3-7 Cavalry, which had to fight a tenacious enemy at As Samawah, in Iraq, on 23 March 2002, and again along "Ambush Alley" the next day. When the cavalry hit the first ambush, Alpha Troop's fire support officer, 1st Lieutenant Wade, said it looked like "Star Wars, with the tracer bouncing off of the vehicles." The enemy closed to within fifteen yards of the vehicles, and the firefight lasted two hours. Fortunately, 3-7 Cavalry was well armed and armored, and it was able to battle through without suffering casualties.[10]

Or consider Capt. Edward Twaddell III, reading from his journal to a combat interviewer about his experience in al-Fallujah, Iraq, in November 2004, in command of Alpha Company, 2d Squadron, 7th Cavalry Regiment, in November 2004: "About 1130, 1st Platoon is still out with the XO, came into contact. Staff Sergeant Santillana's squad had chased an insurgent that they had seen running across an alley into a building. They seized a foothold in the courtyard, prepped the entrance with a grenade, and kicked in the door. Reports were that between 10 and 20 insurgents were waiting for them. Sergeant Abdelwahab was on point. He was immediately hit in the right leg and left arm. Specialist Howard was the number-two man. He grabbed 'Abe,' dragged him back. Simultaneously, the squad started taking fire from a sniper positioned across the street. Specialist Jose Velez sprayed the window across the street with a squad automatic weapon (SAW), stopped in the open to reload, and was shot just below the neck in the right shoulder. Grenades came out of the original target house and exploded, wounding Sergeant Bristol, Specialist Goodin, and Specialist Benny Alicea. Somehow they got everyone back in the Brads and began casualty evacuation. . . ."[11]

Perhaps the army's plan to create an essentially generic "Objective Force" (now "Future Force") that can conduct any mission now performed by the separate branches—which implies the disappearance of the Cavalry altogether—will resolve this issue.[12] Or perhaps the strategy of transformation, like earlier attempts to base force structure on theory, will be tossed aside by combat commanders who will do what it takes to win, even if that means re-creating specialized forces such as the Cavalry.

★★★

Once, in the distant mists of time, the chariot dominated the battlefield with its mobility, but it gradually gave way to the much more flexible horse-mounted soldier. The cavalryman in his various incarnations held sway for nearly 2,500 years, finally to step aside in the mid-twentieth century for the mechanized trooper mounted on his steed of steel. One might think that the mechanized cavalryman of World War II had started a new mounted tradition that would last as long as the internal combustion engine drives war machines. But only our descendents are likely to know whether the new cavalryman will keep his place for a similar age.

U.S. CAVALRY IN THE ETO

Corps Attachments by Campaign

Group	Normal Sqdrns	Start Date	Army	Normandy	North France	South France	Ardennes	Rhineland	Central Europe
2d		7/19/44	Third	ADSEC	VIII, XII		XII, XX	XII	XII
	2d		Third	ADSEC	VIII, XII		XII, XX	XII	XII
	42d		Third	ADSEC	VII, XII		XII, XX	XII	XII
3d		8/10/44	Third		XX		XX	XX	XX
	3d		Third		XX, XII		XX	XX	XX
	43d		Third		XX		XX	XX	XX
4th		6/18/44	First	VII	VII		VII	VII	VII
	4th		First	VII	VII		VII	VII	VII
	24th		First	VII	VII		VII	VII	VII
6th		8/2/44	Third	(Army)	(Army)		III	VIII	VIII
	6th		Third	(Army)	(Army)		III	VIII	VIII
	28th		Third	(Army)	(Army)		III	VIII	VIII
11th		12/14/44	Ninth					XIII	XIII
	36th		Ninth					XIII	XIII
	44th		Ninth					XIII	XIII
14th		12/11/44	First				VIII	III	
			Third					XVIII	III
	18th		First				VIII	III	
			Third					XVIII	III
	32d		First				VIII	III	
			Third					XVIII	III
15th		7/44	Third	ADSEC	ADSEC				XIX
			Ninth		VIII			XVI	XVI
	15th		Third	ADSEC	ADSEC				XIX
			Ninth		VII			XVI	XVI
	17th		Third	ADSEC	ADSEC			XIX, XIII	XIX
			Ninth		VIII			XVI	XVI
16th		3/10/45	Third						XII
			Fifteenth					XX	XX, XXII
	16th		Third						XII
			Fifteenth					XX	XX, XXII

Group	Normal	Start Date	Army	Normandy	North France	South France	Ardennes	Rhineland	Central Europe
	19th		Third					XX	XII
			Fifteenth						XX, XXII
101st	101st	2/9/45	Seventh					XV, XXI	XXI
	116th		Seventh					XV, XXI	XXI
			Seventh					XV, XXI	XXI
102d	102d	6/12/44	First	V	V		V	V	V
			Seventh					VI	V
	38th		First	V	V		V	V	V
			Seventh					VI	V
			First	V	V		V, VII, XIX	V	V
106th	102d	7/6/44	First	VIII	XV			XV	XV
			Third		XII		XV		
	106th		First	VIII	XV			XV	XV
			Third		XII		XV		
	121st		First	VIII	XV			XV	XV
			Third		XII		XV		
113th	113th	7/4/44	First	XIX	XIX			XX	XIX
			Ninth					XIII	XIII
	125th		First	XIX	XIX			XX	XIX
			Ninth				Ninth Army XIX	XIII	XIII
			First	XIX	XIX			XX	XIX
			Ninth				Ninth Army XIII	XIII	XIII
115th	113th	3/12/45	Fifteenth	(66th Inf Div)					VI
			Seventh						
	125th		Fifteenth	(66th Inf Div)					VI
			Seventh						
117th	104th	8/15/44	Seventh			VI		VI	VI
	117th								VI

ADSEC = Advance Section, Communications Zone

Source: "U.S. Cavalry in the ETO," *Cavalry Journal*, May–June 1946, 15.

NOTES

Chapter 1: From Horse to Horsepower

1. Maj. George S. Patton Jr., "What the World War Did for Cavalry," *Cavalry Journal*, April 1922, 168–69.
2. Ibid., 167–68.
3. "Armored Cars for Cavalry Units," *Cavalry Journal*, January 1923, 92.
4. Lieutenant General Grazioli, "Modern Cavalry and Fast Moving Composite Units," *Cavalry Journal*, April 1923, 137–46.
5. George F. Hofmann, *Through Mobility We Conquer: The Mechanization of the U.S. Cavalry* (Lexington, KY: The University Press of Kentucky, 2006), 101–2. (Hereafter Hofmann.)
6. Matthew Darlington Morton, "Men on 'Iron Ponies': The Death and Rebirth of the Modern U.S. Cavalry," doctoral dissertation, Florida State University, 2004, 32–33. (Hereafter Morton.)
7. Brig. Gen. Adna Chaffee, "Mechanized Cavalry: Lecture Delivered at the Army War College, Washington, DC, September 29, 1939." (Hereafter Chaffee.) Hofmann, 103.
8. Maj. C. C. Benson, "Mechanization—Aloft and Alow," *Cavalry Journal*, January 1929, 58–62. Hofmann, 107.
9. Chaffee.
10. Maj. E. C. McGuire, "Armored Cars in the Cavalry Maneuvers," *Cavalry Journal*, July 1930, 386.
11. Ibid., 387–88.
12. Ibid., 391.
13. Field Marshal Viscount Allenby, "The Future of Cavalry," *Cavalry Journal*, January 1929, 2.
14. Maj. George S. Patton Jr. and Maj. C. C. Benson, "Mechanization and Cavalry," *Cavalry Journal*, April 1930, 235ff. (Hereafter Patton and Benson.)
15. Lt. Col. Scott Cunningham, note to author, March 2007.
16. Morton, 48–50. Chaffee.
17. Patton and Benson, 239.
18. Lt. Col. K. B. Edmunds, "Tactics of a Mechanized Force: A Prophecy," *Cavalry Journal*, July 1930, 410–17.
19. Morton, 50–58.
20. Hofmann, 157.
21. Chaffee. Morton, 50–58. Hofmann, 157ff.
22. Capt. F. T. Bonsteel, "The Employment of a Mechanized Cavalry Brigade," *Cavalry Journal*, September-October 1933, 19.
23. Ibid., 24.
24. Morton, 105.
25. Col. M. Wiktorin, "The Modern Cavalry Regiment," *Cavalry Journal*, April 1929, 205–6.
26. Morton, 113–14.
27. Chaffee.
28. R. W. Grow, "New Developments in the Organization and Equipment of Cavalry," *Cavalry Journal*, May-June 1939, 206.
29. Gen. Donn A. Starry, "Introductory Essay," George F. Hofmann, *Through Mobility We Conquer: The Mechanization of the U.S. Cavalry* (Lexington, KY: The University Press of Kentucky, 2006), 12.

30. Alex Buchner, *Das Handbuch der Deutschen Infanterie, 1939-1945* (Wölfersheim-Berstadt: Podzun-Pallas-Verlag GMBH, not dated), 49–50. (Hereafter Buchner.)

31. "German Horse Cavalry and Transport," *Intelligence Bulletin*, March 1946, online version available at Lone Sentry, http://www.lonesentry.com/articles/germanhorse/index.html, as of March 2007. (Hereafter "German Horse Cavalry and Transport.")

32. Morton, 167, 172.

33. Mary Lee Stubbs and Stanley Russell Connor, *Armor-Cavalry, Part I: Regular Army and Army Reserve* (Washington, DC: Office of the Chief of Military History, U.S. Army, 1969, online edition, http://www.army.mil/cmh-pg/books/Lineage/arcav/arcav.htm), 58. (Hereafter Stubbs and Connor.)

34. Col. Charles K. Graydon, "With the 101st Cavalry in World War II: 1940-1945," 1st Battalion, 101st Cavalry, http://members.tripod.com/1-101cav/ww2.html as of October 2006. (Hereafter Graydon.)

35. Chaffee.

36. Morton, 167, 178.

37. Robert Stewart Cameron, *Americanizing the Tank: U.S. Army Administration and Mechanized Development Within the Army, 1917–1943*, dissertation, Temple University, August 1994. UMI Dissertation Services: Ann Arbor, MI, 1996, 492–93. Houston, *Hell on Wheels, The 2d Armored Division* (Novato, CA: Presidio Press, 1977), 33–34. (Hereafter Houston.)

38. Cameron, 492–93. Houston, 33–34.

39. Cameron, 492–93.

40. Ibid., 493. David E. Johnson, *Fast Tanks and Heavy Bombers, Innovation in the U.S. Army 1917–1945* (Ithaca, NY: Cornell University Press, 1998), 121.

41. Maj. Louis A. DiMarco, "The U.S. Army's Mechanized Cavalry Doctrine in World War II," master's thesis, U.S. Army Command and General Staff College, 1995, 17. (Hereafter DiMarco.)

42. Col. Harold Samsel, "The Operational History of the 117th Cavalry Reconnaissance Squadron (Mecz.), World War II," manuscript contained in WW II Survey 1530, Military History Institute, Carlisle, PA. (Hereafter Samsel, operational history.) Robert Lutz, "History of the 117th Cavalry Reconnaissance Squadron (MECZ)," 1. (Hereafter Lutz.)

43. Kent Roberts Greenfield, Robert Palmer, and Bell Wiley, *The Organization of Ground Combat Troops: United States Army in World War II, The Army Ground Forces* (Washington, DC: Historical Division, U.S. Army, 1947), 278. (Hereafter Greenfield, et al.)

44. Maj. I. D. White, "The Armored Force: Reconnaissance Battalion, Armored Division, *Cavalry Journal*, May-June 1941, 48–52. (Hereafter White.) History, 81st Armored Reconnaissance Battalion.

45. White, 48–52.

46. FM 17-22, *Armored Force Field Manual: Reconnaissance Battalion*, 18 August 1942.

47. DiMarco, 26.

48. History, 89th Armored Reconnaissance Battalion.

49. Ibid.

50. Telephone interview with Gen. William Knowlton (ret.), 87th Cavalry Reconnaissance Squadron, October 2006.

51. Lt. Col. Scott Cunningham, note to author, March 2007.

52. History, 91st Reconnaissance Squadron, 1st Cavalry Division. History, 91st Cavalry Reconnaissance Squadron. History, 92d Reconnaissance Squadron. FM 2-10, *Cavalry Field Manual: Mechanized Elements*, 8 April 1941. "U.S. Army Military History Research Collection, Senior Officers Debriefing Program: Conversation Between General Hamilton Howze and Lieutenant Colonel Robert Reed," U.S. Army Heritage Collection Online, http://www.ahco.army.mil/site/index.jsp as of December 2006. (Hereafter Howze.)

53. FM 2-30, *Cavalry Field Manual: Cavalry Mechanized Reconnaissance Squadron*, 29 March 1943.
54. Morton, 232.
55. Greenfield, et al., 356–57.
56. The Second Cavalry Association Regimental History Site, http://history.dragoons.org as of August 2006. (Hereafter The Second Cavalry Association Regimental History Site.)
57. T/O&E 2-25, *Cavalry Reconnaissance Squadron, Mechanized*, 15 September 1943.
58. AARs, 9th Cavalry Reconnaissance Troop.
59. Morton, 184.
60. Telephone interview with L'Cainian Evans, 40th Reconnaissance Troop, October 2006. Telephone interview with Ben Rosenthal, 45th Reconnaissance Troop, October 2006. "1st Airborne Reconnaissance Squadron and Parachute Squadron Association," http://www .airbornerecce.com/oca/ as of March 2007. (Hereafter "1st Airborne Reconnaissance Squadron and Parachute Squadron Association.")
61. Morton, 205–6. Telephone interview with George Trentacosti, 37th Reconnaissance Troop, October 2006.
62. Capt. M. M. Cutler, "Cooperation with the Infantry," *Cavalry Journal*, January-February 1945, 28.
63. AARs, 9th Cavalry Reconnaissance Troop.
64. Samsel, operational history.
65. The Second Cavalry Association Regimental History Site.
66. FM 2-30, *Cavalry Field Manual: Cavalry Mechanized Reconnaissance Squadron*, 29 March 1943.
67. James Deerin, "Prelude to Conflict," manuscript contained in WW II Survey 1530, Military History Institute, Carlisle, PA. (Hereafter Deerin.)
68. History, 43d Cavalry Reconnaissance Troop.
69. "Private Charles Raney," Pegasus I, http://www.pegasus-one.org/pow/charles_raney.htm as of June 2006. (Hereafter Raney.)
70. Sgt. Ivan Marion, WW II Survey 6316, Military History Institute, Carlisle, PA. (Hereafter Marion.)
71. Graydon.
72. Combat interviews, 3d Cavalry Group, NARA.
73. Telephone interview with Gen. William Knowlton (ret.), 87th Cavalry Reconnaissance Squadron, October 2006.
74. History and diary, 25th Cavalry Reconnaissance Squadron. History, 89th Armored Reconnaissance Battalion.
75. Chaffee.
76. R. W. Grow, "Mechanized Cavalry," *Cavalry Journal*, January-February 1938, 30–31.
77. *The American Arsenal* (London: Greenhill Books, 2001), 75. (Hereafter *The American Arsenal*.)
78. History, 45th Cavalry Reconnaissance Troop.
79. Steven Zaloga, *M8 Greyhound Light Armored Car 1941–91* (Botley, UK: Osprey Publishing, 2002), 5–10. *The American Arsenal*, 66.
80. AAR, 96th Cavalry Reconnaissance Troop.
81. "Technical Observers Report, European Theater of Operations, 9 February to 23 March 1945," 12 April 1945, General Staff G-2 Section Intelligence Reports, Numerical File, 1943–46, folder 283, NARA.
82. Notes of Maj. Gen. Omar Bradley on visit to the 1st Armored Division, 1 March 1943, records of the 1st Armored Division.

83. *Catalog of Standard Ordnance Items*, Office of the Chief of Ordnance Technical Division, 1944.
84. AAR, 96th Cavalry Reconnaissance Troop.
85. Morton, 219.
86. *The American Arsenal*, 105.
87. FM 2-30, *Cavalry Field Manual: Cavalry Mechanized Reconnaissance Squadron*, 29 March 1943.
88. Morton, 222–23. History, 45th Cavalry Reconnaissance Troop.
89. Morton, 221.
90. Graydon.
91. *The American Arsenal*, 102.
92. Armored Force Board report 138, 30 June 1941, NARA, RG 156, Chief of Ordnance, Box J-358.
93. *The American Arsenal*, 10–17.
94. *Catalog of Standard Ordnance Items*, Office of the Chief of Ordnance Technical Division, 1944.
95. Ibid. *Memorandum*, "Reports on Combat Experience and Battle Lessons for Training Purposes," Headquarters, 1st Armored Regiment, 9 June 1943, NARA, RG 94, Box 14926.
96. *The American Arsenal*, 50.
97. Ibid., 45.
98. History, 25th Cavalry Reconnaissance Squadron.
99. Maj. Gen. H. C. Ingles, Chief Signal Officer, "Signal Equipment and the Armored Forces," *Cavalry Journal*, May-June 1946, 47–49. TO&E 2-27, *Cavalry Reconnaissance Troop, Mechanized*, 15 July 1943.
100. Salter, 128.
101. Clark Lee, "The Fighting 26th," *Cavalry Journal*, March-April 1943, 3.
102. History, 91st Cavalry Reconnaissance Squadron.
103. Fred Salter, *Recon Scout* (New York, NY: Ballantine Books, 1994), xiii, 20–23. (Hereafter Salter.)

Chapter 2: North Africa: A Concept Tested

1. AAR, 1st Reconnaissance Troop.
2. George F. Howe, *Northwest Africa: Seizing the Initiative in the West: United States Army in World War II, The Mediterranean Theater of Operations* (Washington, DC: Office of the Chief of Military History, Department of the Army, 1957), 124–28. (Hereafter Howe.) Memorandum, Headquarters Blackstone, "Final Report on Operation Blackstone for period 072400Z-110730Z, 1942," 28 November 1942.
3. Howe, 142ff. AAR, Combat Command B, 2d Armored Division. History, 2d Armored Division.
4. AAR, 81st Reconnaissance Battalion. Howe, 386ff. Thomas E. Griess, ed., *The West Point Military History Series, The Second World War, Europe and the Mediterranean* (Wayne, NJ: Avery Publishing Group Inc., 1984), 173. (Hereafter Griess.)
5. Lt. Col. Charles Hoy, "Reconnaissance Lessons from Tunisia," *Cavalry Journal*, November-December 1943, 17. (Hereafter Hoy, "Reconnaissance Lessons from Tunisia.")
6. Lt. Col. Charles Hoy, "Mechanics of Battlefield Reconnaissance," *Cavalry Journal*, May-June 1944, 24. (Hereafter Hoy, "Mechanics of Battlefield Reconnaissance.")
7. Ibid., 26.

8. AAR and journal, 81st Reconnaissance Battalion. Hoy, "Mechanics of Battlefield Reconnaissance," 25. L. E. Anderson, *Return to the Rapido: Company D/F, 81st Reconnaissance Battalion, First Armored Division* (Bennington, VT: Merriam Press, 2005), 125–29. (Hereafter Anderson.)

9. Griess, 173–74.

10. Operations report, 1st Armored Division. Anderson, 132–35.

11. AAR and journal, 81st Reconnaissance Battalion. Hoy, "Reconnaissance Lessons from Tunisia," 16–17. Sgt. Thomas Domando, WW II Survey 1593, Military History Institute, Carlisle, PA. (Hereafter Domando.)

12. Operations report, 1st Armored Division.

13. Hoy, "Reconnaissance Lessons from Tunisia," 20. Hoy, "Mechanics of Battlefield Reconnaissance," 24.

14. AAR and journal, 81st Reconnaissance Battalion. "Commander-in-Chief's Dispatch, North African Campaign, 1942-43."

15. AAR, 81st Reconnaissance Battalion.

16. Lang, *Oberst* Rudolf, "Report of the Fighting of Kampfgruppe Lang (10. Pz. Div.) in Tunisia from December 1942 to 15 April 1943," MS # D-166, 6 June 1947, National Archives. (Hereafter Lang.)

17. AAR, 81st Armored Reconnaissance Battalion. Hoy, "Mechanics of Battlefield Reconnaissance," 27–28.

18. "German Tactical Doctrine, Military Intelligence Service, Special Series No. 8," U.S. War Department, 20 December 1942, online version available at Lone Sentry, http://www .lonesentry.com/manuals/german-tactical-doctrine/index.html, as of March 2007.

19. Hoy, "Reconnaissance Lessons from Tunisia," 17.

20. Ibid., 17–18. Hoy, "Mechanics of Battlefield Reconnaissance," 29.

21. Hoy, "Reconnaissance Lessons from Tunisia," 17.

22. Ibid., 18–19.

23. Unit history, 899th Tank Destroyer Battalion.

24. Griess, 177.

25. "1st Airborne Reconnaissance Squadron and Parachute Squadron Association." "A British Soldier Remembers," http://www.britishsoldier.com/logistic.htm#regorg as of March 2007.

26. Report of Operations, 9th Infantry Division. History, 91st Reconnaissance Squadron. Lt. Col. Harry Candler, "91st Reconnaissance Squadron in Tunisia," *Cavalry Journal*, March-April 1944, 14. (Hereafter Candler.) Capt. Jack Ficklen, "A Reconnaissance Squadron in Tunisia," *Cavalry Journal*, July-August 1943, 16. (Hereafter Ficklen.) Marion. S.Sgt. William De Groat, WW II Survey 1474, Military History Institute, Carlisle, PA. Howe, 616–17.

27. Salter, 63–67. G-3 journal, 9th Infantry Division.

28. Salter, 71–82. G-3 journal, 9th Infantry Division.

29. Hoy, "Mechanics of Battlefield Reconnaissance," 28.

30. History, 91st Reconnaissance Squadron. Hoy, "Reconnaissance Lessons from Tunisia," 14. Ficklen, 16. Salter, 93ff, 110–20.

31. Marion. Domando. Lt. Col. John Huff, WW II Survey 1466, Military History Institute, Carlisle, PA.

32. "Report of Observations at European Theater of Operations and North Africa Theater of Operations," 1 August 1943, General Staff G-2 Section Intelligence Reports, Numerical File, 1943–46, folder 22, NARA.

33. Buchner, 51. "German Horse Cavalry and Transport."

34. "Observer Report on the Italian Campaign during the period 22 Dec 43 to 8 Mar 44,

Inclusive," not dated, General Staff G-2 Section Intelligence Reports, Numerical File, 1943–46, folder 86, NARA.

35. AAR, 34th Cavalry Reconnaissance Troop.

36. Report of Operations, 9th Infantry Division.

37. "Report of Visit to the North Africa Theater of Operations," 7 May 1943, General Staff G-2 Section Intelligence Reports, Numerical File, 1943–46, folder 49, NARA.

38. "Observer Report, Team No. 3," 22 August 1943, General Staff G-2 Section Intelligence Reports, Numerical File, 1943–46, folder 28, NARA.

39. FM 2-30, *Cavalry Reconnaissance Squadron Mechanized*, 28 August 1944. Stubbs and Connor, 71–73.

40. "Interview with Domenic Melso," Rutgers Oral History Archives, http://oralhistory .rutgers.edu/Interviews/melso_domenic.html as of June 2006. (Hereafter Melso.)

41. Raney.

42. "1st Airborne Reconnaissance Squadron and Parachute Squadron Association."

43. Melso.

Chapter 3: Sicily and Italy: Mechanization Meets the Mountains

1. Telephone interview with Ben Rosenthal, 45th Cavalry Reconnaissance Troop, October 2006.

2. Journal, 45th Cavalry Reconnaissance Troop. "Amphibious Intelligence Training," not dated, General Staff G-2 Section Intelligence Reports, Numerical File, 1943–46, folder 105, NARA.

3. History, 91st Cavalry Reconnaissance Squadron. *Sicily*, CMH Pub 72-16 (Washington, DC: U.S. Army Center of Military History, not dated), 1, 6. (Hereafter *Sicily*.)

4. *Cavalry Reconnaissance Number 5* (Fort Riley, KS: The Cavalry School, not dated), 5–6. (Hereafter *Cavalry Reconnaissance Number 5*.)

5. Houston, 158–59, 164.

6. *Sicily*, 10–11.

7. Houston, 164–65.

8. Ibid., 158–59.

9. *Sicily*, 15, 17.

10. Houston, 172–74. History, 2d Armored Division.

11. Memorandum, Headquarters 2d Armored Division to the commanding general, Seventh Army, "Sicilian Campaign," 8 September 1943.

12. *Cavalry Reconnaissance Number 5*, 15–16.

13. History, 45th Cavalry Reconnaissance Troop.

14. History, 91st Cavalry Reconnaissance Squadron.

15. Report of Operations, 9th Infantry Division.

16. History, 91st Cavalry Reconnaissance Squadron. Salter, 152.

17. Lt. Col. Charles Ellis, "Demolition Obstacles to Reconnaissance," *Cavalry Journal*, May-June 1945, 29.

18. *Sicily*, 20–21.

19. *Cavalry Reconnaissance Number 5*, 22–23. AAR, 3d Cavalry Reconnaissance Troop.

20. Report of Operations, 9th Infantry Division.

21. "Sicilian Campaign," 26 August 1943, General Staff G-2 Section Intelligence Reports, Numerical File, 1943–46, folder 51, NARA.

22. Fifth Army History.

23. AAR, 36th Cavalry Reconnaissance Troop.

24. Journal, 45th Reconnaissance Troop.

25. Griess, 234.
26. Journal, 45th Reconnaissance Troop.
27. AAR, 3d Cavalry Reconnaissance Troop.
28. "Report of Officer Returned from Overseas," 12 February 1944, General Staff G-2 Section Intelligence Reports, Numerical File, 1943–46, folder 65, NARA.
29. "Thrice-Wounded Infantry Lieutenant at Air Base," *The Columbia Record*, 12 April 1945.
30. Fifth Army History.
31. Journal, 91st Cavalry Reconnaissance Squadron.
32. History and journal, 91st Cavalry Reconnaissance Squadron. Salter, 260, 263. Journal, 117th Cavalry Reconnaissance Squadron.
33. *The First Armored Division* (Germany: The 1st Armored Division, 1945), np.
34. "Report of Officer Returned from Overseas," 12 February 1944, General Staff G-2 Section Intelligence Reports, Numerical File, 1943–46, folder 65, NARA. "Extracts from Overseas Reports," not dated, General Staff G-2 Section Intelligence Reports, Numerical File, 1943–46, folder 81, NARA.
35. "G-2 Report on Italian Campaign," 15 June 1944, General Staff G-2 Section Intelligence Reports, Numerical File, 1943–46, folder 110, NARA.
36. "Report by Major Edwin O'Connor Jr.," 12 February 1944, General Staff G-2 Section Intelligence Reports, Numerical File, 1943–46, folder 82, NARA. "Extracts from Overseas Reports," not dated, General Staff G-2 Section Intelligence Reports, Numerical File, 1943–46, folder 81, NARA.
37. AAR, 3d Cavalry Reconnaissance Troop.
38. History, 81st Armored Reconnaissance Battalion.
39. Ibid.
40. Ibid.
41. Untitled and dated report by Lt. Col. Robert Williams, General Staff G-2 Section Intelligence Reports, Numerical File, 1943–46, folder 93, NARA.
42. "Extracts from Overseas Reports," not dated, General Staff G-2 Section Intelligence Reports, Numerical File, 1943–46, folder 91, NARA.
43. *Outline History of II Corps* (Italy: 12th Polish Field Survey Company, 1945), 6–7.
44. History and journal, 91st Cavalry Reconnaissance Squadron.
45. Fifth Army History.
46. Lt. Col. Michael Popowski, "The 81st Reconnaissance Squadron Fights Way to Rome," *Cavalry Journal*, January-February 1945, 35. (Hereafter Popowski.)
47. AAR, 3d Cavalry Reconnaissance Troop.
48. Fifth Army History.
49. Ibid.
50. Journal, 45th Cavalry Reconnaissance Troop. Telephone interview with Ben Rosenthal, 45th Cavalry Reconnaissance Troop, October 2006.
51. G-3 journal, 45th Infantry Division.
52. Telephone interview with Robert Flynn, 45th Cavalry Reconnaissance Troop, October 2006.
53. Fifth Army History.
54. History and journal, 91st Cavalry Reconnaissance Squadron.
55. Samsel, operational history. Journal, 117th Cavalry Reconnaissance Squadron.
56. S.Sgt. Philip Schriel, WW II Survey 1527, Military History Institute, Carlisle, PA.
57. Lutz, 5.
58. Samsel, operational history. Journal, 117th Cavalry Reconnaissance Squadron.
59. Fifth Army History.
60. Popowski , 35.

61. Ibid., 36–37. History, 81st Armored Reconnaissance Battalion.
62. Thomas M. Sherman, *Seek, Strike, Destroy! The History of the 636th Tank Destroyer Battalion* (Published by author: 1986), 88. Popowski, 37.
63. History and journal, 91st Cavalry Reconnaissance Squadron.
64. Fifth Army History. AAR, 88th Cavalry Reconnaissance Troop.
65. Ibid.
66. Samsel, operational history. Robert Lutz, phone interview with author, July 2006.
67. Fifth Army History.
68. *General der Kavallerie* Fridolin von Senger und Etterlin, "Kriegstagebuch des Italienischen Feldzuges—Die Vereitelung des Feindlichen Durchbruches Zwischen den Geschlagenem Deutschen 10. und 14. Armeen; Rückzug zum Arno," MS # C-095c, 14 January 1953, National Archives.
69. Fifth Army History.
70. History, 81st Armored Reconnaissance Battalion.
71. Samsel, operational history. Lutz, 9. Journal, 117th Cavalry Reconnaissance Squadron.
72. History and journal, 91st Cavalry Reconnaissance Squadron.
73. History, 81st Armored Reconnaissance Battalion.
74. History and journal, 91st Cavalry Reconnaissance Squadron.
75. Griess, 275.
76. Glen Norris, "Journal Entries of a Soldier in the 91st Reconnaissance Squadron from 1942-45," U.S. Army Garrison Schweinfurt Web site, http://www.schweinfurt.army.mil/sites/1-4/history.htm as of July 2006. (Hereafter Norris.)
77. Ibid.
78. History, 81st Armored Reconnaissance Battalion.
79. Norris.
80. Memorandum draft, "Cavalry Reconnaissance Squadron, 11 July 1944," contained in the journal, 117th Cavalry Reconnaissance Squadron.
81. Popowski, 34.
82. Fifth Army History.
83. Ibid. *The First Armored Division* (Germany: The 1st Armored Division, 1945), np.
84. History, 91st Cavalry Reconnaissance Squadron.

Chapter 4: The Pacific, Part I:
War of the Cavalry Reconnaissance Troops

1. "World War II (Asia-Pacific Theater)," Center of Military History Online, http://www.army.mil/cmh-pg/reference/apcmp.htm as of July 2006. (Hereafter "World War II.")
2. "Report of Colonel Harry Knight, Cavalry, covering Observations in the Southwest Pacific Theater During the Period October 16 to December 30, 1942," not dated, General Staff G-2 Section Intelligence Reports, Numerical File, 1943–46, folder 6, NARA.
3. "Tactical Employment of Japanese Cavalry," 25 July 1945, General Staff G-2 Section Intelligence Reports, Numerical File, 1943–46, folder 212, NARA.
4. John Miller Jr., *Guadalcanal: The First Offensive, The United States Army in World War II, The War in the Pacific* (Washington, DC: Center of Military History, United States Army, 1989), 212–17. (Hereafter Miller, *Guadalcanal.*) AAR, 25th Cavalry Reconnaissance Troop.
5. Miller, *Guadalcanal*, 303. AAR, 25th Cavalry Reconnaissance Troop. Distinguished Service Cross citation for Capt. Teddy Deese.
6. "New Guinea: 24 January 1943-31 December 1944." Center of Military History Online, http://www.army.mil/cmh-pg/brochures/new-guinea/ng.htm as of July 2006. (Hereafter "New Guinea.")

7. "World War II." "New Guinea."
8. *Combat Lessons: Number 4*, U.S. Army, 1944, 53–56.
9. Lt. Col. Clay Bridgewater, "Reconnaissance on Guam," *Cavalry Journal*, May-June 1945, 46.
10. AAR, 43d Cavalry Reconnaissance Troop.
11. "Aleutian Islands," Center of Military History Online, http://www.army.mil/cmh-pg/brochures/aleut/aleut.htm as of July 2006.
12. Ibid. AAR, 7th Cavalry Reconnaissance Troop.
13. "World War II."
14. "New Guinea."
15. Leonard Daloia. *37th Cavalry "Recon." Troop*. Self-published, 1988. (Hereafter Daloia, journal.) AAR, 37th Cavalry Reconnaissance Troop.
16. Telephone interview with George Trentacosti, October 2006.
17. "Lessons Learned—Bougainville Campaign," records of the 37th Infantry Division.
18. Daloia, journal.
19. History and AAR, 21st Cavalry Reconnaissance Troop.
20. *Combat Lessons: Number 2*, U.S. Army, 1943 (?), 55ff.
21. "Night Operations in Pacific Ocean Areas," 14 March 1945, General Staff G-2 Section Intelligence Reports, Numerical File, 1943–46, folder 270, NARA. "Night Operations in Pacific Ocean Areas," 1 April 1945, General Staff G-2 Section Intelligence Reports, Numerical File, 1943–46, folder 284, NARA. "Battle Experience Against the Japanese: Report No. 54," 13 August 1945, General Staff G-2 Section Intelligence Reports, Numerical File, 1943–46, folder 231, NARA. "Battle Experience Against the Japanese: Report No. 58," 13 August 1945, General Staff G-2 Section Intelligence Reports, Numerical File, 1943–46, folder 231, NARA. AAR, 27th Cavalry Reconnaissance Troop.
22. John Miller Jr., *Cartwheel: The Reduction of Rabaul, The United States Army in World War II, The War in the Pacific* (Washington, DC: Office of the Chief of Military History, United States Army, 1959), 351ff. (Hereafter Miller, *Cartwheel*.)
23. Daloia, journal.
24. Miller, *Cartwheel*, 359.
25. Daloia, journal.
26. Telephone interview with George Trentacosti, October 2006.
27. Daloia, journal.
28. Telephone interview with George Trentacosti, October 2006.
29. Archivist Greg Bradsher, NARA, message to author, 16 November 2006.
30. Daloia, journal.
31. Miller, *Cartwheel*, 377.
32. "World War II."
33. Lt. Col. S. L. A. Marshall, "Cavalry in Dismounted Action," *Cavalry Journal*, September-October 1944, 34ff. AAR, 7th Reconnaissance Troop.
34. AAR, 6th Cavalry Reconnaissance Troop. "The Battle of Lone Tree Hill," manuscript, records of the 20th Infantry Regiment.
35. AAR, 31st Cavalry Reconnaissance Troop. *History of the 31st Infantry Division in Training and Combat: 1940–1945* (Baton Rouge, LA: The 31st Infantry Division, 1946), 21–23, 97–98, 101. (Hereafter *History of the 31st Infantry Division.*) AAR and journal, 31st Infantry Division.

Chapter 5: The Pacific, Part II:
The Mechanized Cavalry Finds Roads

1. "World War II." "Leyte," Center of Military History Online, http://www.army.mil/cmh-pg/brochures/leyte/leyte.htm as of July 2006. (Hereafter "Leyte.")
2. AAR, 7th Reconnaissance Troop.
3. AAR, 24th Cavalry Reconnaissance Troop.
4. "Leyte."
5. AAR, 33d Cavalry Reconnaissance Troop.
6. "Luzon: 1944-1945," Center of Military History Online, http://www.army.mil/cmh-pg/brochures/luzon/72-28.htm as of July 2006. (Hereafter "Luzon: 1944–1945.")
7. "World War II."
8. Field Order 1, Luzon operation, 43d Infantry Division.
9. S.Sgt. Paul Gerrish, WW II Survey 1384, Military History Institute, Carlisle, PA. (Hereafter Gerrish interview.)
10. History, 37th Cavalry Reconnaissance Troop.
11. Sgt. Dick Small, *The Invincible 37th Recon* (Self-published, not dated), 13. (Hereafter Small.) AAR, 672d Amphibian Tractor Battalion.
12. Journal, 37th Cavalry Reconnaissance Troop.
13. AAR, 6th Cavalry Reconnaissance Troop. Field Order 1, 6th Infantry Division, 28 November 1944. Telephone interview with Robert Beutlich, 6th Infantry Division, October 2006.
14. "Luzon: 1944-1945." S.Sgt. Paul Gerrish, "My Army Days," manuscript contained in WW II Survey 1384, Military History Institute, Carlisle, PA. (Hereafter Gerrish, "My Army Days.")
15. History, 37th Cavalry Reconnaissance Troop.
16. Lt. Stephen Perry, "Hair, Wheels, or Tracks," *Cavalry Journal*, July-August 1945, 13–14. (Hereafter Perry.)
17. AAR, 6th Cavalry Reconnaissance Troop. Telephone interview with Robert Beutlich, 6th Infantry Division, October 2006.
18. History, 37th Cavalry Reconnaissance Troop.
19. Gerrish, "My Army Days." Perry. Sixth Army report of the Luzon Campaign.
20. Sixth Army report of the Luzon Campaign.
21. Robert Ross Smith, *Triumph in the Philippines: The United States Army in World War II, The War in the Pacific* (Washington, DC: Office of the Chief of Military History, Department of the Army, 1963), 170ff. (Hereafter Smith.)
22. Gerrish, "My Army Days." Journal and history, 640th Tank Destroyer Battalion.
23. Telephone interview with George Trentacosti, October 2006.
24. Gerrish, "My Army Days." Gerrish interview. Telephone interview with Robert Buschur, 40th Cavalry Reconnaissance Troop, December 2006. Smith, 175ff.
25. AAR, 6th Cavalry Reconnaissance Troop.
26. Sixth Army report of the Luzon Campaign.
27. AAR, 25th Cavalry Reconnaissance Troop.
28. AAR, 32d Cavalry Reconnaissance Troop.
29. AAR, 302d Cavalry Reconnaissance Troop. "World War II." "Luzon: 1944–1945." Smith, 215–16.
30. Small, 18.
31. Ibid.
32. Decoration citations and history, 37th Cavalry Reconnaissance Troop.
33. Small, 24.

34. Gerrish, "My Army Days."
35. AAR, 6th Cavalry Reconnaissance Troop.
36. Sixth Army report of the Luzon Campaign.
37. Ibid.
38. AAR, 33d Cavalry Reconnaissance Troop.
39. AAR, 37th Infantry Division. Small, 27–34.
40. Gerrish, "My Army Days." Gerrish interview. AAR, 40th Cavalry Reconnaissance Troop.
41. Ibid.
42. AAR, 24th Cavalry Reconnaissance Troop.
43. AAR, 31st Cavalry Reconnaissance Troop.
44. Roy E. Applebaum, James M. Burns, Russell A. Gugeler, and John Stevens, *Okinawa: The Last Battle: United States Army in World War II, The War in the Pacific* (Washington, DC: Center of Military History, United States Army, 1993), passim. (Hereafter Applebaum, et al.)
45. AAR, 96th Cavalry Reconnaissance Troop.
46. AAR, 7th Cavalry Reconnaissance Troop. "Observers Report—Okinawa Operation," 1 May 1945, General Staff G-2 Section Intelligence Reports, Numerical File, 1943–46, folder 309, NARA.
47. AAR, 77th Cavalry Reconnaissance Troop.

Chapter 6: Normandy: Cavalry in the Hedgerows

1. "Mechanized Cavalry Units," The General Board, United States Forces, European Theater, May 1946, 6. (Hereafter "Mechanized Cavalry Units.")
2. *Normandy*, CMH Pub 72-18 (Washington, DC: U.S. Army Center of Military History, not dated), 21. (Hereafter *Normandy*.)
3. History, 24th Cavalry Reconnaissance Squadron. Lt. Col. John Rhoades and Technician 5th Grade Dale Strick, *"Fightin' Fourth"* (Frankfurt am Main, Germany: The squadron, 1945), 1. (Hereafter Rhoades and Strick.) "Reconnaissance in Normandy—'Y' Cavalry Reconnaissance Squadron (MECZ) June 6-July 1," *Cavalry Journal*, November-December 1944, 12. Maj. Roland Ruppenthal, *American Forces in Action: Utah Beach to Cherbourg (6 June–27 June 1944)* (Washington, DC: Center of Military History, United States Army, 1990, online edition at http://www.army.mil/cmh-pg/books/wwii/utah/utah.htm as of June 2006), 43. (Hereafter Ruppenthal.)
4. *Normandy*, 26–32. Griess, 295. AAR, 4th Cavalry Reconnaissance Troop.
5. Lt. Thomas Fernley, "Normandy to Brest," *Cavalry Journal*, January-February 1945, 18. (Hereafter Fernley.) AAR, 29th Cavalry Reconnaissance Troop. Telephone interview with Harold Smith, 29th Cavalry Reconnaissance Troop, October 2006. Lt. Edward Jones, "Scouting for the Enemy, A Memoir of Lt. Edward Jones, 29th Cavalry Reconnaissance Troop, 29th Infantry Division," unpublished manuscript, 29th Infantry Division archives. (Hereafter Jones.) *Normandy*, 26–32. Griess, 295.
6. AAR, 1st Cavalry Reconnaissance Troop.
7. Ruppenthal, 53. Maj. Robert Tincher, "Reconnaissance in Normandy—In Support of Airborne Troops," *Cavalry Journal*, January-February 1945, 12. (Hereafter Tincher.)
8. *Normandy*, 34.
9. "Comments from Combat," *Cavalry Journal*, November-December 1944, 17.
10. Gordon A. Harrison, *Cross-Channel Attack: United States Army in World War II, The European Theater of Operations* (Washington, DC: Center of Military History, United States Army, 1993), 336. (Hereafter Harrison.) Griess, 307.
11. Tincher, 12–14.

12. Telephone interview with John D'Agostino, 29th Cavalry Reconnaissance Troop, October 2006.
13. Tincher, 12–14.
14. Rhoades and Strick, 2.
15. Griess, 308.
16. Fernley, 18.
17. Jones.
18. "Mechanized Cavalry Units," appendix 7, 3–4.
19. Maj. Charles Rousek, *A Short History of the 38th Cavalry Reconnaissance Squadron (Mechanized)* (Prestice, Czechoslovakia: The Squadron, 1945), np. (Hereafter Rousek.)
20. History, AAR, 102d Cavalry Reconnaissance Squadron.
21. Maj. Thomas Moore, et al., eds., *The 106th Cavalry Group in Europe, 1944–1945* (Augsburg, Germany: The Squadron, 1945), 9. (Hereafter Moore, et al.)
22. Report of Operations, 9th Infantry Division.
23. AAR, 2d Cavalry Reconnaissance Troop.
24. History, 25th Cavalry Reconnaissance Squadron.
25. *Normandy*, 36. Griess, 311.
26. "In Capture of Bourge de Lestre: 'Y' Reconnaissance Squadron in Cherbourg Campaign," *Cavalry Journal*, January-February 1945, 15–17.
27. AAR, 4th Cavalry Group. Report of Operations, 9th Infantry Division. Rhoades and Strick, 3–4.
28. Jones.
29. Griess, 316.
30. Rhoades and Strick, 2.
31. Houston, 199–200.
32. AAR, 83d Armored Reconnaissance Squadron.
33. History, 113th Cavalry Reconnaissance Squadron.
34. AAR, 113th Cavalry Reconnaissance Squadron.
35. Jones.
36. Ibid. Joseph Balkoski, *Beyond the Beachhead: The 29th Infantry Division in Normandy* (Mechanicsburg, PA: Stackpole Books, 1999), 267.
37. Telephone interview with Harold Smith, 29th Cavalry Reconnaissance Troop, October 2006.
38. Fernley, 18.
39. Jones.

Chapter 7: The Breakout from Normandy

1. *Northern France*, CMH Pub 72-30 (Washington, DC: U.S. Army Center of Military History, not dated), 7. (Hereafter *Northern France*.) Report of operations, First Army. AAR, VIII Corps.
2. AAR, V Corps.
3. See the S-3 Journal, 745th Tank Battalion, which records an order to this effect from Headquarters 1st Army, as does the S-3 Journal of the 747th Tank Battalion.
4. Griess, p. 317.
5. AAR, 6th Cavalry Reconnaissance Squadron.
6. *Northern France*. Report of operations, First Army.
7. *Generalleutnant* Fritz Bayerlein, "Panzer Lehr Division: 24 to 25 July 44," MS # A-902, 12 July 1949, National Archives.
8. *Northern France*, 89.

9. Martin Blumenson, *Breakout and Pursuit: United States Army In World War II, the European Theater of Operations* (Washington, DC: Center of Military History, 1993), 253–54. (Hereafter Blumenson, *Breakout and Pursuit*.)

10. AAR, 83d Armored Reconnaissance Squadron. AAR, Combat Command B, 3d Armored Division. Combat interviews, 3d Armored Division, NARA.

11. Blumenson, *Breakout and Pursuit*, 262–63.

12. Ibid., 255.

13. Combat interviews, 4th Cavalry Group, NARA.

14. Blumenson, *Breakout and Pursuit*, 270.

15. Combat interviews, 2d Armored Division, 82d Armored Reconnaissance Battalion, NARA.

16. Ibid. Blumenson, *Breakout and Pursuit*, 273–74.

17. Earl Mazo, "Yard-By-Yard Fight Closed the Trap," *Stars and Stripes*, 31 July 1944.

18. AAR, 83d Armored Reconnaissance Squadron.

19. Moore, et al., 17.

20. AAR, VIII Corps.

21. AAR, 6th Armored Division. Combat interviews, 6th Armored Division, 86th Cavalry Reconnaissance Squadron, NARA.

22. History, 25th Cavalry Reconnaissance Squadron.

23. Report of operations, First Army.

24. Rhoades and Strick, 8–9. AAR, 4th Cavalry Reconnaissance Squadron.

25. AAR, 741st Tank Battalion.

26. AAR, 2d Cavalry Reconnaissance Troop.

27. History and AAR, 102d Cavalry Reconnaissance Squadron.

28. Rousek.

29. History and AAR, 6th Cavalry Reconnaissance Squadron.

30. History, 28th Cavalry Reconnaissance Squadron.

31. Griess, 334. Blumenson, *Breakout and Pursuit*, 348–49.

32. Blumenson, *Breakout and Pursuit*, 357.

33. History, 25th Cavalry Reconnaissance Squadron.

34. Blumenson, *Breakout and Pursuit*, 361–63.

35. "WW2 History of the 8th Recon Troop," Militaria.com, http://www.militaria.com/8th/8recon.html as of October 2006.

36. AAR, 6th Armored Division.

37. Blumenson, *Breakout and Pursuit*, 370.

38. Combat interviews, 6th Armored Division, 86th Cavalry Reconnaissance Squadron, NARA. AAR, 6th Armored Division.

39. AAR, 86th Cavalry Reconnaissance Squadron.

40. History, 15th Cavalry Reconnaissance Squadron. History, 15th Cavalry Group.

41. Chester Wilmot, *The Struggle for Europe* (Ware, England: Wordsworth Editions Limited, 1997), 394–95, 400. (Hereafter Wilmot.)

42. G-3 operations diary, Third Army. AAR, XV Corps.

43. *Oberst* Erich Helmdach, "Measures Taken by the German Seventh Army in the Rear Area After the Breakthrough at Avranches," MS # B-822, 25 March 1948, National Archives. (Hereafter Helmdach.)

44. G-3 operations diary, Third Army. AAR, XV Corps.

45. AAR, XV Corps. AAR, 90th Cavalry Reconnaissance Troop.

46. Moore, et al., 27–28.

47. History, 80th Cavalry Reconnaissance Troop.

48. AAR, XV Corps. Moore, et al., passim.

49. XX Corps Personnel, *The XX Corps* (Osaka, Japan: Mainichi Publishing Co., Ltd, 1945 [?]), 68ff. (Hereafter *The XX Corps*.)
50. Combat interviews, 3d Cavalry Group, NARA. AAR, 87th Cavalry Reconnaissance Squadron. AAR, Combat Command B, 7th Armored Division.
51. Rousek.
52. AAR, 83d Armored Reconnaissance Squadron.
53. AAR, 4th Cavalry Reconnaissance Troop.
54. AAR, 84th Cavalry Reconnaissance Troop.
55. AAR, V Corps. Blumenson, *Breakout and Pursuit*, 590ff.
56. AAR, V Corps. History and AAR, 102d Cavalry Reconnaissance Squadron.
57. Blumenson, *Breakout and Pursuit*, 614–15.
58. Rousek.
59. History and AAR, 102d Cavalry Reconnaissance Squadron.
60. Rousek.
61. Moore, et al., 48.
62. AAR, XV Corps.
63. "Armored Reconnaissance in the European Theater of Operations," not dated, General Staff G-2 Section Intelligence Reports, Numerical File, 1943–46, folder 157, NARA.
64. Capt. Reuben Trant, "Troop C: From Paris to Belgium, 125th Reconnaissance Squadron in Pursuit of Routed Germans," *Cavalry Journal*, March-April 1945, 13–15.
65. Combat interviews, 113th Cavalry Group, NARA. Medal citations, 113th Cavalry Reconnaissance Squadron. AAR, 125th Cavalry Reconnaissance Squadron.
66. Rhoades and Strick, 13.
67. Rousek.
68. AAR, 38th Cavalry Reconnaissance Squadron.
69. AAR, 87th Cavalry Reconnaissance Squadron.
70. History, 25th Cavalry Reconnaissance Squadron.
71. AAR, 121st Cavalry Reconnaissance Squadron.
72. *The XX Corps*, 108.
73. Combat interviews, 3d Cavalry Group, NARA.
74. AAR, XII Corps.
75. Rousek.
76. AAR, 38th Cavalry Reconnaissance Squadron.
77. AAR, 4th Cavalry Group. "Mechanized Cavalry Units," appendix 6, 8. Combat interviews, 4th Cavalry Group, NARA.
78. *General der Infanterie* Erich Straube, "Einsatz des Generalkommandos LXXIV. Armeekorps (Sept. bis Dez. 1944)," MS # C-016, not dated, National Archives.
79. AAR, XII Corps.
80. AAR, XV Corps.
81. Memorandum from Medical Detachment, 102d Cavalry Reconnaissance Squadron, to the Surgeon General, European Theater of Operations, "Narrative History of the Medical Detachment, 102d Cavalry Rcn Sq Mecz," 20 January 1945.
82. Capt. Lawrence Loewinthan, M.C., "Medical Evacuation with a Reconnaissance Squadron," *Cavalry Journal*, March-April 1945, 35–37.

Chapter 8: Southern France: The Strategic Cavalry Charge

1. AAR, 3d Cavalry Reconnaissance Troop.

2. Lutz, 14. Combat interviews, 36th Infantry Division, Major Samsel, executive officer, 117th Cavalry Reconnaissance Squadron, NARA. (Hereafter Samsel, combat interview.) Journal, 117th Cavalry Reconnaissance Squadron. Capt. Paul H. Seidel, WW II Survey 1596, Military History Institute, Carlisle, PA. (Hereafter Seidel.)

3. Lt. Gen. Lucian K. Truscott, *Command Missions* (New York, NY: E. P. Dutton and Company, Inc., 1954), 407. (Hereafter Truscott.) G-3 journal, VI Corps. Brig. Gen. Frederic Butler, "Butler Task Force," *Armored Cavalry Journal*, published in two parts, January-February 1948 and March-April 1948, 13. (Hereafter Butler.) R. Manning Ancell, with Christine M. Miller, *The Biographical Dictionary of World War II Generals and Flag Officers* (Westport, CT: Greenwood Press, 1996), 43.

4. Truscott, 414ff.

5. Maj. Percy Ernst Schramm, "OKW War Diary (1 Apr–18 Dec 1944)," MS # B-034, not dated, National Archives, 84ff, 104. Obkdo. Armeegruppe G: "Kriegstagebuch Nr. 2 (Führungsabteilung)" 1.7.-30.9.1944. Ralph Bennet, *Ultra in the West: The Normandy Campaign of 1944–45* (New York, NY: Scribners, 1980), 159.

6. Unless otherwise noted, the story of Butler Task Force is derived from the following sources: Butler; Samsel, combat interview; AAR and journal, 117th Cavalry Reconnaissance Squadron; Capt. Kenneth Barnaby Jr., "Face-Lifting a Cavalry Squadron," *Armored Cavalry Journal*, July-August 1946, 8–12; G-3 journal, VI Corps; and Vincent M. Lockhart, *T-Patch to Victory: The 36th Infantry Division from the Landing in Southern France to the End of World War II* (Canyon, TX: Staked Plains Press, 1981), 19ff.

7. G-3 journal, VI Corps. "Field Order #2 (Dragoon)," Seventh Army G-3 records. Journal, 117th Cavalry Reconnaissance Squadron. Lutz.

8. G-3 journal, VI Corps. "Field Order #2 (Dragoon)," Seventh Army G-3 records.

9. Truscott, 424. Jacob L. Devers, "Operation Dragoon: The Invasion of Southern France," *Military Affairs*, Summer 1946, 30.

10. G-3 journal, VI Corps.

11. Obkdo. Armeegruppe G: "Kriegstagebuch Nr. 2 (Führungsabteilung)" 1.7.-30.9.1944.

12. *Generalleutnant* Wend von Wietersheim, "The 11th Panzer Division in Southern France (15 August–14 September 1944)," MS # A-880, 4 June 1946, National Archives, 4. Report of operations, Seventh Army.

13. AAR, 3d Cavalry Reconnaissance Troop.

14. Truscott, 426.

15. Report of operations, Seventh Army.

16. AAR, 753d Tank Battalion. Samsel, combat interview.

17. AAR, 753d Tank Battalion.

18. Butler, 36.

19. AAR, 753d Tank Battalion. Butler, 36. Combined G2 and G3 journal, Task Force Butler. Samsel, operational history.

20. G-3 journal, VI Corps.

21. AAR, 753d Tank Battalion.

22. G-3 journal, VI Corps.

23. AAR, 753d Tank Battalion. Butler, 37.

24. Ibid.

25. Samsel, combat interview. S-3 journal, 141st Infantry Regiment. Butler, 37. "2d Bn 141st Infantry: Montelimar," contained in combat interviews, 36th Infantry Division, NARA. (Hereafter "2d Bn 141st Infantry: Montelimar.")

26. AAR, 141st Infantry Regiment.

27. Von Wietersheim, 7.

28. Report of operations, Seventh Army.

29. Capt. Thomas Piddington, "Briancon, France Operation During World War II," contained in WW II Survey 1616, Military History Institute, Carlisle, PA.
30. AAR, S-3 journal, daily unit report, 143d Infantry Regiment. "3d Bn 143d Inf," combat interviews, 36th Infantry Division, NARA.
31. AAR, 753d Tank Battalion. AAR, Task Force Butler. Samsel, combat interview.
32. AAR, Task Force Butler.
33. AAR, 753d Tank Battalion.
34. AAR, Task Force Butler. Samsel, combat interview.
35. *The Story of the 36th Infantry Division* (Germany: 36th Infantry Division, 1945), 16.
36. Samsel, combat interview.
37. G-3 journal, VI Corps.
38. G-3 journal, AAR, VI Corps. Von Wietersheim, 14–15. Journal, 117th Cavalry Reconnaissance Squadron. Arthur Funk, "Mandate for Surrender," *World War II*, March 1990, 28–33.
39. AAR, 3d Cavalry Reconnaissance Troop.
40. Journal, 45th Infantry Division.
41. Telephone interviews with Ben Rosenthal and Robert Flynn.
42. Journal, 45th Infantry Division.

Chapter 9: The Reich's Tough Hide

1. Rousek.
2. Moore, et al., 61.
3. Lutz, 32.
4. Charles B. MacDonald, *The Siegfried Line Campaign: United States Army in World War II, The European Theater of Operations* (Washington, DC: Office of the Chief of Military History, Department of the Army, 1993), 237. (Hereafter MacDonald, *The Siegfried Line Campaign*.)
5. AAR, 87th Cavalry Reconnaissance Squadron. MacDonald, *The Siegfried Line Campaign*, 237ff.
6. AAR, 87th Cavalry Reconnaissance Squadron.
7. Ibid.
8. MacDonald, *The Siegfried Line Campaign*, 246.
9. Telephone interview with Gen. William Knowlton (ret.), 87th Cavalry Reconnaissance Squadron, October 2006.
10. Griess, 362.
11. AAR, 29th Cavalry Reconnaissance Troop.
12. Telephone interview with Harold Smith, 29th Cavalry Reconnaissance Troop, October 2006.
13. AAR, 83d Armored Reconnaissance Squadron.
14. History, 24th Cavalry Reconnaissance Squadron.
15. Combat interviews, 3d Cavalry Group, NARA. *The XX Corps*, 149ff.
16. *The XX Corps*, 195.
17. AAR, XII Corps.
18. The Second Cavalry Association Regimental History Site.
19. Combat interviews, 10th Armored Division, Brig. Gen. Kenneth Althaus and other officers, NARA.
20. AAR, XV Corps.
21. Samsel, operational history.
22. Vernon H. Brown Jr., *Mount Up! We're Moving Out!* (Bennington, VT: Merriam Press, 2005), 25–26. (Hereafter Brown.)

Chapter 10: The Battle of the Bulge

1. AAR, 38th Cavalry Reconnaissance Squadron.
2. AAR, VIII Corps. Combat interviews, 14th Cavalry Group, NARA. AAR, 14th Cavalry Group. Charles B. MacDonald, *The Battle of the Bulge* (London: Guild Publishing, 1984), 83, 103ff. (Hereafter MacDonald, *Battle of the Bulge*.) "Antwort auf den Fragebogen Über die Ardennenoffensive; *Generalfeldmarschall* Wilhelm Keitel and *Generaloberst* Alfred Jodl," MS # A-929, 14 May 1950, National Archives.
3. Lt. Col. Joseph Haines, "106th Cavalry Reconnaissance Troop in the Battle of the Bulge," http://ice.mm.com/user/jpk/106th_Recon.htm as of October 2006.
4. Wilmot, 580.
5. Griess, 380.
6. AAR, CCB, 9th Armored Division. Combat interviews, 9th Armored Division, Combat Command B, NARA. AAR, VIII Corps.
7. AAR, VIII Corps.
8. AAR, Combat Command B, 7th Armored Division. Combat interviews, 7th Armored Division, Brig. Gen. Robert Hasbrouck, NARA. AAR, VIII Corps.
9. Combat interviews, 14th Cavalry Group, NARA. Combat interviews, 7th Armored Division, Brig. Gen. Robert Hasbrouck, NARA. Combat interviews, 7th Armored Division, Capt. Henry Williams, NARA. MacDonald, *The Battle of the Bulge*, 83, 103ff.
10. Combat interviews, 7th Armored Division, 87th Cavalry Reconnaissance Squadron, Capt. Donald Johnson, NARA. AAR, CCB, 9th Armored Division.
11. AAR, CCB, 9th Armored Division. AAR, Troop D, 89th Cavalry Reconnaissance Squadron.
12. Raney.
13. Combat interviews, 7th Armored Division, 87th Cavalry Reconnaissance Squadron, Sgt. Leonard Ladd, Sgt. Joseph McKeon, and Lt. Arthur Olson, NARA.
14. AAR, CCB, 9th Armored Division.
15. Combat interview, Lt. Arthur Olson, 87th Cavalry Reconnaissance Squadron, 7th Armored Division, copy posted at U.S. 7th Armored Division Association Unofficial Home Page, http://members.aol.com/dadswar/7ada.htm as of October 2006.
16. Combat interviews, 14th Cavalry Group, NARA. Combat interviews, 7th Armored Division, Brig. Gen. Robert Hasbrouck, NARA.
17. AAR, 87th Cavalry Reconnaissance Squadron.
18. U.S. 7th Armored Division Association Unofficial Home Page, http://members.aol.com/dadswar/7ada.htm as of October 2006.
19. AAR, VIII Corps.
20. AAR, 90th Cavalry Reconnaissance Squadron. Combat interviews, 10th Armored Division, Col. William Roberts, NARA. *Terrify and Destroy: The Story of the 10th Armored Division* (Germany: U.S. Forces European Theater, 1946), 6. (Hereafter *Terrify and Destroy*.)
21. AAR, 90th Cavalry Reconnaissance Squadron. *Terrify and Destroy*, 6.
22. MacDonald, *The Battle of the Bulge*, 500. *Terrify and Destroy*, 6.
23. Col. Robert S. Allen, *Patton's Third Army: Lucky Forward* (New York, NY: Manor Books Inc., 1965), 174–79.
24. Brig. Gen. Michael J. L. Greene, "Contact at Houffalize," "Our History," http://www.11tharmoreddivision.com/history/Link-up_History.html as of June 2006. AAR, VIII Corps.
25. AAR, 41st Cavalry Reconnaissance Squadron.

26. Obkdo. Heeresgruppe G: "Anlagen (Chefsachen) zum Kriegstagebuch Nr. 3 der Führungsabteilung v. 1.10.-31.12.44." *Oberst (I.G.)* Horst Wilutzky, "The Attack of Army Group G in Northern Elsass in January 1945," MS # B-095, 8 September 1950, National Archives. (Hereafter Wilutzky, "The Attack of Army Group G.") Report of operations, Seventh Army.

27. Ibid. Sixth Army Group history.

28. Ibid.

29. Combat interviews, Seventh Army, NARA.

30. Samsel, operational history.

31. Report of operations, Seventh Army. *Generalmajor* Alfred Philippi, "361st Volksgrenadier Division (24 Dec 1944-12 Jan 1945," MS # B-428, 22 February 1947, National Archives.

32. Robert Lutz, phone interview with author, July 2006.

33. Bronze Star citation for Arnold Lasner. Samsel, operational history. Lutz, 43ff.

34. Brown, 57ff.

35. AAR, 94th Cavalry Reconnaissance Squadron. Capt. Joseph Carter, *The History of the 14th Armored Division* (The Division: 1945 [?]), np. (Hereafter Carter.)

36. Combat interviews, 14th Armored Division, NARA. Carter. AAR and S-3 journal, 117th Cavalry Reconnaissance Squadron. Samsel, operational history. Lutz, 46.

37. AAR, 94th Cavalry Reconnaissance Squadron. Carter.

Chapter 11: On to Victory

1. Capt. Paul H. Seidel, WW II Survey 1596, Military History Institute, Carlisle, PA.

2. Rousek.

3. Rhoades and Strick, 26.

4. History, 25th Cavalry Reconnaissance Squadron.

5. "Mechanized Cavalry Units," 10.

6. Greenfield, et al., 439–466.

7. "G-3 history," 36th Cavalry Reconnaissance Squadron.

8. AAR, 83d Armored Reconnaissance Squadron. Charles B. MacDonald, *The Last Offensive: United States Army in World War II, The European Theater of Operations* (Washington, DC: Office of the Chief of Military History, Department of the Army, 1993), 188. (Hereafter MacDonald, *The Last Offensive.*)

9. Combat interviews, 4th Cavalry Group, NARA. History, 24th Cavalry Reconnaissance Squadron. MacDonald, *The Last Offensive,* 187.

10. AAR, 83d Armored Reconnaissance Squadron.

11. MacDonald, *The Last Offensive,* 185, 192.

12. AAR, 14th Cavalry Group. AAR, 89th Cavalry Reconnaissance Squadron.

13. "Mechanized Cavalry Units," appendix 19.

14. Lutz, 58.

15. Ibid., 60.

16. AAR, XV Corps. Moore, et al., 104.

17. Report of operations, Seventh Army.

18. Operations report, 106th Cavalry Reconnaissance Squadron.

19. AAR, 113th Cavalry Reconnaissance Squadron.

20. AAR, XV Corps.

21. AAR, 121st Cavalry Reconnaissance Squadron.

22. Journal, 36th Cavalry Reconnaissance Squadron.

23. Brown, 102.

24. Kenneth Moeller, "Memories: The European Theater of Operations 1944-45," The 11th Armored Division, http://www.11tharmoreddivision.com/history/moeller_memories.htm as of October 2006.
25. AAR, VIII Corps.
26. History, 89th Cavalry Reconnaissance Squadron.
27. Combat interviews, 3d Cavalry Group, NARA. *The XX Corps*, 346ff.
28. AAR and S-3 journal, 101st Cavalry Reconnaissance Squadron. Graydon.
29. Graydon.
30. Capt. Stuart Seborer, "From Escherhausen to Einbeck," *Cavalry Journal*, September-October 1945, 17.
31. AAR, 38th Cavalry Reconnaissance Squadron.
32. Combat interviews, 4th Cavalry Group, NARA.
33. *Forever Forward* (Germany: The 99th Cavalry Reconnaissance Troop, 1945), reproduced at Forever Forward, http://deddygetty2.home.comcast.net/ as of October 2006.
34. "Observe and Report."
35. Telephone interview with Harold Smith, 29th Cavalry Reconnaissance Troop, October 2006. Journal, 29th Cavalry Reconnaissance Troop.
36. *The XX Corps*, 374.
37. "Mechanized Cavalry Units," appendix 6, 3. Combat interviews, 3d Cavalry Group, NARA. *The XX Corps*, 378.
38. *Yank: The Story of World War II as Written by the Soldiers* (New York, NY: Brassey's (US), Inc., 1991), 134.
39. AAR, 125th Cavalry Reconnaissance Squadron. Ben L. Rose, "Brief History of the 113th Cavalry Group (Mecz.): From Normandy to the Link-Up with the Russians," http://www.geocities.com/stellargames/113th.html as of September 2006.
40. Graydon.
41. AAR and journal, 116th Cavalry Reconnaissance Squadron.
42. Maj. Dominic J. Caraccilo, "World War II: 71st Division's Cavalry Reconnaissance Troop Find the German Army Group South," Historynet.com, http://www.historynet.com/magazines/world_war_2/3035156.html as of October 2006.
43. AAR, 6th Cavalry Reconnaissance Squadron.

Chapter 12: A Brilliant Legacy

1. "Mechanized Cavalry Units," 7. "1st Airborne Reconnaissance Squadron and Parachute Squadron Association."
2. Ibid., 9ff.
3. Hofmann, 39.
4. "The Legacy of the Mechanized Cavalry," Combat Reform, http://www.combatreform.com/mechanizedcalvary5.htm as of August 2006. *Blood and Steel! The History, Customs, and Traditions of the 3d Armored Cavalry Regiment* (Fort Carson, CO: Fort Carson Office of Historical Programs, 2002), online edition, http://www.carson.army.mil/ UNITS/3RD %20ACR/main%20pages/3d%20ACR%20History.pdf as of August 2006.
5. Maj. Edward Chesney, "The 11th Armored Cavalry Regiment in Vietnam, January 1969 Through June 1970," master's thesis, U.S. Army Command and General Staff College, 2002, 1, 6, 10–11. (Hereafter Chesney.)
6. Maj. J. Bryan Mullins, "Defining the Core Competencies of U.S. Cavalry," Combined Arms Research Library, U.S. Army Command and General Staff College, http://cgsc.Leavenworth.army.mil/carl/contentdm/home.htm as of October 2006, passim.
7. Ibid., 48.

8. Chesney, 6.

9. Mullins, 47.

10. Col. (ret) Gregory Fontenot, Lt. Col. E. J. Degen, and Lt. Col. David Tohn, *On Point: The United States Army in Operation Iraqi Freedom*, online edition, Center for Army Lessons Learned, http://www.globalsecurity.org/military/library/report/2004/onpoint/ as of October 2006.

11. "Interview with CPT Edward Twaddell III," Command and General Staff College Digital Library, http://www-cgsc.army.mil/carl/contentdm/home.htm as of October 2006.

12. Maj. Louis B. Rago, II, "Cavalry Transformation: Are We Shooting the Horse Too Soon?" monograph, U.S. Army Command and General Staff College, 2002, 2–3.

GLOSSARY

AAR	After-action report
AP	Armor piercing
Capt.	Captain
Col.	Colonel
CP	Command post
Cpl.	Corporal
Djebel	Hill
Dough/doughboy	American infantryman
ETO	European theater of operations
G-2	Intelligence staff
G-3	Operations staff
Gen.	General
GI	American infantryman
Goumier	Ethnic Berber Moroccan mountain infantryman
HE	High explosive
Lt.	Lieutenant
Lt. Col.	Lieutenant Colonel
Lt. Gen.	Lieutenant General
Maj.	Major
Maj. Gen.	Major General
NCO	Non-commissioned officer
OP	Observation post
Panzer	German tank
Panzergrenadier	German armored infantry
Pvt.	Private
S-3	Operations staff
Sgt.	Sergeant
SHAEF	Supreme Headquarters Allied Expeditionary Force
Squadron	Battalion-size cavalry unit
S.Sgt.	Staff Sergeant
TO&E	Table of Organization & Equipment
Troop	Company-size cavalry unit
wadi	Valley carved by sporadic rains

BIBLIOGRAPHY

Books and Booklets

Allen, Col. Robert S. *Patton's Third Army: Lucky Forward.* New York, NY: Manor Books Inc., 1965.

The American Arsenal. London: Greenhill Books, 2001. The Greenhill volume is essentially a reprint of the U.S. Army's *Catalog of Standard Ordnance Items* of 1944.

Ancell, R. Manning, with Christine M. Miller. *The Biographical Dictionary of World War II Generals and Flag Officers.* Westport, CT: Greenwood Press, 1996.

Anderson, L. E. *Return to the Rapido: Company D/F, 81st Reconnaissance Battalion, First Armored Division.* Bennington, VT: Merriam Press, 2005.

Applebaum, Roy E., James M. Burns, Russell A. Gugeler, and John Stevens. *Okinawa: The Last Battle: United States Army In World War II, The War in the Pacific.* Washington, DC: Center of Military History, United States Army, 1993.

Balkoski, Joseph. *Beyond the Beachhead: The 29th Infantry Division in Normandy.* Mechanicsburg, PA: Stackpole Books, 1999.

Bennet, Ralph. *Ultra in the West: The Normandy Campaign of 1944-45.* New York, NY: Scribners, 1980.

Blumenson, Martin. *Breakout and Pursuit: United States Army in World War II, The European Theater of Operations.* Washington, DC: Center of Military History, 1993.

Brown, Vernon H. Jr. *Mount Up! We're Moving Out!* Bennington, VT: Merriam Press, 2005.

Buchner, Alex. *Das Handbuch der Deutschen Infanterie, 1939-1945.* Wölfersheim-Berstadt: Podzun-Pallas-Verlag GMBH, not dated.

Cameron, Robert Stewart. *Americanizing the Tank: U.S. Army Administration and Mechanized Development Within the Army, 1917-1943.* Dissertation, Temple University, August 1994. UMI Dissertation Services: Ann Arbor, MI, 1996.

Carter, Capt. Joseph. *The History of the 14th Armored Division.* The Division: 1945 (?).

Cavalry Reconnaissance Number 5. Fort Riley, KS: The Cavalry School, not dated.

Combat Lessons: Number 2. U.S. Army, 1943 (?).

Combat Lessons: Number 4, U.S. Army, 1944.

Daloia, Leonard. *37th Cavalry "Recon." Troop.* Self-published, 1988. This work is a copy of Daloia's journal from Bougainville with brief introductory material.

The First Armored Division. Germany: The 1st Armored Division, 1945.

Greenfield, Kent Roberts, Robert Palmer, and Bell Wiley. *The Organization of Ground Combat Troops: United States Army in World War II, The Army Ground Forces.* Washington, DC: Historical Division, U.S. Army, 1947.

Griess, Thomas E., ed. *The West Point Military History Series, The Second World War, Europe and the Mediterranean.* Wayne, NJ: Avery Publishing Group Inc., 1984.

Harrison, Gordon A. *Cross-Channel Attack: United States Army in World War II, The European Theater of Operations.* Washington, DC: Center of Military History, United States Army, 1993.

History of the 31st Infantry Division in Training and Combat: 1940-1945. Baton Rouge, LA: The 31st Infantry Division, 1946.

Hofmann, George F. *Through Mobility We Conquer: The Mechanization of the U.S. Cavalry.* Lexington, KY: The University Press of Kentucky, 2006.

Houston, Donald E. *Hell on Wheels, The 2d Armored Division.* Novato, CA: Presidio Press, 1977.

Howe, George F. *Northwest Africa: Seizing the Initiative in the West: United States Army in World War II, The Mediterranean Theater of Operations.* Washington, DC: Office of the Chief of Military History, Department of the Army, 1957.

Koyen, Capt. Kenneth. *The Fourth Armored Division: From the Beach to Bavaria.* Munich, Germany: The Division, 1946.

Lockhart, Vincent M. *T-Patch to Victory: The 36th Infantry Division from the Landing in Southern France to the End of World War II.* Canyon, TX: Staked Plains Press, 1981.

MacDonald, Charles B. *The Battle of the Bulge.* London: Guild Publishing, 1984.

——. *The Last Offensive: United States Army in World War II, The European Theater of Operations.* Washington, DC: Office of the Chief of Military History, Department of the Army, 1993.

——. *The Siegfried Line Campaign: United States Army in World War II, The European Theater of Operations.* Washington, DC: Office of the Chief of Military History, Department of the Army, 1993.

Miller, John Jr. *Cartwheel: The Reduction of Rabaul, The United States Army in World War II, The War in the Pacific.* Washington, DC: Office of the Chief of Military History, United States Army, 1959.

——. *Guadalcanal: The First Offensive, The United States Army in World War II, The War in the Pacific.* Washington, DC: Center of Military History, United States Army, 1989.

Moore, Maj. Thomas, et al., eds. *The 106th Cavalry Group in Europe, 1944-1945.* Augsburg, Germany: The Squadron, 1945.

Normandy. CMH Pub72-18. Washington, DC: U.S. Army Center of Military History, not dated.

Northern France. CMH Pub72-30. Washington, DC: U.S. Army Center of Military History, not dated.

Outline History of II Corps. Italy: 12th Polish Field Survey Company, 1945.

Rhoades, Lt. Col. John, and Technician 5th Grade Dale Strick. *"Fightin' Fourth."* Frankfurt am Main, Germany: The Squadron, 1945.

Rousek, Maj. Charles. *A Short History of the 38th Cavalry Reconnaissance Squadron (Mechanized).* Prestice, Czechoslovakia: The Squadron, 1945.

Salter, Fred. *Recon Scout.* New York, NY: Ballantine Books, 1994.

Sherman, Thomas M. *Seek, Strike, Destroy! The History of the 636th Tank Destroyer Battalion.* Published by the author, 1986.

Sicily. CMH Pub72-16. Washington, DC: U.S. Army Center of Military History, not dated.

Small, Sgt. Dick. *The Invincible 37th Recon.* Self-published, not dated.

Smith, Robert Ross. *Triumph in the Philippines: The United States Army in World War II, The War in the Pacific.* Washington, DC: Office of the Chief of Military History, Department of the Army, 1963.

Spearhead in the West. Frankfurt, Germany: 3d Armored Division, 1945.

Starry, Gen. Donn A. "Introductory Essay," George F. Hofmann, *Through*

Mobility We Conquer: The Mechanization of the U.S. Cavalry. Lexington, KY: The University Press of Kentucky, 2006.

Stubbs, Mary Lee, and Stanley Russell Connor. *Armor-Cavalry, Part I: Regular Army and Army Reserve*. Washington, DC: Office of the Chief of Military History, U.S. Army, 1969, online edition, http://www.army .mil/cmh-pg/books/Lineage/arcav/arcav.htm.

Terrify and Destroy: The Story of the 10th Armored Division. Germany: U.S. Forces European Theater, 1946.

Truscott, Lt. Gen. Lucian K. *Command Missions*. New York, NY: E. P. Dutton and Company, Inc., 1954.

The Victory Division in Europe, Story of the 5th Armored Division. Gotha, Germany: 5th Armored Division, 1945.

Wilmot, Chester. *The Struggle for Europe*. Ware, England: Wordsworth Editions Limited, 1997.

XX Corps Personnel. *The XX Corps*. Osaka, Japan: Mainichi Publishing Co., Ltd, 1945 (?).

Yank: The Story of World War II as Written by the Soldiers. New York, NY: Brassey's (US), Inc., 1991.

Zaloga, Steven. *M24 Chaffee Light Tank 1943-85*. Botley, UK: Osprey Publishing, 2003.

——. *M8 Greyhound Light Armored Car 1941-91*. Botley, UK: Osprey Publishing, 2002.

Articles and Internet Resources

"1st Airborne Reconnaissance Squadron and Parachute Squadron Association." http://www.airbornerecce.com/oca/ as of March 2007.

"26th Infantry Division." http://www.ww2-museum.org/content/units/Recon/ Recon.php as of June 2006.

"Aleutian Islands." Center of Military History Online, http://www.army.mil/cmh-pg/brochures/aleut/aleut.htm as of July 2006.

Allenby, Field Marshal Viscount. "The Future of Cavalry." *Cavalry Journal*, January 1929, 2.

"Armored Cars for Cavalry Units." *Cavalry Journal*, January 1923, 92.

Barnaby, Capt. Kenneth Jr. "Face-Lifting a Cavalry Squadron." *Armored Cavalry Journal*, July-August 1946, 8–12.

Benson, Maj. C. C. "Mechanization—Aloft and Alow." *Cavalry Journal*, January 1929, 58–62.

Blood and Steel! The History, Customs, and Traditions of the 3d Armored Cavalry Regiment. Fort Carson, CO: Fort Carson Office of Historical Programs, 2002. Online edition, http://www.carson.army.mil/UNITS/3RD %20ACR/main%20pages/3d%20ACR%20History.pdf as of August 2006.

Bonsteel, Capt. F. T. "The Employment of a Mechanized Cavalry Brigade." *Cavalry Journal*, September-October 1933, 19–26.

Bridgewater, Lt. Col. Clay. "Reconnaissance on Guam." *Cavalry Journal*, May-June 1945, 46–47.

"A British Soldier Remembers." http://www.britishsoldier.com/logistic .htm#regorg as of March 2007.

Butler, Brig. Gen. Frederic. "Butler Task Force," *Armored Cavalry Journal*, published in two parts, January-February 1948, 12–18, and March-April 1948, 30–38.

Candler, Lt. Col. Harry. "91st Reconnaissance Squadron in Tunisia." *Cavalry Journal*, March-April 1944, 14–22.

Caraccilo, Maj. Dominic J. "World War II: 71st Division's Cavalry Reconnaissance Troop Find the German Army Group South." Historynet.com, http://www.historynet.com/magazines/world_war_2/ 3035156.html as of October 2006.

Chaffee, Brig. Gen. Adna. "Mechanized Cavalry: Lecture Delivered at the Army War College, Washington, DC, September 29, 1939."

Chesney, Maj. Edward. "The 11th Armored Cavalry Regiment in Vietnam, January 1969 Through June 1970." Master's thesis, U.S. Army Command and General Staff College, 2002.

"Comments from Combat." *Cavalry Journal*, November-December 1944, 16–18.

"Creation of the 91st Reconnaissance Squadron." U.S. Army Garrison Schweinfurt Web site, http://www.schweinfurt.army.mil/sites/1-4/ history.htm as of July 2006.

Cutler, Captain M. M. "Cooperation with the Infantry." *Cavalry Journal*, January-February 1945, 28.

Devers, Jacob L. "Operation Dragoon: The Invasion of Southern France," *Military Affairs*, Summer 1946, 2–41.

DiMarco, Maj. Louis A. "The U.S. Army's Mechanized Cavalry Doctrine in World War II." Master's thesis, U.S. Army Command and General Staff College, 1995.

Edmunds, Lt. Col. K. B. "Tactics of a Mechanized Force: A Prophecy." *Cavalry Journal*, July 1930, 410–17.

Ellis, Lt. Col. Charles. "Demolition Obstacles to Reconnaissance." *Cavalry Journal*, May-June 1945, 28–30.

Fernley, Lt. Thomas. "Normandy to Brest." *Cavalry Journal*, January-February 1945, 18–19.

Ficklen, Capt. Jack. "A Reconnaissance Squadron in Tunisia." *Cavalry Journal*, July-August 1943, 16–18.

Fontenot, Col. Gregory (ret.); Lt. Col. E. J. Degen, and Lt. Col. David Tohn. *On Point: The United States Army in Operation Iraqi Freedom.* Online edition, Center for Army Lessons Learned, http://www.globalsecurity.org/military/library/report/2004/onpoint/ as of October 2006.

Forever Forward. Germany: The 99th Cavalry Reconnaissance Troop, 1945. Reproduced at Forever Forward, http://deddygetty2.home.comcast.net/ as of October 2006.

Funk, Arthur. "Mandate for Surrender." *World War II*, March 1990, 27–33.

"German Horse Cavalry and Transport." *Intelligence Bulletin*, March 1946. Online version available at Lone Sentry, http://www.lonesentry.com/articles/german horse/index.html, as of March 2007.

"German Tactical Doctrine, Military Intelligence Service, Special Series No. 8." U.S. War Department, 20 December 1942. Online version available at Lone Sentry, http://www.lonesentry.com/manuals/german-tactical-doctrine/index .html, as of March 2007.

Graydon, Col. Charles K. "With the 101st Cavalry in World War II: 1940–1945." 1st Battalion, 101st Cavalry, http://members.tripod.com/1-101cav/ww2.html as of October 2006.

Grazioli. Lieutenant General. "Modern Cavalry and Fast Moving Composite Units." *Cavalry Journal*, April 1923, 137–46.

Greene, Brig. Gen. Michael J. L. "Contact at Houffalize." "Our History," http://www.11tharmoreddivision.com/history/Link-up_History.html as of June 2006.

Grow, R. W. "Mechanized Cavalry." *Cavalry Journal*, January-February 1938, 30–31.

——. "New Developments in the Organization and Equipment of Cavalry." *Cavalry Journal*, May-June 1939, 204–7.

Haines, Lt. Col. Joseph. "106th Cavalry Reconnaissance Troop in the Battle of the Bulge." http://ice.mm.com/user/jpk/106th_Recon.htm as of October 2006.

Hoy, Lt. Col. Charles. "Mechanics of Battlefield Reconnaissance." *Cavalry Journal*, May-June 1944, 24–29.

——. "Reconnaissance Lessons from Tunisia." *Cavalry Journal*, November-December 1943, 16–20.

"In Capture of Bourge de Lestre: 'Y' Reconnaissance Squadron in Cherbourg Campaign." *Cavalry Journal*, January-February 1945, 15–17.

Ingles, Maj. Gen. H. C., Chief Signal Officer. "Signal Equipment and the Armored Forces." *Cavalry Journal*, May-June 1946, 47–49.

"Interview with CPT Edward Twaddell III." Command and General Staff College Digital Library, http://www-cgsc.army.mil/carl/contentdm/home.htm as of October 2006.

"Interview with Domenic Melso." Rutgers Oral History Archives, http://oralhistory.rutgers.edu/Interviews/melso_domenic.html as of June 2006.

Lee, Clark. "The Fighting 26th." *Cavalry Journal*, March-April 1943, 3–4.

"The Legacy of the Mechanized Cavalry." Combat Reform, http://www.combatreform.com/mechanizedcalvary5.htm as of August 2006.

"Leyte." Center of Military History Online, http://www.army.mil/cmh-pg/brochures/leyte/leyte.htm as of July 2006.

Loewinthan, Capt. Lawrence, M.C. "Medical Evacuation with a Reconnaissance Squadron." *Cavalry Journal*, March-April 1945, 35–37.

"Luzon: 1944-1945." Center of Military History Online, http://www.army.mil/cmh-pg/brochures/luzon/72-28.htm as of July 2006.

Marshall, Lt. Col. S. L. A. "Cavalry in Dismounted Action." *Cavalry Journal*, September-October 1944, 34–41.

Mazo, Earl. "Yard-By-Yard Fight Closed the Trap." *Stars and Stripes*, 31 July 1944.

McGuire, Maj. E. C. "Armored Cars in the Cavalry Maneuvers." *Cavalry Journal*, July 1930, 386–99.

Moeller, Kenneth. "Memories: The European Theater of Operations 1944–45." The 11th Armored Division, http://www.11tharmoreddivision.com/history/moeller_memories.htm as of October 2006.

Mullins, Maj. J. Bryan. "Defining the Core Competencies of U.S. Cavalry." Combined Arms Research Library, U.S. Army Command and General Staff College, http://cgsc.Leavenworth.army.mil/carl/contentdm/home .htm as of October 2006.

"New Guinea: 24 January 1943–31 December 1944." Center of Military History Online, http://www.army.mil/cmh-pg/brochures/new-guinea/ ng.htm as of July 2006.

Norris, Glen. "Journal Entries of a Soldier in the 91st Reconnaissance Squadron from 1942–45." U.S. Army Garrison Schweinfurt Web site, http://www.schweinfurt.army.mil/sites/1-4/history.htm as of July 2006.

"Observe and Report: Half as Big-Twice as Tough, *69th Cavalry Reconnaissance Troop (Mechanized)*." The Fighting 69th Infantry Division, http://www .69th-infantry-division.com/histories/69recon.html as of June 2006.

Patton, Maj. George S. Jr. "What the World War Did for Cavalry." *Cavalry Journal*, April 1922, 165–72.

Patton, Maj. George S. Jr., and Maj. C. C. Benson. "Mechanization and Cavalry." *Cavalry Journal*, April 1930, 234–40.

Perry, Lt. Stephen. "Hair, Wheels, or Tracks." *Cavalry Journal*, July-August 1945, 13–14.

Popowski, Lt. Col. Michael. "The 81st Reconnaissance Squadron Fights Way to Rome." *Cavalry Journal*, January-February 1945, 34–37.

"Private Charles Raney." Pegasus I, http://www.pegasus-one.org/pow/charles _raney.htm as of June 2006.

Rago, Maj. Louis B. II. "Cavalry Transformation: Are We Shooting the Horse Too Soon?" Monograph, U.S. Army Command and General Staff College, 2002.

"Reconnaissance in Normandy—'Y' Cavalry Reconnaissance Squadron (MECZ) June 6-July 1." *Cavalry Journal*, November-December 1944, 12–14.

Rose, Ben L. "Brief History of the 113th Cavalry Group (Mecz.): From Normandy to the Link-Up with the Russians." http://www.geocities .com/stellargames/113th.html as of September 2006.

Ruppenthal, Maj. Roland. *American Forces in Action: Utah Beach to Cherbourg (6 June-27 June 1944)*. Washington, DC: Center of Military History, United States Army, 1990, online edition at http://www.army.mil/ cmh-pg/books/wwii/utah/utah.htm as of June 2006.

Seborer, Capt. Stuart. "From Escherhausen to Einbeck." *Cavalry Journal*, September-October 1945, 16–17.

The Second Cavalry Association Regimental History Site, http://history .dragoons.org as of August 2006.

The Story of the 36th Infantry Division. Germany: 36th Infantry Division, 1945.

"Thrice-Wounded Infantry Lieutenant at Air Base." *The Columbia Record*, 12 April 1945.

Tincher, Maj. Robert. "Reconnaissance in Normandy—In Support of Airborne Troops." *Cavalry Journal*, January-February 1945, 12–17.

Trant, Capt. Reuben. "Troop C: From Paris to Belgium, 125th Reconnaissance Squadron in Pursuit of Routed Germans." *Cavalry Journal*, March-April 1945, 12–15.

"U.S. Army Military History Research Collection, Senior Officers Debriefing Program: Conversation Between General Hamilton Howze and Lieutenant Colonel Robert Reed." US Army Heritage Collection Online, http://www.ahco.army.mil/site/index.jsp as of December 2006.

U.S. 7th Armored Division Association Unofficial Home Page, http://members.aol.com/dadswar/7ada.htm as of October 2006.

White, Major I. D. "The Armored Force: Reconnaissance Battalion, Armored Division. *Cavalry Journal*, May-June 1941, 48–52.

Wiktorin, Col. M. "The Modern Cavalry Regiment." *Cavalry Journal*, April 1929, 205–14.

"World War II (Asia-Pacific Theater)." Center of Military History Online, http://www.army.mil/cmh-pg/reference/apcmp.htm as of July 2006.

"WW2 History of the 8th Recon Troop." Militaria.com, http://www.militaria .com/8th/8recon.html as of October 2006.

Unpublished Studies

"Antwort auf den Fragebogen Über die Ardennenoffensive; *Generalfeld-marschall* Wilhelm Keitel and *Generaloberst* Alfred Jodl." MS # A-929, 14 May 1950. National Archives.

Bayerlein, *Generalleutnant* Fritz. "Panzer Lehr Division: 24 to 25 July 44." MS # A-902, 12 July 1949. National Archives.

Blaskowitz, *Generaloberst* Johannes. "Fighting by Armeegruppe 'G' in Southern France until the Middle of September 1944." MS # B-800, 16 May 1947. National Archives.

Cameron, Robert Stewart. "Americanizing the Tank: U.S. Army Administration and Mechanized Development Within the Army, 1917–1943." Doctoral dissertation, Temple University, August 1944.

Deerin, James. "Prelude to Conflict." Manuscript contained in WW II Survey 1530, Military History Institute, Carlisle, PA.

De Groat, S.Sgt. William. WW II Survey 1474, Military History Institute, Carlisle, PA.

Domando, Sgt. Thomas. WW II Survey 1593, Military History Institute, Carlisle, PA.

Gerrish, S.Sgt. Paul. "My Army Days." Manuscript contained in WW II Survey 1384, Military History Institute, Carlisle, PA.

——. WW II Survey 1384, Military History Institute, Carlisle, PA.

Helmdach, *Oberst* Erich. "Measures Taken by the German Seventh Army in the Rear Area After the Breakthrough at Avranches." MS # B-822, 25 March 1948. National Archives.

Huff, Lt. Col. John. WW II Survey 1466, Military History Institute, Carlisle, PA.

Jones, Lt. Edward. "Scouting for the Enemy, A Memoir of Lt. Edward Jones, 29th Cavalry Reconnaissance Troop, 29th Infantry Division." Unpublished manuscript, 29th Infantry Division archives.

Lang, *Oberst* Rudolf. "Report of the Fighting of Kampfgruppe Lang (10. Pz. Div.) in Tunisia from December 1942 to 15 April 1943." MS # D-166, 6 June 1947. National Archives.

Lutz, Robert. "History of the 117th Cavalry Reconnaissance Squadron (MECZ)."

Marion, Sgt. Ivan. WW II Survey 6316, Military History Institute, Carlisle, PA.

"Mechanized Cavalry Units." The General Board, United States Forces, European Theater, May 1946.

Morton, Matthew Darlington. "Men on 'Iron Ponies': The Death and Rebirth of the Modern U.S. Cavalry." Doctoral dissertation, Florida State University, 2004.

Piddington, Capt. Thomas. "Briancon, France Operation During World War II." Contained in WW II Survey 1616, Military History Institute, Carlisle, PA.

Samsel, Col. Harold. "The Operational History of the 117th Cavalry Reconnaissance Squadron (Mecz.), World War II." Manuscript contained in WW II Survey 1530, Military History Institute, Carlisle, PA.

Schramm, Maj. Percy Ernst. "OKW War Diary (1 Apr–18 Dec 1944)." MS # B-034, not dated, National Archives. The "war diary" was an unofficial compilation (circa March 1945) of notes and summaries based on meetings and original documents, many of which were destroyed.

Schriel, S.Sgt. Philip. WW II Survey 1527, Military History Institute, Carlisle, PA.

Seidel, Capt. Paul H. WW II Survey 1596, Military History Institute, Carlisle, PA.

Straube, *General der Infanterie* Erich. "Einsatz des Generalkommandos LXXIV. Armeekorps (Sept. bis Dez. 1944)." MS # C-016, not dated. National Archives.

Von Senger und Etterlin, *General der Kavallerie* Fridolin. "Kriegstagebuch des Italienischen Feldzuges—Die Vereitelung des Feindlichen Durchbruches Zwischen den Geschlagenem Deutschen 10. und 14. Armeen; Rückzug zum Arno." MS # C-095c, 14 January 1953. National Archives.

Von Wietersheim, *Generalleutnant* Wend. "The 11th Panzer Division in Southern France (15 August–14 September 1944)." MS # A-880, 4 June 1946. National Archives.

Wilutzky, *Oberst (I.G.)* Horst. "The Attack of Army Group G in Northern Elsass in January 1945." MS # B-095, 8 September 1950. National Archives. Wilutzky was the army group operations officer.

INDEX